HOLLYWOOD IRISH

John Ford, Abbey Actors
and the Irish Revival in Hollywood

To the Carney Family and the Shields Family

HOLLYWOOD IRISH

John Ford, Abbey Actors and the Irish Revival in Hollywood

ADRIAN FRAZIER

THE LILLIPUT PRESS
DUBLIN

First published 2011 by
THE LILLIPUT PRESS
62–63 Sitric Road, Arbour Hill
Dublin 7, Ireland
www.lilliputpress.ie

This publication was grant-aided by the Publications Fund
of National University of Ireland, Galway.

ISBN 978 1 84351 181 6

1 3 5 7 9 10 8 6 4 2

A CIP record for this title is available
from The British Library.

Set in 10.5 pt on 14 pt Minion with Trajan display titling by Marsha Swan

CONTENTS

	Acknowledgments	*vii*
	Introduction	*3*
I	John Ford as an Irish Author	11
II	Barry Fitzgerald and *The Plough and the Stars* on Stage and Screen	55
III	*The Long Voyage Home*: Arthur Shields, John Ford, Eugene O'Neill and Irish Exile	99
IV	Sara Allgood, *Juno and the Paycock* and *How Green Was My Valley*	147
V	Irish Hollywood in the 1940s	175
VI	*The Quiet Man* and *The Playboy of the Western World*	205
	Afterword	239
	Notes	245
	Bibliography	273
	Index	279

ACKNOWLEDGMENTS

After a draft of Chapter II of this book had been written, a conversation with the scholar-author W.J. McCormack changed what would become the rest of the book. He gave me a tip that led to Christine Shields in Oakland, California, who was Arthur Shields' daughter, Barry Fitzgerald's niece, and Sara Allgood's goddaughter. These are the three great Abbey actors whose work is traced here.

Arthur Shields had been a bookish person, a keeper of mementos and careful manager of his own archive. Fortunately, his daughter was too. On being contacted, she let a visiting scholar come to her home and go through the papers. Christine Shields and her cousins Judith Lunny and Susan Slott then made a gift of this precious archive to the National Library of Ireland, Galway. The photographs alone transformed this book; the letters gave it a heart. As 'keepers of the flame', Christine Shields, Judith Lunny, and Susan Slott were helpful whenever asked; never when not asked. Their gift of the archive to the library of NUI Galway has already attracted other scholars and will benefit many more in the future.

I began with a desire to picture performances of the early Abbey Theatre. Those historic productions of the Irish dramatic revival were unique and unrepeatable events, never captured, either on film or in writing. But the actors so famous in the 1920s did go on to careers in film. It was in following those careers that one became aware that the great Abbey actors carried the Revival along with them to California, and then carried Hollywood back to Galway in *The Quiet Man*. That is the simple thesis and trajectory of this book.

A number of friends, family members, and colleagues were kind enough to read the manuscript. My thanks to Kevin Barry, Ros Dixon, John Carney, Kieran Carney, Helen Frazier, Rufus Frazier, Nicholas Grene, John Kenny, Thomas Kilroy, Jim MacKillop, Mike McCormack, Dearbhla Mooney, Riana O'Dwyer, and many times over, Cliodhna Carney. Also to be thanked are those who invited me to lecture on the subject: Marc Conner at Washington and Lee University; Nicholas Grene at the Synge School of Drama in Wicklow; Dennis Kennedy at the Samuel Beckett Centre, Trinity College Dublin; Lucy McDiarmuid at Montclair State University; Paul Muldoon at Princeton University; and Seán Crosson, Tony Tracy, and Rod Stoneman at the Huston School of Film and Digital Media, NUI Galway.

Richard English and Cormac O'Malley gave aid in understanding Ernie O'Malley's relationship to John Ford. Joseph Hone worked with Ford when a young man: my thanks for providing an early look at what became *Wicked Little Joe*. Patrick McGilligan and Scott Eyman – two well-known authors with a vast knowledge of American filmmakers, Ford in particular – were each helpful, the first with publication advice, the second with images from his own archive.

While this book has been in preparation, three other monographs touching on its subject have been published: Ruth Barton, *Acting Irish in Hollywood: From Fitzgerald to Farrell*; Barry Monahan, *Ireland's Theatre on Film: Style, Stars and the National Stage on Screen*; and Michael Patrick Gillespie, *The Myth of an Irish Cinema: Approaching Irish-Themed Films*. There is surprisingly little overlap between the four books. That is partly because the history of Irish cinema is a large field of inquiry, with much left to explore, and partly because there are many ways to come at it. The Internet Movie Database (imdb.com) and its purchasing feature enable one to order cheaply hundreds of historic films that not long ago would have been very difficult to access.

One of the pleasures of writing a biographically ordered story is that it takes one to great libraries. The National Film Information Service at Margaret Herrick Library, the Academy of Motion Picture Arts and Sciences, in the Douglas Fairbanks Center, Beverly Hills, California, is one of the sweetest, best-run places to study; my thanks to Kristine Kruger for the help rendered after my departure. Lauren Buisson at the Arts Library Special Collections, Young Research Library, UCLA, gave assistance in finding a way through the RKO and 20th Century Fox papers. The Lilly Library at Indiana University has the papers of John Ford and Lord Killanin; my thanks to David K. Frasier for dealing with email queries after my visits there. Karen Nangle of the Beinecke Rare Book and Manuscript Library, Yale University, provided the Sara Allgood photographs. My thanks to Bruce Kellner Trustee, Estate of Carl Van Vechten, for permission to use Vechten's portraits of Allgood.

The special collections librarians at NUI Galway were continuously helpful; my thanks to Fergus Finlay, Marie Boran, and especially Kieran Hoare.

I must officially render my thanks, and am happy to do so sincerely, to the Grant-in-Aid of Publications scheme at NUI Galway (which enabled this book to be richly illustrated); and to the Millennium Fund, NUI Galway, which made possible my travel to archives. I was the beneficiary of an NUI Galway one-year sabbatical, during which much of this book was written; my thanks to colleagues in the English department who covered my teaching responsibilities, particularly Patrick Lonergan and John Kenny. My thanks to Irene O'Malley and Dearbhla Mooney, the English Department administrators, for daily making the work environment truly pleasant.

Jonathan Williams, who established Ireland's first literary agency, takes remarkable care in the reading of a manuscript, and then the proofs; he has an eagle eye and a perfectionist's knowledge of form. My thanks to him for placing the book with Antony Farrell's Lilliput Press. There it has been enhanced by the editing of Fiona Dunne, and designed by Marsha Swan. Lilliput has rightly earned a name for publishing not just good books but beautiful ones. Helen Litton gets credit for the index.

There is one final personal nest of motives for writing this book that I wish to uncover. At the time of its beginning, I was the father of two small girls, and did not have time to read a lot of books, much less travel to archives. However, I could, while carrying an infant in my arms, watch movies. What is more, my wife and in-laws were caught up in writing screenplays, directing movies, acting in movies, talking about movies, and arguing about whatever movie they were watching. Steps needed to be taken to catch up at least a little with their expertise. So my heartfelt thanks to Frances Knott and Martin Carney, Jim, John, and Kieran Carney, Lucy Miller and Marcella Plunkett, and, most of all, my wife, Cliodhna Carney.

And, of course, to Clea and Lesy Carney Frazier, no longer infants at all, but very much little ladies who neither would nor could now be carried by me. Without them, I would never have thought to write this book. Now it is Delia Carney Frazier who is the babe in arms, and a reminder of how small a thing, in balance, any book is.

HOLLYWOOD IRISH

Members of the Abbey Theatre company treated to a lunch with the RKO *production team on the set of* The Informer, *February 1935. John Ford is at the last table, far right. (Shields family papers)*

INTRODUCTION

In 1931, 1932 and 1934, the Abbey Theatre company left Dublin for long tours of its repertoire through the United States. The third tour brought the Irish actors to Hollywood in February 1935. At the time John Ford, an Irish American with a passion for Ireland and its literature, was making a movie for RKO Studios of Liam O'Flaherty's novel *The Informer.* A great admirer of the Abbey, Ford staged a welcome banquet for the players on the set of *The Informer*, which represented a lamp-lit Dublin city street.

The photograph opposite is a key piece of evidence for this book. The event it records is not simply a photo opportunity for Irish visitors with RKO celebrities; it was an occasion of some historical significance. Then and there, creative collaboration between Irish actors and a great Hollywood film-maker got underway.

The following Friday night, a number of Hollywood stars joined the Abbey cast on stage in crowd scenes from *The Playboy of the Western World.* Ford arranged for Denis O'Dea, the Abbey's juvenile male, to do a turn as a street singer in *The Informer.* The assistant director's daily call sheet already listed duties for two Abbey veterans who had since settled in Hollywood, J.M. Kerrigan and Una O'Connor. Before the current Abbey troupe left town, Ford took steps to get RKO producers to bring them all back again a year later for the filming of O'Casey's two masterpieces, *The Plough and the Stars* (1936) and *Juno and the Paycock* (this second project was abandoned). The collaboration would continue over many years, bearing fruit in great motion pictures, the last of which was *The Quiet Man* (1952).

While *The Plough and the Stars* did not turn out to be one of these unquestionably great motion pictures that sprang from Ford's collaboration with Abbey actors, the movement of O'Casey's play from stage to screen itself makes a great story, with Irish sectarian trouble at its heart, and the global entertainment market for background.

The original authors and directors of the Irish National Theatre Society at the time of the Abbey Theatre's opening in 1904, W.B. Yeats, Lady Gregory and J.M. Synge, were all Protestants, descendants of the post-sixteenth-century English colony in Ireland; 90 per cent of the country's residents were Catholics. Even though these three authors were all committed nationalists working for Irish independence from Britain, they found themselves in the questionable position of giving dramatic representations of Catholic life from what their audiences expected to be a Protestant point of view. The famous riots over the production of Synge's *The Playboy of the Western World* (1907) had their roots in this sectarian suspicion, or suspicion of sectarianism (arguments over whether the balance of blame lay with the audience or the author are continuing). A similar sectarian conflict heated up among the company's actors in the 1920s, and it boiled over at the time of the first production of *The Plough and the Stars*, which also caused riots: Protestant actors sided with the Protestant O'Casey, and Catholic actors for the most part found the author to be at fault for the incendiary impact of the play.

O'Casey, partly out of disgust with the lack of support he received from both the Abbey's actors and its audiences, and tempted by rich offers from London producers, left Ireland in 1926 and never worked there again. Barry Fitzgerald, one of the stars of the company, followed O'Casey to London. Sara Allgood had already left the Abbey for good, carried on the tide of her success in the title role of *Juno and the Paycock* in 1924. O'Casey's *Juno and the Paycock* and *The Plough and the Stars* became two of the most popular plays in the English-speaking world, and not just popular, but recognized to be great in the sense that Shakespeare's plays are great: literary, human, profound, tragi-comic and pleasurable. These plays paved the way for actors, and other Irish plays, to go from Dublin to London, New York and finally to Hollywood.

After 1926 the Abbey itself resumed its pre-O'Casey decline. Both political parties in the new Irish Free State were conservative, Catholic and theoretically anti-English language. A vigorous censorship of books and films was instituted, and the government – by virtue of its subsidy of the Abbey from 1925 – was able to place a representative on the theatre's board of directors. The War of Independence (1919–21) and Civil War (1922–3) had left the Irish economy in a poor state. The 1929 worldwide depression further sank the standard of living. By 1931 the Abbey, just to keep afloat, found it necessary to undertake the first of what would be four major tours of North America in that decade. The aim was to capitalize on the international popularity of Irish drama in general and O'Casey's plays in particular. In the first 1931/32 tour alone, the Abbey played in 74 cities and gave 238 performances. By the time the 1932/33, 1934/35 and 1937/38 tours were completed, the Abbey was known in nearly every city and town of North America.

It was the custom in the era of the early 'talkies' for Hollywood talent scouts to take up to fifty orchestra seats on Broadway opening nights in order to spot new acting talent.[1] Sara Allgood had played Broadway in *The Plough and the Stars* (28 November-December 1927), *Juno and the Paycock* (19 December 1927–January 1928), Paul Vincent Carroll's *Shadow and Substance* (26 January 1938–September 1938) and a revival of *Juno* (16 January–13 April 1940). Barry Fitzgerald and his brother Arthur Shields had been in Broadway productions of plays by O'Casey and Carroll, a writer now forgotten but in the 1930s regarded on Broadway as the successor to Shaw and O'Casey. By creating a public for Irish drama, and exposing its stars to talent scouts, Abbey tours of the USA opened the door for its actors to enter Hollywood studios.

Research for this book benefited by a stroke of author's luck: a hoard of papers belonging to the key actors in this whole transition of Irish Revival drama from Dublin to Hollywood fell into my lap. At a conference in Galway on the performance history of *The Playboy of the Western World*, the scholar-author W.J. McCormack mentioned that he had a cousin who had a cousin who had in her possession the personal papers of Arthur Shields and Barry Fitzgerald. Within a few weeks, Christine Shields set before me in Oakland, California, dozens of boxes of papers and memorabilia – documents of family history, the private letters of her father Arthur Shields, her mother Aideen O'Connor and uncle Barry Fitzgerald, business papers from the Abbey tours of the USA, tax records, contracts with theatres and film studios, and hundreds of photographs from movies, plays and family life. This trove of papers (later donated by Christine Shields to the National University of Ireland, Galway) made it possible to tell the story of the Irish dramatic revival flowing into world cinema as a story of individuals. Arthur Shields, Barry Fitzgerald and Sara Allgood (godmother to Christine Shields) carried the traditions of Abbey acting within their persons – their muscles remembered those traditions, their voices were trained in them, their own inventiveness was governed by them. Where these actors went, the Irish dramatic revival went too.

One particularly significant historical moment revealed by the Shields family archive is the afternoon in September 1938 on which Arthur Shields decided to leave Ireland for the United States. He asked the director and founder of the Abbey, W.B. Yeats, if they might have a talk. The poet invited him to lunch at the Kildare Street Club (an exclusive Dublin resort of the Protestant Ascendancy). Shields had fought by James Connolly's side in the Easter Rising in 1916; he had been one of the last rebels to surrender. At the Abbey Theatre he became the leading man and a person who, in Yeats's words, 'incarnates our traditions'.[2] But by the late 1930s Ireland had grown impossible for Shields. He complained that now you had 'to say your prayers in Gaelic' to get on at the Abbey, and Shields had neither Gaelic nor prayers. More particularly, though married and with a child, he was in love with a young actress in the company, Aideen O'Connor. Offers to direct on Broadway and to do film-acting in Hollywood had been extended to him, with the chance of parts for Aideen too. He hated to leave the Abbey, but it no longer felt like home. The old poet replied that, all things considered, perhaps it was best for Shields himself that he take up one of his offers; however, as long as Yeats had anything to do with the Abbey, Shields would be welcome to return. By the following month Arthur Shields was in New York to direct M.J. Farrell and John Perry's *Spring Meeting*, and within seven months, Yeats was dead and John Ford had sent Shields a contract for a new part that had been specially written for him into Twentieth Century Fox's *Drums Along the Mohawk*.

The rapid transition by Arthur Shields from creative teamwork under W.B. Yeats to work under John Ford is startling. It is not customary to see a connection between these two great artists. They belong to different media, different levels of culture, different continents, and almost different centuries, in that Yeats emerges from 'the long nineteenth century' and Ford is a significant figure in post-World War II cinema history. You look for one in *The Norton Anthology of English Literature* and for the other in Turner's Classic Movies. Nonetheless, the author and the auteur are linked, and by more than the fact that Arthur Shields was an actor: each of them trusted as a human means of expression of their own individual talents. Ford wanted to contribute to the Irish Revival too, the revival that Yeats more than anyone had started. Ford made certain movies that he conceived of as additions to that movement. That is why it made sense to him to work with actors like Sara Allgood, Barry Fitzgerald, Arthur Shields, J.M. Kerrigan and Una O'Connor. That is why he sought out Irish writers like Liam O'Flaherty, Sean O'Casey, Maurice Walsh, Eugene O'Neill and Frank O'Connor, and directed movies based on their works. That is why he named the village in *The Quiet Man* after Yeats's famous poem 'The Lake Isle of Innisfree'.

The factual record of the movement of the Irish Revival into world theatre and then into global cinema is so rich, and so little known, that the best way to treat it is by a documentary narrative, and to let the facts speak for themselves. My previous books were a theatre history, *Behind the Scenes: Yeats, Horniman, and the Struggle for the Abbey Theatre* (University of California Press 1990), and the biography of a writer, *George Moore 1852–1933* (Yale University Press 2000). They left me with some experience of, and a preference for, a biographical and documentary approach.

To get at the mere truth of things, one has to overcome unusual obstacles in film studies. The number of those involved in making a Golden Age studio movie was huge, so reading a film in the light of any particular person's artistic contribution is complicated. Contemporary documents about the movies are often driven by myth-making and profit-driven press releases, interviews and reviews; they obviously cannot be taken at face value. Baseless anecdotes become almost scriptural in their authority by means of repetition, like the one about John Ford, who, when pressed by a producer for being behind schedule, supposedly ripped an elaborate battle scene out of the script, then declared, 'Now we're on schedule' (see Chapter III for a debunking of this myth). Manufactured witticisms are put into the mouths of Hollywood personalities who, except when reciting, never said a witty thing in their lives. Indeed, one of the difficulties in writing a book about actors and Hollywood people, as compared with writers, is that their letters are not often particularly quotable. Complaints about life on the road or spells of unemployment figure largely. Because of the unreliability of information about Hollywood, or the lives of actors in general, it was judged appropriate to print endnotes to this narrative; primary sources in archives are used wherever possible; gossip is held up to scrutiny.

The life adventures of the characters in this book were often extraordinary, although not in the case of the best actor among them, Barry Fitzgerald (his grumpy, kind, and shy offstage personality could have belonged to any decent civil servant, Fitzgerald's day job for twenty years). On the other hand, although an unusually modest man, his brother Arthur Shields was a real-life hero of the Easter Rising, as well as the Abbey Theatre's leading man and a Hollywood character actor with scores of credits to his name. John Ford was a boaster and a bully, but he was also a genius, and felt to be so by all those around him. Dishonest on occasion, he honestly earned his decorations for heroism in World War II and his five Oscars from the Academy of Motion Picture Arts and Sciences. In this book these figures are seen not from below as on a pedestal, or from above as if looking down on popular entertainers, but close and on the level, as individuals whose importance to the public is beyond doubt and merits an accurate account.

It will be obvious to readers that the story of early Abbey actors in Hollywood movies far extends in significance its importance as an ethnic success story. That more general significance can be illuminated by a pair of paradoxes from the writings of Oscar Wilde. Speaking of the relation between art and life, Wilde says in 'The Decay of Lying' that 'No great artist ever sees things as they really are.' He uses Japanese painting as his proof:

> The Japanese people are the deliberate self-conscious creation of certain individual artists. If you set a picture by Hokusai, or Hokkei, or any of the great native painters, beside a real Japanese gentleman or lady, you will see that there is not the slightest resemblance between them. The actual people who live in Japan are not unlike the general run of English people; that is to say, they are extremely commonplace, and have nothing curious or extraordinary about them. In fact, the whole of Japan is a pure invention. There is no such country, there are no such people.[3]

In similar fashion one could say, in relation to the writings of the Irish Revival, the whole of Ireland is a pure invention. There is no such country, there are no such people. They were invented by a magically gifted generation of writers, mostly Protestant (James Joyce is the catastrophically huge exception), who took as their artistic material the customs, folklore and literature of a Gaelic-speaking, Catholic civilization. When Abbey Theatre audiences shouted during the first performances of *The Playboy of the Western World* (1907) 'That's not the West!' and 'That's not Ireland!' they had a point. Ireland is more 'commonplace' and has less that is 'curious and extraordinary' about it. But audiences pleaded in vain, because Synge's play was a great play, just as Hokusai's watercolours are great paintings.

In the same essay Wilde spins out a second paradox about the relation of art to life, and it partially contradicts the first: 'Life imitates art far more than Art imitates Life.' As soon as a great work of art has made known a new type of person, 'Life tries to copy it, to reproduce it in a popular form, like an enterprising publisher.'[4] The efforts of fact to reproduce fiction are amply evident in the case of the Irish Revival. Again and again in the story that follows one finds people testifying that they were inspired to take patriotic action by a single incendiary play, *Cathleen ni Houlihan* (1902). Yeats has come in for a degree of scholarly ridicule for asking himself near the end of his life, 'Did that play of mine send out/Certain men the English shot?' ('Man and the Echo'). Yet the problem is not that (in the words of W.H. Auden) 'poetry makes nothing happen'. The play did indeed send out a lot of men to fight for Ireland; whether or not they were among those who were shot is open to question. (It is the phrase 'that play of mine' that is particularly suspect, because Lady Gregory wrote much of *Cathleen ni Houlihan.*[5]) The overriding, unpedantic point is that in the Easter rebellion, life imitated art, and the Irish Revival in general was a forerunner of the Irish rebellion.

Life again follows in the footsteps of literature in the case of the excoriated *Playboy*. Whether or not there were women in Ireland like Pegeen Mike before the play was performed, there certainly were after it. The proud, belligerent, well-fortuned and love-hungry Mary Kate Danaher in *The Quiet Man* is modelled on Pegeen Mike, not upon the average female in mid-twentieth-century County Mayo. Maureen O'Hara's performance ensured that Irish women at home and abroad who saw *The Quiet Man* would have a self-image to live up to. In doing so they would enact (though at several removes) the fantasies of J.M. Synge, an unmarried, indeed, possibly virginal, Protestant gentleman who died in 1909.[6] That is at once unbelievable and true.

There is a possible resolution of the dizzying contradiction between Wilde's two paradoxes: artists do not see life as it really is, and life imitates art, which would have life eternally attempting to resemble something that is attempting to resemble something that it is not. The resolution is that people are not 'extremely commonplace', with 'nothing curious or extraordinary about them', as blithely affirmed in Wilde's deliberate insult to average citizens. Humans are not fixed forever in one ethnic form, much less a unitary, trans-ethnic 'human nature'. Today's ordinary and commonplace pass away, to be replaced tomorrow by things somewhat different, themselves soon to be experienced as ordinary and commonplace. The story of representations (how people appear in plays and movies) matters not simply because plays and movies provide so much of our pleasure, but also because in the story of social change, representations are both the mirror and the lamp, as art may both reflect reality and light the way forward to new realities.

The concept of symbolic ethnicity, developed first by Max Weber and modified by Herbert Gans, is explained in Chapter I. It is a key to this book. Ethnic identities are continuously remade by cultural industries – that is, on the individual level, by poets, playwrights, novelists and film-makers. Movies in particular, given the mass market appeal of some of them, have the power to fashion identities that hearken back to countries of origin. This was a power that John Ford was keen to seize upon. Along with some other directors, he wanted to lift the status of Roman Catholics in predominantly WASP America. He also wanted to depict Irish people as the prototypical immigrants in a democratic land, those who were the country's first sheriffs, doctors, generals, mayors and freedom fighters. He wanted to celebrate the high art, modernist magnificence of twentieth-century Irish literature by doing justice to certain key texts in motion pictures. Finally, he wanted to be seen within Ireland as an Irish artist himself, and contributor to the Irish Revival, with something to say of value as a result of his American experience. In *The Quiet Man*, he said it.

The narrative in this book is fast-paced and by its nature complicated. It criss-crosses several countries and three major cities, Dublin, New York and Los Angeles. It encompasses literature, history, drama and film. It has not one but four starting points: John Ford, Barry Fitzgerald, Arthur Shields and Sara Allgood. Time schemes overlap in the first four chapters, which are dedicated to each of their careers in turn. Sometimes events recur in the narrative, as seen from the points of view of their different participants. By virtue of being the story of individuals, it demonstrates how culture forms people, and the fact that it is people who make culture. Every chapter in the book includes extensive consideration of at least one movie by John Ford, so instrumental in bringing Abbey actors to Hollywood, and so reliable an employer for them thereafter. Thus, this book about the Irish Revival doubles as a book about John Ford. On the belief that readers, like the author, have come to care for the people involved, an afterword tells what finally became of Barry Fitzgerald and his remarkable brother Arthur Shields.

I

JOHN FORD AS AN IRISH AUTHOR

Previous page: *John Ford in uniform, World War II. (Lilly Library)*

'My name is John Ford; I am a director of Westerns': thus Ford presented himself – famously, sham-modestly, and misleadingly.[1]

The occasion on which he first deployed the formulation is crucial. The date was 22 October 1951, at a Screen Directors Guild Meeting in the Beverley Hills Hotel. The organization, like the country as a whole, had been in crisis for several years over the hunt for Communist Party members obedient to Moscow. Cecil B. DeMille wanted the Guild to compel each of its members to take a loyalty oath to the United States of America.[2] By this means he also hoped to reduce the power and influence of directors of foreign birth, people like the German-born Billy Wilder and William Wyler and the Italian-born Frank Capra – men with 'accents', as DeMille framed the category of un-Americanness. If directors refused to take the oath, then they would be blacklisted by Hollywood producers, who had by 1951 been well and truly terrified by Joseph McCarthy's House of Un-American Activities Committee in the US House of Representatives.

John Ford and Merian Cooper (his producer and partner in Argosy Pictures) were indignant at the thought of being subjected to any loyalty test except one administered by the US government. Surely no one had a right to question *their* patriotism. Cooper, producer of *King Kong* in 1933, had become a brigadier general in the army; Ford had climbed to the rank of admiral in the navy while running the photographic unit of the intelligence service in every major theatre of World War II. He had been awarded the Purple Heart for an arm wound received in the Battle of Midway.[3] Yet the loyalty-oath issue went deeper than questions of service to country. It also went deeper than party politics. Both Ford and Cooper were Republicans, just like DeMille, who advocated the oath, and like Joseph L. Mankiewicz, the current Guild president, who opposed it. Certainly, matters of professional formation were involved: 'We organized this guild to protect ourselves against producers,' Ford reminded his colleagues. An oath would require the surrender of a degree of professional freedom. Beyond national service, party politics, or profession, however, the issue raised questions of ethnicity in an American's artistic identity, and that is why Ford opened his remarks by saying who he was.

Among the 298 delegates in the Crystal Ballroom, there can hardly have been one that did not know that the six-foot tall, stooped and slack-jowled man wearing an eye-patch and baseball cap went by the name of John Ford and that he had directed Westerns, scores of them. In the world of movie-makers, he was as quintessential an American figure as Buffalo Bill. By 1951 he had been in Hollywood for 37 years and had made 118 movies. In December 1935, he was one of the twelve who founded the Screen Directors Guild. The modesty of his self-introduction was fake modesty, a rhetorical irony to undercut DeMille's pomposity. Because DeMille had been the first director to make a full-length movie in Hollywood (*The Squaw Man*, 1914), and because he subsequently made many high-grossing epic spectaculars (*The King of Kings*, 1927; *Cleopatra*, 1934), this son of English immigrant theatre people had come to regard himself as old stock, a native aristocrat.[4] Ford countered by staking his claim to the one uniquely American genre, the Western, more or less as if he had said, 'My name's Hancock, John Hancock, and I wrote the Declaration of Independence.'

It was a strong opening, and after some further remarks, half-belligerent ('I don't like C.B. DeMille') and half-friendly ('but I admire him'), and with very little further eloquence or argumentation, Ford proposed that the motion for an oath be dropped, the current board of directors be asked to resign, and the meeting adjourned. DeMille 'shrivelled and shrank' as Ford spoke.[5] He knew he had been trumped by another patriot patriarch.

Ford would have been entitled to introduce himself quite differently. He might, for instance, have said, 'I am a director of Shirley Temple movies,' for he had made *Wee Willie Winkie* (1937) for Twentieth Century Fox and later cast the actress as an adult in a Western, *Fort Apache* (1948). That would be a twisted take on his filmography, but it would not have been unreasonable for him to have said, 'I am a director of films about Lincoln and Lincoln's America.' Ford's series of Southern and Midwestern films starring Will Rogers (*Dr Bull*, 1933; *Judge Priest*, 1934; *Steamboat Round the Bend*, 1935), his two films about the life of Lincoln (*Prisoner of Shark Island*, 1936; *The Young Mr Lincoln*, 1939), his other American historical films starring Henry Fonda, whether in 1776 Massachusetts (*Drums Along the Mohawk*, 1939), 1881 Tombstone (*My Darling Clementine*, 1946) or Dustbowl Oklahoma and Depression California (*The Grapes of Wrath*, 1940), creatively defined an American fair-minded, homespun, democratic individualism in an array of geographical and historical settings. His ability to create a historical screen poetry was seized upon by producer Winfield Sheehan of Fox Studios, and adeptly developed by Darryl Zanuck when he took over the amalgamated Twentieth Century Fox Studios in 1935.

In light of his achievements within the studio system, Ford could have simply said to his colleagues in the Screen Directors Guild, 'I am a successful money director,' for he had done the work assigned to him by Sam Goldwyn, RKO, Fox and Twentieth Century Fox through several decades, always on schedule and within budget, winning four Academy Awards, and with very few losing propositions, whether the movies were Westerns, war movies, Americana, historical costume dramas (*Mary of Scotland*, 1936) or Shirley Temple vehicles.

Finally, to bring into discussion the aspect of his artistic identity that will be examined at length here, John Ford was a director of art films of Irish interest. But, although he was at work on his fifth such project at that moment (*The Quiet Man*, 1952), an ethnic self-presentation would hardly have suited his purpose at the Screen Directors Guild meeting in 1951.

2

Nor would it have been, when replying to DeMille's nativist arguments, appropriate for Ford to introduce himself by saying, 'My real name is Sean Martin Aloysius O'Feeney.' In 1894 those were the names given the thirteenth child of John Feeney, an immigrant bootlegger and saloon-keeper. Ford was not ashamed of this Irish background. Far from it. He told friends to call him 'Sean', not John. No one could have known John Ford for long without learning that his father came from the village of Spiddal outside Galway on the west coast of Ireland, and his mother's people from the Aran Islands, off that same coast and within sight of Spiddal.

Although by 1951 Ford had made only three or four short visits to Ireland, in conversation he made much of his familiarity with the country. He arrived for the first time in Spiddal on a four-day visit to Ireland in December 1921, during a truce in the War of Independence. In Connemara Ford evidently met Michael Thornton, an IRA cousin on the run from the British army. Could a wealthy relative like himself have refused to contribute some cash to the cause? Subsequently, Ford anecdotally ballooned his brief sympathetic association with Michael Thornton into active service in the fighting.[6]

John Ford with his cousins in their Spiddal cottage, either in 1951 or 1955. Ford's son Pat is third from left. (Lilly Library)

At a Hollywood party he would announce, 'I'm an Irish rebel, freedom fighter. Bet you didn't know that.'[7] On movie sets Ford sometimes even pretended to fluency in the Irish language by mixing gibberish with the few catch-phrases he remembered from childhood (Maureen O'Hara, who had some school Irish, was induced into conspiring in the hoax).[8] The fantasy element in Ford's ego-identification as Irish is nicely symbolized by the sailboat he purchased in 1934, thereafter the central vehicle of his recreation. He named the hundred-foot ketch *Araner*, after the islands from which his mother's people came. The boat and its name highlighted both the continuity between John Ford and his pre-Famine Irish forebears, and his distance from them in the splendid Californian triumph at which their descendant had arrived.[9] That there was an element of fantasy in Ford's Irishness does not mean that it was unreal or unimportant to his identity. It suggests the opposite: that his Irishness was a wish in need of fulfilment, a gap in his American identity that had to be filled.

Like many other Americans, Ford required an ethnic personality profile as an intermediary between the abstract individualism of the capitalist metropolis and the nation state. The pressures upon first-generation immigrants to adapt to the language, the ethnically mixed churches, the secular public education, and the mobile employment markets of America were immense. Emigrate or starve had been the dilemma in their home countries, and integrate or starve was often their only choice in America. The ideology of the United States aimed to create national solidarity among immigrants by means of a theory of the equality of each citizen – at least each non-African, non-Asian and non-Hispanic citizen – at the level of individuality, which implied the surrender of group loyalties to one's community of descent and a promise of blind justice on the part of the state with respect to hierarchies of groups.

The huge waves of immigration of the late nineteenth and early twentieth centuries, of Germans, Irish, Italians and Russian Jews, raised fears during World War I of their '100 per cent Americanism' in the majority population, especially after 1917, when the USA entered the war on the side of Britain and against Germany.[10] In 1924 the US Congress, still concerned about the threat of newcomers to national solidarity, passed an immigration bill that fixed an annual quota of immigrants for each country based on its place in the national origins of the US population in the census of 1920, the involuntary immigrants from Africa and Asia excepted.[11] As a consequence 70 per cent of the future immigration to the USA would be from Ireland, the United Kingdom and Germany, all 'white' and Western countries, envisioned in 1924 to be the core of a future uniform American identity. But even second- and third-generation white Americans from these countries would often yearn to retain features of their group identity before the last shreds had melted away.

An ethnic profile could, as Emile Durkheim suggested, provide citizens of a modern state with spiritual guidance and consolation, helping them steer clear of the despair that attends complete normlessness ('anomie').[12] A remnant of 'symbolic ethnicity' could serve a still vital function even if it amounted only to the celebration of national holidays (e.g. St Patrick's Day), the determination of one's religious affiliation (Irish Catholic), rare overseas holidays in the 'homeland' ('the ould sod'), identification with the high culture of one's ancestral nation (the Irish Renaissance), and the attribution of personality features to inheritance from one's ancestors (alcoholism, orality, pugilism).[13]

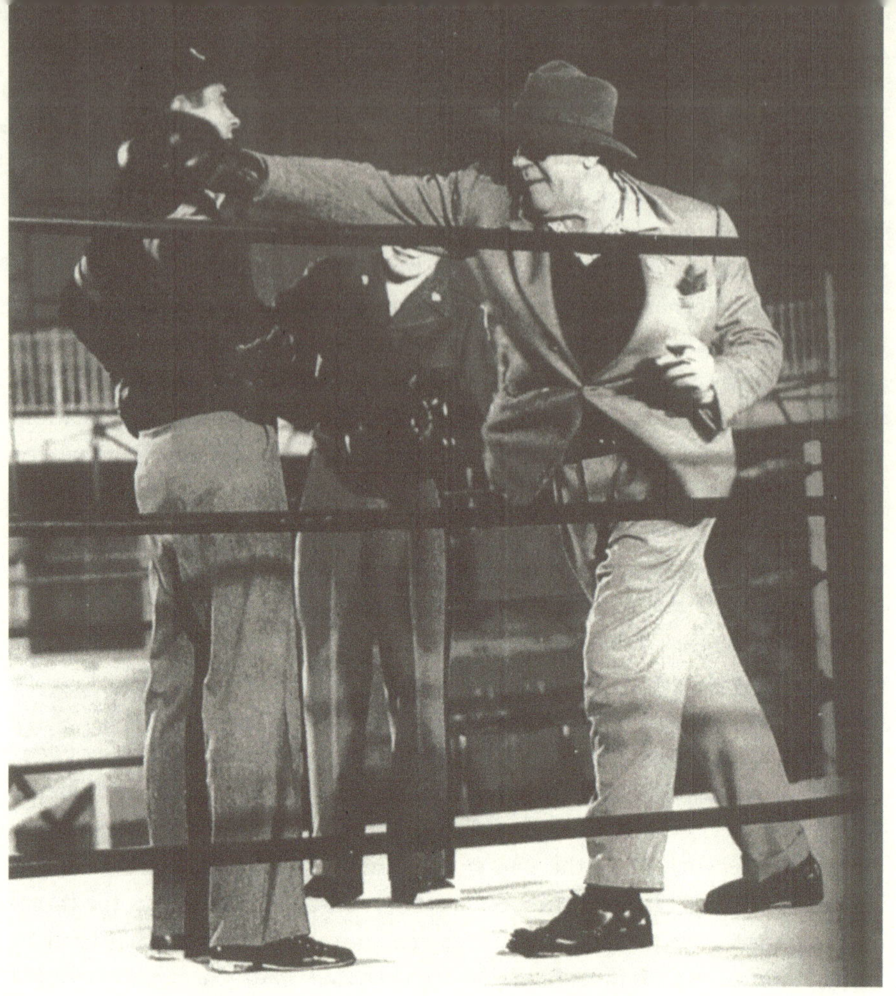

John Ford illustrates how to throw a punch, Long Gray Line, *1955.*
(Courtesy Scott Eyman)

3

For instance, if one self-medicated by means of alcoholic binges, as Ford often did once he had wrapped a film, one could point to heavy drinking as just part of the personality kit of an Irish male, a mark of group belonging. One could even require one's drinking buddies and crewmen on the *Araner* – people like John Wayne and Ward Bond, men of no immediate Hibernian ancestry – to be Irish too. Or how could one excuse one's physical violence against friends, subordinates and women? For sometimes John Ford unpredictably sucker-punched people.

He did it even to actors with whom he had worked again and again, such as Henry Fonda (Ford 'suddenly jumped up and slugged him in the face'),

Maureen O'Hara ('He turned on me and socked me square in the jaw. I felt my head snap back and heard the gasps of everyone there'), and Dobe Carey ('So I'm smiling, and boom! Ford hits me right here [in the jaw]).'[14] Such bewildering, unforgivable acts Ford could hope to understand, or get others to interpret, as just part of a romantic Irish personality, the ethnic burden he had to bear. Ford was not a highly articulate man. 'Ford can't write,' screenwriter Nunnally Johnson reported, 'it just runs him nuts.'[15] His sole gift in self-expression was telling through pictures, with words – where essential – provided by others. His surviving letters show very little of the character, humorous charm, elegance and depth embodied in his best movies. So he could not lay claim to the Irish 'gift of the gab'.

But he certainly had an artist's creative nature, and he protected its freedoms by evasiveness in relation to truth. His reports on life took the form of fabulations – not transcriptions of an event but heightened, complex translations of it. In interpersonal relations he carried statements one step past irony. An ironic statement is one in which what is meant is different from what is said, but also a statement in which one's intention is still to be understood. Ford's conversation, as many producers, stars, and especially interviewers would come to learn, was filled with statements that were plainly misleading. He was, in fact, an unrepentant liar. But this personality attribute could be at least partly transvalued from vice to virtue by being understood as an aspect of his Irish heritage, for the Irish are stereotyped as people of powerfully imaginative natures. In 1937 Ford wrote to a nephew fighting on the Republican side in the Spanish Civil War that he was glad the boy had inherited 'the good part of the O'Feeney blood'. He had to admit that his own temperament carried strains both good and bad: 'Some of it is awful, very God-damned awful – we are liars – weaklings – and selfish drunkards, but there has always been a stout rebel quality in the family and a peculiar passion for justice.'[16]

Ford's claims to Irishness carved out a dimension of freedom in an American civil society that, partly because of its Protestant origins, and partly because of the centrality of the free market to its way of life, officially valued sobriety, self-discipline and speech of almost promissory plainness. If drinking, fighting and tale-telling were Irish habits, they had to be tolerated on the grounds that all ethnic forms of life ought to be equally valued.

An ethnic personality profile might serve not only in justifying personal habits that American civil society treated as vices, but in providing the security of given virtues in a social marketplace of excessive freedoms. Ford's 'Irish' and patriarchal sense of family and his Catholic notions of marriage are important here. In a civil ceremony in 1920 Ford married 28-year-old Mary McBryde Smith, of Scottish and Irish descent. As a Catholic, Ford could not marry in church a woman who was either Protestant or divorced, and she was both. In December 1941, after the death of Mary Ford's first husband and her conversion to Catholicism, they were married a second time in the National Cathedral, Washington DC. In divorce-happy Hollywood the Fords treated marriage as indissoluble. Ford admitted he was not an ideal husband: it was his ethnic inheritance that made him so difficult, he apologetically explained to Mary. In a sentimental letter written in New York in 1943 while awaiting his departure to the Asian theatre of war, Ford concluded:

> I pray to God [the war] will soon be over so we can live our life together with our children and grandchildren and our *Araner* – Catalina [Island] would look good now! God bless and love you Mary darling – I'm tough to live with – heaven knows & Hollywood didn't help – Irish and genius don't mix well – but you do know you're the only woman I've ever loved – God bless m'darling.[17]

Secure in her position and her house, but aware that Hollywood husbands could sometimes only think of their 'lousy, stinking tail[s]',[18] Mary Ford somewhat ominously recommended that Hollywood wives take to heart the old saying, 'Don't believe any of what you read, and only half of what you see.'

4

Not that there was a great deal of gossip about John Ford, even in a town where Hedda Hopper and Louella Parsons had turned gossip into an international industry.[19] There is little evidence that Ford had a nature that was particularly passionate sexually, or single-mindedly disposed towards either women or men. Yet through the sexist system of procurement operating fairly openly in film studios, he would have been exposed to what for another would be stiff temptations. For instance, at Twentieth Century Fox where Ford was employed in the 1930s and 40s, head producer Darryl Zanuck would have sex with a starlet at four o'clock each afternoon, the identity of the starlets changing regularly.[20] In the same period, as leading director for the studio, Ford did not make use of his office couch for casting purposes.

He did become romantically entangled with Katherine Hepburn during the filming of *Mary of Scotland* in March 1936 and kept up the flirtation at least until January 1937. He took her home to meet his family in Portland, Maine, and had dinner with hers ('Is it true your people are Irish Catholics?' Hepburn's

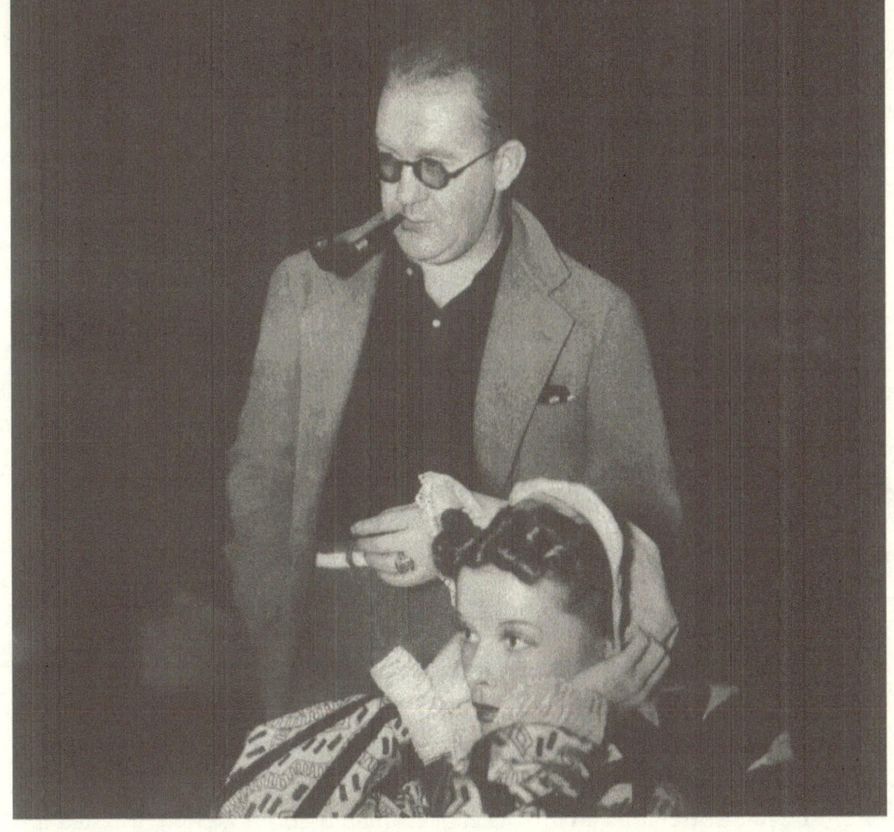

Katherine Hepburn and John Ford on the set of Mary of Scotland, *1936.*
(RKO/Photofest, © RKO)

blueblood aunt inquired in mock disbelief). He brought Hepburn out for a sail on the *Araner*, during which she posed for a photograph giving him an on-deck foot-massage. There is, however, no evidence that Hepburn was lying when she said, 'He never made a pass at me.'[21] While on tour around the Midwest in a stage play, Hepburn wrote to Ford that his spirit went with her; he 'occup[ied] a wonderful place suspended in mid-air below the [theatre] balcony',[22] a tough, fatherly, yet finally appreciative image before which she could perform in hope of applause. But it was an image that could be relied upon never to become a man, and never to require that she should stop performing and start being a woman. It suited them both, Hepburn's recent biographer William J. Mann hypothecizes, that Ford was a married man unlikely ever to leave his wife. Thus, they were each protected by his monogamy from what they did not really want in any case. Sexual intercourse could have brought their romance to a catastrophic end. Hepburn's 'Dear John' letter (actually addressed to *Dear Sean*) of 10 April 1937 pointedly complains of a lack of clarity on both her part and his during the relationship, and concludes that '*Maybe* [was] a feeble way of saying *no*.'[23]

Ford had other flirtations. One not noticed by his all-but-all-knowing biographer Joseph McBride has been identified by William J. Mann in *Kate: The Woman Who was Katherine Hepburn.* After January 1937 when Hepburn dropped Ford and literally flew off with pilot, film-maker and millionaire Howard Hughes, Ford found a new darling among Hepburn's Hollywood friends, the ginger-haired Irish-American Mimi Doyle (1914–79). She was the daughter of a Los Angeles banker and sister of actress Eve March.[24] Mann proves that Mimi Doyle is the author of a mysterious love letter in the Ford archive, one that takes the form of a catty playlet reporting Hepburn's private conversation about her past romance with Ford. But Mann does not go on to observe that on the evidence of this letter Ford may have set Mimi Doyle up in an apartment, for which she appears to thank him: 'Little boy, the new apartment is wonderful. I have a big picture of you and somehow I'm not quite so lonesome with that to look at first thing in the morning and the last thing at night (oh my I love you).'[25] He also found her a part as a telephone operator in *Four Men and a Prayer* (1938) and other bits in five subsequent films, the final one as 'Mamie Burns' in *The Last Hurrah* (1958).

To what degree this affair was consummated and how long it lasted are things unknown. Perhaps to Mimi Doyle as to Katherine Hepburn, Ford came no closer than floating in the middle distance. In spite of the frank intimacy of her phrasing – *the last thing at night (oh my I love you)* – it is rather hard to imagine 44-year-old Ford in bed with this 28-year-old. He had certain habits that were likely to render his person unattractive. For instance, he rarely took his pipe out of his mouth, except when replacing it with a cigar or a handkerchief. His favourite tobacco is described by seasoned reporters as 'unfragrant' (read *stinking*).[26]

Apart from his smoking, a widespread and sexualized pastime in any case for men and women in the period (remember Garbo exhaling clouds of cigarette smoke in the faces of her leading men?), Ford had the unique habit of chewing a large white handkerchief. Evidently, this was some secondary form of suckling behaviour, and one that loosed his mind to reverie. He sucked his handkerchief in script conferences; he sucked it while in his director's chair on set during filming. He went through handkerchief after handkerchief. The lifelong habit overstimulated his salivary glands. When he would relax with a drink from the tension of creative thought, his lips would grow wet with slobber. Dobe Carey, who was kissed by Ford when drunk, found the experience embarrassing, and needed to wipe himself afterwards, which enraged Ford.[27] So Dobe Carey had a double surprise: first the wet kiss, then a sucker punch. Still, whatever may have been the features of John Ford's physical person, geniuses, millionaires and leaders of men – and Ford was certainly all those – have a supervening attractiveness for women and men. After all, one of the most beautiful, intelligent women in the western world, Katherine Hepburn, had fallen for him.

When separated by World War II duties from his wife, Ford flirted with his wartime secretary, who called him an 'old goat' and always said 'No' to what were only joking offers.[28] Finally, during the preparations for filming *The Quiet Man*, he wrote Maureen O'Hara rather corny, stilted love letters, possibly composed when drunk. In them he worked himself into a fantasy that he was the Trooper Thornton hero of that film, later to be played by John Wayne, opposite O'Hara as the heroine Mary Kate Danaher.[29]

5

O'Hara, from what mixture of motives it is hard to say, relays anecdotes in her 2004 autobiography that suggest a counter-explanation of Ford's monogamy. According to her, Ford never had a sexual love for another woman not because of his Irish Catholic mores, but because his passionate feelings were primarily for men. O'Hara says that in 1954 she went to see the director about costume tests for *The Long Gray Line*. He did not get up from his desk where he was drawing on a pad. When O'Hara came close, she saw what he was drawing: 'Penises. Big ones and small ones. Thin ones and fat ones.' She declined to acknowledge what she saw, and what he knew she had seen, for he continued his drawing. They did not speak of the matter. A few days later, she came into his office without knocking, and this time caught Ford kissing someone, who, when he left Ford's embraces turned out to be a famous leading man, O'Hara says, without naming the person in question.[30]

There is admittedly a strain of malice in O'Hara's reminiscences: she is far more likely to offer shocking revelations about others than about herself. For instance, in the context of a child-custody battle, she reports hearing that her ex-husband was, literally, a 'cocksucker'.[31] While she was grateful to Ford as the one director who 'allowed her talent to triumph over her face', and gave her more scope for acting than she was allowed in her 'tits and sand' swashbucklers, O'Hara did not like being punched, abused verbally on set, harassed by pseudo-love letters, and upbraided for divorcing her drunk, bankrupt and unfaithful husband – all of which she had to put up with from her old friend and fellow Irish patriot John Ford.[32]

Apart from the slobbery kiss when drunk applied to Dobe Carey, there is only one other story of male–male love in Joseph McBride's long biography. Woody Strode (1914–94), a famous African-American decathlon star (kept out of the 1936 Olympics only by a UCLA academic requirement),[33] became one of Ford's favourite actors. In 1960 Ford took the financially risky step of giving Strode, often cast by others as one of many black extras in fourth-rate Tarzan remakes, a leading-role in a Western, *Sergeant Ruttledge.* The movie is about a soldier in a Negro cavalry regiment who is falsely accused of rape. Strode in some scenes is posed as the archetypal 'buck', that virile representation of white suspicions that black men really are better.

Sergeant Ruttledge guides his troops by means of his faith that 'Some day', 'Maybe, but not yet', black Americans will get the freedom that Lincoln promised them. On that expectation he is 'crazy' enough to 'fight the white man's war' against the Indians. His faith in America's future is precariously vindicated in the climactic trial scene, in which Strode, although exposed along the way to what is depicted as casual and wholly customary courtroom racism, is found Not Guilty of rape by the military tribunal.

Three years later, when Ford was ailing and lonely, Strode temporarily left his own wife and children to move into the director's house to look after him, sleeping at the foot of his bed. Strode stayed for four months. He gave the old man massages and tried to curtail his alcoholism. The relationship, McBride concludes, had a 'homoerotic element' but, as McBride rightly adds, it also matches the affectionate, mutually respectful, master–servant relationship between Pompey and the despairing Tom Doniphon in *Liberty Valance* (1962), roles played just a year earlier by Strode and John Wayne.[34] Anyone who can remember Strode's body – he plays the spear-carrying gladiator in the duel with Kirk Douglas in *Spartacus* – will be able to understand what a potent symbol of the life force that physique could be, perhaps especially for a patient undergoing the late stages of bodily decrepitude. What Ford got from Woody Strode seems to have been more therapeutic, medicinal and psychological than sexual. It is a mysterious affair, and one can only wonder at the humanity of Strode, involving a sensitivity beyond shame, in volunteering for the intimate real-life role of male nurse.

The relationship with Strode played a part in John Ford's emerging appreciation of the value not just of his own ethnicity, but of multi-ethnicity. Ford had been one of the directors to make most regular use of Stepin Fetchit, the jive-talking, lazy and pseudo-stupid 'coon' minstrel star. Ford cast him in *Judge Priest* (1934), *Steamboat Round the Bend* (1935) and *The Sun Shines Bright* (1953), and wanted to put him in *My Darling Clementine* (1946).[35]

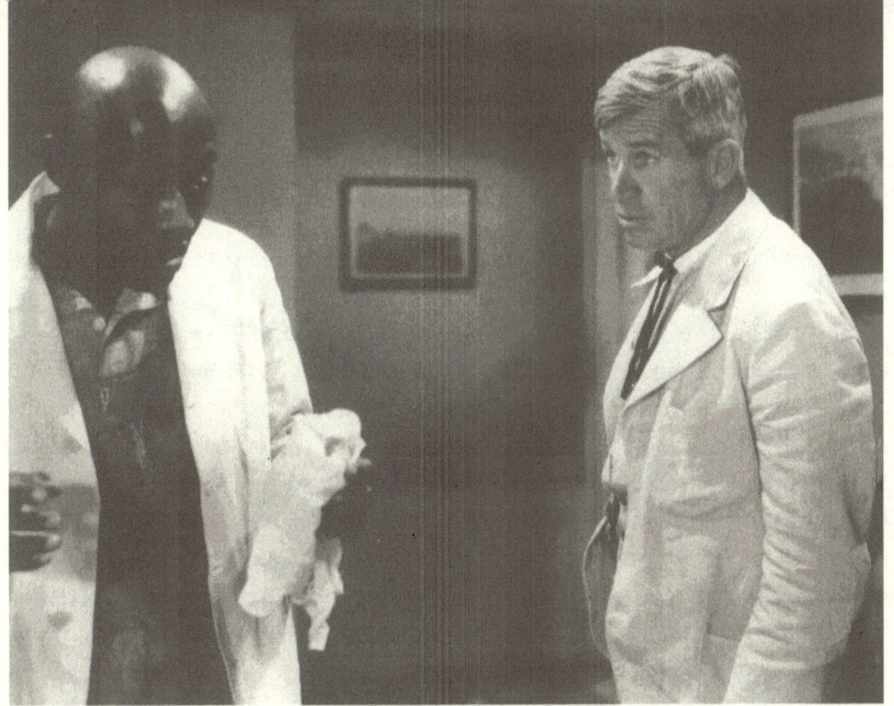

Stepin Fetchit (left) as Jeff Poindexter and Will Rogers as Judge Priest in Judge Priest, *1934. (Google Pictures)*

Furthermore, for decades Ford's Westerns depicted Native Americans in the customary way as simply the Other, against whom the post-Civil War, ethnic immigrants would unite into an American community, their past differences white-washed. Yet *The Searchers* (1956) tackled the murderous racism and fear of miscegenation lingering in the white population after the Civil War, a national race psychosis underlying American mass-culture narratives of the twentieth century. If *Sergeant Ruttledge* was, as Ford claimed, 'the first time we had ever shown the Negro as a hero',[36] *Cheyenne Autumn* for the first time made the Indians both sympathetic individuals and collective victims of unspeakable injustice and inhumanity. 'Let's face it,' Ford told Peter Bogdanovich on the set, 'we've treated [the Indians] very badly ... we've cheated and robbed, killed, murdered, massacred and everything else, but they kill one white man and, God, out come the troops.'[37] The film depicts the Cheyenne's trail-of-tears migration from an Oklahoma reservation to their old buffalo-hunting grounds in Wyoming. With *The Searchers*, *Sergeant Ruttledge* and *Cheyenne Autumn*, the old director made a radical change of direction in his storytelling about blacks and Indians. The self-described Irishman had come to understand that in a multi-ethnic society, to quote Emile Durkheim, 'the image of the one who completes us', the image of the Other, must become 'inseparable from ours ... It thus becomes an integral part of our conscience.'[38]

6

One last key figure in Ford's life sheds light on Maureen O'Hara's suggestion that Ford was fundamentally homosexual. Although he has been little written about (two brief references in McBride's big biography), this man was a significant long-term interest in Ford's life, and especially in its Irish dimension.

About the sexuality of Brian Desmond Hurst (1900–86) there can be no doubt. Christopher Robbins opens his memoir of Hurst with a characteristic anecdote. Late in his life, Hurst arrived at a Belgravia pub for his customary mid-morning breakfast of a raw egg in a glass of champagne. One labourer seated at a table of three shot off his mouth: 'Fucking old queen.' Hurst ordered the men a round of pints, and then swanned over to them. After a friendly toast, he said, 'By the way, gentlemen, I am *not* an old queen … *I am the Empress of Ireland.*'[39] Hurst was indeed a flamboyantly indiscreet lover of soldiers, policemen and working-class boys.

He had been born in Belfast. His father was a Protestant and a blacksmith in the shipyards. Hurst joined the British army and in 1915 was wounded at the Battle of Gallipoli. After the war, he shed his Belfast working-class Protestant heritage, and declared his utter different-ness by becoming both an Irish Republican and a Catholic. While enrolled as a student of painting at the Ecole des Beaux-Arts in Paris, he met James Joyce and Liam O'Flaherty. In 1928 Hurst turned up in Los Angeles, where he got work as an artist, scene-painter and extra. In Ford's silent *A Hangman's House*, starring Victor McLaglen, Hurst had a part as an extra (as did, for his first time on screen, John Wayne, then still called Marion Morrison). Watching Ford on set, Hurst decided to become a director himself.[40]

Ford took a friendly interest in his fellow Irishman; he called him 'cousin'. For Ford, the word was significant, not just fanciful. Ethnic membership is based not just on a common religion, language and customs, a shared history and dates of commemoration, but also on the idea of a common ancestry in a certain place, and thus actual kinship ties, even if these are untraced genealogically. Ethnically conceived, all Irishmen thus belong to a single family.[41] The kinship is fictive, of course. The Galway Catholic Feeneys and Belfast Protestant Hursts did not have a common religion, shared history, or single ancestral stock; they descended from what for centuries had been and still remained warring groups. Ireland was not a multi-ethnic society like the United States of America; it was a segmented, internally colonized, plural society, largely as a result of Britain's re-conquest and Protestant plantation of the island in the seventeenth century. But Ford's readiness to treat individuals who self-identified as Irish in

Hollywood as if they were long-lost cousins in need of a helping hand was a very important part of both his personality and his work as a film-maker. It was an American custom, perhaps especially among the Irish, for those immigrants already settled in an ethnic community to provide a job, a loan, a bed, a meal, or just advice to the bewildered newcomers from 'home'. In the ethnically rich, rapidly transforming metropolis of movieland, the custom had important consequences for the films themselves.

Ford bought a painting by Hurst and invited him home to dinner. In turn Hurst introduced Ford to his Anglo-Irish aristocrat friend, the outlandish Harry Clifton (the man who gave Yeats a massive piece of sculptured lapis lazuli in 1935, inspiring one of Yeats's greatest late poems).[42] So that he might learn his trade, Ford took Hurst on as a gofer on the production team for *Arrowsmith* (1931). When Liam O'Flaherty arrived in Hollywood trying to sell his novels to the movies, Hurst, Ford and O'Flaherty together drew up some initial plans for the filming of *The Informer* (1935).[43]

But Hurst was friendly not only with Ford. In Los Angeles he found, for instance, a boyfriend in Michio Ito (1892–1961), the dancer who in 1916 had performed as a hawk in one of Yeats's Noh plays, but who in 1933 was choreographing *Madame Butterfly* for Paramount.[44] Hurst had also found his way into the George Cukor set of Hollywood homosexuals. At one time when he was living at Ford's house, Hurst told his host he was going to Cukor's for dinner. Returning late at night, he discovered that Ford had waited up for him. Who was there? Ford wanted to know. It was a surprise to learn that his fellow Irish-American Spencer Tracy was at the party.[45] But Ford easily accepted that Garson Kanin and professional sissy Clifton Webb would have been among the crowd.[46] Next Ford wanted to know about all the rooms in the house, and Hurst obliged, describing the pool, the drawing room, the study, but admitted he could not give an account of Cukor's bedroom, because he did not go there. Ford said, 'Brian, I am proud of you.'[47]

That was the first time, Hurst says, the two men mutually acknowledged the homosexual side of Hurst's life. But what about the homosexual side of Ford's life? As characterized in the anecdote, Ford is eager to learn about Hollywood's closeted community of men, and he takes no trouble to distance himself from friends whom he knows to be homosexual, like Cukor and Hurst, but he wishes them to believe he would be happier if they would not act upon their desires.

Hurst began his career as a director in 1934 working with DuWorld Pictures in Hollywood on a version of Poe's *The Tell-Tale Heart*. He then returned to Ireland to make a film of J.M. Synge's *Riders to the Sea* (1935), starring Abbey actors Sara Allgood, Ria Mooney and playwright Denis Johnston, with costumes borrowed from the Abbey Theatre, Dublin.[48] In London Hurst soon got a long-term contract with producer Alexander Korda to direct major motion pictures, such as *This Lion Had Wings* (1939), with Merle Oberon and Ralph Richardson.

While working in the Office of Strategic Services, Ford visited Hurst in London during 1942.[49] On his return to London in 1944 to supervise the filming of the D-Day invasion, Ford spent a weekend in the country with his friend. Hurst then left to film George Bernard Shaw's *Caesar and Cleopatra* in Denham.[50] In 1947 the two men exchanged gifts (blue dressing-gown for Ford, cigars for Hurst) and began to talk of making films in Ireland.[51]

Director Brian Desmond Hurst is shown on the set of Hungry Hill, *1947.*
(Courtesy Universal Pictures/Ronald Grant/Photofest)

Along with Michael, Lord Killanin, Brian Desmond Hurst was brought into the planning for *The Quiet Man.* Initially it was Brian's producer, Alexander Korda, who was to provide funding for that film.[52] Ford, Hurst and Killanin joined up at Ashford Castle, County Mayo, in November 1950 to scout locations. On this occasion Ford and Hurst together took out a two-year lease on the rectory cottage on Killanin's estate in Spiddal, where they would have free use of a trout stream and the beaches of Galway Bay.[53] Upon his return to the USA Ford sent his Irish friend a present of two blue silk shirts, and sought advice about possibly casting Siobhan McKenna in *The Quiet Man* (though not as Mary Kate Danaher).[54]

Busy with his own production schedule, Hurst was unable to be on hand during the filming of *The Quiet Man* during the summer of 1951. The following October, in the wake of the excitement created by the visit of Hollywood to County Galway, Hurst stayed for two weeks in the cottage he had leased with Ford in Spiddal. Killanin and Hurst believed *The Quiet Man* opened the door to a new possibility. They proposed that Ford join them in forming a film production company based in Galway, with their films distributed by Arthur Rank. The focus of the company would be on adaptations of works from the Irish Literary Revival. In the offer letter they mentioned as possibilities film treatments of Liam O'Flaherty's *Famine* and James Stephens's *The Demi-Gods*.[55] On 24 October 1951 Ford replied by telegram: 'COUNT ME IN.' He concurred 'one hundred per cent'. Strangely enough, Ford sent this telegram just two days after the Screen Directors Guild meeting at which he introduced himself as an all-American movie-maker ('I am a director of Westerns').

Ford's first idea for the Irish production company was to use still-surviving participants in 'The Troubles' for a story about Republican martyr Kevin Barry (1902–20). Barry was a university student who led an attack against a lorry of British soldiers at the start of the Anglo-Irish war, killing six (the first British casualties in the campaign). He was arrested and hanged, in spite of his request to die by firing squad – hanging was for criminals, not soldiers. Ford intended to make the Kevin Barry story into a 'patriotic' and 'anti-British' movie, but one to be done with such 'showmanship' that even the British would 'welcome' it.[56]

Lord Killanin argued that a nationalist exaltation of Kevin Barry would reawaken divisions within the Irish population (presumably between Republicans and Unionists). So Ford dropped the idea, consenting to the view that the products of the new Four Provinces Films should not 'antagonize any National group', presumably in particular the Protestant group in the province of Ulster: 'I don't mind killing them, but I am very tender-hearted and don't care to hurt their feelings.'[57] This bravura piece of self-contradiction tells us something: Ford was conscious of the degree to which his 'I'm an Irish freedom-fighter' pose was just a pose, and he expected others to allow for an ironical reading of it. Ford admitted to Killanin that, on second thought, his idea for the Kevin Barry film was unworkable, an 'arty' combination of 'documentary' and 'romantic' approaches.

Lord Killanin (right) with unidentified man, during filming of The Rising of the Moon, *1957. (Lilly Library)*

Brian Desmond Hurst visited Ford twice in 1952: 'We … really had a wing-ding.' Ford wrote to Killanin, 'Did him no end of good. We squeezed in a trip to Hawaii by air. Mary, Brian, and I – swell!'[58] Their joint venture in turning the Irish Literary Revival into a golden era of film-making in the west of Ireland ultimately led to two limited achievements. Ford made three short unrelated stories (from a Lady Gregory play, a Michael J. McHugh tale and a Frank O'Connor story) into the triptych feature *The Rising of the Moon* (1957). It is recognizably a Ford film but does not rank in his top twenty, even though Ford handpicked the stories, cast the actors, and partly produced the whole enterprise.

Hurst filmed J.M. Synge's *The Playboy of the Western World* in County Kerry locations, with Siobhan McKenna as Pegeen Mike (1962).[59] This was the last film he was to make. *The Rising of the Moon* is a great director's not very good piece of work; Hurst's *Playboy* is a not very good director's bad work. These two films constitute the total output of Four Provinces Films. Both are literary (though Ford's handling of the scripts is characteristically free). Neither won high praise nor made the least bit of money, yet they suggest something else that might have been, something Ford long dreamed about: a full identification of the film-maker with the great Irish literary tradition, in a form profitable to Ireland and ennobling to its people worldwide. The happy success of *The Quiet Man* had made the realization of this dream seem possible.

*John Ford (*centre; *unidentified either side) near Oughterard, County Galway, filming 'Guests of the Nation', part of* The Rising of the Moon', *1957. (Lilly Library)*

John Ford with actors from the Taidbhearc Theatre, Galway, preparing to film The Rising of the Moon, *1957. (Lilly Library)*

This aspiration – nurtured by Ford from the early 1930s to the mid-1950s – coincides with his relationship with the unlikely figure of Brian Desmond Hurst. Through these decades Brian Desmond Hurst served as one of Ford's primary personal contacts with an Irish citizen, but his Irish 'cousin' was as untypical and fantasticated an Irishman as it would be possible to find, unless one looked backward to Oscar Wilde or across to the Dublin actor and impresario Micheál Mac Liammóir (an Irish-speaking 'Catholic' born in London as Michael Willmore). Wilde was an Irishman who invented modern queerness; Mac Liammóir a queer who invented his Irishness. Like both, Hurst had enormous personal charm and style.

To judge by Christopher Robbins's memoir, Hurst was a preposterously funny man. Furthermore, he truly loved Ford; loved him as a father and a friend and a film-making genius. But not as a lover. Hurst kept few secrets about men's love lives. Robbins's book includes very funny, indiscreet stories about, for instance, Noel Coward and Sir Michael Redgrave, though it is mostly himself that Hurst takes pleasure in outing. One has to conclude that if John Ford was not actively homosexual with Hurst or in Hurst's demi-monde, he was not actively homosexual, beyond what was supposedly spied by Maureen O'Hara.

The strong bond between John Ford and Brian Desmond Hurst seems to have been woven of several strands: Hurst idolized Ford and Ford liked to be idolized; they both identified from afar with Irishness; both loved film-making; both were visually gifted but with a striking receptivity to literature; like Micheál Mac Liammóir, both identified in a highly romantic way with the Irish Literary Revival, that *fin de siècle* cultural movement led by W.B. Yeats, which united nationalism with the worship of beauty and artistic expressiveness. Finally, both Ford and Hurst existed in a mental world of wild creative possibility.

7

Ford's films are often described as love stories among men. He liked to make films of *Men Without Women* (1930), to quote the title of one; films about soldiers and sailors and cowboys. In such stories, the relationships among the male principals are, as they must be for the sake of the films' drama and profundity, necessarily intimate. Even in those Ford movies where a woman appears in a romantic leading role, she often serves as the prize in pursuit of which two men engage in intimate combat. In *The Man Who Shot Liberty Valance*, for instance, the struggle of educated Easterner Rance Stoddard and natural cowboy Tom Doniphon is literally for the love of Hallie Stoddard. She functions archetypally as mother of the American future: will it be ordered by the law and institutions or by the gun and individual mettle?

In another sense, Hallie Stoddard is just the beard who socially enables a relationship between the two men. Those male–male intimacies in Ford's films between the Rance Stoddards and the Tom Doniphons, the Wyatt Earps and the Doc Hollidays (in *My Darling Clementine*), are never manifested in kisses, genital touches, or even an ever-so-fleeting consciousness of physical attraction. Ford, or his playmates John Wayne and Ward Bond, would knock you silly for suggesting any such thing. The adolescent frat-house nature of their fun is captured in an entry by Captain Ford in the logbook of the *Araner*: 'Caught the first mate [Wayne] pissing in [Ward] Bond's flask this morning – must remember to give him a raise.' The rules are strict indeed under which male tenderness can flourish in the straight world.

8

In the long life of a Hollywood director, working with beautiful stars in nearly 150 movies, this is a rather uneventful sexual history, whether with attractive men or women. Given that Ford was furious at Maureen O'Hara for seeking a divorce from her wholly useless husband Will Price (even though a year earlier Ford himself had been romancing O'Hara in letters), that he was torn up about John Wayne's divorce from his first wife, and that he began the sundering of his relationship to his own son Pat partly on account of his divorce, one must conclude that Ford took seriously the indissolubility of marriage (inherited from his Irish Catholicism) as a valuable standard in the normless flux of modernity.

It is appropriate to put it this way rather than to say that Ford opposed divorce because he believed in the orthodox Catholic teaching on marriage. Asked if he was Catholic, Ford replied, 'I am, but not very.'[60] More significantly, after World War II, when starting a new production company, Argosy Pictures, Ford, along with his screenwriter Dudley Nichols (1895–1960), made a huge effort and financial investment in producing a film of Graham Greene's *The Power and the Glory*. *The Fugitive* (1947) is a terrible film. Henry Fonda – prototype of an American Protestant if there ever was one – is miscast as the last remaining Catholic priest, wearing a sarape and riding a donkey through a dystopian, socialist Mexico, in which both religion and drink have been outlawed. The theological point of Greene's novel was that a drunken, adulterous Catholic priest who does not acknowledge his own children can still be a true priest; he may yet serve as the instrument of God's grace. The scenario of Ford and Nichols completely misses this point. Their hero does not have sex with a woman, much less father a child, and he gets drunk only once, and then unwillingly.

But the message with which Greene's point is replaced reveals something about John Ford.[61] The screen narrative becomes a simple allegory to demonstrate that people cannot bear too much reality. They need a drink sometimes. Equally, they require faith and magical rites such as baptism and psychological rituals like confession, just as they require their daily bread and five o'clock tequila. Even if you stamp out all signs of religion and kill all the priests, ministers of faith will as if by magic reappear. People will reassemble humbly and dreamily around them. There is something of Voltaire's bleak Catholic atheism in the movie's moral: if there were no God, it would be necessary to invent Him. This is only a coy way of saying, 'There is no God, but the chaos of instinct would be intolerable without belief.'

John Ford and screenwriter Dudley Nichols were also interested, it seems, in giving high art cinematic status to their Catholicism, just as they had sought such status for Catholic Irishness in *The Informer* (thus the extreme camera angles, tableau groupings, and imposing chiaroscuro in both films). All that emerges in *The Fugitive*, however, is a slow-paced, pretentious allegory without any real religious feeling whatsoever. Apart from the fact that *The Fugitive* saddled Argosy Pictures with a debt from which it never escaped, even though all the company's subsequent films were profitable, it reveals something about Ford's attitude to religion. He had, the film shows, a functionalist view of the importance of dogma and religious institutions. Catholicism, like ethnicity, was a necessary fiction.

9

That ethnicity is a fiction, according to Max Weber, is its defining characteristic: 'Ethnic membership (*Gemeinsamkeit*) differs from kinship group precisely by being a presumed identity, not a group with concrete social action, like the latter.' Ethnic groups, he says, 'entertain a subjective belief in their common descent because of similarities of physical type or customs or both, or because of memories of colonization and migration'.[62] Weber here suggests that an ethnic community is maintained in the present by its observance of customs it imagines to have received down the generations from a mythically unitary ancestral past. The members of each new generation commune with each other by imaginatively communing with the past of forefathers in the motherland. They observe the tribe's dietary traditions (if any), learn its original language (if any), play its native sports, practise its local religion, marry within the tribe, perhaps monopolize certain trades, and maybe build certain kinds of dwellings or arrange domestic interiors in a traditional way. But this notion of even a fictive 'primordial' ethnic core has been critiqued by contemporary social anthropologists. In 'The Poverty of Primordialism', Jack Eller and Reed Coughlan argue that ethnic identities are not given and long-established, but are 'renewed, modified, and remade in each generation. Far from being self-perpetuating, they require creative effort and investment.'[63]

Included among the processes by which ethnic identities are continuously remade are the cultural industries, which themselves feed upon the inventions of poets, novelists, popular historians and film-makers. The power of cinema in particular to shape social attitudes was recognized, with a high degree of worry, by churches and government representatives. The centralization of the power to fashion identity in one industry concerned American authorities sufficiently that, in spite of the Constitutional protections of the freedom of speech and freedom of the press, the US government was ready to create an official film censorship at the very start of the silent era. This move was only stopped in 1922 by the producers' pre-emptive appointment of Will Hays, a Republican politician, to run a system of self-censorship, the Motion Picture Producers and Distributors Association [MPPDA]. Hays proved insufficiently aggressive for the Catholic Legion of Decency, so their representatives, Irish-Americans Joe Breen and Martin Quigley, put teeth into the MPPDA by creating a 'Production Code', enforced with very little change from 1934 to 1952.[64] As a result of Breen's invisible but very Catholic hand, blue-pencilling every single script prior to shooting, crime never paid, divorce was never mentioned, unmarried couples always kept their feet on the floor, homosexuals were not to be seen, and priests appeared frequently on screen as cheery good fellows.

While the Production Code Administration kept its eye upon sex and crime (and through them the proper mating between social groups and the protection of private property), Congress was vigilant about the representation of nationalities. In 1941 the USA was governed by a Neutrality Act with respect to the warring parties in World War II. Two senators on the Committee on

Interstate Commerce accused Hollywood producers of allowing foreign-born directors to attempt to drag America into the war, by means of pro-British epics like *That Hamilton Woman* (1940, dir. Alexander Korda) and anti-German thrillers like *Manhunt* (1941, dir. Fritz Lang). Darryl Zanuck, appearing before the Committee, defended Hollywood by saying the movies 'sold the American way of life not only to America but to the entire world'.[65] Zanuck was thinking perhaps of pictures he himself had recently produced, starring Henry Fonda, and directed by John Ford: *Drums Along the Mohawk*, *Young Mr Lincoln* and *The Grapes of Wrath*. Not only did these films market the American way of life to Americans and others, they participated in the invention of that way of life. The self-recognition of Americans as American came through identification with stars like Henry Fonda in stories of the country's past. As a role model, he was a lesson to immigrants and a clarification to old inhabitants.

John Ford's claim to be the great film fashioner of American identity (the implicit role in which he appeared at that 1951 meeting of the Screen Directors Guild) was already secure by the end of the 1930s. In 1939, his miraculous year of triumphs, he also made one more classic, *Stagecoach* (1939). In it, John Wayne has his first successful starring role in an A-list movie. *Stagecoach*, like Ford's post-war Cavalry trilogy, gives profound and entertaining expression to abiding issues of American culture – freedom versus law, race and democracy, violence and what George W. Bush called the 'homeland', a Fordian touch meant to evoke both national destiny, domestic decency, and a circle-the-wagons alert to the core white ethnicities, to unite against the Absolute Other.

If one sees Ford as an American among Americans, and director of Westerns, then *The Quiet Man* of 1952 is a charming freak of Irish-American sentiment, with little precedent in his career, and less bearing on Irish realities. And that is how Ford's career is often represented. But Ford's career did not look this way to other people in the 1930s, and it may be doubted that it looked that way to him. In his own mind he was not just an American who made stories about America, but an Irish artist. Just as Yeats, Synge, O'Casey, Liam O'Flaherty and others had invented an heroic modern Irish identity in literature, he wished to do the same in films. He developed contradictory plans either to transplant to Hollywood the remaining geniuses of that cultural revival, or to go to Ireland to join in the building up of the Irish Free State. In *The Rise of the American Film: A Critical History*, published in 1939, Lewis Jacobs gives a solid account of Ford's biographical background and the stages of his stylistic development. Jacobs concludes: 'It is safe to say that the best of [Ford's future] pictures will be painted with the green hills of Ireland as a background.'[66] This raises two questions: first, since none of Ford's films up to then had been made in Ireland, on what evidence might a bright man like Lewis Jacobs think this was a safe thing to say in 1939? Second, why did that prediction turn out to be so incorrect?

10

A key collaborator in Ford's Irish cultural enterprises was Dudley Nichols. The son of a doctor in a small town in Ohio, Nichols served with the navy in World War I and then became a journalist for the *New York World.* With the emergence of talkies, opportunities arose in Hollywood for writers of every kind. At the urging of Winfield Sheehan, production chief of Fox Studio, Nichols came west to seek his fortune in June 1929. Assigned to work with Ford, Nichols recalled that, even on first meeting, 'I liked him. I am part Irish and we got on.'[67] Being part Irish was a big help in getting on with John Ford.

Another man working on the story was James Kevin McGuinness (1893–1950), along with Ford, Nichols and Winfield Sheehan, a person of Irish ancestry. They agreed to work together on a submarine story, but Nichols said that while he knew about the navy, and he knew how to write a play, he had no idea how to construct a screenplay. Well, Ford said, could you write a play in fifty or sixty scenes? Nichols answered that of course he could tell a story not just in three acts but in many scenes. Ford and Nichols also came to agree that film dialogue should be scantier and plainer than dialogue in a play or novel.[68] The collaboration went smoothly, and the two men thereafter 'worked together as much as possible'.[69]

While many directors and screenwriters worked separately from one another in the studio system (the director was given a completed script produced by a team of writers and re-writers unknown to him, or a writer and director were randomly matched project by project by the producer), Nichols and Ford collaborated as a production unit on five films over the next four years. Yet these were still films assigned to them by the producer. They might seek to discover their own film style. They might stuff the cast with Irish actors – J. Farrell MacDonald, Spencer Tracy, George O'Brien, Walter McGrail, Robert Emmett O'Connor, Jack Murphy, Maurice Murphy, Sally O'Neill and so forth. But what they really wanted to do, initially in company with James McGuinness, was a film of Liam O'Flaherty's *The Informer.* In such a film they would bring on board the composer, set designer and photographer from the very start, even before the screenplay was written, so that the entire project would be an integrated collaboration, rather than a producer-managed factory enterprise with complete division of labour and no creative autonomy for the artisans.[70] However, in the emerging structure of the studio system in Hollywood, it was not the business of writers or directors to pick subjects or organize the sequence of their development; those were jobs for the producer.

Fox Studios refused their request to buy the rights to O'Flaherty's novel. McGuinness then moved from Fox to Metro Goldwyn Meyer, and Ford and Nichols worked variously for Universal, Columbia, MGM and Fox, before arriving at RKO, a studio formed in 1928 by Joseph Kennedy. In the 1960s, while John F. Kennedy was president, Ford told Peter Bogdanovich that it was the president's father Joe Kennedy who had brought him into RKO. Offered scripts for some Westerns, Ford said he was tired of them. 'I've got a story here written by my cousin Liam O'Flaherty.'[71] The line producers at RKO were furious at the rejection by a director of his assignment. Their understanding was as follows: John Ford is a director of Westerns; here were some Westerns; his job was to direct them. RKO was not long after declaring bankruptcy, and still under bank supervision, and Westerns were dependable money-makers. Joe Kennedy then said, according to Ford in 1963, 'An Irish story? That ought to be good; why don't you let him make it?'

This is a fine story of 'Micks on the make', and was especially newsworthy since JFK was then president, but things did not happen this way. Joe Kennedy sold the last of his stock in RKO in 1931, while Ford's first picture with the studio was *The Lost Patrol* in 1934. According to a 1935 interview with the *New York Times*, the producer who approved the purchase of *The Informer* was an Irishman, but it was not Joe Kennedy; it was J.R. McDonough, co-executive producer at RKO from February 1934. He had been persuaded to back the film partly through the efforts of assistant producer, Cliff Reid (after Ford showed him the novel, Reid said, 'I was crazy about it; I saw it had great stuff in it').[72]

Learning that *The Informer* had been given a green light, the other executive producer at RKO and guardian of the bottom line, B.B. Kahane, threw a fit.[73] It was a 'criminal waste of money', an Irish story would never sell.[74] To sweeten his proposition, Ford offered to forswear his fee and direct the film for 12.5 per cent of the profits. Even so, Ford recalled, 'They wouldn't let me work on the lot [on Melrose Avenue] – they sent me across the street to a dusty old stage [at California Studio] ... They wouldn't build us any real sets ... the city of Dublin was just painted canvas.'[75]

It was Ford's custom as a director, having fully invested himself in the story, to take his ideas for how to stage scenes from the setting.[76] He liked to choose locations that were already poetry, as in his famous preference for Monument Valley, Utah, its arid grandeur serving more as a dreamscape and heroic threshold of the American West than as a possible place of habitation, or even a historical route to areas of settlement. In the case of *The Informer*, however, the cheaply constructed set was unevocative. But Ford had the help of a photographer of genius, Joe August (1880–1947). August had been filming in Hollywood since 1913, and he was not only an old hand, but an ambitious visual artist. Like Ford, August had been awestruck by the style of F.W. Murnau, the great German director, in *Sunrise* (1927), starring George O'Brien, one of Ford's own leading men. O'Brien plays a farmer torn between two women, in a melodrama that poses city against country and bad mistress against decent wife.[77]

In February 1935 at California Studio, with only a dusty stage and painted flats to stand in for 1922 Dublin, Ford released Joe August to do what he could in the *Sunrise* style, with light, camera angles and dissolves. Ford animated the space within the set by means of a wind machine and an overworked fog machine (magically, wind and fog exist together, as in nature they cannot). The beauty of *Sunrise* was invented within the camera, with toy trains, fake marshes, mock-up German cities in the night, luminous mists, and boats on dark waters taking on a convincing surreality by careful, frame-by-frame superimpositions. It is a magic lantern illusion of light and dark, not an optical register of the physical world.

Liam O'Flaherty's somewhat Dostoevskian tale is a psychological study of a classic Irish stereotype, the man who out of cowardice, drink, poverty, or all three, betrays a secret nationalist organization to the British authorities, thus thwarting once again the goal of Irish independence.[78] The film is faithful to the novel's innovative representation of an individual not at the level of consciousness but as a sort of hungry, melancholy animal moved by deep but dull instincts amid the deterministic complications of an only dimly apprehended society. Although big and powerful, the anti-hero, Gypo, is so unenlightened he is past being contemptible; he becomes the pitiable victim of circumstances.

A large part of the work of capturing O'Flaherty's new conception of human individuality (similar to the heroes in Eugene O'Neill's *The Hairy Ape* [1922] and Richard Wright's *Native Son* [1940]) was achieved by casting. RKO producers tried to foist well-known heavies on Ford, but he was determined to get Victor McLaglen.[79] While McLaglen's surname was perhaps a sufficient basis for Ford to call him cousin, he was not actually Irish.[80] Born in Kent, McLaglen was the son of the Anglican bishop of Tunbridge Wells. He served with the Irish Guards of the British army during World War I (and was made Privy Marshal of Baghdad when General Allenby captured the city),[81] fought as a professional boxer across Canada, and travelled right around the world. Arriving in Hollywood in 1924, he became a leading man and a personality in the 'Hollywood Raj.' He started a United Services club to welcome officers of British ships docking in California harbors.[82] McLaglen had a huge, muscled 6′3″ frame and people sometimes thought he had no more than that, but he was an articulate, gentle and even elegant man off-screen. On screen he was well able to play parts besides those of the heavy – cast as a Russian spy in the 1931 *Dishonored*, he is the love interest for Marlene Dietrich.

Victor McLaglen with his Oscar, 1 January 1937. (Time and Life Pictures/Getty Images)

After reading O'Flaherty's novel, he was 'dubious' about the part. By 'shrewd salesmanship', Ford gradually brought McLaglen round to the view that he was born to play Gypo. 'Physically and mentally, he was the informer,' Ford told a reporter, and then corrected himself: 'Just make that physically.'[83] This is a typical stroke of Ford's humour – slightly sadistic. Indeed, McLaglen, with his huge hands and beetling Neanderthal brow, was physically right for the part. Furthermore, he was flexible enough an actor to give the role what it required. However, McLaglen was a far cry from the instinctual, cowardly beast that was Gypo. It was not for who he was, but for what he could do, that Ford cast Victor McLaglen as Gypo. He needed a big-framed star from an earlier era of screen acting to play a completely inarticulate man, to play him, that is, as he would be played in a silent movie, with big gestures and a face that displayed emotional messages with the rapidity and unsubtlety of bulletins on an electronic billboard.

The opening sequence of the film rapidly lays out the plot and creates a remarkable mood of inevitability without any dialogue whatsoever. Gypo comes upon a poster offering £20 for information leading to the capture of Frankie McPhillip, wanted for murder. Gypo, with his slow ooze of mentation, takes a while to digest the information – thinking is an alimentary process for him. The poster activates a memory trace: himself and Frankie, uniformed and armed with rifles, merrily drinking bottles of stout in a pub. The image is briefly superimposed on the poster. Throughout the movie, Gypo's phases of consciousness take shape as hallucinations. In silent movies this was a device for showing a character's thoughts, but in the sound era it suggests a character who does not have thoughts; Gypo is sub-conceptual. His consciousness is a screen on which sense-impressions, memory traces and fantasies appear and dissolve.

Victor McLaglen as Gypo Nolan in The Informer, *1935. (Courtesy RKO)*

Frowning, Gypo tears down the poster, crumples it in his big meaty hand, and drops it on the street. With slow rocking strides, he makes his way down the foggy streets and then bumps his head into an overhanging street sign. With a scowl, he looks up at the sign's advertisement for 'Fish and Chips', a little two-second incident that rapidly establishes Gypo's abnormal height, his hunger, and his poverty. He comes upon a crossroads where a street singer (Denis O'Dea) under a lamp gives a tremulous rendition of the 'Rose of Tralee'. Brought to a stop by the song's sentimentality, Gypo suddenly feels the crumpled poster, blown down the street, sticking to his trouser leg. The fog in which Gypo is surrounded, and the gusts of wind that drive him down the streets, are plainly expressionist symbols of his interior life, for the poster is a chillingly animated symbol of his doom.[84] He shakes his leg once, twice, before he rids himself of the poster. He is then jerkingly startled by the sight of a platoon of five armed soldiers frisking pedestrians. He pulls his cap down on his head, as a man on the run would do.

Down the street under another lamp stands a young woman (played by Margot Grahame) in a Madonna-like attitude: shawl around head and shoulders, sad uplifted eyes. Opposite, a middle-aged man in a bowler hat eyes her up. He smiles meaningfully. In a famous magical transformation, she heaves a sigh of resignation, lowers her gaze to the man, and throws back her shawl, revealing a head of blonde hair, a décolleté dress, and a cute little hat perched on her head – the perfect Magdalene. The transition from virgin to whore is achieved in a single second.[85] She sidles toward the man, and he sidles toward her, until he is close enough to exhale his cigarette smoke into her face. Meanwhile, the wanted poster has blown down the street and is sticking this time to her ankle, and again it has to be kicked loose.

Gypo comes upon the scene. He picks up the gentleman as if he were a lightweight manikin and tosses him five yards out into the street. Margot Grahame then has the first line of spoken dialogue in the film: 'O Gypo! O, Gypo! What's the use? I'm hungry and can't pay the room rent.' In a shop window, she sees an advertisement offering boat passage to America for £10. Twenty pounds, and we would both be free, she tells him. He is startled with rage and fear at what he takes to be her suggestion that he should rat out his old friend. But the idea has been planted in the thick's brain. Again and again, like hallucinations, the images of the wanted poster with the £20 reward and the advertisement for the £10 tickets are superimposed on what Gypo sees around him. When Frankie McPhillip later finds Gypo over his dinner in a lodging house, Gypo stares astonished at his old friend's face, seeing *Twenty Pound*

Reward written all over it. It is no time before Gypo informs the British police, Frankie is shot, and the reward is paid.

From that point on, the focus of McLaglen's acting is Gypo's belief that every single person, even the blind man in the street, can see that he is a Judas. In a painful paradox, everything he does to hide it stupidly makes his guilt more visible. A ferocious boxer, he slugs everyone who looks at him crossways. Buying a bottle of whiskey to quell his fear and guilt, he flashes his money to a surprised barman, to whom Gypo is well known to be chronically penniless. He brags to his girlfriend that he has come into possession of her fare to America. Half-drunk, he goes to Frankie's wake and accidentally spills gold coins onto the floor in front of everyone there, including men in belted trench-coats from the IRA. While all the mourners watch, he hands over a large donation to Frankie's mother (Una O'Connor).

Called to account by the commandant of the IRA (Preston Foster), Gypo admits he has not had a job in six months. He is soon buying fish and chips for all his new hanger-on friends. One particularly determined leech (J.M. Kerrigan), calls him 'King Gypo' and (the classic Irish cliché) 'a king and the descendant of kings'. By means of such simple flattery, Gypo is led to a whore-house for further fleecing. This is not a detective story of little clues slowly adding up to the truth, but of the truth known from the start and the procession of its painfully obvious consequences.

At 1 am, at the end of Gypo's long day of shame, a court of inquiry is held by the IRA. McLaglen, breaking down, asks the Volunteers and the jury of ordinary citizens, 'Is there anyone here who can tell me why I did it?' They cannot, but, led by a jury foreman in a long grey beard (played by Francis Ford), they condemn him nonetheless. After some terrific fighting by McLaglen with his would-be executioners, a chase around the streets and up and down stairs, he is at last mortally wounded and staggers into a church where Frankie McPhillip's mother is praying. The next-to-last line in the movie is hers: 'I forgive you, Gypo. You didn't know what you were doing.' The final reconciliation scene is unsatisfactory to some modern movie-goers – too allegorical, pretentious and Catholic for contemporary tastes – but it is an admirably deft piece of writing by Dudley Nichols, whereby, through a little verbal echo, the blind patriarchal judgment of the courtroom is washed away by the Christian mercy of the holy mother, and, arms spread as if on a cross, the Irish Judas becomes a Jesus.

Gypo is not the sole representation of Irish ethnicity in the movie. Another is Dan Gallagher, the IRA commandant. Played by handsome leading man Preston Foster, he is a sober, alert, Catholic and fair-minded, but unsentimental patriot. (In O'Flaherty's novel, this figure had been a murderous, repellent communist.)[86] He broods over the threat of Gypo to the movement. Not only has he betrayed one man to the police; with what he knows he could go on to destroy the whole organization. Clearly, with his obvious character flaws – sentimentalism, drink, belligerence, self-flattery, hunger for popularity with the crowd, and ignorance – Gypo Nolan, however lovable a brute, cannot be trusted with the country's destiny. He and all he represents must be killed off for Ireland to be free.

11

The Informer is a famous case of a 'sleeper', a movie that after little studio promotion and a slow start with the public becomes a commercial success as a result of good reviews and 'word-of-mouth' advertising. While there are certainly estimable qualities in *The Informer*, it received favourable treatment from critics partly because it bucked the trends of 1935 Hollywood. Still in the first flush of talkies, movies at the time were in love with dialogue, often borrowed from stage plays; *The Informer* reverted to the aestheticism of the silent era. It was deliberately arty, while the moguls of the entertainment business were anti-art. When big studios like MGM promoted their million-dollar epics on the basis of their conspicuous expenditure – big stars, casts of thousands, fairyland sets – *The Informer* was shot in three weeks for about $250,000. One critic, Pare Lorentz of *Vanity Fair*, made much of the fact that its one star, McLaglen, is never allowed by the director to 'control the *mise en scène* … It is the film and its collective that work, as opposed to the Hollywood norm where all … is thrown aside that the one personality may be blown to the skies.'[87]

Ultimately, the artistic-political significance of *The Informer* came to a head in the debate over the Academy Awards of 1936. The awards were made by the Academy of Motion Picture Arts and Sciences (AMPAS). This was an organization controlled by a cabal of the studio producers. The same group of producers had alienated other interested parties in the studio system – writers, directors, actors and cameramen – by demanding an across-the-board 50-per cent pay-cut in 1933, supposedly to save the industry from the effects of the Depression. The producers, however, spared themselves any belt-tightening. In the struggle for financial and artistic power within Hollywood, screen actors, screenwriters and screen directors each formed guilds, all of them in conflict with the producers, and sometimes with each other. In an article published by *The New York Times* before the Awards were announced, *The Informer* was defined as evidence that the writer and the director, working freely, were the secret of motion-picture success.[88] Bossy producers and vain actors either stole the credit that belonged to others, or actually got in the way of the truly creative people.

Ford and Nichols themselves gave this same spin to the publicity for *The Informer*. Nichols, an activist in the Screenwriters Guild, declared that even if offered an Academy award for his work on *The Informer*, he would not accept it, because there were few writers in the Academy of Motion Picture Arts and Sciences – only 35 – as opposed to 990 in the Screenwriters Guild. The vote of so few of his colleagues would be no honour at all. (Nichols was given the award, and he did refuse it.)

Ford gave one interview about *The Informer* in which he said that all that producers want to do is make money, and a lot of money. That was fine; he conceded that the art form depended on capital. But the only way producers knew how to make money was by doing once again what made money the last time. In fact, they knew nothing about what made a movie successful. Ford himself doubted that success had any more to do with stars than with producers. 'You don't think *The Informer* went over because of McLaglen, do you? … I'm no McLaglen fan you know.'[89]

Ford had given out the story that, the night before filming the climactic courtroom scene, he had sent people out to get McLaglen drunk. The following morning, Ford made the actor stumble unrehearsed through the scene, ad-libbing, repeating himself, and looking lost.[90] He was not acting as if he were stressed, it was implied; he was stressed. The genius of the performance (for which McLaglen got the Award for Best Actor), Ford not very subtly suggested, derived from himself, the invisible director (who also got an Academy Award for *The Informer*).[91] Indeed, he told a reporter that credit for the movie, nominated for five Oscars and winner of four, belonged to 'Nichols and me – We did *The Informer*.'[92]

This interpretation prevails in the present. On the current trailer for *The Informer* on 'The John Ford Film Collection' (a set of five DVDs), Peter Bogdanovich is interviewed:

> What had happened was that Ford told McLaglen that he didn't have to work the next day and he came back and it was the most important scene in the picture. McLaglen told him he was miserable about it and couldn't do it. [Here a film clip is inserted in the trailer, McLaglen saying in the trial scene, 'I couldn't, I don't, I don't know what I'm doing'.] That's what made it so good. Ford knew that if he'd (McLaglen had) acted … [Ford] wanted him to be almost incoherent. And that's how he got the Oscar.

That is not what happened. This is auteur-worship, an idol of the tribe. McLaglen may have gone out the night before with some Japanese people, as Joseph McBride claims. He may have had some drinks, as he was accustomed to do anyway. He was given a direction by Ford to ad-lib during the trial scene, to ask questions, and express confusion, and he drew upon his skills as a professional actor to do so. And that's how he got the Oscar.

By whatever complexity of men and means, *The Informer* turned out a huge success, to the surprise of the RKO producers. But 'does that make it any easier to go ahead with O'Casey's *The Plough and the Stars*?' Ford asked. 'Not for a second!' He and Nichols were 'fighting to have the Abbey Players imported intact and we're fighting the censors and fighting the so-called financial wizards at every point'. Creation was conflict in 1930s' Hollywood. The interviewer asked Ford what was the ultimate purpose of his struggle with the studios. Did he 'believe, as a director, in including your point of view in a picture about things that bother you?' Ford looked at him as if 'to question the necessity of an answer': 'What the hell else does a man live for?'[93] Thus, in 1935, John Ford staked his claim to being the author of the films he directed.

12

The *auteur* theory as a theory was developed by cinephiles in France in the early 1950s. Truffaut, Godard and others, instead of seeing new releases one by one, got a chance to look at the whole tranche of American movies Occupied France had missed during World War II. They were struck by the personal distinction of some directors' careers (Howard Hawks, Alfred Hitchcock and a few others, but not Ford) and the incoherent and therefore impersonal nature of the output of others. Their theory was that film could be an art form only when a great director imposed authorial control over the medium. The director's work would then be thematically and artistically coherent. When, as was often the case in Hollywood, a director does not pick the subject, write the script, cast the actors, perform the roles, operate the camera or edit the footage, it can be difficult to trace the director's hand in the final product.

Obviously, film is always an absolutely collaborative art. While the public is eager for an artist's signature (preferably in the bottom right-hand corner of the painting), all the arts are, in fact, social and collaborative. Film-making is more so. The credits roll at the end of a Hollywood movie, and one sees hundreds, even thousands of names. There is no other art form like that.

Can one then really claim that a movie, like a poem, has a single author, and expresses that one person's point of view?

It is clear from the case of *The Informer* that the *auteur*-theory of film was not simply an academic question arising in the 1950s and 60s; it was the subject of labour conflicts within the film-making industry in the 1930s. Creative control was struggled over between professionals with divided and yet equally essential responsibilities. In the context of the 1936 Academy Awards and the push by producers to impose discipline on the factory system of production, Ford and Nichols railed against producers, ridiculed star Victor McLaglen, and rather ignored the contributions of cameraman Joe August and music composer Max Steiner.

But we never find either Nichols or Ford on screen or soundtrack. Why not say that what is really relevant to understanding the meaning of this work of art is the ethnic background, sexual history, artistic influences and aesthetic views of Victor McLaglen, or Joe August, Max Steiner or J.R. McDonough, who, as producer, envisioned the potential success of Ford as director for this literary property? For that matter, why not look to the biography of Liam O'Flaherty? He is the one who came up with the basis for the whole affair.

John Ford did aspire, as he told the interviewer in 1935, to express himself through film. But so did the others involved in the making of *The Informer.* What else did Joe Kerrigan live for, the old Abbey Theatre actor who plays the leech Terry, but to express himself? Why did Una O'Connor, the ex-Abbey Theatre actress who plays the bereaved mother of Frankie McPhillip, launch herself on the wandering life of a theatre and film actress? She too lived to express her talent. All the participants in such a venture are talented people with real vocations.

Yet Ford's job as a director was unique. He alone had to work with each and every creative partner in the film and orchestrate the contributions of all. To the extent that John Ford had genius, and that was to a very great extent, it was a genius for collaboration. A director's collaboration in movie-making, the most complicated of all cultural industries, has many sides. One side, sometimes impeded by the studio system of long-term contracts, is picking one's collaborators. Ford tended to pick people of Irish ancestry, his widespread if fictive cousinage. He entertained an absolute faith in the brandname of the Abbey Theatre as a store of quality actors. In the case of cinematographers in particular, he simply went for men of talent, like Joe August, Gregg Toland and Winton Hoch. He also tended to work with the same people again and again, in a sort of team, or even family – the loosely affiliated 'John Ford

Stock Company'. Membership required not just personal creativity but loyalty to Ford, belief in Ford, and subservience to Ford. A poem written by Ford's regular crew concludes:[94]

We love him like we love the Lord;
We're the students of the great John Ford.

A second side of the director's art of collaboration was the capacity to appraise accurately the creative potential of his co-workers. In some films, for instance, Ford would tell the cameraman where to put the camera and he would strictly limit the amount of footage shot, so as to curtail the freedom of the editor. In cases like *The Informer*, however, Ford would, out of a respectful understanding of the cameraman's capacity, set him free to do what Ford had anticipated he was capable of. In other words, Ford expresses himself by his understanding of how Joe August will express himself and by his permission for the photographer to do so.

A similar anticipation of an artiste's expressive capacity is crucial to the casting of actors: 'You've got to tell your story through the people who will portray it,' Ford explained to a reporter.[95] While he seems to have seized the freedom to cast *The Informer*, studio executives often picked the stars, or they insisted on the director at least drawing upon those the studio had under long-term contract. Even in those cases, however, Ford claimed the right to cast the minor parts. For these he tended to choose former stars or else veterans of the Abbey Theatre ensemble:

> I'm able to see that these ex-stars will, after all, give a better performance even in the smallest parts than any casual extra would; and it's my contention that the bits in any picture are just as important as the starring role, since they round out the story – complete the atmosphere – make the whole plausible. You've seen, certainly, a good many really fine scenes spoiled suddenly by a background player who is obviously reciting his lines, or blundering awkwardly through his action. I won't have that.[96]

Once he had chosen his actors, he did not try to tell them how to do their work, as Maureen O'Hara noticed: 'The most wonderful thing in watching Mr Ford work was the freedom he gave his actors … He never gave specific directions, and I learned over time that this was the best compliment Mr Ford could give.'[97] It was not in doing his collaborators' work for them, or in predetermining the outcome, but in setting free the creative initiative of members of a trusted crew that Ford excelled as a director.

A third side of Ford's art of collaboration was his preference for working with a screenwriter from early on in the development of the story. While he could not write a script himself, his nightmare was being a hack studio director handed a few pages on the set each day to film, with no overview of the story, his only role being to tell the actors where to stand.[98] In his favourite method of collaboration, he and Dudley Nichols would go on a voyage on the *Araner*. Ford would suggest something; Nichols would suggest something, back and forth. Then the writer would produce a draft, and Ford would give his opinion before redrafting. They would return to port with a finished script.

This happened in the case of *The Informer*. The draft screenplay for *The Informer*, dated 18 December 1934, begins in the dining room of a Dublin lodging house and a long, wordy exposition by way of a conversation between Gypo Nolan and Frankie McPhillip, the man he will betray. Not until page 12 of this draft does Gypo read the wanted poster, the first thing he does in the finished script. After this draft was written, however, Nichols went with Ford on a voyage on the *Araner*. The script that was completed upon their return, used for shooting in February 1935, and thereafter followed closely by Ford, begins with detailed action and no dialogue:

> WIDE ANGLE SHOT of a Dublin street corner. Thick fog. Somewhere in the distance a street singer is singing to a fiddle. Before us is a blank brick wall where diverse bills are posted, some tattered, some new, but all vaguely seen through the fog. A lamp post on the corner lights this wall and throws shadows up this side street. Around the corner past his lamp post is a brighter street – our Dublin street which extends for a short block past a fish and chip shop to the public house on the corner. But all that is out of the scene now. Out from the fog down this dark street emerges the slouching figure of GYPO NOLAN. Desolate and down and out. Hands shoved in his pockets. An old felt hat on his head. An old white muffler wrapped round his throat. In this FULL SHOT we see him come out of the fog like some strange fish out of a mysterious ocean of mist. He halts near the corner and stares at a small poster ...[99]

In an important 1951 article published in *Films in Review*, Lindsay Anderson argued that Ford did not understand his own genius; he had been led astray in a string of movies by Dudley Nichols into 'sentimental simplification of issues and characters, a highly self-conscious striving for significance, and a fundamental unreality'.[100] The great Ford films, according to Anderson (and he was ready to make the largest of claims for their value) were American stories produced by Darryl Zanuck, like *Drums Along the Mohawk*, *Young Mr*

Lincoln and *My Darling Clementine.* There is no question but that Nichols had an influence on Ford, but was it a good influence?

The films made without Nichols do not, to name but one difference, have the same degree of respect for literature (Irish literature especially) or an equal ambition to discover filmic equivalents for literary effects. In the mid-1930s, through figures like Dudley Nichols and John Ford, as well as bookish Jewish producers like Irving Thalberg and David O. Selznick, movies were ambitious to match the expressive reach of literature.[101] In the case of Nichols and Ford, the goal was to realize and add, in particular, to the achievements of the Irish Literary Revival. If Nichols made a difference to Ford, Ford also made a measurable difference to Nichols. The drafts of *The Informer* screenplay before and after the voyage on the *Araner* force one to conclude that Nichols wrote in ready collaboration with Ford's own notions about the *mise-en-scène* and screen continuity. *The Informer* – story, dialogue and camera set-ups as encapsulated in the script – is the result of collaboration.

In gratitude for being allowed to collaborate with the writer, Ford would invite Nichols onto the set, usually forbidden to writers, partly because the studio had to pay the writer for his time there, and partly because many actors and directors were wary of writers, who tended to keep guard on the verbatim realization of their photoplays. In a 1930s' survey of Hollywood writers, Ford and Nichols, along with the writer-director pair of Robert Riskin and Frank Capra, were overwhelmingly named as the colleagues most admired. Those partnerships had enviable creative identity.

A final side of Ford's skills as a collaborator is his dark side. He was a bully who loved a scapegoat. He would single out a person – actor, producer, cameraman, or whatever – and humiliate him or her in front of the assembled production team. Sometimes he would pursue his victim for days and days afterwards. Even stars like Jimmy Stewart and John Wayne did not always escape such public spectacles of humiliation. A case has been made that the bullying was part of a crafty motivational strategy by which the director got the best out of an actor. The treatment of McLaglen in the courtroom scene, for instance, can be read (though not convincingly) as the prototype for such motivational stratagems. But often an artistic pretext is not apparent for what seems unmotivated, disproportionate public cruelty.

In his book on John Wayne, Garry Wills concludes that Ford was just a son of a bitch who abused his position of power.[102] Certainly, many of the tales of Ford's explosions on set relate to this power. He turned nasty whenever the director's authority was the least bit called into question. For instance, Cliff

Reid, assigned to be associate producer for *The Informer*, arrived on set the first day. Normally, it would be his job to keep a close eye on the day-to-day progress of filming – numbers of lunches eaten, extras used and pages shot – and thus on the project's budget. Ford called the company together. 'This,' he said, pointing to Reid, 'is an associate producer.' He took Reid's chin in his hand, and turned his head into profile. 'Take a good look at him, because you will not see him again until the picture is finished shooting. Thank you, Cliff, I'll see you at the rushes.'[103] Disgraceful conduct to a colleague without whom the project might not have been green-lit! But in this way the director succeeded in getting freedom from further interference by the associate producer.

Left to right: John Ford, Margot Grahame, unidentified man and Victor McLaglen, filming The Informer, *1935. (Courtesy Scott Eyman)*

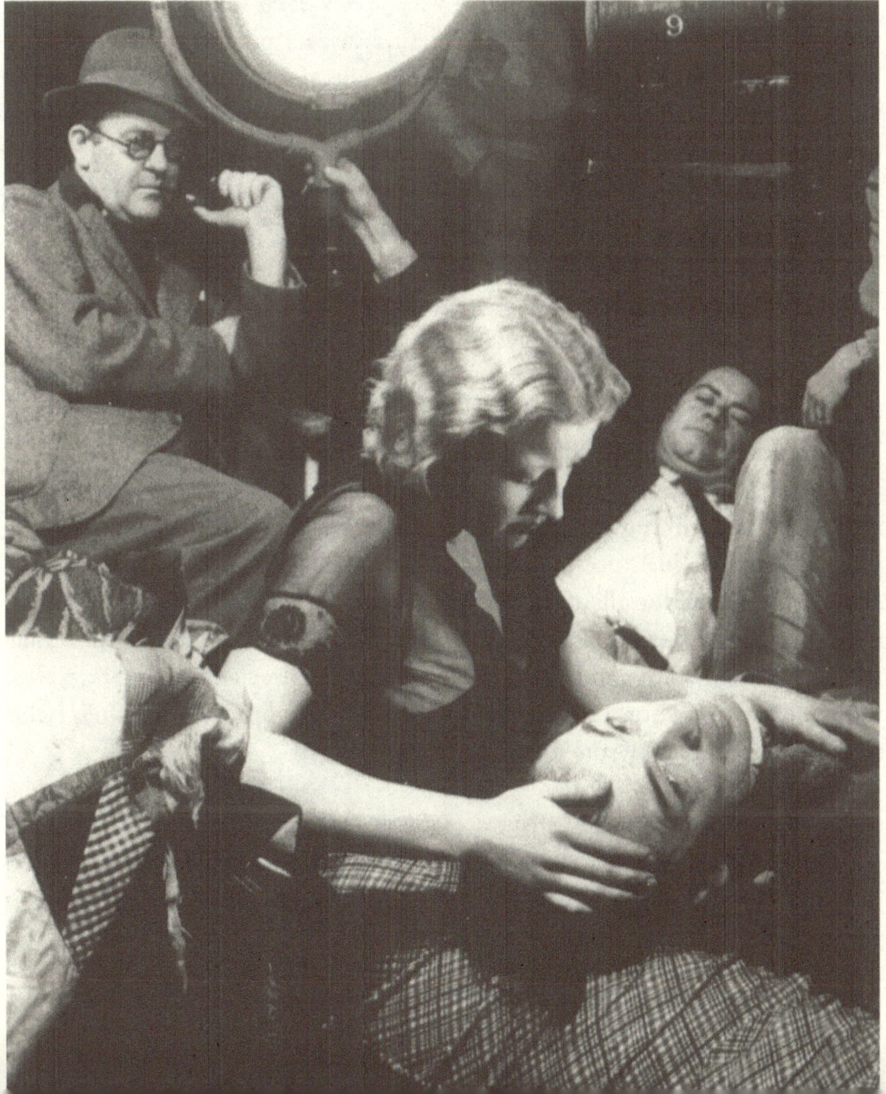

On the same day, the schedule called for the first scene to be shot at eight o'clock in the morning. It was a scene involving Margot Grahame, the English stage actress cast as Gypo's streetwalking girlfriend. But at 8 am, Miss Graham was not on the set. Ford said to his brother Eddie O'Fearna, 'For chrissakes, Eddie, it's her first day. Let's not panic just because the actress is a bit late. Let's give her some time.' He took a few puffs on his pipe, then said, 'What time is it now?' 'Two minutes after eight.' 'Well,' Ford said, 'let's give her until seven minutes after. There's no reason to make her nervous on the first day.' O'Fearna ran off to the wardrobe department, but at 8.07, there was still no Margot Grahame, and Ford informed Joe August that they would move on to another scene. When the actress followed by her assistant arrived at 8.45, Ford complimented her on her make-up, her clothes and her hair, and then said he wished she had been there at eight o'clock. Now there was no time for that scene. 'We'll just eliminate it from the script. It's a very pretty dress though.' The actress's assistant wept.[104] Of course, this treatment, however pseudo-polite, not only made Miss Grahame nervous, it terrified the whole cast, and ensured that for the next three weeks of filming, the actors, a class of people not known for being on time, paid close attention to the shooting schedule.

What really riled Ford was getting advice, or even the least suggestion, from one of the crew. When he was making *Mary of Scotland*, leading lady Katherine Hepburn volunteered an idea. Watched by a reporter from the *LA Times*, Ford said, 'All right, if you know so much, you direct,' and walked off the set. Hepburn, unfazed, mugged looking through the camera. Such a fit was childish, but it also made it clear to everyone that Ford was not going to be bossed around by his star, no matter how brilliant, beautiful and nervy she was. Ford explained to his wife that 'As exec,' he had 'to be an SOB.'[105]

Whether he had to be an SOB or not, John Ford was one, and it did not seem to come to him with difficulty. The director kept his stock company on pins-and-needles in expectation that he might stage one of his on-set sideshows of personal humiliation. 'Will I be next?' they wondered. Nonetheless, a lot of talented people liked to work with Ford. One reason was that their talents were shown to good effect in the movies he directed. When *Stagecoach* premiered in New York city, it got rave reviews, and Dudley Nichols (who wrote the screenplay) wrote to congratulate Ford:

> If there was ever a picture that was a director's picture, it was that one. I tried to make that clear to everyone who complimented me in New York. I feel I was a very happy collaborator; and tried to do my best, as did Bert Glennon [cameraman],

> Tollubov [art director], Lovey [editor], and the rest. That is one thing you invariably do, inspire your whole crew including the writer to pitch in and do their best. I don't believe you will ever have a bad crew.[106]

13

As soon as *The Informer* was wrapped, Ford was alive with plans for more Irish films. The Abbey Theatre company was on tour in the USA in 1935, and it happened to play in Los Angeles while Ford was filming O'Flaherty's novel. He had already put into the film's cast two former Abbey stars, J.M. Kerrigan and Una O'Connor. With the Abbey in town, he added current member Denis O'Dea, who plays the street singer. Ford then came up with the idea of making a movie of one of the Abbey's biggest repertory successes, Sean O'Casey's *The Plough and the Stars*, using the whole Abbey cast. Just after shooting on *The Informer* concluded, RKO purchased the rights to the play, and announced that Ford would be the film's director and Dudley Nichols the screenwriter.[107] Plans were afoot to follow *The Plough and the Stars* with *Juno and the Paycock*.[108] What thus far had not been settled was whether or not Ford would get his way and be allowed to import the whole cast for the production from the Abbey.

A year later, on 25 February 1936, well before filming began on *The Plough and the Stars*, Ford bought the rights to a short story by Maurice Walsh, 'The Quiet Man'. Evidently, RKO was not interested in making a commitment to this project, so Ford began to look for a producer, and to look, and look. It would be sixteen years before the film was made. That was not entirely owing to the fact that no American producer could see the value in making a film either based on a play James Agee had recently called the best since Shakespeare, or one based on a short story about an American boxer going home to live in the west of Ireland. By 1939, when Lewis Jacobs published his book, things were shaping up nicely for Ford's plan to make movies with 'the green hills of Ireland as a background', or at the least, for making Irish-interest films in Hollywood with the best of Ireland's actors playing parts in them. But Jacobs, writing in early 1939, could not know that in September of that year, World War II would break out. Ford could not know that. The Abbey actors who came over for *Plough and the Stars* and got studio contracts could not know that war would make it impossible for them to go home to their families.

World War II changed everything. In Ireland Irish neutrality, the emigration of talent, and an oppressive attitude to freedom of expression had put an end to the Irish Revival. In the USA Ford began to side with Britain even before the USA entered the conflict: England, he told Anna Lee (matron of British Hollywood), was one of the bravest countries the world had ever known.[109] That change in attitude to Britain would necessitate not only a new take on his Irish nationalism, but the complete erasure of Maurice Walsh's setting of *The Quiet Man*, the evils of the Black and Tans and the heroism of the IRA flying columns. Ultimately, Ford would be led by his experience of war away from Irish nationalism and toward a multi-ethnic appreciation of American democracy. As a writer on Ford's post-war Westerns puts it, the director developed an old strain in his vision of life, his pluralistic multi-culturalism. The Irish become the Ur-Ethnics, but there also appear various tribes of 'Native Americans, Mexicans, African Americans, Slavs and Poles, Frenchmen and Italians, Swedes and Germans, poor whites and Southerners'.[110] He was led by history away from the celebration of the pure virtues of ethnicity and toward a celebration of the USA, at a time when it really was a democracy of immigrants based on tolerance, ethnic difference and respect for individuality.

14

However, before war broke out, by bringing Abbey stars to America, Ford imported the Irish cultural revival, especially as it was literally embodied in the performers of the plays of Sean O'Casey. The actors carried the Revival's heritage within their own expressive capacities. Their acts of self-expression were the means by which Ford often told his stories and expressed himself. Furthermore, the range of their work in Hollywood, for both John Ford and other leading directors, would disseminate the Revival throughout the world.

II

BARRY FITZGERALD AND *THE PLOUGH AND THE STARS* ON STAGE AND SCREEN

Previous page: *F.J. McCormick (left) as Joxer and Barry Fitzgerald as Captain Boyle in* Juno and the Paycock, c.1935. *(Shields family papers)*

In March 1933 the Abbey Theatre company was a long way from Hollywood, and a long way from Dublin too. It was in Chicago that Barry Fitzgerald was playing Captain Boyle, a spluttering, five-foot-six, profane Jupiter, to Eileen Crowe's Juno, in *Juno and the Paycock*, while Crowe's husband, F.J. McCormick, gave his famous rendering of Joxer Daly, the Captain's 'ratty yes-man'.[1]

Fitzgerald's 'querulous voice and pompous futility when he was strutting on stage' set the whole theatre rocking.[2] Sean O'Casey's tragicomedy, set against the backdrop of the Irish Civil War, had been the world's favourite Irish play since its 1924 debut. It was still a money spinner in Chicago. Since embarking at Galway on 1 October 1932, the troupe had played in New York for four weeks, then Pittsburgh, Philadelphia and Baltimore. After Chicago, they would head for Washington DC, and then New York again. Not until July 1933 would they be back on stage in Dublin.

The tour was the second of three long circuits of North America by the Abbey players following the Great Depression. The Abbey Theatre itself was left dark, while the troupe was sent out on the roads to spread its fame, and, more essentially, to keep the actors in cash and on contract.[3] While on tour, actors received double pay and had the pleasure of travel, even if by third-class accommodation.[4] Dublin audiences missed them, but the actors (at least those without small children) enjoyed the long stays in America.[5] After the first tour, Barry Fitzgerald found himself miserable back in Dublin. He would do anything, he told Sean O'Casey, to get back to the USA – the 'only live, vital country' he had ever seen.[6]

The Abbey board of directors – W.B. Yeats, Lady Gregory, Lennox Robinson and Walter Starkie – were in a bind.[7] If the company did not tour, its actors could only just afford to live in Dublin on the proceeds of the box office (small audiences paying low prices) and the £1000-per-year state subsidy. The best actors would one day be picked like ripe cherries by Hollywood agents and London producers, leaving green understudies behind. Some already had been plucked away, including Sara Allgood, who had featured in several of Alfred Hitchcock's films. And in 1929 Fitzgerald had been induced by Sean O'Casey and Charles Cochrane to come to London for parts in O'Casey's *The Silver Tassie* and in Cochrane's 1930 revue.[8]

Abbey Theatre company on tour, 1934/35. (Shields family papers)

The Silver Tassie, with a breathtaking set design by Augustus John, was a critical rather than commercial success at London's Apollo Theatre on 11 October 1929, but Cochrane's revue was the opposite. Crowds flocked to its variety of entertainments: a ballet by Balanchine and Moscow's Boris Kochno, dances by 'Cochrane girls' (Sheilah Graham, F. Scott Fitzgerald's last love, was one of them), and skits and songs by popular comedians like Ada May, Jack

Powell and Barry Fitzgerald each taking several turns. It was clowning, but clowning of a superior sort.[9] The revue ran from March until October 1930. Fitzgerald's take-home pay was £25 a week, over three times the maximum on the Abbey salary scale.[10] Furthermore, at this time Alfred Hitchcock – upon O'Casey's urging – hired Fitzgerald to play a part in the film of *Juno and the Paycock*.[11] Another pay cheque was added to the £700 total the actor collected from Cochrane's revue. In order to take those London parts, Fitzgerald had given up not just the Abbey, but his daytime job in the civil service, Department of Unemployment, where he had over ten years' seniority and the assurance of a good pension in retirement. The risk had been great. Now he was flush with success, although somewhat weary of doing the same gags night after night, month after month, with a director who had little interest in Fitzgerald's own notions of how to play his parts.[12]

During its own season, without Barry Fitzgerald, the Abbey company as a whole – all the actors, in all the plays – had takings of only £671 in Dublin, less than Fitzgerald had made on his own in London. The situation was 'disastrous'. 'The loss of Barry Fitzgerald is very serious,' Lady Gregory confided to her diary on 26 June 1930, 'and that Revue [in which he is playing] seems [to be] going on interminably.'[13] Lennox Robinson, Abbey author and manager, was dispatched to London in October to tell Fitzgerald how much he was missed by Lady Gregory, Robinson himself, the Abbey cast, and its audience too: they all wanted him to come home.[14]

Barry Fitzgerald – Will Shields (1888–1961) was his real name – was an old friend of Robinson. He and his brother Arthur Shields (1896–1970), also a leading member of the Abbey company, used to spend Sundays at Robinson's cottage, 'The Lodge', on Sir Horace Plunkett's estate in Foxrock, County Dublin. In the early and mid-1920s O'Casey would sometimes come along too. All four were bookish, patriotic Irish Protestants with a love of the stage. The Shields brothers thought well of Lennox Robinson's plays too, especially the comedy *The Whiteheaded Boy* (1916)[15] and *The Big House* (1926), a Chekhovian tragedy on the demise of the patriotic fraction of the Irish landlord-class.[16] When Robinson called upon Fitzgerald in London, at first the actor would promise nothing, but by December 1930 he was back on the Abbey payroll and the Abbey stage, playing St Leger Alcock in *The Big House*.

With Fitzgerald's return, attendance picked up slightly, but only slightly, not enough to enable the directors to give actors a significant raise in pay.[17] It seemed that the only way to keep the best actors in the company was to send the company on tour. A circuit of sixty-six American and seven Canadian cities was organized, beginning with Wyncote, Pennsylvania, on 21 October 1931. However, in the long run, would American tours solve the Abbey's problems? As a side-effect, they showcased potential stars to those cherry-picking Hollywood and Broadway talent-scouts the Abbey management was trying to keep at bay.

In the mid-1930s half the population of the USA went to the cinema every single week. In Ireland 1271 films were screened in 1935, the majority from Hollywood; over 18 million tickets were sold in the Free State, even though Pope Pius XI declared films an evil worse than books, temptations deemed sufficiently pernicious in themselves.[18] The world's money, scarce everywhere else, was flowing as rapidly into Hollywood as bathwater down a drainpipe, and soon enough, wouldn't the actors follow it?

2

In March 1933 while in Chicago, Udolphus Wright gave a backward-looking interview to a reporter for that city's Sunday *Times*. Wright was the longest-serving member of the ensemble. He had joined the Irish National Theatre Society in 1903, a year before there even was an Abbey Theatre, and he had remained with the company all along, except for a period of enlistment with the Royal Engineers in World War I.[19] Udolphus Wright's reminiscences were mostly of those actors who had left the Abbey over the years, and made good in other countries.

The first wave of departures came shortly after the foundation of the Irish National Theatre Society in 1902. P.J. Kelly, Dudley Digges (1879–1947), and his wife Maire Quinn, three of the ten founding members of the theatre, their idealistic patriotism rattled by Synge's *Shadow of the Glen* (1903), left to put on Irish plays in the 1904 St Louis World's Fair. Thereafter, they remained to make their fortune in America. Digges married Maire Quinn and became a big shot on the Broadway stage (with the Theatre Guild). In recent years he had begun to work in Hollywood. He is the Chief Detective in the 1933 cinema sensation, *The Invisible Man.*

The second wave of departures saw the creators of the Abbey style leave. Frank Fay, a 'fanatical elocutionist', had trained the voices of the actors, so that stage whispers could be heard in the back rows of a theatre, 'like feathers borne on puffs of wind'.[20] His brother W.G. Fay drilled the company in 'teamwork' and 'restraint':[21] no stars, no flashy movements, and all eyes on the speaker, giving the effect of a spotlight moving from one actor to the next in the course of a dialogue. But the English owner of the theatre, Annie Horniman, could not stomach the Irish impertinence of W.G. Fay, short but tough and insistent that the manager should manage, without interference from the woman who owned the building. In early 1907 Horniman had Yeats bring in Ben Iden Payne, a 26-year-old Englishman, to take over the company on several times Fay's own salary. The Fay brothers hung on for another year, but, raging, and having lost control of the company and the confidence of the Abbey directors, they both quit on 13 January 1908 and went to England.[22] Frank Fay died in 1931 after years of bitterness in Dublin, during which he refused even to go to the Abbey.[23] W.G. Fay was still a jobbing director in Glasgow and London, occasional broadcaster with the BBC ('More Irish Stories', 10 February 1931), author of books on acting (*Merely Players*, 1932), and sometimes a character-actor in a West End play, such as *Storm in a Teacup* (April 1936).[24]

Udolphus Wright as Lieut. Langon in The Plough and the Stars, *Majestic Theatre, Brooklyn, Christmas week, 1934. (Shields family papers)*

As Udolphus Wright remembered it, the third wave of departures from the Abbey troupe began with the tours that first showed America what gems the Abbey had, and showed the Abbey players what gems America had. Una O'Connor was tempted out of the cast after the second Abbey tour of 1912/13. She remained active in Hollywood, exercising a taste in expensive dresses and a talent for bit parts.[25] Along with Digges, she could be seen in *The Invisible Man*, as the Innkeeper's Wife.

In Sara Allgood's case as well, touring with the Abbey led to breaking from the Abbey. From her debut in 1904, she had made a name as a comic and poignant Irish actress of beautiful voice, mostly through parts in the plays of Synge and Lady Gregory. In fact, Gregory felt the success of her own plays depended on Sara Allgood taking part in them.[26] By 1916, however, Allgood had become a bankable star – too plump and plain for an ingénue role on the London stage, but charming and deep in every other respect. With the Abbey's profits dropping from the start of World War I, then plunging steeply after the Easter Rising, Allgood received an offer to star in a production of *Peg O' My Heart* headed for Australia, and she snapped it up. After several years 'down under', a marriage, then a bereavement, the widowed Allgood returned to the London stage and finally to the Abbey. Her career-defining triumph in *Juno and the Paycock* (3 March 1924) led to offers to revive the play with a different cast in London. In March 1926 off she went to play Juno at the Royalty Theatre to Arthur Sinclair's Captain Boyle.[27]

Caught without an engagement in London in 1928, and in the red, Sara Allgood offered to return to the Abbey yet again ('My whole heart is in it; it would kill me to be cut off from it,' Allgood sobbed to Gregory),[28] but not at less than £15 a week. And would the Abbey clear her £200-debt as well? Fifteen pounds a week was double the highest rate in the Abbey salary scale, and, dashing Lady Gregory's hopes and Allgood's vanity, no such fat contract was extended by manager Lennox Robinson. Allgood remained in London, where she got parts in *Blackmail* (1929) and *Juno and the Paycock* (1930), Alfred Hitchcock's first two talkies.[29] In 1933, at the time Udolphus Wright was giving his interview to the *Chicago Times*, Sunday edition, Allgood was in a London production of *The Things That Are Caesar's* by Paul Vincent Carroll, along with a cast made up of ex-leading ladies and gentlemen of the Abbey: Sara's sister Molly Allgood (stage name: Maire O'Neill), Kathleen Drago, J.A. O'Rourke and Fred O'Donovan.

Some of those in the cast of the 1933 *The Things That Are Caesar's*, Udolphus Wright explained, had left *en masse* just after the Easter Rising. That was

Sara Allgood (left), Arthur Sinclair (second from left) and Marie O'Neill (third from right) celebrate their apparent good fortune, 29 July 1927, after Sean O'Casey's play, Juno and the Paycock, *was staged at Golders Green Hippodrome, London. (Sasha/Getty Images; misdated on Getty website)*

largely because of mismanagement by the Belfast playwright St John Greer Ervine, unwisely appointed director of the Abbey by Yeats in the autumn of 1915. Right away he began to treat the actors like a boss in a shipyard. Actors not rehearsing were driven from the green room: one had to be busy, even if one had no business on stage.[30] In public lectures St John Ervine described the Irish people – that is, his own audience – as a 'sick nation', 'very nearly a lunatic' one.[31] After the Easter Rising, on 24 April 1916, St John Ervine would remove the qualification 'very nearly'; heart and soul a Unionist, for him the insurrection was madness. Outrageously (from his point of view), one of his own players, 20-year-old Arthur Shields, was arrested at the end of the rebellion with other members of the Irish Citizen Army in the General Post Office; another, Seán Connolly, had been one of the first men killed in action.

It was obvious to Ervine that many of the rest of the company, even if they had not shouldered weapons, were on the rebels' side too. He gave them all notice of dismissal, and demanded that they reapply for their jobs on new and stricter terms. By a month after Easter Monday they had had enough.

When daily playgoer Joseph Holloway went to the Abbey at 8 pm on 29 May 1916, handbills were being distributed, printed up by the actors. They apologized to their public, but declared the players 'WOULD NOT APPEAR ... under the present Manager, MR ST JOHN ERVINE.'[32] It was a repeat of the Easter rebellion.

Even though the manager resigned in July, Arthur Sinclair, Sydney Morgan, Kathleen Drago and others had left by then. The biggest loss was Sinclair (1883–1952). A law student, he had joined the Irish National Theatre Society for Yeats's *On Baile's Strand* on 27 December 1904, the opening night of the newly refurbished Abbey Theatre.[33] He then became a stalwart of the company, good in both comedies and tragedies. Upon quitting the Abbey, Sinclair and J.B. Fagan set up a rival company called 'Arthur Sinclair and His Company, The Irish Players, Late of the Abbey Theatre, Dublin'.[34] Many Abbey veterans took part in its tours of Ireland, Britain, Australia and North America. One of those veterans, J.M. Synge's beloved Molly Allgood (1887–1952), became Sinclair's wife. The last time Udolphus Wright had seen him, Sinclair was acting with Fred O'Donovan, a former actor and manager of the Abbey. Sinclair, O'Donovan and Maire O'Neill staged a farce, *Old Man Murphy*, at the Savoy Theatre, London, in March 1932.[35]

Arthur Sinclair, c.1920. *(Shields family papers)*

'Dull as ditchwater' offstage, the carrot-haired Sinclair had only to walk on stage to become the part. Instantly people would begin to smile and laugh, especially when he came on as Michael James O'Flaherty in Synge's *Playboy*, with 'the most realistically drunken gait' a London *Times* reviewer had ever seen on stage.[36] Sinclair rarely knew what was going on in the scenes in which he had no lines; the significance of the play as a whole had no interest for him. When asked how his stage success was achieved, Sinclair shrugged, 'Personality … I have it. I don't know what it is, but I have it.'[37] Well into the 1930s reviewers continued to call Arthur Sinclair the greatest Irish actor of them all.

At the end of Udolphus Wright's interview, it might well have seemed to the Chicago *Times* reporter that there were more great ex-Abbey players, more by far, than present Abbey players. Indeed, during their four weeks in New York, one reviewer made the odious comparison in question. This company 'doesn't have the virtuoso playing of the Irish Company from five years previous', the reviewer said, 'a company that included Arthur Sinclair, Sara Allgood, Maire O'Neill and Sydney Morgan'.[38]

3

Yet there were virtues to being in the Abbey that might be lost outside it. Not long after Udolphus Wright was being interviewed by the Sunday *Times*, Barry Fitzgerald was talking to a reporter for the Chicago *Daily News*. Yes, he had done a spell on the London stage, with vast crowds and a big pay cheque, but still he wanted to go back to the Abbey:

> There was such a difference in rehearsals. In London the directors told every actor just what to do, with the result that the cast could get no further than the limitations of the one director. I'd no liking for the commercial theatre … Mind you, I like money too, but I like the Abbey style better. There every actor, once he has shown himself to be one of the company, is allowed to develop his role with more liberty than anywhere else … We don't make the money [they] do in commercial theatre, but we're more secure. [39]

In addition, as Fitzgerald made clear, he took a personal interest in great drama and in Irish cultural nationalism. From the time he was a young man, just starting out in the civil service, Fitzgerald was caught up in the enthusiasms of the Irish Literary Revival. He and his brother revered Yeats and Gregory. In the years before 1916 he went to the Abbey every night. Sara Allgood, Maire O'Neill, Joe Kerrigan, Arthur Sinclair were his idols, and he thought the plays in which they appeared – the works of T.C. Murray, Lennox Robinson, Lady Gregory and Synge – were important to the emergence of the Irish nation. His brother Arthur Shields had been doing walk-on parts since 1912, when he was just sixteen.[40]

Fitzgerald himself joined the company in 1915 when he was twenty-seven. He took roles part-time, the basis of all his Abbey work between 1915 and 1927. He would bicycle from his job in Dublin Castle to the Abbey for lunch hour in order to rehearse, then 'grab a sandwich and hurry back to work'.[41] When his workday ended, Fitzgerald would return to the Abbey for a short rehearsal before dinner. Rehearsals went on constantly. The Abbey custom was to run a programme (normally a one-act and a full-length play) for one, two or three weeks, then put up a new programme, in incessant repertory while the season lasted. As a result, players on stage in one show were usually rehearsing a second show in the daytime. Obviously, Fitzgerald loved being on stage in those plays, before that particular audience: a man would not work that hard otherwise.

After actors resigned in 1916 in protest against the management of St John Ervine, Fitzgerald got his chance. Roles were there for the taking, and he took them. The first time Lady Gregory saw him on stage was December 1917 in *Blight*, a play by Joseph O'Connor and Oliver St John Gogarty about the disastrous state of public health in Dublin's tenement housing. Micheál Mac Liammóir (later the star actor and designer of Dublin's Gate Theatre) played a crippled boy in a tenement;[42] Arthur Shields was Medical Dick; and Barry Fitzgerald was a labourer. It was a small role, just a few words to say and moments on stage, but Lady Gregory could tell, any one could tell, that whatever it was Arthur Sinclair had, Fitzgerald had it too.[43]

Yet it was not until O'Casey wrote a part with him in mind that Fitzgerald achieved greatness. After the production of *The Shadow of a Gunman* (12 April 1923), O'Casey began to frequent the Abbey and befriend the players. Barry Fitzgerald was rooming with another civil servant in the Abbey company, Gabriel Fallon, in a flat off St Stephen's Green.[44] The two actors loved the Dublin music-hall greats – their names mean nothing now, but they were beloved by their large audiences in the 1920s. O'Casey, reportedly, had never been to a music hall, that most working-class of Dublin entertainments. The young O'Casey was priggishly idealistic. On 23 April 1922, he wrote Lennox Robinson that the '[Abbey] Theatre, the country, the National Gallery and the Botanic Gardens – with certain Authors – are the only things I worship'.[45] So the two actors took him along to the 2000-seat Theatre Royal whenever they could.[46] The impact of the genre is all over the play O'Casey was writing at the time, *Juno and the Paycock*: the songs of Joxer, the exits through the window by Joxer (in flight from his 'buttie's' wife), the over-the-top fears of a real job on the part of the Captain, the straight-man/buffoon duet of Joxer and the Captain, the fed-up-with-it-all exasperation of Juno.

O'Casey was writing the part of gasbag grandiloquent Captain Boyle just for Barry Fitzgerald. Seeing Fitzgerald as the Captain trying to say a polysyllable was like watching a man struggling to keep a slippery eel in his mouth: eyes bulged, spittle flew, and his jaw nearly unhinged. The character was apparently based on a real-life model of O'Casey's acquaintance, one of many work-shy layabouts, but this one claimed, falsely, to have once been a sea captain. Barry Fitzgerald was just the man to impersonate him, but not because Fitzgerald was like the man in question. No one could be less so. Fitzgerald was a man who spoke slowly, measuring his words; he worked constantly; he earned a good deal of money; he liked to play golf on Sundays; his best friend was J.J. O'Leary, owner of a printing works.[47] O'Casey thought Fitzgerald perfect for the part because Fitzgerald had a talent for 'taking off' Dublin's dissolute and eccentric city characters, those rich in personality and in nothing else.

Barry Fitzgerald (left) and J.J. O'Leary, 1946. (Shields family papers)

Most of the Abbey actors loved to impersonate people from different parts of Dublin; they were natural mimics. F.J. McCormick, a pious, married-with-family-in-the-suburbs Catholic, excelled in the imitation of gurriers from Dublin's northside. In the Abbey acting school, such as it was, one teaching practice was to take the students to a pub in Donnybrook, a suburb in south Dublin.[48] The teacher would say, 'Now study that barman.' After the teacher had finished his pint of Guinness, they would all return to the Abbey stage, and the students would attempt to reproduce the mannerisms and especially the accent – the right Dublin accent was crucial – of the barman. Another day, the teacher would take them to a pub in a different part of town, maybe the Liberties or Drumcondra, where the manners and accent were in each case perceptibly different. Barry Fitzgerald revelled in such mimicry. He did it in his spare time for laughs, after work in Dublin Castle or on the golf course. While *Juno and the Paycock* was being written, Fitzgerald listened night after night to O'Casey in his flat at 422 North Circular Road, right in the parish of the fictional Boyle family. 'I took my cues from [his] descriptions and impersonations,' Fitzgerald told the Chicago reporter.[49]

The Abbey Theatre was one of those rare theatres in which an ensemble of actors could regularly work at close quarters, time and again, with the leading playwrights of the nation, while living in community with the models of their *dramatis personae.* That was one of the virtues and comforts that might be found in the Abbey, and lost outside of it.

4

It would be a mistake, however, to think of the Abbey as harmonious even in its glory days of the mid-1920s, with the great O'Casey plays coming one right after another, in the wake of the national events they represented: the 1919–21 War of Independence (*The Shadow of a Gunman*), the 1922–3 Civil War (*Juno and the Paycock*), and the 1916 Rising (*The Plough and the Stars*). If the country was divided by these conflicts, so too were the Abbey players and authors. O'Casey, for instance, was 'exasperated beyond endurance' by the direction in which the country had gone since 1916.[50] The anti-Catholic, anti-Republican and anti-Free State furies that he expressed and re-expressed in his autobiographies were already gathering heat within him.

A false picture of O'Casey as one of the type of Dublin working-class people he put into his plays has come down to us; even Yeats sometimes had this view of him.[51] O'Casey himself had the slightly alienated, but still affectionate, relationship to his characters that Fitzgerald had. Nicholas Grene has rightly called attention to the implications of a stage-direction concerning Minnie Powell in *The Shadow of a Gunman*: '[L]ike all of her class, Minnie is not able to converse very long on one subject.'[52] 'Like all of her class,' Grene observes, 'not mine, the playwright's, or yours, the reader's.'[53] O'Casey's parents were neither working-class nor Catholic. His father was a clerk in the Protestant Church Missions, with tenancy of a sizable house on Dorset Street. This lower-middle-class family of evangelists was surrounded by working-class Catholics on the northside of Dublin, so O'Casey grew up in 'uncomfortably close quarters' to the sort of characters who feature in his Dublin plays.[54]

Of all the characters in his plays, O'Casey as a young man most resembled 'The Covey' in *The Plough and the Stars*, a priggish young socialist who quotes the theses of 'Jerensky' to Rosie Redmond, a prostitute in a pub, and then prudishly upbraids her for being what she is. The Covey is the furthest thing from Fluther Good, the moral and ethnic centre of that play, who offers to fight The Covey for insulting the lady, and then, once The Covey is put out of the pub, stands Rosie Redmond a drink, and perhaps other things as well. As an older man – he was forty-three when writing *The Plough* – O'Casey had perhaps come to see the silliness of his doctrinaire youth, and to make sport of it in The Covey. By then he could also appreciate the comic charm of loquacious boasters like Fluther and Captain Boyle. But he was not much like those characters himself, apart from becoming an equally loquacious boaster in his many autobiographies. In other respects, he was an author, a socialist and a Protestant, three degrees of separation from the Dubliners who take the central roles in his two best plays.

The exteriority of the relationship of O'Casey to such characters is part of the particular qualities of *Juno and the Paycock* and *The Plough and the Stars*. Owing to that exteriority, the plays compass usually incompassible qualities: the handling of a character like Captain Boyle takes huge pleasure in his outsize pretensions to be a naval officer, philosopher and gentleman; it also condescends to those pretensions and, in a rather Protestant fashion, morally condemns them as a cover for the abandonment of his duty to provide for his family and stand by them through thick and thin. Here is Boyle's reaction when he finds out that his unmarried daughter is pregnant, and the one who did it to her, the schoolteacher and part-time solicitor Bentham, has bunked off to England.

> Oh, isn't this a nice thing to come on top o' me, an' the state I'm in! A pretty show I'll be to Joxer an' to that oul' wan, Madigan! Amn't I afther goin' through enough without havin' to go through this!
>
> ...
>
> Where is she? Where is she till I tell her off? I'm tellin' you when I'm done with her she'll be a sorry girl![55]

As if Mary were not a sorry girl already. Boyle's comedy had always been the comic effect of incongruity, not saying the right thing for the occasion. But his heartlessness and self-indulgence in this situation, where a father most needs to show his heart and forget himself, is not funny; it is brutal and chilling. It makes the pleasure the audience has taken in the Captain a terrible mistake, something the audience should now feel guilty about. Spectators are thus, to quote Milton, 'surprised by sin'.

Indeed, when it dawns on the audience that the plot element of a spoiled will – taken for a piece of old theatrical lumber – is actually a parody of the December 1921 Treaty that half the Republicans could not accept, there is more still to feel guilty about. The peace dividend had already vanished by 1924. The play suggested that informers like Johnny Boyle would continue to finger neighbors like Mrs Tancred's son, and 'Irregulars' would once again carry off war-cripples like Johnny in tit-for-tat assassinations, as if the drink, illegitimacy and capitalist exploitation that continued to beset the poor were not troubles enough. In this tragi-comedy, it is after the laughter dies that the tragedy sinks in.

5

The slight sectarian edge to O'Casey's Dublin plays, and within some of the Abbey players that acted them, was part of the trouble that erupted for Ireland's most popular playwright with the staging of his third masterpiece, *The Plough and the Stars.* How the conflicts did not emerge sooner is a mystery. F.J. McCormick (real name: Peter Judge) was a civil servant with the Department of Education and a very pious Catholic. In *The Shadow of a Gunman*, he had the part of Seamus Shields, a door-to-door pedlar who shares a tenement room with Donal Davoren (played by Arthur Shields). Davoren is a would-be poet who allows others to believe he is an IRA man, with fatal consequences for his girlfriend. On stage, Shields noticed that McCormick kept saying the Dublin expletive 'Jaysus' (for 'Jesus').[56] Shields himself gave no quarter to pious prudes. When playing Christy Mahon, it was his custom to pronounce the most lurid phrases from *The Playboy of the Western World*, usually left out in deference to the Catholic nationalist opinion.[57]

So one night after *Shadow of the Gunman*, Shields teasingly brought it to McCormick's attention that he was saying 'Jaysus' right, left and centre. Indignant, McCormick said he had never used such a word on stage in his life. The next night, Shields put a mark in a prop notebook (his character was a writer) each time McCormick said, 'Jaysus'. Thirty-three times. McCormick was flabbergasted. He had been that lost in the part, he had not noticed.

Arthur Shields (left) as Christy Mahon, Barry Fitzgerald as Michael James, and Eileen Crowe as Pegeen Mike in The Playboy of the Western World, *New York, 1932. (Shields family papers)*

Rehearsing *The Plough and the Stars* in early January 1926, however, McCormick had his wits about him. He did not want, as Jack Clitheroe, to use the word 'snotty' of his stage-wife Nora. It was a filthy word for a filthy thing. And his real-life wife Eileen Crowe, cast as Ginnie Gogan, a charwoman with a small baby and a long-dead husband, refused to say from the stage the following line: 'Any kid, livin' or dead, that Ginnie Gogan's had since [her marriage], was got between th' bordhers of th' Ten Commandments.'[58]

That assertion of propriety, she felt, would evoke a mental picture of a quite unspeakable impropriety – adulterous tenement sex – and so was itself unspeakable.

Wife and husband Eileen Crowe and F.J. McCormick, c.1936. (Shields family papers)

Pretty young Ria Mooney was beginning to worry about playing Rosie Redmond, her first big part: 'I had reached twenty-three years of age without knowing what precisely was meant by a "prostitute".'[59] They were thick on the footpaths all around the Abbey premises, but Mooney was not sure exactly what those women did for money, although she knew it was very bad.[60] When light dawned on her, she doubted she wanted to be one, even on stage. Characters in the play over and again enforced their points with intensifiers like 'Jaysus', 'Christ', 'lousy', 'lice', 'bastard', 'bitch' – it was 'beyond the beyonds' to represent the slum conditions of Dublin's Catholic population in this indecent way, M.J. Dolan (another veteran player) declared.[61]

On 10 January 1926 O'Casey wrote to the play's director, Lennox Robinson, saying he would rather withdraw the play entirely than remove such words at the request of actors. By 'snotty', O'Casey explained that he had obviously meant 'sarcastic', not that they had runny noses. The other words had been used by other Irish playwrights, if not all in one play. 'I draw the line at a Vigilance Committee of Actors ... things have happened since Synge: the war has shaken some of the respectability out of the heart of man ... and the USSR has fixed a new star in the sky. Were corrections of this kind allowed, the work would be one of fear.'[62]

In the stand-off between actors and author, part of the corps remained on O'Casey's side. Cast members Shelah Richards, Barry Fitzgerald, Arthur Shields and Gabriel Fallon loved the play. So the company was split, and, except for Fallon (a Catholic, if at this stage in his life a broadminded one)[63] it was split along sectarian lines: Catholic actors hostile to O'Casey, and Protestant ones in favour of him.

Yeats stepped in to settle the dispute. He made O'Casey drop most of the 'bitches', but not the great one at the end from Bessie Burgess to Nora Clitheroe: 'Merciful God, I'm shot, I'm shot, I'm shot! ... I've got this through ... through ... through you, you bitch, you!'[64] He also required the author's permission to leave out the 'Dancing a Jig in the Bed' song by Rosie Redmond.[65] Then Yeats rounded on Eileen Crowe and told her she had a choice: either say Ginnie Gogan's line about children begotten between the borders of the Ten Commandments, or else give up the part. She said she would have to consult her priest. Having done so, she gave up the part to May Craig. Yeats allowed McCormick to leave out the word 'snotty', but he made Shelah Richards act as if McCormick had said it, and reply, 'I will not be called snotty!' – a delightful trick of stage illusionism, and a credit to the old magician.[66] All in all, Yeats had been a brilliant field marshal. And he was clearly beginning to enjoy himself.

6

For months Yeats had been alive to the possibility that *The Plough and the Stars* would cause trouble. *The Plough and the Stars* was one of the first plays produced under the new government subsidy, announced on 8 August 1925; the Abbey had become in some sense a state theatre. But in what sense? Part of the new arrangement was that the government could appoint a member to the Abbey board of directors. This man, George O'Brien, saw himself as the 'watchdog of the subsidy'.[67] Once he had seen the script, and confidentially talked with M.J. Dolan about it, he sent Yeats a long letter on 5 September 1925 enumerating five categories of objection, with lists of page numbers for offences under each category. He wanted Rosie Redmond, the prostitute, out of the play.

Yeats did not quibble about every point, and said modifications were always made as a matter of course in rehearsal, but the prostitute, like the drunkards and wastrels, was essential to the play's great theme: the contrast of 'the ideal dream' and the 'normal grossness of life', and could not be essentially altered.[68]

As a reading of the play, this is on the mark. O'Casey's play is in the realist tradition of Ibsen, in which the playwright, as the enemy of lies, shatters romantic illusions. However, the 'ideal dream' was, in this case, the basis for the state: that the Easter Rising was a heroic and ultimately successful fight for freedom from England, leading to all the good the people now enjoyed, and to none of the evils they suffered. Newspaper reviewers of the play got this point straight away. According to O'Casey, the rebellion was 'not worth it': 'One drop of the milk of human kindness is worth more than the deepest draughts of the red wine of idealism.'[69] That message was bound to be especially indigestible to the diehard, anti-Free State, Republican followers of Éamon de Valera. They still carried the torch of the 1916 rebels. In an Ireland not fully free from an oath to the king of England, and without the Six Counties in the North, their war was not finished. As for the widows, sisters and mothers of those who had died in 1916 – a class of person with an almost sacred status in the new Ireland – for them Nora's speaking of the soldiers as cowards, as betrayers of their marriages, could be received only as a sacrilege. After the trauma of their own personal losses, such a characterization was unacceptable, unforgivable.

The Plough and the Stars is a play about the Easter rebellion that does not depict Irishmen rebelling. It depicts what other Irishmen did while a small number rebelled, or it depicts the rebels going to, and then running from, the action. The silhouette of Patrick Pearse, leader of the rebels, can be seen through the window of a pub, and can be seen from this point of view only. Inside the pub, heated up by his bloody-minded rabble-rousing rhetoric, flag-bearing soldiers down glasses of drink. A prostitute complains that the men are so hot for fighting that they have gone cold on her.[70] There is no scene in the GPO, headquarters of the rebellion.

No scene anywhere depicts Irishmen dying like heroes. They die aplenty in other ways. A scene depicts young Mollser sinking away with tuberculosis. Bessie Burgess, a loyalist, is shot twice through a window by a Tommy on the street, trying to stop a nationalist rooftop sniper. Lieutenant Langon, who had said he would be proud to die for Ireland, is horrified to discover – his stomach ripped open by a bullet – that that is just what he was going to have to do, die: 'Me clothes seem to be all soakin' wet. It's blood ... My God, it must be my own blood!'[71]

It was at once historically true, and a heresy, that many Dubliners at first had neither sympathy for nor interest in the rebellion; the main interest of a sizable number was looting. By 1926, however, a surprising portion of the people in Dublin claimed either to have been in the GPO, or to be closely related to someone who was. This is not so hard to believe. A genealogist could probably show that tens of thousands of Irish people were at least third-cousins of the 1600 Volunteers out on Easter Monday.[72] But the same genealogist could probably also show that just as many Dubliners or more were closely related to the looters. In any new state, some things are worth remembering and others best forgotten. It was the things often forgotten that O'Casey reminded Dubliners about. In the play, the delight of characters in pillaging is given ample stage-time. Uncle Peter, Fluther, The Covey, Bessie Burgess and Mrs Gogan all steal from the smashed shops. Only three Irish characters in the play do any fighting, and that is off stage: Jack Clitheroe, Captain Brennan and the unfortunate Lieutenant Langon. For the others, the rebellion is a people's carnival and a temporary suspension of the laws of private property.

Yeats, a senator in the new Free State, surely knew the play would give trouble, and where it would give most trouble: with the de Valera Republicans who rejected the Free State, in whose Senate he served. He was not disappointed at the prospect.

7

While the play was in rehearsal, the Abbey actors gave a benefit performance of *The Shadow of the Gunman* for the Free State soldiers at the Curragh, a military camp near Dublin. The benefit was hosted by Senator W.B. Yeats. After the show, Yeats was relaxing with the actors, and telling stories of early days at the Abbey. Would the theatre ever again see events, Arthur Shields asked, like those at the first performance of *The Playboy of the Western World*? Excited, Yeats rose from his chair, and lifted his hand: 'Shields, I shall tell you in a fortnight's time.'[73]

On opening night, Monday, 8 February 1926, Yeats made sure the packed theatre had a ballast of government supporters. During the interval, he led a procession of government ministers – Ernest Blythe, Kevin O'Higgins and Lord Chief Justice Hugh Kennedy – down to the green room to congratulate the cast. As the party went up the stairs to the stalls, Joseph Holloway raised his voice, 'There they go, the bloody murderers.'[74] These three had been key figures in the government's decision to execute prisoners in reprisal for Republican assassinations of state officials. Tension was high, on stage and off.

On the second night there was a bit of hissing from the sister of Kevin Barry, poster child of Irish Republican martyrs. On Thursday night protest blazed up. In the first act, an aisle of six Republican women – including Mrs Pearse, Mrs Tom Clarke and Mrs Hanna Sheehy Skeffington – hissed and booed and stamped their feet. As the curtain went up on the pub scene, with Pearse's words heard behind the stage-flats, the six women began to sing songs and make speeches from the pit. The demonstration spread. A man yelled out, 'That flag was never in a public house!'[75] Not everything could be heard from the stage. In the third act, when Nora Clitheroe (Shelah Richards) began to describe the cowardice at the heart of the men in uniform, the Republican widows and their supporters, about a dozen in all, tried to get up on the stage. More of the crowd then rushed the stage. A man took a swing at Maureen Delaney (playing Unionist Bessie Burgess). Barry Fitzgerald socked him on the chin, and the man fell into the stalls – a sounder blow than Fitzgerald's character, the fantasy pugilist Fluther Good, had ever dealt. Missiles were targeted at Rosie Redmond, frightening Ria Mooney, the young actress in the role. A woman protester was trying to set fire to the stage curtains; Shelah Richards clawed her hair.[76] Two stage lamps were broken. A curtain was torn. F.J. McCormick – so famous for absorption in his part – went out of character, and pleaded with the audience: 'The author is to blame, not the players!' The curtain came down on a scene of mayhem.

Then Yeats, who had been pacing in the wings as if preparing for a part, came on stage, and held up his hand for silence. None came. Shelah Richards took off a shoe and hurled it at a protestor, who picked up the shoe and threw it at Yeats, just missing.[77] Or did it graze him? Yeats paid it no attention. 'You have disgraced yourselves again!' the poet declared. People shouted back, 'Pensioner Yeats!' As a poet of the English language, Yeats had been in reception of a Civil List pension from the Crown since 9 August 1910; to Republicans, this made him a lackey of the British government. Yeats bulled onward: 'Is this to be an ever-recurring celebration of the arrival of Irish genius? Once more you have rocked the cradle of genius ... The fame of O'Casey is born tonight. This is his apotheosis.'[78] The audience shouted over him: 'Take the play to England! We don't want it here.'[79] Arthur Shields regarded Yeats with astonishment. Shields still cherished the memory in his sixty-seventh year: Yeats 'didn't give a damn. Stood there with his hands up, flaying hell out of them with his tongue.'[80] Finally, Yeats strode back into the wings and telephoned for the police, then left the theatre for the office of *The Irish Times* just across the Liffey, and gave the editor a copy of the speech he had recited from the stage.

Portrait of William Butler Yeats, 1923. (Spicer-Simson/Hulton Archive/Getty Images)

Late one night on 12 February, a motor car arrived at the St Stephen's Green flat of Barry Fitzgerald; men demanded he come out. It was like a scene from an earlier O'Casey play, where Johnny Boyle was murdered by Republican gunmen. But Fitzgerald was not like Boyle, always at home.[81] He had gone to a dance after the show, and not come back for supper. In the middle of the night there had also been strange knocks on the doors of Shelah Richards and Ria Mooney, frightening knocks they pretended not to have heard.[82] On Saturday the directors locked the actors in the theatre between the matinee and evening shows, just to make sure they were not abducted or assassinated.

When the curtain rang down on the Saturday evening show, the scheduled week of performances was complete. As Yeats predicted, the fame of O'Casey went forth from the theatre across the world, and soon London and New York were calling for productions of *The Plough and the Stars.* But those audiences, while well able to enjoy its splendid roles, could hardly comprehend the intimate and profound exasperation the play gave to a post-revolutionary and post-colonial Irish Catholic people. O'Casey had wound them up as only one near and dear can do, and then blasted all their pieties.

8

A few weeks after *The Plough and the Stars* closed, O'Casey unwisely accepted an invitation to debate the merits of his play with Hanna Sheehy Skeffington, a smart, tough and able orator. The venue selected was the university Republican Club on Merrion Row, so Hanna Sheehy Skeffington had home-field advantage. Her own husband, the much beloved pacifist and feminist, Francis Sheehy Skeffington, had been murdered by a British officer during the Easter Rising. She spoke first and brought the crowd wholly onto her side. Calmly and seriously, she said the playwright, while his works had the 'mark of genius', was a 'grouch' who could pick out and assemble only squalid incidents. It was a pity, but he did not have it in him to do justice to 'what was great and fine in 1916'.[83] O'Casey rose, and then, a few sentences into his speech, faltered, and sat down again. After a rest, he got to his feet again, and began to defend his play with a point-by-point rebuttal of Sheehy Skeffington's speech; he did not make a good job of it.[84] In the debate, he had been beaten by a woman, and well beaten.

Late that night his friend Gabriel Fallon found O'Casey at 422 North Circular Road with a ticket to London in his hand, sent to him by the producer J.B. Fagan. If he used the ticket, the playwright reflected, he might never come back to live in Ireland. Very soon afterwards, he did use it, and he did not come back. The mass rage at his unCatholic iconoclasm had burnt him badly. In London he was lionized; he found a lovely young wife. Two years later, he received in the post the Abbey's rejection of *The Silver Tassie* just as his first child was born, 30 April 1928. That trauma sealed the bitterness within him, and cut him off from his imagination's home, Dublin.

9

The great Dublin plays continued to hold the stage wherever English was spoken. Yet something seems to have happened to the Abbey productions of these classics, quite apart from the bowdlerization of the Abbey acting version of *The Plough and the Stars* (the cuts actors had sought in rehearsal were conceded by the directors after the riots). In *Juno and the Paycock* and *The Plough and the Stars*, speech after speech became a set piece, like an aria in an opera. Character was everything to the Abbey players, plot and atmosphere nothing, a New York critic observed.[85] The performance of *Juno* was 'more an exhibition than a play', though admittedly an exhibition by a half-dozen maestros. Barry Fitzgerald 'fairly SMELT his part of the Captain. His voice performed incredible feats of comedy, and his great earthy frame oozed alcoholic amiability.'[86] In his rendition, a fake pomposity from Boyle, such as – 'Ever since the Will was passed I've run hundreds o' dockyments through me han's, I tell you, you have to keep your wits about you' – could reveal twists and turns of screwball mirth.[87]

Maureen Delaney and Barry Fitzgerald, 1932/33 tour. (White Studios/Shields family papers)

Like Fitzgerald, Maureen Delaney had the ability to 'lift up the house on [her] appearance on stage'.[88] In the eyes of American critic George Jean Nathan, however, her 'winking, snorting, and mugging ... wreck any serious play'.[89] But were the O'Casey plays still serious plays? They had become Dublin character comedies.

In Chicago, the reviewer for the *Herald and Examiner* compared the Abbey to an American football team: 'all star at the right moment',[90] an observation that leaves unaddressed whether or not a play should be like a sporting contest.

The early Abbey style, in which no one moved while a character spoke, and all eyes were on that character, evolved into a sequence of solo turns, and each turn was an opportunity for individual display, rather like a session of jazz musicians – the pianist finishes, now here's a riff from the man on the sax! In rehearsal, much of the business was left for the actor to devise. Only voice mattered to director Lennox Robinson. During rehearsal, he 'put his elbow on the arm of his seat and his hand over his eyes ... [S]ets did not matter to him, nor did costumes, and ... he never looked at the players' make-up.'[91] The result of this setting of the actors loose to devise their own by-play struck American spectators as odd. In the October 1932 New York performance of *The Whiteheaded Boy*, Barry Fitzgerald seemed 'a comedian a little too conscious of his comicality'. The audience was being invited to enjoy the way well-known parts were played, to focus on the actor, not on the authenticity of the person represented.

The American custom, whether on Broadway or in Hollywood, was to spend a great deal of money on a leading man and leading lady, guarantee spectators lavish set and costumes, and focus on a through-line for the plot, leading to the happy ending. The productions of *Juno and the Paycock* and *The Plough and the Stars* that toured American in the early 1930s lacked these ingredients. They meandered comically towards unhappy endings, with startlingly vivid lowlife characters sporting their eccentricities in front of cheap, painted scene-flats.

10

The 1934/35 Abbey tour took the company for the first time to Los Angeles, where *Juno* and *The Plough and the Stars* were staged. At the time, John Ford was filming Liam O'Flaherty's *The Informer* at California Studio on Melrose Avenue.[92] O'Flaherty (1896–1984) came to Hollywood in 1932 in search of script work. As soon as O'Flaherty arrived, Ford befriended him. The novelist was from the Aran Islands. Ford's own father, John Feeney, had been born in 1856 in Spiddal, on the mainland just miles from Aran, a rocky strip of coastline as hard hit by the 1845–9 famine as any place in Ireland. As mentioned in Chapter I, Ford christened the splendid yacht he bought in 1934 the *Araner*,[93] and in O'Flaherty, he had a pal who actually was an Araner, someone whose first language was Irish, and who had fought on the anti-Treaty side in the Civil War. O'Flaherty evidently did his best to turn Ford into a communist like himself. For a time Ford became sympathetic to the rights of labour, or, at the very least, to the rights of a film director's labour.[94]

While the Abbey actors were in Los Angeles Ford hired Denis O'Dea out of the company to play as a wandering street singer in the film. Una O'Connor and J.M. Kerrigan, former Abbey players then resident in Hollywood, were already in the cast. The touring company was treated by Ford to a lunch on the set of *The Informer.*

By the end of April 1935 John Ford had financing from RKO Studio for a film of *The Plough and the Stars.* It was his wish to put the entire Abbey cast of the play under contract and bring them to Los Angeles, but RKO did not allow that. The studio executives insisted on two film stars for Jack and Nora Clitheroe, the Irish-born Preston Foster (a frequent lead in RKO pictures), and 29-year-old Barbara Stanwyck (original name, Ruby Stevens, of Scots-Irish parentage). Ford was permitted to ask the Abbey management to release actors for the remaining speaking parts in the film.

The Abbey had earlier resisted such requests. In the summer of 1932, after MGM Studio gave Abbey ingénue Kitty Curling a screen test, talent scouts were dispatched to Dublin. They asked Lennox Robinson to suggest others who might be suitable for the screen. Robinson said members of the Abbey company were under 'fast contract'. He did nothing to facilitate interviews between the MGM agents and specific players. Word got out after the agents left town, and some players, like Barry Fitzgerald, were bitter at the missed opportunity.[95]

F.J. McCormick, Eileen Crowe, Barry Fitzgerald and Arthur Shields leaving from New York for Hollywood, June 1936. (Shields family papers)

John Ford had a more definite and restricted offer than the overture by MGM agents; he had a lot of money to spend as well. The budget for *The Plough and the Stars* was approximately sixty times the annual subsidy for the Abbey in 1936.[96] On 19 July 1935 Hugh Hunt, former President of the Oxford University Dramatic Society, had been appointed artistic director of the Abbey, and it was the young Englishman who had the job of dealing with John Ford and RKO. In late February Miss Reissa, the London agent for RKO, arrived in Dublin to propose paying the Abbey Theatre for the release of its leading actors for July and August of that year and for the use of its name in advertising; they offered $750.[97] The Abbey Board made a counterproposal of $5000. A deal was struck for $1000. The actors themselves were to be paid princely sums by any standard except Hollywood's (though the Abbey made them agree to pay 10 per cent back to the company for the loss of their services): Barry Fitzgerald, $750; Denis O'Dea, $600; Eileen Crowe, $450; F.J. McCormick, $450; Arthur Shields, $500.[98]

Not all the actors would come back at the summer's end, and of those who came back, not all of them would remain long in Dublin. Barry Fitzgerald had been restless in Dublin since he had given up on the London stage in December 1930. At first he suspected that his Abbey fans were 'off' him: 'People who go away as I did [to act in the London *Silver Tassie*] are disapproved of by Dublin people.'[99] The prejudice continued, he thought, even a year later. Notices of the Abbey plays often left him unmentioned and heaped praise on F.J. McCormick. Maybe it was because he was a Protestant and McCormick was not, 'for Dublin is very Catholic now'.[100] In September 1932, having seen the United States, and loved it, Fitzgerald found it 'hard luck' when Lennox Robinson blocked the actors from negotiations with agents from MGM.[101]

On 12 August 1935 Fitzgerald reprised his role as Sylvester Heegan in *The Silver Tassie*, a very funny part. But the Dublin press slated the play, and Catholic clergy objected to the cross in Act 2 as a blasphemy. Brinsley MacNamara, a Catholic playwright on the Abbey board, attacked the play, and so was forced by fellow directors to resign. More priests and laymen joined in the brouhaha. Dublin was getting very Catholic indeed.[102]

The audience only wanted Fitzgerald to make them laugh; they would laugh even before he had done anything to make them do so. When he took serious roles, critics complained that he was 'hopelessly miscast'; they were a waste of his 'comic genius'.[103] According to Dublin critical opinion, 'Barry Fitzgerald is a clown.'[104] So it may be assumed that he was one actor who was very happy to be setting sail in June 1936 in order to get his chance in Hollywood.

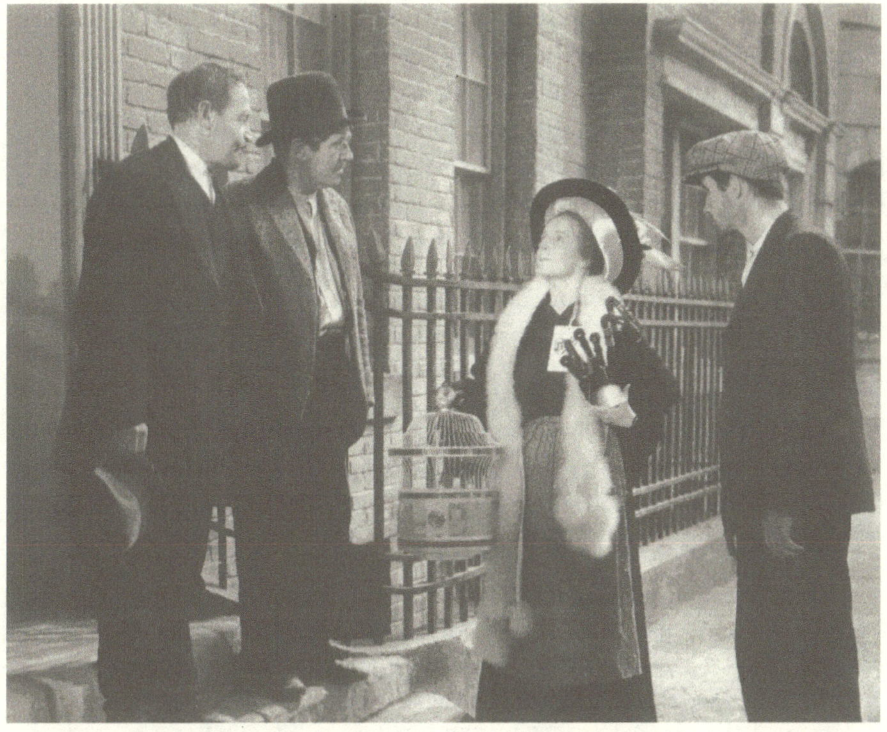

Barry Fitzgerald, J.M. Kerrigan, Eileen Crowe and Denis O'Dea in The Plough and the Stars, *1936. (Courtesy RKO Pictures/Shields family papers)*

11

Barry Fitzgerald was not among the actors when they arrived back in Dublin, but the others were returned safely to the Abbey. Greeted by interviewers, they said they had been vastly impressed with John Ford, a genius and an Irishman. 'If the Saorstat Government can afford to finance a real Irish picture that would be typical of Irish life and embody the real spirit of the country,' they should get John Ford to direct it: 'It would be magnificent propaganda,'[105] F.J. McCormick predicted. Evidently, McCormick continued to believe that O'Casey's play should have been, and was not, any of those things: typical of Irish life, instinct with its spirit, or magnificent propaganda for the country to outsiders. Ford's American film, he hoped, would be more like what was needed by the young Free State as a representation of its own 'Declaration of Independence' and 'Revolution'. Even if there were parallels between Ireland and

America, Hollywood itself did not seem like home to Mr and Mrs McCormick. Eileen Crowe was frightened by the ups and downs of celebrity.

Some of the extras in the crowd scenes for the film, she learned, had been stars just a few years earlier. American fame could be 'very brief indeed'. In leading actresses, youth was at a premium, and narrowly calculated.[106] It sounds as if Crowe had read Robert Frost's poem about the Los Angeles cleaning woman, once 'the beauty Abishag,/The picture pride of Hollywood':

> No memory of having starred
> Atones for later disregard
> Or keeps the end from being hard.[107]

On 23 December 1936 all the actors who had returned from Hollywood – F.J. McCormick, Eileen Crowe, Denis O'Dea and Arthur Shields – gathered in the censor's office for a private screening of *The Plough and the Stars*. Holloway recorded the general disappointment:

> It was a sentimentalizing of O'Casey's play with Barry Fitzgerald standing out on his own as 'Fluther Good'; [Joe] Kerrigan was colourless as 'Peter Flynn', and all the other characters of O'Casey were more or less dwarfed out of recognition by the producer. The storming of the GPO was effectively done. The film story is a sentimentalized rendering of the Clitheroes' story and as such makes an effective picture, but as a screen telling of O'Casey's play it is not a success.[108]

Such a judgment – 'not as good as the book' – is typically made of films based on great literary works. The review of Ford's *The Plough and the Stars* in the London *Times* is similar: it harped on the virtues of the play 'from which this film claims to be adapted':

> It is a device of the theatre, but not of the cinema, to suggest great events by their echoes within a small room, and the movement of crowds by the conversation of a few people. Mr Sean O'Casey's play, from which this film claims to be adapted, makes a brilliant use of this device, and it is inevitable that the greater scope and expansion of the cinema would destroy this artifice. Here the events of 1916 are shown at large, the meetings and the marches, the defence and capture of the Dublin Post Office, the looting of shops, the snipers on the roofs, and the hair's breadth escapes of individual fighters. All this is very well done and successfully conveys the horror of fighting in the streets of a modern town; the settings and the photography are good and there is a continuous suspense. But the merits of the film have little or no relation to the merits of the play, and even the story as it affects the chief characters is radically altered ...[109]

It is true that the film version of *The Plough* substitutes exterior street scenes and rooftop vistas (built on a studio production lot) for box-sets on a small stage. It is also true that it often substitutes action for talk, and thus plot for character. Yet the *Times* review does not really investigate what the merits of the film are, aside from noticing that they are not the merits of the play.

Certainly Ford encountered mass-market demands by the RKO producers that even he found shocking. Sam Briskin, the new production chief at the studio, could not understand O'Casey's play, or why Ford should have wanted to film it. Why were the Irish fighting the British in the midst of World War I anyway? Were they on the German side? Truly Irish-American, Ford replied that Patrick Pearse wanted the same thing that George Washington did: liberty. After Ford finished shooting on 20 August 1936, Briskin remained puzzled. 'Why make a picture where a man and woman are married? The main thing about pictures is love or sex. Here you've got a man and woman married at the start – who's interested in that?'[110] Briskin wanted Ford to write scenes of Jack and Nora Clitheroe as unmarried. Ford refused to shoot any more film, and went on a drinking binge, or a voyage on the *Araner*, or both. After looking at the preview reports from RKO employees on 30 September Briskin ordered second-line directors George Nicholls and Ed Donahue to retake the scenes between Preston Foster and Barbara Stanwyck, and these were shot on 10, 11, 17 and 18 October, but, while the fact of their having been filmed infuriated Ford – he broke relations permanently with RKO – the new scenes of unmarried Clitheroes were not seen by the film's reviewers, and they are not available to be seen today.[111]

However bad the new material may have been, Briskin had a point. The film was not being made for Irish and Irish-American people who knew O'Casey's play. It was being made for many millions of other people who neither knew *The Plough and the Stars* nor cared about Ireland. Furthermore, it is a shortcoming of O'Casey's play that the parts for both Jack and Nora Clitheroe are weak; Yeats, Lady Gregory and George O'Brien all realized this on a first reading of the submitted manuscript. In the stage version Jack and Nora Clitheroe do not even have the effect of being the leading characters. Fluther Good, Bessie Burgess and Ginnie Gogan are the most brilliant of the many minor characters; there are no major characters in the play. The Clitheroes had to be restructured.

In many respects the story of the central couple had been strengthened by Ford and Dudley Nichols in their original screenplay. As the film begins, Jack and his wife Nora are alone in their upstairs flat. It is just after dinner. Jack, disgruntled, sits on the edge of an armchair smoking a cigarette. He has reluctantly agreed not to spend his evenings at meetings of the Citizens Army, but he cannot relax at home. Leaving the plates on the table, Barbara Stanwyck (as Nora) sits at his feet, laying her torso into his lap, and looks up into his face. The arrangement is, from a male point of view, pleasantly suggestive and promising. Yet Jack is on guard.

'Isn't it time to do the dishes?' he asks.

'There are more important things than dishes.'

'What?'

'You.'

This little catechism picks up the fundamental theme of O'Casey's play, and encapsulates it at the start. What in life is of most worth? In dialogue from the play that is used unchanged later in the film, Clitheroe says to Lieutenant Langon before the rebellion:

'You have a mother, Langon.'[112]

'Ireland is greater than a mother,' Langon replies.

'You have a wife,' Captain Brennan tells Clitheroe, who answers, 'Ireland is greater than a wife.'

Such comparisons between relative goods continue in the film. Finally, it is made clear that Ireland is held by the Republicans to be greater than love, family, neighbours, or an individual life.

12

After her womanly, love-centred version of what matters most in life, Nora then asks Jack to kiss her, and he does, deeply. She hands him his squeeze-box: 'Play for me.' Jack takes up the air of a street singer outside. Rising and smoothing her dress back down over her hips, Nora takes a slow, sexy walk over to the lamp. She turns it down low, stands quietly, head slightly bent beside the hearth; firelight glows on her front. Jack amuses himself with the accordion. It is palpable that Nora now means to make love to her husband. She crosses to pull the curtains over the windows, and sees the street singers in the fog under a streetlamp. Suddenly, a man in uniform appears on the footpath. She pulls down the shade and jerks the curtains closed.

'What's the matter?' Jack asks.

'Nothing,' Nora lies, as she bolts the door. 'Promise me you'll never go away and leave me!' There is a loud knock at the door and a short: 'Clitheroe!'

'That's Brennan!' Jack says with surprise.

Brennan is played by a lean F.J. McCormick. If one wanted to see the long-vanished early Abbey style of concentrated expressiveness, this short scene is where to find it. Brennan stands silently after handing over a dispatch from General Connolly. Jack reads the letter. McCormick/Brennan stares at Nora; Nora stares back. When Jack, finding he has been appointed Commandant, asks why he was never told before, McCormick half-smiles, saying nothing.

'But word was brought to you.' McCormick gives an ever so slightly mocking emphasis to 'was'.

'Who did you give it to?'

Pause. 'I think I gave it to …' Slow burn. '… Mrs Clitheroe over there.' And was that a smile on McCormick's face? Not quite. A subtext is written in stares and silences: Brennan is long familiar with Mrs Clitheroe; he both lusts after her and hates her. He hates her because she inspires sexual desire in him but belongs to Jack, not to him.

The sexualization of this scene as a whole – emphatically erotic, if within the rules of the Hollywood Production Code – can be justified as in the spirit of the play. If McCormick shows off the best of the Abbey style, Stanwyck's performance demonstrates what Hollywood had and the Irish theatre did not: the self-conscious, controlled erotics of star-power (one senses the sad unsatisfied desire in Stanwyck's Dublin housewife, like a depressed spring). If only Preston Foster had had the wherewithal to match her, or at least to fail in dramatic fashion.

Preston Foster as Jack in The Plough and the Stars, *1936, with John Ford and the production team reflected in the window-glass. (Lilly Library)*

But maybe even Spencer Tracy, to whom the part had been offered, and by whom it was rejected as too weak, could not have saved the plot. The play can do without a hero; the film cannot.

It is important to the story in the film that the values of sex, marriage, and family are woman-centred values and crucial to life, and that men are centrifugal from those values. They have to be coaxed and held near the hearth. The film-script's sexualization of the opening scene is not far from O'Casey's intention. As first written, and promptly squashed by George O'Brien, the play opened with a hot scene of married delight. Nora says to Jack, 'You can; come on, put your leg against mine – there.' Jack murmurs (it would be up to the actors to improvise the accompanying actions): 'Little rogue of th' white breast.'

13

Lovers of the play felt painfully the stripping out of so much of the rich loquacity of the scenes with minor characters. Indeed, with *The Informer*, it had become the passion of Ford and Nichols to set themselves against the infatuation of other film-makers with dialogue in the post-1930 talkie era. They wanted to make *The Informer* intelligible by atmosphere, soundtrack, action and cinematography alone, even to one who wholly ignored the slight bits of dialogue in the film. In the case of *The Plough and the Stars*, Ford was neither so programmatically anti-talkie, nor so expressionistically atmospheric in his film technique. Nonetheless, it is noteworthy just how many scenes in the movie version of *The Plough and the Stars* have only a few lines of speech or none. Nichols stripped away the playwright's words to a minimum, and then Ford as director set the actors free to manifest the spirit of the play.

The first appearance in the film of Barry Fitzgerald as Fluther Good is one such scene, and it is a triumph. It enables one to understand why Mary Pickford of United Artists signed Fitzgerald up to an exclusive contract once the film was released. After an exterior shot of men in uniform marching in formation down a city street, with rifles shouldered, Fluther Good is shown ducking into a pub. He spies three partial glasses of stout on the bar, abandoned by those who have rushed out to see the soldiers pass. The barman is watching the soldiers through the window. Fluther quickly and expertly empties the contents of the three glasses into a fourth partly drunk glass, making one brimful pint. He drinks this down with manifest relish, glug, glug, glug, never taking the glass from his lips until it is empty. The barman turns as he hears Fluther leave by the door, and sees four empty glasses on the bar. He shakes his head with disapproval and picks up a blackboard. On the slate already appears the name, FLUTHER GOOD with five 'x's beside it; the barman chalks four more crosses. In his appetite to scrounge free drink, Fluther has been charged for more than he in fact swallowed.

Arthur Shields as an IRA leader and political orator. This scene not used in the version of The Plough and the Stars *now extant. (Shields family papers)*

There is not a word spoken, yet the spectator has a very complete introduction to Fluther Good in its thirty-seconds of screen-time. As two RKO viewers from the advertising department put it in preview reports, 'The byplay was corking!' 'Fluther ... practically steals the show.'[113] Another prize piece of acting by Fitzgerald is in the fight scene between Fluther and The Covey over remarks of a rude nature the young man passed about Rosie Redmond. Fitzgerald takes off his jacket, rolls up his sleeves, and with fantastically silly imitations of the noble art of pugilism, squares up to fight. With his hands opened palm outward (he makes no fist at all of fighting), one flourished to the front, the other half-tucked behind him, he bobs and weaves until he has made himself dizzy, by which time, no blows having been exchanged at all, The Covey has been hustled by others out of the pub. Putting on his coat again, Fluther says, 'The second time I hit him, I thought I'd killed him!' Such scenes would be said by cinéastes to be 'director's touches', because Ford's distinction was the invention of humorous, folksy grace notes in a serious story. The invention of the business for the scenes, however, and the panache with which that business is carried off, are all Barry Fitzgerald. One of the things he had loved about the Abbey was that, unlike the commercial London stage, it allowed actors to improvise. A Hollywood director like Ford did the same. He cast actors that he knew had within them the power to invent parts of the story that the director wished to film.

Another example of a 'Fordian touch' occurs in a subsequent scene in the bar. Fluther Good is at a table with Mrs Gogan and her baby. They are toasting the Republic with glasses of whiskey. Bessie Burgess, Dublin Protestant Unionist and street fruit-vendor, comes in, loud with sarcasm about the nationalist toy soldiers; her own son, she boasts, is bravely fighting in the trenches in France. After Bessie Burgess accuses Ginnie Gogan of having been the mother of one bastard after another, Ginnie places her current infant into the arms of a bewildered Uncle Peter, and, putting up her fists, speaks her line, 'Any kid, livin' or dead, that Ginnie Gogan's had since, was got between th' bordhers of th' Ten Commandments.' The sentence so objectionable to Eileen Crowe in January 1926, although spoken in the film, is nearly undetectable; it is lost in the hubbub of the fight that has broken out between the two women.

The rest of the scene has no real dialogue at all, just a tumult of shouts, yet in the film it is more memorable and enjoyable than the cross-talk between the women that precedes it. The barman throws Bessie Burgess out into the street. She picks up a paving stone and pitches it through the pub window. He sadly shakes his head at the damage to his premises. Inside, amid the crowd, Ginnie Gogan is still squawking and fussing. He takes her by the arm and puts her out.

She too picks up a paving stone, and hurls it through a second window. The discouraged barman comes back in, and is met by Uncle Peter, still holding Ginnie Gogan's baby, who is even more disconsolate now that she has gone off without it. In dumbshow, he tries to get the barman to take the infant. Not having any of it, the barman puts Uncle Peter and baby out the door. Returning, now totally exasperated, the barman finds that one of the clients inside the pub has picked up one of the two stones thrown into the pub. The barman disarms the customer, and pitches the stone away over his shoulder ... straight into his one remaining unbroken window. Double takes all around among those still in the bar.

Barbara Stanwyck as Nora Clitheroe and Barry Fitzgerald as Fluther Good in The Plough and the Stars, *1936. (*RKO*/Shields family papers)*

The acting in this scene may have been partly directed by Arthur Shields (he received a credit as assistant director), but the outbreak of folksy comedy is Ford's hallmark. It perfectly sets up a poignant scene that follows between Mollser and Nora Clitheroe, in which Mollser – seeing how worried Mrs Clitheroe is about her husband – wonders if she herself would ever want to be married. 'Make no mistake, Mollser,' Nora says kindly but firmly, 'you'll want a man beside you. There's no happiness for a woman but a man. For it's a woman's nature to love, just as it's a man's nature to fight, and neither can help it more than the other.' This sad but beautiful oppositional balance of rights between men and women is also Fordian. Yet it is untypical of O'Casey, whose sympathies in the play were all on the side of the women's sense of what is important. The socialist playwright certainly believed men could, and should, change; the film-maker did not.

14

John Ford fundamentally altered the meaning of *The Plough and the Stars* to suit his own values. He meant to do this from early on. On 9 March 1936 he had written O'Casey a long letter about his intention to have Jack Clitheroe at the picture's end look up at the Plough and the Stars flag and 'utter a prophetic speech to the effect that at some day that flag will be hoisted again'. Ford then told a long story about two visits he had made to his family village of Spiddal. During his first visit, when he hurried to the help of the Feeneys (his way of telling it) 'during the trouble of 1921', the thatched cottage of the Thorntons was being burnt by the British. On his most recent visit, eighteen months earlier, Michael Thornton was a schoolteacher of Irish and English to well-dressed, enthusiastic children. The new government had 'carefully achieved an amazing change in the economic and social lives of people'.[114] In short, the Easter rebellion that O'Casey's play mocked was actually, Ford believed, both great and good, the work of heroes not cowards, and he intended his film to make this point clear. A director who romanticized the IRA was taking on a film that was a classic anti-romantic debunking of nationalist revolutionaries.

Did Ford choose to make a film of *The Plough and the Stars* simply because he liked the title, the theme of the Easter Rising, the bit parts by the Abbey players, and the great public acclaim of the masterpiece? Because to turn it into a celebration of the achievement of Irish freedom through heroic violence required not just that the play be gutted, but that it be given a new backbone. O'Casey, the son of a man who worked in the Protestant mission, was at heart a pacifist; he deplored war. Ford, the son of a tavern-keeper, regarded a barroom brawl as fine manly entertainment, and he was devoted to, even infatuated with, the military. He was as much at odds with O'Casey's vision as Yeats was when he rejected *The Silver Tassie* partly because O'Casey could not see 'the mere greatness of the world war'.[115] Yet to turn *The Plough and the Stars* into a sort of Western in which the gunfight is the resolution, Ford had little to go on. Primarily, what he had as a means for the conversion of O'Casey's weak males into heroic Irish freedom fighters was Preston Foster, and Foster, who had to carry the flag, had at his disposal neither lines, nor deeds, nor charisma. No one thinks the result a success. With the failure of the director-led enterprise, Ford blamed Briskin and RKO for interference. They blamed Ford for being so provincial a Hibernophile that he had neglected to consider the American market.

One addition to the play, which is successfully achieved, is an underlying but reiterated identification of the Irish struggle for freedom from Britain with the American revolution of 1776. This is not done crudely but it is emphatic. Ford introduces to the scenario a scene in a dark committee-room lit by a single lamp. The Proclamation of the Irish Republic is read out in solemn tones by the one figure standing (Arthur Shields as Patrick Pearse). With marmoreal gravity, James Connolly and six other men seated around the table listen, and then sign the document one after another. The first man's name is not John Hancock, nor are others Benjamin Franklin and Thomas Jefferson, but the tableau of solemn signatories strongly suggests the famous witnesses of the American Declaration of Independence.

The identification between Ireland and America is even more effectively created by means of the Tricolour the Irish rebels run up a pole above the GPO. The flag appears four times between battle scenes in which the British increase their use of fire-power. Each time it is more bullet-ridden than before. In the final scene of the film, British Tommies take it down the flagpole and cast the banner away over the side of the building. As some Irish people gathered beside Mollser's coffin at the church door look up, the flag in one slow tracking shot is shown billowing downward through the upward-rising smoke of the shattered city – a visual allusion to these famous verses:

> O say can you see, by the dawn's early light,
> What so proudly we hail'd at the twilight's last gleaming,
> Whose broad stripes and bright stars through the perilous fight
> O'er the ramparts we watch'd were so gallantly streaming?
> And the rocket's red glare, the bombs bursting in air …

As the final frames of *The Plough and the Stars* fill with the faces of Jack and Nora looking upward to the flag, his arm around her shoulder, the following dialogue closes the picture:

> Jack: The rising is over.
> Nora: What was it all for?

Jack: This is only the beginning.
Nora: Beginning of what? Men lying dead, women sorrowing and grieving … is there no end to it?
Jack: Yes, there is an end. We'll live to see Ireland free, and go on fighting till we do.
Nora: Yes, and we'll go on weeping.

Quite apart from the facts that at the end of O'Casey's play, Jack is dead, Nora has had a miscarriage, and lost her mind as well, this ending completely alters the meaning of the story.

To an American audience, the bullet-ridden flag must inevitably recall the United States national anthem. 'The Star-Spangled Banner' was written by Francis Scott Key following the burning of Washington DC in the war of 1812. The British bombarded Fort McHenry with rockets and bombshells, but the next morning Francis Scott Key saw the Stars and Stripes still flying in the battlesmoke, and composed his verses. By evoking this scene, Ford identifies Ireland and America. In regard to whether nationhood is worth fighting for, the answer as a result will be wholly different from what O'Casey's play suggests. Damn right, American audiences will think; of course liberty is worth fighting for. Remember that Irishman Patrick Henry? *Give me liberty or give me death!*

15

Barry Fitzgerald's brilliant by-play with the half-drunk glasses in the bar bears an uncanny likeness to a nightmare role as a shiftless drunk that the actor had refused to play in an English film being shot outside Dublin in the 1920s, in which a priest lectures the man for drinking whiskey on a streetcorner, and takes away his bottle. The apparently chastened man watches the priest until he turns a corner, then from within his overcoat withdraws a second bottle. With deep self-satisfaction he takes a swig. The bar scene with Fluther Good also has a shambling, work-shy Irishman, the drink, the incorrigible taste for same, the semi-respectful half-compliance with an arrogant clergyman, and the life that is a joke. Add to it the hilarious bar fight with The Covey, and one has a fairly complete picture of the stereotype of an Irish male. It was a stereotype that Barry Fitzgerald would get lots of opportunities to perfect in twenty years of movie-making, whether in Irish, British, Western or modern-American settings (though these would certainly not be his only opportunities). In 1941 he even did a turn in the African jungle as a staggering, lovable Irishman, with

Maureen O'Sullivan and Johnny Weismuller defending *Tarzan's Secret Treasure.* And in 1952 Fitzgerald brought it all back home in *The Quiet Man.*

So what does this story reflect? It is a story of a certain style of acting that was carried to the world's millions, one in which actors--trained by Frank Fay, or in his tradition--learned to speak words with quiet force, like feathers borne on puffs of wind, and learned also, after Fay left the company, to invent all their own stage business. It is a story, on another level, of globalization, the star system and the triumph of stereotypes in media for the masses. It is the story of Protestants in Dublin, however patriotic, still with a mimetic and parodic relationship to Catholic culture. It is a story of Protestants who found their home becoming no home at all in a Free State more like Franco's Spain than the Republicans' Spain. And of course it is a story of Ireland becoming a brand name – much loved, and often consumed in a glass.

16

The Plough and the Stars began shooting on 7 July 1936 and finished filming on 20 August. After the other Abbey players departed from Hollywood for Dublin, Barry Fitzgerald did not inform the theatre company of what he himself intended to do. Pressed for a reply, he cabled that he could not give a definite date of return. Told on 2 October 1936 that his roles would be assigned to another for the upcoming Abbey tour to Glasgow, Fitzgerald sent his regrets.[116] It occurred to him that, now that he had some money saved up, it might be interesting to travel around the world, perhaps by motorcycle.[117] But by the new year he had been signed to an exclusive contract by the Mary Pickford Company. After signing, he waited and waited for a part, and eventually was loaned on 28 April 1937 to Paramount Studios for *Ebb Tide,* based on a Robert Louis Stevenson story, and starring Frances Farmer, Ray Milland and Oscar Homolka. Fitzgerald got $550 a week, with a guarantee of four weeks' work.[118] Captain Boyle of *Juno and the Paycock* was going to sea at last.

While *Ebb Tide* was being filmed in July 1937, Dudley Nichols was working with Hagar Wilde on a script for Howard Hawks to direct, *Bringing up Baby.*[119] A part was introduced for an Irish gardener with a drinking problem. The addition of a cliché was not a problem for this movie; the script was full of them already. There is a professor of palaeontology (Cary Grant), and he is predictably absent-minded and unworldly. In a surprise that ought to be no surprise, a trained leopard gets mixed up with a wild one. The madcap, fast-talking, dizzy dame (Katherine Hepburn) sits on the proper, but very handsome hero's top hat. The two quarrel and when she tries to walk away, he happens to be standing on the train of her silver-lamé dress, so the whole back panel is torn away, unbeknownst to her, exposing her French panties; so he must cover her bottom with his crushed top hat. Later, when she sends his dirtied suit to the cleaner, he is forced to wear a woman's negligee with a fur border. The clever dog buries a valuable object, the intercostal clavicle of a brontosaurus, and that is the single piece the professor needs to complete the skeleton's reconstruction. The lost clavicle permits a raft of unsubtle double-entendres between Grant and Hepburn, along the lines of 'Where's the bone?' 'The bone's in the box.' Hepburn tries to awaken a gentleman by throwing bigger and bigger pebbles at his window, and just as he puts out his head, hits him with a sizable rock. These are all clichés, the *New York Times* reviewer complained when the film came out, and added that he – like much of the 1938 viewing public – found Katherine Hepburn 'fatiguing'.[120] The film was not a hit.

So why is *Bringing up Baby* now regarded as possibly the best of all the screwball comedies? She is so airy, he is so earnest. She is so svelte, he is so springy. The dialogue is merrily tight and rapid in its pell-mell tumble of silly jokes:

> David Huxley: [*trying to prove to Susan that she's playing his ball on a golf course*]: You see, a PGA has two lines and Crow-Flight has a circle.
> Susan Vance: [*blithely driving his ball to the green*]: Mm-hm. I'm not superstitious about things like that.

After she has sunk an amazingly long putt, he retrieves his ball from the cup, and points to a mark:

> David Huxley: You see, it's a circle.
> Susan Vance: Well, of course, do you think it would roll if it were square?

Nothing is really too silly for these deadpan-delivery stars, even Hepburn's line when Grant tells her there's a leopard in the bathroom and she has to get out of the apartment: *I can't. I have a lease.* If there were a pause for a laugh on a line that so little deserves one, the present-day viewer might groan with disgust, but the pace is sufficiently rapid that two or three other gags, pratfalls, or cock-ups have occurred before a measured judgment can be passed on that one bad pun.

Director Howard Hawks famously gave Cary Grant the note for his performance: imitate Harold Lloyd, the silent comedian. Lloyd's most famous roles were as an upright, 'average' young man in spectacles who in his ambition to fulfil his dreams is comically exposed to one danger after another. This hint evidently worked for Grant, but it was not the sole key for the comedy in the film. The key for Hepburn's acting is that she loves this man. Whenever she looks at him, her eyes melt. So she must think fast, and talk fast, and never take no for an answer, stopping at nothing to get her man, who is in fact engaged to be married the day after she first meets him. 'Everyone contributed anything and everything they could to that film,' Hepburn recalled.[121] Charlie Ruggles as Major Applegate was allowed to do again what he had been doing so well already in forty-five movies in the 1930s alone – to say *ahem*, look confused, and carry on as best he could regardless. He is given the perfect set-up for his skill when Aunt Random (a Lady Bracknell figure out of Oscar Wilde) tells him at dinner he is to 'bring out' the Cary Grant character, who is, she says (because that's what she's been told), a big-game hunter like Major Applegate, but one who has recently had a nervous breakdown. At dinner, whatever question Major Applegate asks, David Huxley (Grant) replies, *No*, since he is not what he has been said to be, and his whole attention is upon the little dog who has buried his precious brontosaurus bone, and might at any point run out to reveal its whereabouts. With each *No*, and dash from the room by Professor Huxley, Ruggles gets a chance to give a variation on his professional theme of the 'fluster'.

By the same token, Barry Fitzgerald is given a chance to do his party piece. The originality of the joke is not the point; familiarity is. The better to identify him, Fitzgerald is given a hat, vest and rumpled suit exactly like the ones he wore as Fluther Good in *The Plough and the Stars* film and in the scores of stage performances in the same role across the USA. He has the same droopy stage-moustache too.

Playing a gardener named Gogarty (this is Nichols's joking allusion to his New York pal Oliver St John Gogarty), Fitzgerald's main scene occurs during the dinner party when the dog keeps coming and going from the house, followed by the nutty professor: 'Drive a man crazy!' Gogarty complains, 'And then they say keep away from the bottle! Not even to steady one's nerves!' Mumbling, he heads to the garage where he has a bottle stashed, but also where 'Baby', the leopard, is shut up. He gets his bottle, and the leopard follows him out the garage door.

In the garden gazebo, a tipsy Gogarty mumbles grumpily to himself. The dinner guests have come into the garden, and Major Applegate is repeating, for Aunt Random's pleasure, his imitation of the cry of a leopard. 'Instead of sitting decently at table and eating their dinner,' Gogarty grumbles, 'I can't stand it.

Howling and roaring like a lot of banshees. If one more thing happens to upset me, I'd be seeing things.' Just then (inevitability is the essence of the fun in this movie), Baby leaps up beside him in the gazebo and begins to purr loudly. After one long-drawn terrified look, bushy eyebrows raised high, Gogarty rushes into the kitchen and grabs the cook: 'Me gun! Me gun! Hand me me gun! I saw, I saw, I saw a cat, as big as a cow, with eyes like balls of fire.' Susan and David lock gazes – Baby is loose!

Fitzgerald has a few other scenes in the film, but this scene establishes his function. It is to reprise, or quote from, a great O'Casey role, Fluther Good, in its bibulousness, shambling gear and self-infatuated pugnacity. Contemporary reviewers of *Bringing up Baby* often mention that Fitzgerald is once again doing his drunken Irishman bit in an American movie. Actually, this is the first time in which he did it (indeed, there would be others). With his 'querulous voice' and 'pompous futility', the role of Gogarty (alias Fluther Good) makes up a distinguished part of a great movie in which many kinds of comedy have been thrown together, stripped down to their essentials, strung one to the next by a plot, and directed with pace and panache.[122] Barry Fitzgerald would come to play other kinds of character, but he got his start as one who could bring a Captain Boyle or Fluther Good sort of character into the mainstream of world cinema.

III

THE LONG VOYAGE HOME: ARTHUR SHIELDS, JOHN FORD, EUGENE O'NEILL AND IRISH EXILE

Previous page: *Young Arthur Shields and his library, 1913–16. (Shields family papers)*

In early September 1938 Arthur Shields (1896–1970), actor and frequently the director of plays at the Abbey Theatre, was in great trouble of mind. He was not sure he could stick it in Dublin. According to his third wife Laurie, Shields was not the sort of man who plotted his life as a writer plots his novel. He took things as they came, just as an actor assumes the part as it is written in the night's play. Trapped in a tight spot, when a door opened, was that not his cue to go through it?

2

That had been the way even in 1916 when Shields took his rifle and followed Commandant Connolly into the Dublin General Post Office. He played the part of a young Irish hero 'to a T', none better.

Arthur was the seventh of eight children of Adolphus Shields, a compositor, journalist and labour leader who founded the Gasworkers' Union and organized the first All-Ireland Labour Conference. His mother, Fanny Sophie Ungerland Shields, was born in 1856 in a middle-class family in Hamburg, Germany, and met her husband in 1881 when the Scottish family for whom she served as governess happened to take an Irish vacation. Mr and Mrs Shields ran a Protestant socialist household dedicated to equality and the full expression of each person's native talents. They lived in many houses – North St George's Street, Vernon Avenue in Clontarf, Seafield Road and others – but a long, parliamentary table in the kitchen was a fixture in them all.

The family was not wealthy. They shifted from rented quarters to rented quarters, and thus the children moved from school to school. The primary place of training of Arthur Shields was the Merchant Tailors' School. If Arthur received an unexceptional formal education, he had a first-rate informal one. He loved to read Russian novels and Irish poets. Yeats was his favourite author. In 1911, aged fifteen, he founded a family drama group, 'The Kincora Dramatic Club'. Its first production was Lady Gregory's rebel play, *The Rising of the Moon.* Later they did works by Yeats, Synge and T.C. Murray.

The turning point of Arthur Shields's early life came in 1913, and it was the classic turning point of young Irish idealists of the period. He attended Yeats and Gregory's incendiary folkplay *Cathleen ni Houlihan.*[1] Set at the time of the 1798 rebellion, and in a peasant cottage in County Mayo, near where the French landed troops in aid of the rebels, the play depicts an old woman, who is Ireland, calling upon a young man to abandon his preparations for a wedding, and to give his life to her, to give her all. Threaded through her incantatory speeches are allusions to rebel ballads and their rebel heroes, figures who are real to her, but paradoxically draw others into a dream of liberation through self-sacrifice. As if entranced, Michael walks out on his family and fiancée and follows Cathleen ni Houlihan. When she is last seen, she is no old woman, but a young one, with the walk of a queen.

At the close of this little fifteen-minute play, Arthur Shields resolved to serve his country. The immediate means by which he meant to serve Ireland was by learning to put on plays like *Cathleen ni Houlihan.* His father paid for tuition at the Abbey school of acting, where he was taught by Una O'Connor, J.M. Kerrigan and Frank Fay.[2] By December 1913 he was appearing in walk-on parts and, by March 1914, in a speaking role.[3]

On 25 May 1914 the Home Rule Bill was passed for the third and final time in the House of Lords, signalling the approach at long last of at least a measure of Irish independence. But from that date plans for a political solution to the Irish difficulty began to unwind. The bill was amended in July to provide for the exclusion of Ulster, where, armed by an April gun-running expedition, a provisional government was being formed by Protestant Unionists opposed to separation from Britain. To stop the splitting of the country, the Irish Volunteers were established and began to recruit soldiers. On 26 July a shipment of guns was landed at Howth just outside Dublin, where paramilitary troop columns waited to receive them. On their return to the city, the Volunteers were challenged by the police and British regiments, but the effort to disarm them failed. Frustrated of their purpose, the British troops were interrupted on their way back along the River Liffey to barracks by a jeering crowd. On Bachelor's Walk alongside the Liffey, the troops fired a volley of live rounds into the crowd, killing four civilians and wounding thirty.

After the atrocity, new recruits poured into the Volunteers, among them Arthur Shields and his best friend, Charlie Saurin, both just eighteen. Far from boasting about his military experiences, Shields left little record of them, but it is possible to reconstruct his activities from other witnesses, primarily Charlie Saurin, who went on to a career in the army of the Irish Free State.

The two boys were issued rifles and drilled in Father Mathew Park in Fairview with the 'F' Company. Shields could not bring his firearm home because his father did not approve of physical force to achieve political ends. Strikes, journalism, plays – yes; guns – no. With the connivance of some actors (veteran J.M. Kerrigan and the juvenile male, Seán Connolly) Shields hid the gun under the Abbey stage.

One other thing Shields hid under that stage was the hand press on which the Proclamation of the Irish Republic was to be printed. Helena Molony, an actress with the theatre and a member of the Republican movement, arrived at the Abbey one night with the press, and said it had been kept in one place after another, but each place had been raided. So Shields shoved it under the stage with some props and old bits of scenery, and there it safely stayed for nine months or a year, until Helena Molony and some others returned late one night with a hand-cart, and wheeled it off to another hideaway.[4]

On the morning of Easter Sunday 1916 Shields returned from an Abbey tour of England to his family home in Seafield Road, Clontarf. In the *Sunday Independent*, a statement by Volunteer chief Eoin McNeill countermanded an order for troops to mobilize for manoeuvres (planned as a cover for the Rising). In the afternoon, an officer from 'F Company', along with Shields's friend Charlie Saurin, called at Seafield Road to give an order to stand by, but the planned five o'clock muster was off. On Monday morning Shields received orders from his company commander to gather at Father Mathew Park. His gun, however, was under the Abbey stage. He also had the typescript of a play that was about to debut, *The Spancel of Death*.[5] Captain Leo Henderson sent him to fetch the gun and return the typescript. Once at the Abbey, Shields feared he would not make it back to the park before the company departed for its positions. So he went round the corner to Eden Quay and down a block into Liberty Hall.

There Commandant General Connolly welcomed him into the ranks of the Citizen Army by saying, 'I hope you will prove as good a man as your father.'[6] At 11.45 am two hundred soldiers fell in. Twenty-five under the leadership of Abbey actor Seán Connolly went to City Hall; one hundred went to St Stephen's Green. Shields remained with a force of seventy under the leadership of Connolly and Joseph Plunkett. They marched along Eden Quay, turned into Lower Abbey Street, wheeled right onto O'Connell Street, and north to the General Post Office. Connolly then called out, 'Left turn. The GPO – charge!' There was no expectation of an attack, and no resistance. At 12.25, Connolly and Pearse came out in front of the post office. Stephen MacKenna, friend of Synge and translator of Plotinus, happened to be on O'Connell Street. He listened as Pearse, 'pale and cold of face', read out the proclamation of the Irish Republic to an indifferent crowd, who gave up 'a few perfunctory cheers'.[7]

Connolly ordered that the Dublin Bread Company at the bottom of O'Connell Street be fortified to protect the telegraphic works there. Shields was part of the six-man squad given this mission.[8] They barricaded the stairwells, broke out the windows, and began to fire at any troops who attempted to make their way toward the GPO. By Wednesday heavy artillery was being used against rebel strongholds. Connolly ordered his men to abandon the Dublin Bread Company. The officer in charge, Fergus O'Kelly, thought retreat was a mistake: 'We're giving them hell from here.'[9] Arthur Shields was next assigned to carry messages from the GPO to Lower Abbey Street and beyond. Five times he was seen, tall (5' 10.5"), bespectacled, rifle in hand, running crouched across O'Connell Street, while 'bullets scored chips out of the tram sets all around him'.[10]

Inside the GPO the mood became tragic. On Thursday Connolly had taken a bullet in the ankle; only injections of morphine could control the pain. Pearse knew from 'those who had been out about the streets on various errands' that not just the British but 'the people were ready to attack them'. He was now convinced that all the men and women around him 'must perish in the Rising to which he had brought them'.[11]

By Friday afternoon, bombarded by the gunship *Helga* anchored in the Liffey, the GPO could be held no longer. Fire was sweeping through the building, and at 3.30 the roof began to collapse.[12] At eight o'clock Pearse called the Volunteers together in the main hall. They were to 'go out and face the machine-guns as though you were on parade'.[13] Under the cover of night they made their way through a network of laneways to a house on Moore Street, Number 16. Oscar Traynor stood at the door and passed the soldiers through,

Corner of Sackville Street and Eden Quay at the end of the Easter Rising, 1916. (Shields family papers)

one by one. When Charlie Saurin arrived, Traynor said, 'Arthur Shields is gone upstairs.'[14] In the top room, Saurin found Shields, rifle in hand, kneeling at a window looking out onto Moore Street.

Dawn revealed a total of seven men in the little room. One was the first signatory of the 1916 Proclamation, Tom Clarke. Republican women arrived downstairs with bandages and sandwiches, and tended to Connolly in the kitchen. Outside, an overwhelming force of British soldiers waited at the corner of Moore Street and Henry Street, and opened fire at anything that moved. A group of seven, including Shields, was ordered to tunnel from building to building, in the direction of Great Britain Street, in the hope of breaking out of the rebels' encirclement, and linking up with forces at the Four Courts. Having tunnelled near to the British barricade, the men were visited by Patrick Pearse, who looked outside, and went away.

Word was brought to the seven men that they were to be given 'the place of honour' in the coming battle. The plan was for them, on a signal, to jump down into Moore Lane, fire a volley, and charge the machine-gun-mounted British barricade. Obviously, they would all be killed, and quickly, but the hope was that this activity would serve as a diversion while the rest of the rebels broke into Moore Street and stormed the less heavily defended barricade at the top of that street.

While awaiting the signal to attack, the seven received a life-saving countermanding order. They were not to open fire on any account, even if the British soldiers entered their building. Shields and Saurin could now see the Tommies at the barricade begin to relax – to chat and smoke cigarettes. At five o'clock the seven men were told to form up and go out into the steet; Sean McDermott read them terms of surrender. Outside, they saw bodies of Volunteers scattered along the lane. A civilian with a white flag lay in his drying blood. They had to clamber over a barricade. Down at their feet on the other side, looking upward, lay The O'Rahilly, dead. He had been the editor of *An Claidheamh Soluis*, the Gaelic League journal, and had opposed rebellion, at last taking up arms as an act of solidarity.

A British soldier told the captive Volunteers to put down their weapons. They would then, he urged, be allowed to go home. The men filed along and pitched their rifles in a heap. Some citizens spat upon the captives, Shields recalled. He was taken with the others to Richmond Barracks, and lined up in a gymnasium. A 'G-man' examined the prisoners in order to pick out the leaders for court martial. Willie Pearse – brother of the president, Patrick Pearse – was pulled from the line and taken away. The detective stopped in front of Shields, who was still wearing his glasses. He looked, though just twenty, like a man of importance. What was his name? Where did he work? The Abbey Theatre? Shields was asked if he knew Philip Guiry, another Abbey actor now held as a prisoner of war. Nothing was said of a third player who had fought in the rebellion, Seán Connolly. On Monday, positioned at City Hall, he had been one of the first to kill a British soldier and one of the first to die.

Within a few days Shields and Saurin were put with other prisoners in the hold of a freighter and shipped to detention camps in Britain – Knutsford in Cheshire, then Frongoch in Wales. It was there that the new Sinn Féin political order rapidly took shape, and it was a Catholic and Gaelic shape. At 9.30 every evening the Rosary was recited in Irish.[15] An executive was elected and subcommittees formed; by July, the one-man, one-vote democracy was dissolved in favour of military rule, a rank-and-file structure with orders of command. Shields was appointed to the 'Amusements' subcommittee. Mostly, he read novels (there was a prison library), smoked cigarettes and lay in bed. The detention camp was cold and damp, and he came down with a chest infection (possibly the origin of his subsequent tuberculosis).

On 12 July he wrote to tell his family that he had spotted an orange sash the previous day, and was thinking of taking up a lunch pan and beating it as a drum to lead a parade (the traditional Ulster celebration of the triumph of

William of Orange over the Catholic King James is held on the Twelfth). The joke was that he was in the last position to throw his sectarian weight around – not that Shields, a socialist and atheist, was sectarian. But he was billeted with fellow internees who were binding themselves together through specifically Catholic devotional practices. The evidence suggests that Arthur Shields underwent a separation from Sinn Féin during his internment, on account of being neither Catholic nor Irish-speaking. Decades later, while living in Hollywood, when asked why he had left Ireland, he replied that it was because he didn't want to pray in Gaelic.[16]

3

By the time Shields got back to the Abbey (he was released from Frongoch in August and appeared in Shaw's *Widowers' Houses* on 9 October 1916), the company had been cleared out after an insurgency among the actors against the author-manager, St John Ervine. In an obvious aftershock of the Easter rebellion, Ervine introduced – as mentioned in Chapter II – an almost military set of rules; for example:[17]

> If a player is late for rehearsal, his or her part will be transferred to another Player, and if the excuse for being late is inadequate, he or she will be deprived of the part altogether.
>
> Players are not to be in the Theatre except when engaged in rehearsals or performance. No Player is to be in the Theatre after 11.30 pm without permission.
>
> ... Any Player keeping the stage waiting [for a curtain call] will be fined half a crown.
>
> Not more than two passes will be given to each Player in one month.
>
> Players are not to take any books from the cases in the Vestibule or Office without permission.
>
> ...
>
> Players are not to enter the Office except on business and then only by invitation from the Manager or Secretary. The Office hours are from 10 am to 1 pm and from 2.45 to 5 pm.

In vain had G.B. Shaw warned Ervine that 'Ulster discipline would never do.'[18] The leading players quit *en masse*. That created openings for Shields and his timid older brother Will, a civil servant in the Department of Unemployment. While Will 'suffered anguish at the thought of confrontation', and seemed happy in a state of vague onward drifting,[19] he proved to be a naturally exuberant actor if put on stage with half-decent lines. Within a few years, the Shields brothers were the mainstays of the Abbey company. Arthur was Christy Mahon in all revivals of *The Playboy of the Western World*, along with other parts for handsome leading men, while Will Shields – under the stage name Barry Fitzgerald – came to shine in comic parts.

When Micheál Mac Liammóir (then called Michael Willmore) arrived in Ireland in March 1917, he was trying to make a living by selling his paintings. The theatre diarist Joseph Holloway bought four, and took Mac Liammóir to the Abbey, where Arthur Shields bought a painting too. Soon the two young men became friends. A.J. 'Con' Leventhal left a vivid record of an evening spent with Shields and Mac Liammóir in 1918:

> Shields has the long face, the strong chin, and the mild pleading look that keeps young ladies eternally romantic. As a cinema star, he could have out-faired Fairbanks. Tall and slim, he sways from the shoulders like a daffodil … Mac Liammóir painted a watercolour of him in which green predominated, Baudelaire's hair dye having become a popular symbol of decadence. And from the pockets of the closely fitting jacket bulging with Parnassian poets, it would not be too rash to judge that the caricaturist believed Shields to be fin de siècle. If a predilection for Wilde, an inclination to the bizarre, a taste for Japanese prints, and Chloes that change with the moon are end of the century characteristics, then he was correctly labelled.[20]

The lads split a bottle of champagne three ways, before going to the theatre, where Shields manages to get them complimentary tickets. He has a crush on the actress. Mac Liammoir and Leventhal soon grow bored, and leave the auditorium. In the stairwell, they read Verlaine to one another, while Shields, inside, keeps his eye on the actress. After the show, the three go round to the Abbey greenroom. A half bottle of Chablis has been left behind by another, which, with the prop bread from the week's performances of *Mixed Marriage*, they happily consume. Sitting hand in hand on the greenroom sofa, they attempt a séance. Yeats did it, didn't he? Mac Liammoir is the one who most expected to contact a ghost, but it is Leventhal who suddenly has an attack of the shakes. According to his friends, his face in that seizure becomes momentarily devoid of features, just 'a wall of flesh'.

After his release from prison camp, Arthur Shields dedicated himself, it appears, to art rather than politics, or rather to art mainly and sometimes to politics through artistic means. He had, as he said, no prayers and no Gaelic, and felt, it seems, out of step.[21] In the country as a whole, Republican activity – purified by Catholicism and the Irish language – had broadened and intensified since 1916. In January 1919 the seventy-three Irish members of parliament elected on the Sinn Féin ticket met in Dublin and adopted a Declaration of Independence. In the same month, in the course of stealing a shipment of gelignite, IRA Volunteers shot two policemen. A protracted war with England was on the horizon. So March 1919 was a significant time for the Abbey directors to put *Cathleen ni Houlihan* on the bill, with its call to arms; it was also significant that they cast Republican activist and actress Máire nic Shiublaigh in the title role.[22] However, the actress – who had not been a regular member of the company since 1905 – did not show up for rehearsals. Waiting on stage on Monday morning Arthur Shields was surprised to find Lady Gregory, looking uncommonly unnerved.[23] Unbeknownst to others, she and not Yeats had been the primary author of that play, and now at last she herself was going to play Mother Ireland.[24] Lady Gregory was at the time 'very, very old', Shields recalled; she had always spoken with a lisp, and she was terrified of going on stage. Once Shields (in the male lead) had to whisper a prompt to her, but only once. In spite of a cold, and shock at the backstage darkness before the curtain went up, she got through the rest of her lines. At the end of the week's final performance she murmured in relief to Shields, 'That was all right.'[25] Her reward was sweet: two curtain calls all to herself.

Lady Gregory as The Poor Old Woman and Arthur Shields as Michael in Cathleen ni Houlihan, *March 1919. (Shields family papers)*

The early 1920s were days of trouble for the country, but great days for the Shields brothers. On an Abbey tour of London, a pretty British soldier of Irish Catholic descent, Bazie McGee, entered a relationship with Arthur Shields, and the two were married. Under the stage name 'Joan Sullivan', Mrs Shields had begun to go on stage in small parts at the Abbey plays by 22 December 1924.[26] Arthur and Will Shields became friends with other nationally minded Protestants who were part of the cultural formation of the new state – people like Micheál Mac Liammóir; Harry Clarke, the stained-glass artist;[27] Lennox Robinson, author and stage manager of the Abbey Theatre; and, from the spring of 1923, Sean O'Casey, who would create some of his best characters with Barry Fitzgerald in mind, such as Captain Boyle in *Juno and the Paycock* (3 March 1924) and Fluther Good in *The Plough and the Stars* (8 February 1926).

4

While rehearsing *The Plough and the Stars* in January 1926, Arthur Shields met the young barrister, later playwright, Denis Johnston.[28] Johnston's diaries are a vivid record of the Dublin theatrical milieu in the twenties. In 1926 he was supposed to be working at the law in London but kept taking the mailboat back for weekends, because he had discovered a new Dublin – not in the suburbs, but 'in Greystones and Merrion Square'.[29] The citizens of this new Dublin 'are called [Lennox] Robinson, [Sean] O'Casey, [Susan] Mitchell, [Sara] Allgood and [W.B.] Yeats'. All these personages were Protestants born; all were fundamental makers of the Irish Revival. Johnston was delighted to get in the swim of the younger members of the set, like the Shields brothers and Johnston's new sweetheart, the fiery young actress Shelah Richards. He would meet them at the Abbey Theatre, join them in doing the Charleston at the Metropole, argue outside the library in Kildare Street, attend 'queer foreign plays' by George Yeats's Dublin Drama League in the School of Art, and argue late into the night with Arthur Shields, nicknamed 'Boss', and his wife Bazie McGee, known as 'Mac'.

The two couples – Shields and wife, and Johnston and girlfriend – became fast friends, fast in both senses of the word. Johnston, the spoiled son of a legal family, and Shelah Richards, the popular girl of the hockey-playing Protestant girls' school, Alexandra College, were always fighting and making up, with 'Mac' the confidante of both. The relationship did not keep Johnston from petting parties with a debutante named Olive, and flirtations with two ingénues from the Abbey, Kitty Curling and Ria Mooney. Even Mrs Shields was added to the list of his summer 1926 conquests.[30]

In a pastiche of Joyce's *Ulysses*, Johnston described joining the Shields couple at the August 1926 Dublin Horse Show, when his first girlfriend 'Doris' – now married – appeared on the scene:[31]

> Where's Mac and Boss Shields? Oh here. Awfully sorry for being late ... Here's Dad too with programmes. No sign of a bit of room here. All right for me – but Mac! Clappyclapclap. Funny to see the Union Jack over there among the foreign flags ...
>
> Good God! Doris!!
>
> She smiled too. Alone ...
>
> Do you see that girl, Mac? The one in green! Yes, Mac, that's my first love. Do you still ride, Doris? Where are you living now? Where's that bloody bald officer you married? ... She's gone now ...
>
> There's Doris again! With a woman. God, she's asking for it! Almost like a pick-up. Look at her looking back! Oh my heart! Shut up, Mac! It's just like the way I used to feel. Isn't that devastating?

'Mac' (Mrs Shields) listens to Johnston's tales of the complications of young love, and later, at her wild birthday party, begs him not to marry Shelah Richards for this reason and that, while Johnston laughs hysterically. By November everyone was 'at sixes and sevens': 'Ambrose [Charlie Pilkington] was chasing Shelah, Shelah chasing T[om] Purefoy, [and] Mac chasing everybody ... Abbey in revolution.'[32]

This wild bohemian demi-monde in the new Catholic Gaelic Free State gets no attention at all in histories of the period, but it was hardly hidden in the late 1920s. When the Gate Theatre Company began to stage plays in the Peacock annex of the Abbey on 11 October 1928, the doors were opened on a homosexual half-world within the bohemian demi-monde. It was aesthetically coded so it did not have to be officially acknowledged, but Irish debuts of Wilde's long-censored *Salomé* and Eugene O'Neill's *The Hairy Ape* (the stoker from an ocean liner passes for rough trade) made clear the dispositions of the loving couple who founded the Gate, Micheál Mac Liammóir and Hilton Edwards.[33] The joke about the Gate and Abbey being, respectively, 'Sodom and Begorrah', was soon making the rounds.

In 1932 Mary Manning (1906–99) – daughter of an Anglo-Irish military man, and another member of this fast crowd – put the Dublin bohemians and their antics on the Gate stage in *Youth's the Season*.[34] Here is Mac Liammóir's description of his part:

> I played a youthful invert in a cyclamen polo jumper ... I painted lampshades in designs of a rather dubious Greek origin, got tight at a party and slapped a boyfriend's face, wept, and said how hard it was to be called Flossie at school, and ended up with a lament for a young suicide after the manner of the page of Herodias in *Salomé*.[35]

The 'young suicide' was Terence Killigrew, a pen-portrait of Denis Johnston, who had the cheek to take the role on stage. Overdoing his elected role of mad poet, Killigrew kills himself not out of heartbreak, though he has been dumped by his girlfriend, nor out of alcoholism, though he is a heavy drinker, but from anxiety of influence. Like T.S. Eliot, he feels himself to be a hollow man, a farce, incapable of originality.

Johnston confided a similar fear of creative sterility to Arthur Shields:

> There's something nasty about [Brinsley MacNamara's 12 April 1926 play] *Look at the Heffernans* ... Lennnox's new play [*Ever the Twain*] in about a month. So I'll see it all right. As for my own play – I see quite clearly now how bad it is. I can hear Boss [Arthur Shields] smile through his horn-rimmers and murmur, 'Ah, no!' I must really write a straight one. A decent one about people I know. One I needn't be ashamed of or in which I try to be clever.[36]

After two more years of Joycean experiment, Johnston's play was consummately an achievement of cleverness. Performed on 19 June 1929, *The Old Lady Says, 'No!'* became the first original play to make a hit at the Gate Theatre. It was like one of those 'queer foreign plays' the Dublin Drama League did, such as Ernest Toller's *Masses and the Man.* Johnston's first play is a dizzying, parodic and bitter expressionist extravaganza of old nationalist songs, poems and stock conceptions, as if the nation, like its protagonist, were in a coma. Sick of his own unoriginality, and sick too of new Ireland's recherché conception of itself, the playwright spat out in scorn all that was old hat.

The young Protestant bohemians of the early Free State were not Roaring Twenties partiers at the end of the Empire in one colonial outpost, or not just that. Many were public-spirited, patriotic intellectuals who had devoted themselves earnestly to the national cause before the revolution, and they wanted to keep doing so after it. However, their contribution to the culture of the new state was perforce a critical one. They were ready to Hibernicize the colony, but they could not in good faith join in the state-organized Savanarolan effort to Catholicize and Gaelicize it.

Lennox Robinson (1886–1958), for instance, had been first inspired one August Saturday afternoon of 1907 when he went to see Yeats and Gregory's

Cathleen ni Houlihan in the Cork Opera House, 'the most important week in my life'. The play 'crystallized forever ... certain national emotions', and he decided to devote himself to the national cause by means of drama.[37] Beginning with *The Cross Roads* in 1909, he contributed a stream of plays in a variety of modes about Irish life. He served long spells as the stage manager of the Abbey. But in the new Free State, he was condemned – not for his alcoholism or bisexuality, which went unmentioned – but for his free thinking. In June 1924 Robinson imprudently gave a potentially impious story to some young Catholic intellectuals (Francis Stuart and Liam O'Flaherty) for their new magazine *Tomorrow*.[38] In sombre tones and with persuasive local colour, the story tells of an Irish countrywoman who, becoming pregnant, thinks she's the new Virgin Mary and bearer of the second coming of Christ. The story's premise is worked out in an elegantly straight-faced manner, as George Moore would have done it.[39]

Clerical authorities were outraged by the story and had Robinson driven from his job as an organizer of the free Carnegie Libraries in Ireland. At a conference of clerics in Ballinrobe, County Mayo, on the question of immoral literature in general, and in particular on whether or not Ireland should accept free libraries from the Andrew Carnegie Trust, Right Rev. Monsignor Macken, Dean of Tuam, gave the clergy's view that reading certain books inflamed and strengthened the passions: 'Reading is food for the mind, mental pabulum, and if the food is unwholesome the living thing consuming it will be weak and decrepit. Then there is the waste of time and consequent neglect of household and other important duties.' Authors and their wares needed, the Monsignor said, to be carefully watched by Vigilance Committees in each and every parish, and the Catholic Truth Society should give its advice 'about particularly Catholic books to be sold at Church doors'.[40] The whole Carnegie scheme was treated by the clergy as highly dangerous, unless by the clergy strictly controlled.

Robinson's feeling of being on the outside rather than the inside of the new Ireland emerges in one of his best plays, *The Big House* (6 September 1926). Shelah Richards, as Kate Alcock, voiced its lament on behalf of the Protestant nationalist section of the Irish population after being marginalized by the new Catholic majority: 'I think I'd like it better if they hated us. That at least would make me feel that we had power, that we counted for something; it's very hard to forgive toleration.'[41] A few years later, when the 1929 Censorship Bill was passed, Robinson would have been happy just with toleration. Indeed, more and more, that became the message of those writers and actors who were neither Irish-speaking nor piously Catholic: toleration of individual difference, toleration of religious difference, and toleration of the varieties of things that may make life pleasant – love, art, gardens, the novel and the foreign.

One is again reminded of Shields's answer to why he left Ireland: 'Because I didn't want to have to pray in Gaelic.'[42] But that was not a full answer to the question.

5

On 3 October 1931 the Abbey Theatre company left for a tour of the USA. The touring company included Shelah Richards (by then married to Denis Johnston), Barry Fitzgerald, Arthur Shields and Mac Shields. Mac Shields did not wish to be simply a mother and housewife. Early in her marriage, Mac felt that if she were to have a child at all, she wanted that child to be a girl. When the nurse held up her newborn infant, saying, 'It's a boy!', Mac, just coming out of anesthesia, replied, 'Ah, damn!' The boy's name was duly recorded, and remained, Adam.[43]

When the time came for the 1931 tour, Adam Shields was still an infant. The decision by both mother and father to leave him behind with Charlie Saurin – who had married Arthur Shields's sister Lini – seemed less strange in Ireland in 1931 than it would today. Families were more widely extended and mutually supportive then. Individuals often had to accept the necessity of leaving spouses or children behind for long periods in order to make money abroad. Arthur Shields took on the job of tour manager for an additional $200 a week, hardly sufficient compensation, he came to think, for the trouble of dealing with the disorganized habits of Lennox Robinson, who served as advanced publicity man, lecturing to 'collections of old frumps'.[44] On Sundays, while Mac was at the movies with others, Boss sat in his hotel doing the accounts. Every time he thought of his son Adam, he got a lump in his throat.

The Abbey players went up and down Pennsylvania, all across Ontario, and down through Michigan into Ohio. Just after Christmas Denis Johnston joined the company in Cincinnati, Ohio, to help rehearse his new play, *The Moon in the Yellow River*.[45] By 30 December 1931, they were in Milwaukee, Wisconsin, where Barry Fitzgerald wrote home that he thought he might skip the next tour already planned for the following year, since 'the company is not a very gay one'.[46] It certainly proved to be very gay the next night, to judge by the account of the Abbey New Year's Eve party by Denis Johnston, given him by Shelah Richards, who was present:

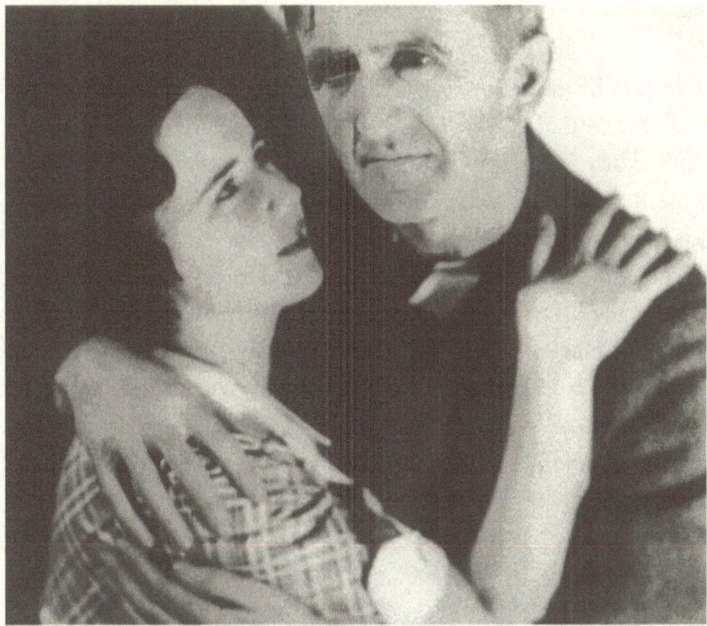

Kitty Curling and M.J. Dolan, publicity still, 1933/34 tour. (White Studios/ Shields family papers)

> Kitty Curling, tight and berserk – could it be? No, it couldn't. Yes, it was! She was interfering with the adjustment of Boss's dress – as we say in the more genteel lavatories. It's really damn funny how that is a thing we will never allow anybody else to do. There is Shelah – a reasonably normal person who slept with me long before we were married, and she goes round swearing and cursing like a Girl's Friendly Woman, saving Kitty from herself – abusing her and browbeating her across Boss's tattered fly-buttons, and Kitty abusing her back and saying damn it all, hasn't she got a husband? – a very reasonable point of view.[47]

The actors ice-skated in Madison, Wisconsin, tobogganed in Winnipeg, played poker on the trans-Canada express out of Calgary, were astounded at the majestic sights of the Great Continental Divide, loved Vancouver (as beautiful as any postcards they'd seen of Switzerland), took drives around the Olympia Mountains in Washington State, bathed in hot springs in Boise, Idaho, then dropped south through Denver, Colorado, and west into the Texan cities of Amarillo, Dallas ('people down here rather uncouth'), Austin, Houston and Waco, then across Alabama and down into Florida before returning up the coast to New York for another circle through New England, embarking at last on SS *Scythia* out of Boston on 2 May 1932.[48]

6

The letters home from this trip by Arthur and Will Shields are mostly cover letters for return bank drafts, itineraries, exclamations at the beauty of the continent, or complaints about the hard slog of a coast-to-coast tour of that continent. However, two reflections on American culture emerge. First, the Shields brothers liked the racial and ethnic diversity of North America and found the racism of the white establishment depressing. Passing time before shows in New York, Barry Fitzgerald would put his hands in his pockets and saunter through Harlem: 'I liked it tremendously. The Negroes there seem to live so casual a life. I see no lack of culture.'[49] Arthur Shields preferred the Pacific coast, especially Vancouver, partly because the city had a Chinese quarter, a Sikh quarter, lots of 'interesting looking oriental people', and 'something queer around every corner'.[50]

Abbey Theatre at Tuskegee University, Alabamba, 2 March 1932. (Shields family papers)

The best day of the whole tour was 2 March 1932 at Tuskegee University, the Alabama teacher training college for 'coloured people', founded in 1880 by Booker T. Washington.

They played Lennox Robinson's *The Whiteheaded Boy*, a comedy about Denis, the pet son of a large family. Everyone sacrifices so Denis can become a doctor, a profession for which he has neither aptitude nor inclination. The family rebels when Denis decides to get married and become a labourer, ambitions that lie within the scope of his abilities. The highly appreciative Tuskegee audience was the theatrical highlight of the year for Arthur Shields:

> You cannot imagine how fine those audiences were. So quick in seeing the humour that is so often lost on white audiences here. It was great to watch them laughing. Laughter seemed to affect them much more than it does us. I saw young men rolling about – throwing their arms and legs up – getting on their feet and doing a little dance. It was extraordinary, and they loved the play. Every now and again, we were held up because a burst of laughter or applause lasted so long. Ah, it was great. I'll never forget it. [51]

When Shields was interviewed in the early 1960s by an American academic, he was asked if the Irish were not the best theatre audiences he had ever encountered. 'Oh, no,' Shields shot back, 'I wouldn't say so. But I can remember playing two of Lennox Robinson's comedies down in Tuskegee …'

'The Negro university?'

'Yes … where we had the most wonderful reception and the most wonderfully perceptive reception.'

'Perceptive?' (sceptically).

'Yes, perceptive – they could almost see before the lines were said what was being led up to.'

'Why were they more perceptive than an audience in New York or Chicago?'

'Because I think they are a more perceptive people. They're watching more. They are watching more than we think.'

The second reflection on North America that emerged during the tour concerned American theatrical culture. Towns no bigger than Dublin had huge, spectacular receiving houses for touring shows. A fortune would be spent on scenery for these shows; stagehands were better paid than Abbey actors. But no plays were being written locally about the local life. The older shows toured from Broadway round the states were like American hotel dishes: they all tasted the same, as if cooked a week before.[52] Shields made his views known to the local press. The trouble with you Americans, he told a reporter in Hartford,

Connecticut, is that you are too much for lavish things: 'The money spent in staging one of [your] more elaborate shows would keep the Abbey Players going for two years.'[53] The Hartford theatre group 'should present plays dealing with life in Hartford or near Hartford and playwrights living in the locality should write such plays'. 'Fluently, though rather slowly, and with a good command of English,' Shields made a related point in Philadelphia in November 1932. Americans were too worried about specialist theatre education and professionalism. The Abbey players did without university courses in drama: 'I may know that a certain rope has to be pulled up and down [backstage] – but I don't know what the name of it is.'[54] Between training theatre professionals and making celebrities of actors, Shields warned, Americans were going to 'ruin the mystery' on which the art depended.

Evidently, in 1932, the Shields brothers did not know about Eugene O'Neill and the Provincetown Players, who had self-consciously followed the Abbey's example in becoming a theatre of new writing about the immediate world in which the audience found itself. What is more, the success of the Provincetown Players had given momentum to a 'Little Theatre' movement in the USA, too little at first to be noticeable to the touring players. Just a few years later, however, Arthur Shields and Barry Fitzgerald would come to know and admire the American offshoot of the Abbey idea. Both men had parts in the Abbey production of O'Neill's *Days Without End* (16 April 1934), the first of several important associations between the Shields brothers and the American playwright's work.[55]

7

There is a small but significant note from 23 August 1933 preserved among the Shields papers. An Abbey Theatre postcard, it invites Miss Una O'Connor of 56 Hollybank Avenue, Ranelagh, to call to the theatre for an interview with Mr Arthur Shields. Una O'Connor, blue-eyed, 'Titian-haired' and five feet four, was the 18-year-old daughter of the Shipping Master of the Port of Dublin.[56] While still a student at the Dominican Muckross Park, O'Connor had shown exceptional promise in school plays. Her parents permitted her to join the Abbey school of acting, under the tuition of M.J. Dolan. Once Kitty Curling – the company's glamour girl – became engaged to a Philadelphia businessman on the previous Abbey tour, her parts had to be filled.[57] By 14 September 1933, after her interview with Arthur Shields, Una O'Connor, under the stage name 'Aideen

O'Connor', was already on stage in *Margaret Gillan* by Brinsley MacNamara, and soon went into all the parts formerly played by Curling: Mollser in *The Plough and the Stars*, Mary in *Juno and the Paycock*, and so forth.

A year later, for the third Abbey tour of the USA, Aideen O'Connor joined the travelling company. In a production still from Lennox Robinson's Pirandellian farce, *Drama at Inish*, she has her hands on Arthur Shields' shoulders. As they stand in close to one another, he looks surprised, and has a grip on her wrists, as if to take her hands off his person. One might imagine there is here some sexual magnetism between Aideen O'Connor and Arthur Shields, but the photograph simply illustrates a scene at the end of Act I. Aideen O'Connor is playing Helena, the hotel maid, who bursts in upon a rehearsal; a character has just practised the line: 'You do not understand – betrayer. [With a great cry.] Michael, Michael, give me back my baby!'

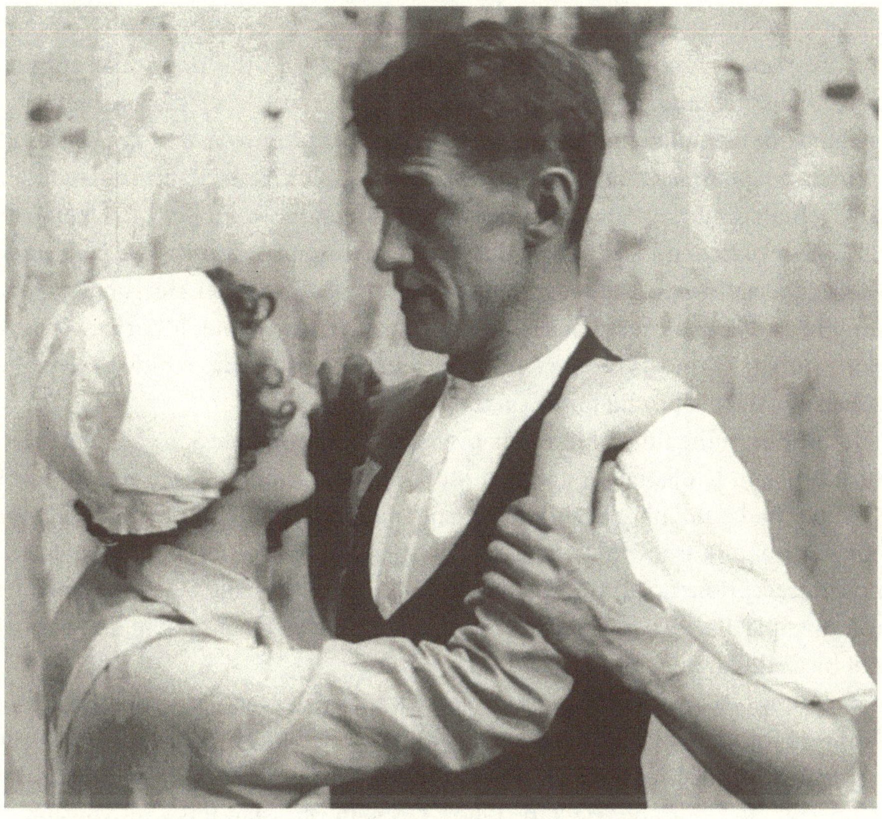

Aideen O'Connor and Arthur Shields, as Helen and Michael, in Drama at Inish, *1934. (Shields family papers)*

Helena gets hysterical, because her lover, the hotel 'boots', is also named Michael. Thinking himself summoned, he rushes in, and the maid throws her arms around his neck, crying 'Michael, Michael, our baby!'[58] As in the photograph of Aideen O'Connor and Arthur Shields, he tries to disengage himself from this public demonstration of their backstairs love. But soon the secret is divulged that Helen's child had died at birth in Dublin. Off stage, the tour of 1934/35 went off without any sign that Arthur Shields was anything more to Aideen O'Connor than the kindly but harassed and troubled manager of the touring company.

8

For 12 August 1935 *The Silver Tassie* was at last to be played at the Abbey Theatre, Dublin. A haughty and misguided letter of rejection from Yeats to O'Casey seven years earlier had set off a firestorm in the press. The subsequent feud had done no good for either the theatre or Dublin's favourite playwright.[59] In the following years the Abbey had not produced, nor had O'Casey written, a better play than *The Silver Tassie*. No doubt, Yeats, Robinson and the Abbey management wished that this 1935 production would bury the hatchet. O'Casey's old friend Arthur Shields was called upon to direct the play, and Barry Fitzgerald was scheduled to reprise the role of Sylvester Heegan, written for him by O'Casey. Harry Clarke's talented cousin, the painter Maurice McGonigal, designed the sets for the Dublin production. All the preparations were in place to make the production a success.

But from the time of the riots over *The Plough and the Stars* (11 February 1926), Ireland had gone on growing more nationalist and more Catholic, and O'Casey had gone on growing more anti-nationalist and anti … well, if not anti-Catholic, outspokenly opposed to Roman Catholic canon law (no divorce, no contraception, no 'impure' literature) becoming the civil law of the state. It was possible that O'Casey might be welcomed back by Yeats and the Abbey, but not by Catholic Ireland.

A host of consuls, ministers, professors and writers accompanied the Yeats family to the opening night. A newspaper listed the following prominent guests: American Minister and Mrs Owsley; French Minister and Madame Guerlet; Monsieur M. Goor and Madame Goor; German Minister and Frau von Juhlmann; Mons Weenink, Consul General for the Netherlands; Madame Ruzicka; Dr Bethel Solomons and Mrs Solomons; W.B. Yeats and Mrs Yeats; Miss Anne

Yeats; Mrs Jack Yeats; Senator and Mrs Ernest Blythe; Desmond FitzGerald and Mrs FitzGerald; Mr and Mrs James McNeill; Swedish Consul; Madame Starkie; Mrs J.M. Starkie; Mr and Mrs R. M. Smyllie (editor, *Irish Times*); Miss Sarah Purser (painter); Mainie Jellett (painter); Mr F.R. Higgins (poet) and Mrs Higgins; Mr Joseph Holloway; Mr S. Waddell and Helen Waddell (scholar and poet); Mr J. Geoghegan, KC; Mr and Mrs Lennox Robinson; the Earl and Countess of Longford.

Another newspaper review, however, was not overawed by the ceremonial blessing of the great and good. It was subtitled 'Play that May Shock Christians' (by Christians, it meant Catholics). For a play that had been well received in London, and at the worst is O'Casey's fourth-best play, the review offered unqualified condemnation: 'cold-blooded obscenity and blasphemy on the stage before an audience of men and women takes on a vileness that is appalling'.[60] The imitation of the Mass in Act 2 was deemed 'a gross insult to Catholics': 'To use sacred music as the tune for a chant about lice, filth, and the other ingredients for war is going too far.'

Members of the audience leaving after the show had been heard to say various things – 'interesting', 'blasphemous', 'queer mixture', 'Yeats was right', 'crude', 'nothing much'. On succeeding nights, however, the house was full, and audiences applauded heartily at the curtains. But from pulpits and in the press, certain Roman Catholic clergy excoriated the Irish national theatre for daring to exhibit such a play.[61] A Catholic member of the Abbey Board, Brinsley MacNamara, published a lengthy attack upon the play (which brought about his resignation).

Reactionary sectarianism was becoming the official voice of Dublin media. Gabriel Fallon, Abbey actor from 1920 to 1928 and emerging cultural commissar in the 1930s, wrote a regular theatre column for *The Irish Monthly*. In his August 1936 article he began with an epigraph from Daniel Corkery's *Synge and Anglo-Irish Literature* (1931): 'What chance of expressing the people of Ireland have those writers who, sprung from the Ascendancy, have never shared the Irish national memory, and are, therefore, just as un-Irish as it is possible for them to be?'

'Ascendancy' was very broadly defined by Corkery and Fallon. To them it simply meant the Protestants in Ireland, not just titled folk, owners of large estates, the Church of Ireland hierarchy, or the magistrates and barristers of the Four Courts and fellows of Trinity College Dublin, whether Protestant or (as some of the ruling elite were) Catholic. Fallon had once been Sean O'Casey's best friend. He had also been a pal of Arthur Shields. He had worked under the direction of Lennox Robinson. All Protestants, they were now equally defined as 'just as un-Irish as it is possible for them to be'. In this article, Fallon applied the Corkery thesis to Lennox Robinson, with special reference to *Drama at Inish.*

Taoiseach of the Republic of Ireland, Éamon de Valera (1882–1975), left, *facing away from Lennox Robinson (1886–1958) at the funeral of W.B. Yeats in Drumcliffe, County Sligo. Yeats died in 1939 in France but his body was finally laid to rest in Ireland, 9 October 1948. (Haywood Magee/*Picture Post*/Getty Images)*

Robinson was not the child of great privilege. His father was a bank manager who retired to become a clergyman in Cork. However, this religious background, according to Fallon, disqualified Robinson as a Irish National Theatre playwright. His unsuitability was further shown by *Drama at Inish.* The premise of Robinson's comedy – an Irish town wanting to produce plays of 'the higher drama' for the improvement of the people – was said by Fallon to be false. Irish Catholics know that it is the business of religion to speak plainly about evil and improve our vision of what is good, while the tendency of 'the higher drama' was to be morally ambiguous.[62] There was no scene in Irish drama as 'small, as mean, as full of acerbity and as lacking in the chivalrous dimensions of dramatic art as the scene in which a maid bursts in upon a rehearsal, where a character is saying in broad burlesque, give me back my baby, and the maid takes up the same cry'.

This bullying by Gabriel Fallon, an ex-bit-part actor, of Lennox Robinson, a man who had devoted his life to the Abbey Theatre since 1908, written a score of steadily successful plays, and stage-managed most of the other repertoire, including the O'Casey classics, is a remarkable sign of the temper of counter-revolutionary Ireland.

9

While the right of Sean O'Casey, Lennox Robinson and W.B. Yeats to be Abbey playwrights was being openly questioned, an able playwright emerged who had been born a Catholic. Surprisingly, his main interest was in dramatizing the shortcomings of the clerical domination of Irish life. Paul Vincent Carroll (1900–68) was the son of a schoolteacher in Dundalk, County Louth. After teacher-training at St Patrick's College, Drumcondra, he decided to leave Ireland and settled in Glasgow.

His first play, *The Things that are Caesar's* (15 August 1932), showed a materialist priest who sides with a young woman's mother in forcing her to marry the son of a wealthy farmer. On 25 January 1937 Carroll's next play, *Shadow and Substance*, debuted at the Abbey, directed by Hugh Hunt. Arthur Shields was in the lead as Canon Skerritt. He gave the best performance the *Irish Independent* reviewer had ever seen him deliver, and one of the best, he judged, ever witnessed on the Abbey stage.[63] With a cast of three priests, three teachers under the priests' management, and two young female house-servants (one a mystic), the play exposed on stage a busy world of celibates and unmarried Catholics. Canon Skerritt, a main character, is an arrogant, Swiftian priest with a continental education. He looks down with scorn on his sport-loving, bumpkin fellow curates and their vulgar images of the Sacred Heart: 'If, for a moment, I felt our Redeemer's heart was akin to that monstrosity on the wall, I should go back to Socrates and be a pagan.'[64]

The school's head teacher, O'Flingsley, wants to enlighten Irish children but finds himself hobbled by clerical louts. The mystic servant, Brigid, loved by both Canon Skerritt and O'Flingsley, is killed by a mob out to get the liberal teacher. The message of the play is Christian, but its clergy are not, and its Irish people are very Irish but not very nice. On 26 January 1938 the play opened in New York, ran for 274 performances, and won the New York Drama Critics Award for best foreign play of the year.

Partly to capitalize on the new popularity of Paul Vincent Carroll, the Abbey once again went on a USA tour in the autumn of 1937. This time, Aideen O'Connor and Arthur Shields went with the travelling company, and Bazie Shields stayed home.

Aideen O'Connor and Arthur Shields in Shadow and Substance, *1937.*
(Shields family papers)

The relationship between Arthur Shields and Aideen had become sexual in 1936. Now they were defiantly continuing it.[65] Aideen O'Connor wrote to her sister Eileen from Hotel Edison in New York on 18 November: 'Mac has not come yet. The general feeling is that when she hears that Boss is to produce *Shadow and Substance* – which means extra money – she'll be out. Well – let her!' After Saturday night's performance in Manhattan, Aideen stayed out at parties and nightclubs until 4 am. She loved the new dance craze – 'the Big Apple, it's called. It's very intricate and quite mad.'[66] She was so tired the next morning, she slept through Sunday mass.

Aideen's father, the Shipping Master of Dublin, had learned something of her private life before she left for America. He was not pleased. His behaviour had been 'too grim'. Aideen pleaded with her sister Eileen to get him to 'relent'; otherwise, Aideen felt she could not go home again.[67] By the time the company had reached San Francisco, she 'adored America ... I dread the idea of leaving it.'[68] A Boston lawyer had proposed to her. She did not love him, but given the situation in her family home, she was seriously considering the proposal.

The Abbey Theatre on tour, 1933/34. Bazie McGee Shields (third from right, back row), Arthur Shields (fourth from left, back row) and Una 'Aideen' O'Connor (second from left, front row). (Shields family papers)

A month later in Los Angeles, she was having a splendid time with Will and Boss Shields. They spent a day at the beach, then went to a party at the Hollywood home of the other and older Una O'Connor, once a member of the Abbey company, and now established as a popular character actress in the movies. The party was crowded with Hollywood Irish celebrities: Maureen O'Sullivan (Tarzan's Jane), J.M. Kerrigan, John McCormack (the great Irish tenor), and some English and American stars as well. On Sunday, 3 April, director John Ford invited the Shields brothers, Aideen, and Denis O'Dea to dinner at his Odin Street home; John and Josephine Wayne were there too. The Waynes gave another party for Aideen and the Shields brothers on 5 April. To her sister, Aideen wrote that she was much fattened and looked 'immense in the chest'; 'I now take 32-inch brassiere.' While that is not immense by Hollywood standards, a film studio had called Aideen for a screen test. Afterwards, she judged her best chance professionally was 'to stick with the Abbey back to Ireland and then go to London'.[69]

Maureen O'Sullivan and Tommy Clifford greeted by J.M. Kerrigan (centre) on their arrival via the Union Pacific Chief to appear in Song of My Heart *(1930) with John McCormack. It was O'Sullivan's first picture. (Library, Academy of Motion Picture Arts and Sciences, Hollywood, California)*

On 28 May 1938 the company left New York to return to Ireland. This tour had been led by F.R. Higgins, a poet and protégé of W.B. Yeats. Higgins, a married man, had a dalliance underway with actress Ria Mooney. The Abbey was rife with love-making. The director of the theatre, Englishman Hugh Hunt, was carrying on a correspondence with sixteen-year-old Phyllis Ryan, who had made her sensational debut as the mystic servant 'Brigid' in *Shadow and Substance* (the part later taken by Aideen O'Connor).[70] On board ship to the USA, F.R. Higgins advanced his affair with Ria Mooney,[71] but he turned against those other lovers, Arthur Shields and Aideen O'Connor.[72]

Back in Dublin, Higgins kept Aideen out of parts. Roles for pretty young females went instead to Ria Mooney, Phyllis Ryan, or Aideen's old friend, Frolie Mulhern. 'Higgins appears to hate me with a deadly hate,' she wrote. 'For Boss's sake I'm keeping my tongue in my cheek but one of these days it'll come unstuck and then I'll tell Higgins what I and the rest of the world think of him – and be fired for ever from the Abbey!'[73]

Front (left to right): Aideen O'Connor, F.R. Higgins, Kate Curling Wall and Arthur Shields; back: possibly Joseph P. Wall, Philadelphia textile manufacturer and husband of Curling, c.1938. *(Shields family papers)*

10

Arthur Shields was cast once again as Christy Mahon in *The Playboy of the Western World* for the Abbey Festival in August 1938 – seventeen plays, many of them one-act classics, running on twelve successive nights. It was an honour to go on stage as the Playboy in the Abbey Festival, the signature role in the classic of the Irish stage. Shields had been the Abbey's Playboy since the early 1920s, and he must have suspected, at age forty-two, that this might be the last time he would do it. The Abbey Festival was conceived by Lennox Robinson and F.R. Higgins as a public tribute to the man they loved, W.B. Yeats, obviously nearing the end of his own life (he died the following 28 January). Shields very much wanted to be part of the celebration. He gave writers his reverence, and above all other writers for him was Yeats. It is no exaggeration to say that Yeats and Yeats's work had shaped his life as a man. To the end of that life, Boss Shields preserved in the 'Green Room' of his home a splendid library of first editions of Yeats's poems, plays and essays.[74]

Arthur Shields and Maureen Delaney as Christy Mahon and the Widow Quin in Playboy of the Western World, *1933/34 tour. (White Studios/Shields family papers)*

At the Gresham Hotel on 9 August 1938 Frank O'Connor gave one in the series of lectures that formed part of the Abbey Festival. Ostensibly, his subject was J.M. Synge, but really his lecture concerned two former mentors: Daniel Corkery and W.B. Yeats. With eloquent humanity, O'Connor condemned Corkery's sectarian thesis in *Synge and Anglo-Irish Literature.* Nationality, O'Connor declared, is as inescapably part of one's being as one's sex or one's hometown. Synge, Gregory and Yeats were Irish without qualification.[75] The great staying power of their writing, he concluded, arose from their audacity and the heroic decision as Protestant writers to stay in Ireland and fight it out.

But how could Arthur Shields stay in Ireland to fight it out, when he was gradually being pushed out of his place in the Abbey by the hostility of (fellow Protestants) F.R. Higgins and Ernest Blythe? On top of that, his marriage was on the rocks, divorce was illegal in Ireland, and he had a deep affair in progress with a young Catholic colleague. Word then arrived from Broadway producers Gladys and Philip Merivale: the offer of a part in a production for the Morosco Theatre of *Spring Meeting* by M.J. Farrell and John Perry. There would also be a part for Aideen.

At this turn of events, Shields asked W.B. Yeats if the two could have a talk. Yeats invited him to tea at the Kildare Street Club, former haunt of the nearly, if not dearly, departed Protestant Ascendancy. Shields – whom Yeats esteemed as 'a man who incarnates [the Abbey's] traditions' – talked of the trouble he had directing the players introduced recently through the Abbey school, a 'prolotariot' with 'misshapen bodies', Yeats called them (and spelled them).[76] Then there was the personality conflict with F.R. Higgins. The fact may have come up that the Abbey board had recently rejected for production Paul Vincent Carroll's new play, *The White Steed*, on the grounds that it was anti-clerical.[77] Shields's marriage was breaking up; he was in love with Aideen O'Connor. And now there was an offer to go into a play on Broadway.

Having heard him out, the poet said that as long as he had anything to do with it, the Abbey Theatre would always have a place for Arthur Shields. However, all things considered, the job in *Spring Meeting* might be a good thing.[78] This blessing evidently meant a lot to Shields: he told the story in detail to his family in later years. On 10 October 1938 the London *Times* announced that Arthur Shields and Aideen O'Connor would be going to New York to appear in *Spring Meeting*, in a production to be directed by John Gielgud.

11

Spring Meeting opened on 8 December 1938 and ran for ninety-eight performances, in Broadway terms a success but not a triumph. The triumph would belong to Barry Fitzgerald, also on Broadway, playing 'with cranky, various humanity' the old Canon in *The White Steed.* Rejected by the Abbey for being anti-clerical, Paul Vincent Carroll's third play opened on 10 January

1939, directed by Hugh Hunt, recently resigned from the Abbey. It received outstanding reviews and would go on to receive the New York Drama Critics' prize for Best Foreign Play of the year, the second year in a row Carroll had won this award. As the USA was also 'plagued by evangelists of repression', *The White Steed* was judged to be both relevant and justified in its defence of individualism.[79]

While in New York, Arthur Shields made an important friend, Eddie Choate. He worked for Lee Shubert of the great Shubert clan of Broadway showmen. Lee Shubert had been the associate producer for the Abbey's 1937 run in New York, so the company was familiar with the Abbey personnel, repertoire and drawing power. Eddie Choate himself wanted to raise capital and produce an Irish play: if possible, the next play by Paul Vincent Carroll, then the hottest writer on Broadway. By March 1939 Arthur Shields was able to secure for Eddie Choate the USA production rights of Carroll's *Kindred*, then still in draft form. In return, Shields was given the right to cast and direct the show, initially scheduled for October 1939. He would get his expenses and 20 per cent of the profits.[80] The long-term aim of the two was to create a Broadway production company for Irish dramas using Irish actors. In place of the Abbey touring, or rather in competition with the touring Abbey, there would be a permanent New York outlet of the Irish dramatic revival, using veterans of the Abbey in plays by Abbey authors. On 9 March 1939, the agreement signed, Arthur Shields and Aideen O'Connor sailed from New York to Ireland.

The partners in Choate-Shields Productions immediately began to correspond over *Kindred*. While they genuinely liked one another, the two men had wholly different approaches to theatre. On one hand, Choate was a wizard at complicated capital creation schemes, profit-sharing percentages for the investors, multi-claused contracts for the artistes, and mathematically adjusted insurance policies – all aspects of the high-risk business of Broadway theatre. The producer loomed large in Choate's conception of a production. For a success, the right team had to be contracted: a director perfectly matched to the concept, a charismatic star, a strong and professional supporting cast, a top artistic designer, and a properly edited script.

On the other hand, Shields came from a state-supported, under-financed, ensemble repertory company of actors on permanent contract, with a general practice of short runs even for hit plays, and a company ethic of complete reverence for the word of the author. The role of the director was a minor one, since every actor was free to develop his role afresh on the night (no fixed blocking), as Shields once explained to a New York journalist:

> The Abbey rehearsal technique is different from the established custom. There is nothing set, no predetermined stance or gesture. We hear with horror that there are directors who chalk the stage so that performers may know where to stand and how to move. The idea of an actor counting steps between lines, seating himself at a definite speech, is almost beyond their comprehension. The Abbey Theatre demands that its players be, first of all, natural.[81]

The set design for an Abbey production might be good and it might be bad (the sets by Tanya Moiseiwitsch and Anne Yeats in the thirties were often imaginative), but an artistic or even realistic set was not essential to what the Abbey deemed a good production. What was essential was natural acting of great dramatic literature.

Immediately, Eddie Choate and Arthur Shields disagreed on the principals. Choate ruled out Hugh Hunt as a director because *The White Steed* was not the success on Broadway that, given the reviews, it ought to have been (it closed after 139 performances). He proposed John Gielgud for the starring role as the two Dermots. Shields, however, had loathed Gielgud's theatrical style in *Spring Meeting.* Apart from being English, Gielgud was, in Shields's view, showy and ill-attuned to an ensemble style of performance. But, Choate argued, for successful presentation on the Broadway stage, Carroll's plays had to be 'taken completely out of the literal mode of Irish drama and done with acute theatrical showmanship'.[82] Shields was shocked. The production of Carroll's play did not, he agreed, have to be completely Irish, but certainly the star had to have 'sympathy with and understanding of its roots', which in the case of *Kindred* was the local culture of Dundalk, County Louth, near the border with Northern Ireland. Gielgud had no connection of any kind with any part of Ireland.[83]

Although off to a rough start, the production of *Kindred* meant a lot to Arthur Shields, and he explained to Choate one reason why: 'I have not seen Aideen since we landed. It is a great loss. However, she will soon be in Dublin, so we will meet every day at the theatre. I never got the opportunity to tell you much about my private affairs, but you can guess that there is more than one reason that I long for the success of *Kindred*.'[84] Shields thought he himself might at least be considered for the key role of the two Dermots. But, when consulted, Hugh Hunt confirmed Eddie Choate's suspicion that casting Arthur Shields in one of the lead roles would be a mistake, 'unless you intend playing the play purely on its value as a script, which might be dangerous'.[85] Choate's further suggestions of Laurence Olivier or Burgess Meredith were both preferable, in Hunt's opinion, to Shields, even though neither was Irish.

Just then news arrived that was to change Arthur Shields's life. On 12 May 1939 he signed a contract with Twentieth Century Fox to play a part in John Ford's *Drums Along the Mohawk*, with options for two further pictures. The contract was for four weeks' work, beginning 17 July, at $600 a week (the Abbey was paying him the equivalent of $35 a week).[86] A new world opened to him. He still had to find a way to get Aideen out of Dublin. Higgins, 'that swine', was 'definitely keeping her out of work'. But if things proceeded according to plan for an autumn production of *Kindred* in New York, Boss would have the power to cast Aideen in Carroll's play. 'America,' he admitted, 'has shocked me and my tastes and responsibilities. Anyway, to hell with everything else. I'll be in New York soon.'[87]

12

Nineteen-thirty-nine was an *annus mirabilis* for John Ford. He was on a streak, a great director in peak form – from *Stagecoach* (released 2 March), directly into *Young Mr Lincoln* and *Drums Along the Mohawk*, before, after three weeks' rest, starting to shoot *The Grapes of Wrath* in September. Of these four great films, all but *Stagecoach* owe a great deal to the producer, Darryl Zanuck. In particular, *Drums Along the Mohawk* benefited from Zanuck's creative talents as a former screenwriter and editor and now kingpin producer for Twentieth Century Fox. Many screenwriters had worked on turning Walter Edmonds's historical novel into a film: Bess Meredith (9 January 1937), William Faulkner (15 March 1937),[88] Sonya Levine (30 December 1938) and Lamar Trotti (5 April and 24 April 1939). In a script conference on 5 April 1939 on Trotti's version, Zanuck brilliantly reconstructed the story, throwing orders right and left: 'As it stands, it is depressing and morbid and would make a flop.' 'Gil and Lana [hero and heroine] are too much alike.'

> Gil and Lana must be of different molds to start with – so that there is an issue between them – that is patched up as the story unfolds. At first she is rebellious – then she … realizes her responsibilities. On the other hand, when that time comes – when the hardships come one on top of the other, the man begins to feel terrific remorse … for having brought her there. You can work this into a very … real human drama.

'Drop the patriotic element … let the audience write in the flag-waving for themselves.' 'Drop the foreword.' 'The first time we hear about the war is when Gil is asked to report for duty. Up to this point, the story should be completely personal.' 'Drop the montages.' 'Drop scenes 107 to 110.' 'We will make the run [for help from Indian attack] the climax of our story. Gil, alone, will make it.'[89]

Two weeks after this script conference (18 April 1939), Zanuck wrote to John Ford and told him Trotti's screenplay was now 'magnificent', and he wanted Ford to direct the picture, beginning no later than 26 June. On 3 May Ford came to a final script conference on Trotti's latest version. He made just two suggestions: he wanted to develop the role of Reverend Rosenkrantz with some comedy moments, and he wanted Arthur Shields to play that part.

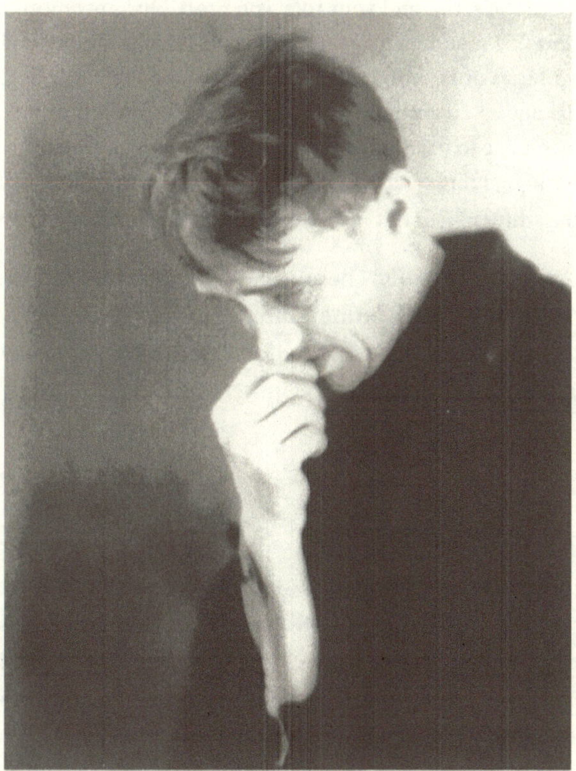

Arthur Shields as Christy Mahon in The Playboy, *1933.*
(White Studios/Shields family papers)

At the same meeting, Zanuck made one further significant change. He pictured for Ford and Trotti how the scene would be played in which the men, defeated, return from battle, and Lana searches in vain for her husband Gil. Just when she is about to give up, she turns and looks in the distance where a lightning flash illuminates a lone silhouette, her husband. Then he will, in a dazed fashion, report the nightmare of the battle.[90]

One of the most famous anecdotes about John Ford as a director concerns this scene. According to the oft-told tale, during the filming Ford was over-budget and behind schedule. Zanuck was panicking. An assistant producer was sent to press Ford to speed up the pace. The next few days' shooting concerned a big battle scene, so Ford picked up a copy of the script, tore out ten pages, and said, 'Now we are on schedule.' In place of the battle, he explained to Henry Fonda:

> 'Henry, I have to shoot a battle scene that I don't want. I had a better idea today. You've studied the script and your role, you probably know more about the battle than I do. Sit down and lean against this wall.' With the camera aimed at Fonda, Ford fired a series of questions: 'So, Henry, how did the battle begin?' And Fonda replied, making up an account. 'And Peter, what happened to Peter?' asked Ford; or 'What was it like to have killed that man, after seeing John die?' And Fonda went on improvising, giving a virtual psychoanalysis of the battle. "Cut!" called Ford, and told the editors: "Cut out my questions and use it as it is." One long take.'[91]

Great story, but not true. There was no such battle scene in any of the later scripts for the film, and Zanuck himself conceived of Fonda's report of the war in Ford's presence. What Ford added to the script was a fuller part for Arthur Shields, and not much else.

13

The filming of *Drums Along the Mohawk* was done in the Wasatch Mountains in Utah, a long way from upstate New York and western Massachusetts where the revolutionary-era story is set. But it increased the patriotic glamour Ford wished to throw over America's dawn to have the mountains and trees ten times taller than possible. Henry Fonda was to play the pioneer farmer who must shoulder a musket against the perfidious British and the marauding Indians. Claudette Colbert was to play Fonda's out-of-place wife – no frontierswoman Claudette, who thought the outside toilet on set took period detail and method acting several steps too far.[92]

Ford had the cast living under a strict regime – only two beers a man at mess. Each evening, a bugler went into the woods to play 'Taps', as if the cast were bivouacking troops.[93] The cast experienced something of what it was like to build a new community in a vast, strange continent. It took bravery, mutual support and hard work. Arthur Shields's role as the preacher Reverend Rosenkrantz is a small one and not essential to the plot, but he made it signify. Paul Vincent Carroll's plays about priests, in which Shields had shone, did the same thing for him that O'Casey's plays had done for Barry Fitzgerald and Sara Allgood. These actors were beloved stars in theatres across the English-speaking world, and each had a certain structured set of meanings.[94] They could take with ease any role in a film that fitted, perfectly or just partly, with those of Canon Skerritt, Fluther Good or Juno Boyle, respectively. Although born a Protestant and by practice an atheist, Shields was identified by casting directors as someone who could play a very convincing clergyman, whether Protestant or Catholic. *Drums Along the Mohawk* presents, as Joseph McBride says, a

> naïve patriotic picture of multi-racial harmony, when Ward Bond runs up the newly arrived American flag over a fort in the Mohawk Valley, watched by pioneer couple Gil and Lana Martin (Fonda in a tricoloured hat, and Claudette Colbert in a red bonnet and blue dress), along with a Christian Indian who salutes the flag (Chief Big Tree) and a happy black servant (Beulah Hall Jones).[95]

But the part given to Shields, and his characterization of it, are not naïve, nor are they patriotic. His great scene is a service in a little church with pews and balcony of rough-hewn wood and clear Protestant church-windows. The citizens of the nascent little community of Americans are gathered together. An organ is played, badly, as the congregation sings a hymn. Reverend Rosenkrantz mounts a raised pulpit, and calls on Almighty God to bring succour and guidance to those parishioners he is about to name: 'First, we are thinking of Mary Wallaber. She is just 16 years old but she is keeping company with a soldier from Ford Dayton. He is a Massachusetts man, O Lord, and thou knowest that no good can come of that.'

'Hallelujah!' cries out Chief Big Tree under his tri-cornered hat with a feather in it. He smiles all round at this condemnation of intermarriage with men from Massachusetts, but his fellow parishioners do not smile back. Whether they realize it, or whether they do not, we still understand with no further comment that the Reverend's prejudice against intermarriage is a savage and ridiculous one, and that the church is nearly always ridiculous when it thrusts itself into the path of true love.

Next, Reverend turns his thoughts to the sick and infirm. 'Peter Paris has the flux real bad. His uncle Isaac who keeps a store in Dayton asks for a prayer, and says he has just got in a new supply of calicos, French broadcloths, fancy handkerchiefs, new hats and heavy boots, all at bargain prices.' The incongruity of the sermon trailing off into a shop advertisement is certainly broad comedy, but the ponderosity of Shields's straight delivery carries it off. The ironic implication that the Protestant Church in America has since the founding fathers basically been a promotional arm of business sails unchecked into the viewer's comprehension. Finally, the Reverend calls down the wrath of God – 'Jehovah, God of Battles' – to aid his people against the Tories and 'the sons of Belial' – his term for the Mohawks, native inhabitants of upstate New York. As Robin Wood says, by making Reverend Rosenkrantz 'comic and quaint', the film manages 'neither to endorse nor reject him', but certainly, as acted by Shields, the treatment of the Reverend is closer to rejection than to endorsement.[96]

14

The famous last line of *Drums Along the Mohawk* is Henry Fonda's quiet statement to his wife, as the Stars and Stripes is being run up a flagpole on the belfry and the national anthem is playing on the soundtrack: 'I reckon we better be getting back to work. There's going to be a heap to do from now on.' After his five weeks and five days of work in Utah and Los Angeles, mostly waiting off set to be called, Arthur Shields felt the helpless weight of nothing to be done at all in the USA. On 23 August 1939 he was still waiting in Hollywood for his release by Twentieth Century Fox (it came on the 29th).[97] Life in California – a swim with Barry Fitzgerald, or golf – seemed 'trivial', 'no initiative'. 'I am depressed.' He could not get accustomed to the heat or the atmosphere in the Los Angeles basin: it 'takes the energy out of one and seems to sap your thinking powers'.

'I don't know what's to be done,' he admitted to Eddie Choate, 'between worry about the future – about [Aideen] and the people in Dublin – I really don't know where I am.' Aideen was waiting in New York for the *Kindred* rehearsals; his son Adam was with Bazie Shields in Dublin. He was sitting in the Hollywood Athletic Club writing a letter.

The world situation was terrifying. Just three days later, on 26 August, Hitler and Stalin signed a pact to remain neutral with respect to a war by either against anyone. That left Germany free to take on the French and British without worrying about its Eastern Front. It also meant the Nazis could drive into Poland without provoking the Russians. And that is what they did on 1 September 1939. On 3 September Britain and France declared war on Germany.

By mid-September Arthur Shields had arrived by train back in New York, where he was reunited with Aideen. Eddie Choate began to go over the text of *Kindred* with him, wanting to rework the play. Carroll had continued his arc of development, from the earnest realism of *Shadow and Substance* through the Yeatsian myth and metaphor that intrude upon *The White Steed*, to full-blown otherworldly allegorical 'Voices' in *Kindred*. This was stylistic development, but not improvement. The playwright had come to regard himself as a Shavian prophet of creative evolution. For the press, he described his play as 'an attack on the cock-eyed values ruling our daily life. It shows the creative minds of humanity in conflict with the mind of the grafter, the money-grubber and the self-seeking politician.'[98] That is not a message likely to go down well in the United States, where it is believed that the money-grubber and self-seeking politician are the creative minds of the country, and that such a state of affairs is not always a bad thing. But if Choate was right to suspect that the play needed work, as is politely said of scripts that are not very good at all, Arthur Shields had the attitude that it was the job of the actors and director to make the script work. This is the attitude of service to literature he had learned at the feet of W.B. Yeats. There could not be anything wrong with the script; a great playwright like Carroll knew what he was doing.

Finally, on 26 December 1939, *Kindred* opened at Maxine Elliott Theatre. Arthur Shields was in the role of one of the Dermots, since no greater stars could be secured. The other Dermot was played by Englishman Wallace Ford (who had recently starred in the film of John Steinbeck's *Of Mice and Men*). Barry Fitzgerald and Aideen each had a part. While seemingly inevitable in hindsight, it was surely as surprising and crushingly disappointing to the cast and production team as to any theatre people in such circumstances when the production proved a flop and an utter flop. The play closed on 6 January 1940 after just sixteen performances.

The situation was desperate. Arthur Shields had a 20-per cent stake in a bankruptcy.[99] The partners owed the backers a return no matter what the result. So it was decided to make the most of the fact that they had a number of actors under contract and a lease on the Maxine Elliott Theatre. In place of *Kindred*, they decided to put up as soon as possible *Juno and the Paycock*, with Barry Fitzgerald and Sara Allgood appearing in the roles they made famous, and that made them famous: Captain and Juno Boyle. Although the reviews of this rapidly concocted *Juno* were mixed on 16 January, the attendance in the following days was good. At any rate, if the show ran out of steam, Choate and Shields planned to try *The Playboy of the Western World*. The Abbey

Theatre concept of a repertory company with short runs might have its uses on Broadway after all.

The stress of 'a heap of work to do' in making a home in the USA took its toll on Arthur Shields throughout the *Kindred* debacle. A terrible pain in his chest would not go away. He got weaker and weaker. A New York doctor performed tests. On 19 January Shields got the diagnosis: TB. On the 20th he left the cast of *Juno*, and on the 22nd entered Lennox Hill Hospital. Part of the 1940 treatment for tuberculosis involved something that sounds like a pre-death experience: his lung was medically collapsed.

Meanwhile, *Juno* continued to draw crowds, so at least Shields was not marked as a failure and a bankrupt during his first year in America. Still, he was weak, exhausted and worried sick when he was released from hospital on 16 March 1940. The possibilities of work for Aideen were limited by her alien status (Equity required that American actors be used unless the play absolutely called for a foreigner).[100] German U-Boats were sinking ships crossing the Atlantic, so there was no question of Arthur Shields going to see his son, or, even should the mother have allowed it, his ten-year-old son coming to join him.

15

In April Arthur Shields, not long out of hospital, got news that John Ford wanted both him and Barry Fitzgerald for parts in a film to be made of a sequence of one-act plays by Eugene O'Neill, entitled *The Long Voyage Home.* On 6 April 1940 Shields left New York for Hollywood.

The O'Neill plays had been performed as a cycle by the Provincetown Players on 3 November 1924, revived in 1925, and once again at the Lafayette Theatre on Seventh Avenue in 1937. The one-acts worked well in sequence because, though written independently, they all involve the crew of a British merchant marine freighter making its passage from the West Indies to London in a time of war. A few simple ideas about men's place in the world knitted the one-acts together: men try to escape through irresponsibility, men feel isolated and far from home, men even in their freedom typically suffer from a sense of being trapped.[101] With impressive coherence, the plays investigate male psychology.

O'Neill also makes a bid to use the ship and its crew – though realistically dramatized – as an allegory of America and its immigrant population, just as Herman Melville had done with the crew on the *Pequod.* The cast of characters includes a range of national types: Yank, the American; Driscoll, an

Irishman; Cocky, a Cockney Englishman; Smitty, a middle-class Englishman; Ivan, a Russian; Olson, a Swedish man; Paul, a Norwegian; Scotty, a Scotsman. Given the multinational emphasis of O'Neill's play,[102] it is surprising that John Ford signed up both Barry Fitzgerald and Arthur Shields for the cast. O'Neill's script required only one Irishman, 'Aloysius Driscoll', and for that part Ford cast an American, Thomas Mitchell. Barry Fitzgerald was chosen to play 'Cocky', but he was not directed to give him a Cockney accent, while Arthur Shields plays 'Donkeyman', the seaman charged with minding the ship's auxiliary steam-engine, and a part in O'Neill's one-act that was much elaborated in the screenplay.

Ford also hired J.M. Kerrigan – another Abbey Theatre veteran. Kerrigan played 'the Crimp', an agent employed to decoy, trap and impress seamen for unscrupulous captains. These Irish casting choices did not eliminate the thematic implication that the ship is an allegory of America, but it gave an impression that the role of Irishmen in the immigrant identity of expatriates was a dominant one.

J.M. Kerrigan, c.1931. (Fox Film Corporation, Gift of Dan Thomas. Library, Academy of Motion Picture Arts and Sciences, Hollywood, California)

An additional effect of the 'Celtification' of the cast by Ford was to restore an Irish quality to O'Neill's dialogue that had been strained out by Dudley Nichols, the screenwriter. Nichols's script is faithful to the spirit of O'Neill's story, but minimalist in its use of dialogue, something no play could be, and a good film should be. O'Neill's language is as baroquely poetic in its dialect as something from Synge's *Playboy*. (In fact, the American had been inspired to write plays by his September 1911 visits to the Abbey Theatre productions then on tour in New York; he went to every one of them.)[103] Here is Driscoll's speech in *Bound East for Cardiff* (1914), an effortful imitation of Syngean dialect poetry:

> The divil's own life it is to be out on the lonely sea wid nothin' betune you and a grave in the ocean but a spindle-shanked, gray-whiskered auld fool the loike av him. 'Twas enough to make saint shwear to see him wid his gold watch in his hand, tryin' to look as wise as an owl in a tree, and all the toime he not knowin' whether 'twas cholery or the barber's itch was the matther wid Yank.[104]

In the screenplay, this becomes simply:

> Driscoll: I'm afraid he's very weak. Please do something, sir.
> Captain: My good man, I'm not a doctor. Keep him quiet, and we'll hope for the best. I'll send him something for the pain, at any rate. [To Yank:] You'll be up tomorrow. You'll be all right! [Captain leaves.]
> Yank: Don't lie, Drisc. I'm going to die. The sooner the better.

This is a brilliant and necessary piece of simplification of the playscript by the screenwriter, but O'Neill's textuality has been heartlessly sacrificed by Nichols. Part of what compensates in the film for the loss of the poetic dialect are the accents of the Irish actors and the visible poetry of their performances. Seeing the footage, Nichols himself was amazed at the transformation of his script, as he admitted to Ford: 'I got a terrific belt out of the rushes. I know you're going to get a terrific picture and I think you know it too. Another 16-inch shell into the MGM glamour empire! I agree with Condon, all you need is a phone book or the contents of an office wastebasket – then get on the set.'[105]

The Long Voyage Home obviously meant a lot to John Ford. Darryl Zanuck, who had Ford under contract at Twentieth Century Fox, had no interest in the project, but he released Ford to produce it with Walter Wanger through Ford's made-to-order production company, Argosy Pictures. On 12 and 13 February 1940, having paid O'Neill $20,000 for the film rights, Ford went with Dudley Nichols to the playwright's Tao House in California.[106] Film-maker, screenwriter and playwright got along famously.[107] In addition to the Irish actors, Ford packed the cast with his friends and members of what, loosely conceived,

Barry Fitzgerald (left) as Cocky, John Wayne (centre) as Ole Olson and John Qualen as Axel Swanson in Long Voyage Home, *1940. (Lilly Library)*

is often called his 'stock company' – such as Ward Bond and John Wayne. John Wayne is required to act a part unlike 'John Wayne'. He has the trouble one would expect with a Scandinavian accent, but Ford worked around it.

When an aspiring director asked Ford how he got such a strong performance out of the cowboy actor, Ford replied: 'Count the times Wayne talks.

That's the answer. Don't let him talk unless you have something that needs to be said.'[108] This is not a very nice thing to say, especially about one's best friend, but Ford was not a very nice man, and loved whipping boys. He wanted Wayne in this role just to look big, handsome and simple, even silly. Wayne was equal to the job. It was close enough to the part Ford made him play in real life. Once, when writer-director Peter Bogdanovich told Ford he'd gotten Wayne a book for his birthday, Ford replied, 'What did you do that for? Wayne's already got a book.'

Although the time-scale of O'Neill's trilogy was moved from World War I to the present as a way of making the story more immediately interesting to movie-goers, this was an art film through and through. Ford got one of the hottest cameramen in Hollyood, Gregg Toland, to do the photography. Toland had just shot the Academy-award-winning *The Grapes of Wrath* for Ford, and he was about to do *Citizen Kane* with Orson Welles. *The Long Voyage Home* opens with a montage of fifty or more cuts of native women on shore and men on the deck of SS *Glencairn*, anchored at night off a Caribbean island – no dialogue at all for nearly five minutes.[109] On the soundtrack native drums are heard and two choruses, one male, one female – who – *ooh-oh! who – ooh-oh!* – answer to one another in the night. The seamen are photographed so that they appear as individuals, separate, wandering the deck, stopping, listening, troubled, not wanting to hear the music. It is a bit like Ulysses passing the island of the Sirens, but when sexual music floats through the fog, the sailors' ears are not plugged with wax.

The plot of the first episode (the play version was entitled *Moon of the Caribbees*) shows the Captain permitting a group of native women to come on board; after all, the men will soon be leaving on what may be the last voyage of their lives. The ship is to pick up arms and ammunition in the USA and then sail to Britain through waters patrolled by German U-boats.

The men turn out to be more interested in the rum that the Caribbean women have brought on board than in the women themselves. Axel the Russian plays a jig, while the sailors and women pair up and clumsily attempt to dance. The seamen are rough and crude with the island women, no gentlemanly charm at all. Their terrified misogyny is apparent. The prettiest of the island women goes aside toward the most handsome of the sailors, the Englishman Smitty [Ian Hunter]. 'Have you got anything to drink?' he rudely asks. She shows him her cleavage as she bends to fetch up a bottle of rum from within her fruit basket. With no eyes for her charms, Smitty grabs the bottle, but is then frustrated: the bottle will not come uncorked. He is about to smash its neck against the gunnels when the Donkeyman [Arthur Shields] stops him, and calmly uncorks the bottle with his pocketknife. Normally close-mouthed, Smitty begins to open up:

> Donkeyman. I did my share of drinking in my time. Doctor said I would have to stop it or die. So I stopped. What's troubling you, Smitty? That singing on the shore getting on your nerves?
> Smitty: If I didn't know we were in the West Indies, I'd imagine we were anchored off some island of the dead. The ghosts are wailing, Donkeyman.
> Donkeyman:The natives is queer. I've known them to keep on singing like that all night long. I used to worry a lot about dying. I don't no more. Take that singing now. Sounds kind of nice and sleepy like to me.
> Smitty: Sleepy? If I listened to it much longer, I'd never get to sleep.
> Donkeyman: What's bothering you, Smitty?
> Smitty: O memories, Donkeyman.
> Donkeyman:The best thing to do with memories is to … forget 'em.
> Smitty: What if you couldn't forget them?
> Donkeyman: Then I'd get drunk. Same as you're doing. Whatever kept you going to sea in an old tramp like this? I suppose there's a woman mixed up in it, eh?
> Every time we get near the land, you get that look in your face. When a man goes to sea, he ought to give up thinking about things on shore. Land don't want him no more. I had my share of things going wrong, and all come from the land. Now I'm through with the land, and the land's through with me.

Ole Olson (John Wayne) is going back to the land, Smitty replies, but Donkeyman doubts he'll make it. He's seen Olson try to go home three times, but he always gets drunk and winds up on another ship.

> Smitty: Well, I'm not going back to England.
> Donkeyman: The ship is.
> Smitty: Mind your own business, Donkeyman.

This is Shields's biggest scene in the film, and the meditative, sorrowful, sympathetic air in which he delivers his lines gives him the authority of the ship's philosopher of alienation.

Smitty – the standoffish English gentleman – tries to jump ship in the USA when they stop to collect the cargo, but is rounded up by the cops and put back aboard SS *Glencairn.* Thus begins the film's second sequence, derived from O'Neill's one-act *In the Zone.* Barry Fitzgerald, playing a 'wizened runt of a man with a straggling grey mustache', has a central part in this sequence.[110] Trim in his yacht cap, bowtie and white belt-length jacket, he imparts some humour to the characterization (as when, discovering the nature of the cargo, he cries out, 'This is not a ship. Just a bomb, a great big dynamite bomb!' with *bomb* pronounced as by Peter Sellers later in *The Pink Panther*). The character of Cocky is a nasty one, and Fitzgerald's natural lovableness did not prevent him from revealing its nastiness.

Cocky reads an article about 'The Fifth Column' and a pair of German spies who sent coded messages to one another disguised as love letters, and he decides that Smitty is such a spy. Isn't that why he tried to get off the ship in the USA? Isn't that why he keeps a locked box in his bunk? And why he opens his porthole at night, allowing German subs to see light from the ship? Cocky has it all figured out.

Having gotten the already paranoid crew to gang up on Smitty, and gag him, they open Smitty's box for safe-keeping only to find letters from his wife. In a scene shot in low illumination, Driscoll reads out a letter:

> 'There is only one thing, Tom Darling, can wreck our lives. This black shadow.' Code word, sure. 'Whenever you are tempted, think of those who love you. Think of Tommy, and Betsey, and your own Elizabeth.' Signed Elizabeth. Here's one addressed to this ship. Same hand, only a little shakier. 'Tom Darling. It is only from your chance meeting with Harry, that I know how to reach you. I know you lied to give me peace of mind, always hoping you could fight it out, and make it come true. My heart broke at the thought of your trial. My heart broke when your letter came as if from the grave, saying that for my sake you would never return to England ... There is no disgrace we cannot go through together. I refuse to tell the children, as you ask, that your father is dead. He can never be dead to me, as I love him. O Tom, Tom, you must come back to us. Elizabeth.'

All the men grow quiet and sad. The 'enemy' that they have captured is a man just like themselves. They turn away and slowly go back to work.

The idea that the curse that drove a man to drink, or to run away, or to work with no end in sight, could be forgiven, had indeed already been forgiven by the wife and child back home, meant something to each member of the crew of the *Glencairn*. There is 'a woman mixed up in it somewhere' in these men's lives, not just the fine lady who comes in a black car to collect the body of Smitty in London, after he's been machine-gunned by a German fighter plane. There is also Ole's mother, who serves as a mother figure for all them, saying, 'You come home now, Ole.' There is the barmaid in the Red Stork in Cardiff, the last person remembered by the dying Yank after his lung is punctured in a squall. The men grow nostalgic for home as if home itself were a wife or mother.

Driscoll, for instance, lying in the sun as the ship nears its destination, says, 'Smell that … the sweet smell of Ireland, the grass and the fields,' until Axel corrects him, 'But that's England, that way.' Driscoll shouts angrily, 'Did I ask you?' and quite rightly too. Cathleen ni Houlihan, the wife and mother allegory of Ireland, is wherever an Irishman's dreaming eyes are cast. The past that is evoked in songs like 'It's a Long Way to Tipperary' and 'Shenandoah' is not the real past they fled, and it evokes for them places they will never reach.

For a Hollywood movie, and one nominated for an Oscar, *The Long Voyage Home* is both oblique and profound. As Eugene O'Neill observed with pleasure, there is no suspense, no love story, and no happy ending, but the theme of exile is emotionally realized with great philosophical power. In the final scene of the film, the Donkeyman (Arthur Shields), with a newspaper in hand, is sitting on the deck of the *Glencairn*, tied up at the docks in London. Littered paper swirls on the wharf, rising in the wind, swirling again before being fetched off by a gust. The men who have gone ashore for a drink – and swearing they'd never come back to the *Glencairn* – file slowly past the Donkeyman and into the forecastle. They say nothing as they pass. So the Donkeyman has to ask, 'Where's Ole?' Axel says, 'Ole go home. Ole go home to Stockholm.'

'Where's Drisc?'

Axel replies, 'Drisc gone. *Amindra.* He sail on that terrible ship, *Amindra.* He's gone. He's gone.'

Shields walks slowly to the side of the ship, and, after a thoughtful moment, lets the newspaper drop into the streaming water below. The camera lets us see down into the water as the front page is being swept away: '*Amindra* TORPEDOED!' are the headlines. The image of men at sea as the litter of life, swept away by wind and water, is left in the viewer's mind, as a long shot of Arthur Shields, head bent, standing at the ship's side, ends the film.

John Ford is famous for his Westerns, stories of American pioneers trying to build a safe home and a good life in the new land, which is the land of the American movie-going public, their country. But *The Long Voyage Home* has an opposite motion, of Irishmen going east, always working, but never arriving. These were a people for whom 'home', as Fintan O'Toole writes, is 'not so much the place you were as the place you wanted to be, a place as much imagined as remembered or experienced'.[111] The Irish were a famine-driven people, 'always roaming with a hungry heart', as Tennyson said of Ulysses, and as they approach the margin of the true Ireland, it fades forever and forever as they move. Arthur Shields comprehended the works of great artists both as a reader and an actor. He embodied the works of W.B. Yeats, Sean O'Casey and John Ford for the public. He had the capacity to understand these works, and in particular to feel how deeply the nature of his own long voyage was probed by John Ford's film.

IV

SARA ALLGOOD, *JUNO AND THE PAYCOCK* AND *HOW GREEN WAS MY VALLEY*

Previous page left: *Sara Allgood as Maurya in* Riders to the Sea, *September 1938;* right: *Sara Allgood as herself, September 1938.*
(Photograph Carl Van Vechten; Beinicke Library, Yale University)

A portrait of Sara Allgood (1879–1950), one of the greatest early Irish actresses, hangs among those of the founders in the Abbey Theatre, the National Theatre of Ireland. Biographical entries in encyclopedias mention that she was with the Abbey when it opened in 1904, that her sister Molly (stage name 'Maire O'Neill') had been betrothed to J.M. Synge at the time of his death, and that 'Sally' Allgood hit her peak as Juno in O'Casey's *Juno and the Paycock* (1924), before going to Hollywood where, having been employed, it is falsely said, in sadly insignificant film roles, she died in poverty on 13 September 1950.

Two clichés meet here: the sad emigrant from the emerald isle and the decline of a national dramatic actress forced into the service of the American entertainment industry. Lost in such a brief biography is not just the detail but the whole shape of Allgood's life. Of her sixty-seven years, fifty-four of them on the stage, she was with the Abbey for only twelve. By 1908, just four years after the Abbey opened, she was breaking away for spells with the Manchester Gaiety and Mrs Patrick Campbell's company in London. The year 1914 found Allgood with Liverpool Repertory starring in John Masefield's *Nan*.[1] The end of that run brought her back to the Abbey for the first six months of 1915.

Soon she was off again, having obtained the lead – for once a pretty *ingénue* role was hers – in a Hibernicized melodrama, *Peg O' My Heart*, scheduled to tour Australia. The next five years 'down under' are a dark, undocumented period of Allgood's life. Major events in a woman's whole life occurred – marriage, the birth of two children, the deaths of husband and both children – of which she almost never spoke upon her return in May 1920.

On her return to Britain, even before her ship had docked, Allgood had arranged work through J.B. Fagan in a touring British production of Lennox Robinson's *The Whiteheaded Boy* among a cast of ex-Abbey players, including her sister Molly and Molly's second husband, Arthur Sinclair.[2] This company of veterans was successful on stage but quarrelsome off it. Sara Allgood, Sinclair later complained, always wanted 'to play flappers, though her waistline had long since vanished'.[3] She came to hate Molly's husband, and queered his pitch by giving him the wrong cues or walking off stage while he still had lines to say to her. 'She thinks she is everybody,' complained Sinclair, who had a right to believe he was somebody too.

In late 1923 Allgood left the London Irish Players for Dublin. It was her good luck to return to the Abbey not long before rehearsals began on Sean O'Casey's new play and first classic, *Juno and the Paycock*. There was no waiting for recognition of her greatness in the lead role; the play was instantly acclaimed upon its debut on 3 March 1924. The following year, Allgood left to join a London production of *Juno and the Paycock* with a different cast, one that included Sinclair and Molly Allgood.[4]

2

November 1937, many years, many theatres, and many films later (including three directed by Alfred Hitchcock), Allgood was in Edinburgh touring in a musical comedy with Douglas Byng (1893–1987), customarily billed as 'bawdy but British'.[5] It was the only berth she could find after the flop in New York of a madcap comedy based on the British love of dogs and fair play, *Storm in a Teacup*.[6] Then arrived a stroke of actor's good fortune: an offer by telegram from Eddie Dowling (1894–1976), one of the Shubert brothers' producers.[7] In 1937 he calculated on the possibility of a Broadway success with a play that had originally opened on 25 January 1937 at the Abbey, Paul Vincent Carroll's *Shadow and Substance*.

In Dublin the production had featured Arthur Shields and sixteen-year-old Phyllis Ryan.[8] Rather daringly for its time, *Shadow and Substance* put a cast of clergymen on stage. An ugly and hysterical society is represented, not wholly unlike the one in Arthur Miller's Salem witchcraft play, *The Crucible* (1953). For the lead in a Broadway production – religion on stage, *à la* Eugene O'Neill, was cutting edge in the USA too – Dowling had secured the knighted British character actor Sir Cedric Hardwicke. Now Dowling aimed to add Sara Allgood to the cast. The failure of the stage version of *Storm in a Teacup* did not, in his judgment, diminish her drawing power. A film of the play with Vivien Leigh and Rex Harrison in the leads and Allgood in her part as a plucky dog-lover had done good business from February 1937.

Obviously, in the casting of *Shadow and Substance,* Allgood could not play the female lead, Brigid, the young, pious and pretty housekeeper. She was no longer young and had never been pretty. It would be her job as 'Jemima Cooper' to illustrate the theme that village society was hysterical and ugly, and, more importantly, by her high billing to advertise a degree of Irish authenticity.

Those who had this authenticity in the fullest measure, the Abbey players, happened to be in New York at the time.[9] At the beginning of October they had arrived under the leadership of F.R. Higgins, commercial publisher (*The Builders' Provider, Irish Oil and Colour Trade Review,* and others), poet, and mate of W.B. Yeats.[10] Through his own pushiness and Yeats's support, Higgins had become the company's latest artistic director, determined to put it on a business footing and bring to an end decades of unprofitability.

But the New World was all new to him. This was his first trip to Manhattan, and Higgins was astonished by skyscrapers – 'You could not see up to them' – and the rooms in the Edison Hotel with their own baths, towels in the bathrooms, and soap in little paper packets. It was amazing. The Edison, he wrote his wife, was ten times bigger than the Shelbourne Hotel, Dublin's finest, and ten times swankier too. But out on the streets, which he conceded were very clean, every second person was black, and Sam, Jacob, and Lee Shubert – promoters of the Abbey tour – were, Higgins concluded, Jewish.[11]

In early November Eddie Dowling approached Higgins about a production of *Shadow and Substance* on Broadway under Abbey auspices, so long as the star be Sir Cedric Hardwicke. Higgins did not trust Dowling: in his eyes, the producer was 'an Italian Jew posing as an Irishman' (what advantage such a pose would secure it is hard to say).[12] Higgins refused the offer point-blank. The Abbey's players would not serve in 1930s' America as supernumeraries in a show with a Jewish manager and an English star. Then how about, Dowling suggested, releasing Arthur Shields to direct five weeks of rehearsals for Dowling's production? Higgins accepted the alternative, but, asserting himself as an experienced businessman not to be fooled, stipulated two conditions: 50 per cent of Shields's $400 a week salary be paid to the Abbey Theatre; a two-week run of *The Playboy* be guaranteed in one of Lee Shubert's New York theatres.[13]

Shadow and Substance opened on 26 January 1938 with Hardwicke playing opposite Julie Haydon and with Allgood in support, and then ran and ran and ran, 274 performances in all. It won the New York Drama Critics' Circle prize for best foreign play of the 1937/38 season. For Sara Allgood, it was all day off in Manhattan, with just a few lines each night, her name in lights on the marquee, and steady money, month in and month out.

3

In September 1938, while the run of *Shadow and Substance* continued, Sara Allgood was contacted by Carl Van Vechten.[14] Having met Allgood after a 21 March 1938 performance of *Shadow and Substance*, he wanted to make a portrait of her, and Allgood consented to sit for him on 13 September 1938.[15] Two plates from this shoot are stunning. One photograph shows the actress, the other the woman. In the first, Allgood is posed in a shawl, part of her costume for a revival of Synge's *Riders to the Sea* (1903), in which she played Maurya of Inishmaan, who has lost the last of her six sons, all to the sea. Hands half-folded as if in prayer or grief, the head slightly inclined and eyes cast down to the side, Allgood falls into the pose of so many Marys in paintings of the death of Jesus. Yet this *pietà* attitude can also be understood as expressive of something both local (a peasant woman in an Irish fishing community) and infinite, in the idea that those who give life cannot prevent the death of the life they have given: 'No man at all can be living forever, and we must be satisfied.'[16]

The other photograph could hardly be more different. Wearing at a jaunty angle a netted hat of a sort then fashionable, Sara Allgood flashes a face lit up with laughter, and a fine set of teeth. Two strings of pearls dip into her open-necked dress. This is not Maurya, but the successful Broadway actress who never appears as herself on stage. There is a great gap between the immemorial and illiterate yet profound emotion of Maurya and the spontaneous and self-pleased high spirits of Sara. What was the woman in the hat like when unprompted by a part? What was it that she brought to her roles?

William Hazlitt, the English essayist, notices what is fundamental to actors' lives. During their time, they may be the most admired people of any profession, yet the public, while fond of particular actors and even familiar with them, do not know who these individuals really are, because when they are heard on stage, as Hazlitt puts it, 'Their very thoughts are not their own.'

They pass from joy to woe at 'the prompter's call'.[17] We simply see them say the words of another and pretend to think.

According to old-timers among theatre-goers, the actors of the past are always the best; they had a greatness never to be seen again. This opinion is both unprovable and incontestable because, as Hazlitt says, the genius of the actor dies with him or her. This fact is frustrating for those interested in Irish theatre of the early twentieth century, when the works of Synge, O'Casey and Shaw were first staged, and when, according to tradition, a glorious and native style of acting prevailed at the Abbey, embodied in famous members of the company like the Fay brothers, the Allgood sisters, Arthur Sinclair and J.M. Kerrigan in the first decade, and Barry Fitzgerald, F.J. McCormick and others during the third decade. There are not even silent films of an Abbey production made during its glory days. The closest one can come is John Ford's 1936 film *The Plough and the Stars*, which, albeit interesting, is unsatisfactory.

However, it is not strictly true that these actors left no record behind of their genius. There are contemporary reviews of their performances, though rarely are these minutely descriptive or even evocative. The laudatory epithets of one era are as useless as those of another, just puffs of mist. Photographs survive of Abbey actors in costume for a variety of plays, many of them publicity stills that capture identifiable dramatic moments of a play. From these, just as from Carl Van Vechten's studio shot of Allgood as Maurya, one can get a feel for the actor's physical attitudes, gestures and 'face work'. Many of the best of the actors from the early Abbey went into films by the 1930s, usually first in London, then in Hollywood. On the soundtracks of the films that circulate on DVD or videotape, we can hear the voices of Sara Allgood, Barry Fitzgerald, Arthur Shields and others, the absence of which makes the publicity stills finally so dissatisfyingly mute a record. And those voices are truly characterful. One can speculate upon what vestiges of an Abbey style of voice, movement and characterization is traceable in such films. Yet these recovered moments of lost time do not tell us much of the person who creates the performance, of the woman in the hat, as opposed to the bereaved mother in an Aran shawl.

4

How important the intelligent individualities of great actors are to the performances they render is an open question. It is one that received several implied answers on 28 September 1932 by the dignitaries gathered together in

Dublin at the Abbey Theatre for the unveiling of a portrait of Sara Allgood by Sarah Purser. The Minister of Finance of the Irish Free State, Seán MacEntee, sent a letter (read by Lennox Robinson on the occasion) that acclaimed Allgood's work as an inspiration to the founders of the new state. MacEntee's compliment was not so 'over the top' as it might seem. Another government minister who had been active in the War of Independence, C.S. ('Todd') Andrews, before that war spent his Saturday nights with Sinn Féin friends in the Abbey Theatre. Nursed on its pageantry, their Ireland became (these are the words of C.S. Andrews): 'an Ireland which had nothing to do with economics, property, or with how people lived or loved or prayed. It had in fact become a political abstraction, and from Caitlin Ni Uallachain [Cathleen ni Houlihan], Roisín Dubh and the Sean Bhean Bhocht proceeded the Republic.'[18] Sara Allgood impersonated Cathleen ni Houlihan in the famously incendiary play of that title, and she was Sean Bhean Bhocht in Lady Gregory's patriotically maudlin *The Old Woman Remembers.*[19] So Allgood served as the very image of Mother Ireland for many young men, future soldiers, 'martyrs' and ministers of state. At the unveiling of the portrait of Sara Allgood, W.B. Yeats was eloquent on her power. Allgood, he said, 'made whole masses of emotion possible which otherwise would have lain latent in the mind of the author. Like other great actresses, and great artists of every kind, she possessed the power to "mould history". '[20] In ceremonies such as this, poets and ministers of state do not speak on oath, and understatement is not the accepted manner of speaking. Nonetheless, Yeats was articulating a long-held belief that great actors could inspire authors to write great plays, and then these same actors would invest the scripted characters with emotion and life.

Yeats himself had tried to write plays for Florence Darragh and Mrs Patrick Campbell to act in: *Deirdre* (1906) and *The Player Queen* (1922). No woman in the Abbey ensemble, Yeats felt, could display the bewitching sexuality of these heroines on stage. When he thought of 'the movements' of Miss Darragh as Salomé in the play by Oscar Wilde, he 'ventured and discovered subtleties of emotion' for his Deirdre that he had never before attempted.[21] He accepted as facts that Sara Allgood was necessary in similar fashion to Lady Gregory's early 'peasant' work and that Molly Allgood had aroused emotions in Synge that found romantic expression in *The Playboy of the Western World* (1907) and *Deirdre of the Sorrows* (1910), emotions which Molly Allgood then embodied on stage.

Yeats's concept of actors as actualizers of emotional potentialities in the mind of a writer, on occasion prior to the act of composition, and initiatory of it, is a startling extension of the Stanislavskian formulation. The Russian director urged actors to draw upon their own past emotions and to find conscious means for reaching unconscious memories. The actor's job was, according to Stanislavski, to actualize emotional potentialities in characters once they had been created, and, quite apart from the authors who created them, to draw not upon the playwright's advice or upon textual study but upon masses of their own personal psychic material.

In addition to the actress-as-Muse model, Yeats entertained another concept of the relation of actors to the parts they play. Perhaps, he thought, they were like spirit mediums, people dispossessed of their own bodies by spirits now seeking self-expression. In *Words upon the Windowpane* (1934), his character 'Mrs Henderson' falls into a trance and speaks with the voice of several ghosts, both men and women, until, shaken by the rage of the spirit of Jonathan Swift, she awakes in ignorance of the characters that she has somehow channelled.

At the 1932 unveiling, Allgood returned Yeats's compliment. Writers, she said, 'had helped her to express something inside her of which she had not been aware at all'.[22] So does the actress, as if under hypnosis, 'act out' something repressed, and only later – if at all – become conscious of it? Perhaps, Allgood implies, the power of the acting is in proportion both to the depth at which an emotion has been buried and to the capacity of great writing to plumb those depths.

By the end of the ceremonial exchange of compliments of Yeats and Allgood, how things stood in the relations between playwright, actor and role was fraught with conflicting possibilities, a sort of uncertainty always prolific for Yeats. A year earlier, in a preface to *Words upon the Windowpane*, he had written of the relations between spirits and mediums, and characters and actors. His key sentence begins 'I consider it certain,' and many words later that sentence concludes that the voice that speaks at a séance 'is first of all a secondary personality or dramatization created by, in, or through a medium.'[23] Alas, whether it is *by*, *in* or *through* is just what one wanted to ascertain. Is shawled Maurya a secondary personality artistically created *by* Sara Allgood, the woman in the netted hat? Is Maurya created *in* Allgood by Synge, who had seen in her both stoicism and the potential to release unexpressed grief?[24] Or is Maurya the effect of the playscript seen and heard by us *through* Allgood, who is a passive medium of a certain quality, like a pane of glass or a phonograph?

The question is important. Whether it is worthwhile to investigate the biography of actors depends on the answer. William Hazlitt was of the opinion that what the public sees of actors on stage is a 'likeness of the world', but a 'bettered likeness … with the dull part left out'. The dull part, he suggested, is the actor's own life, who 'when [she is] alone is nothing'.[25]

5

The early life of the Allgoods is hardly predictable. Sara was born on 31 October 1879, the first of eight children, in an old-fashioned tenant house at 45 Middle Abbey Street, just a few hundred yards west of the theatre where she would make her name.[26] Her first ancestor in Ireland was an English commissioned officer, Edward Allgood, who formed a battalion in Ireland in 1786. Edward Allgood's son Henry married a Catholic (named O'Neill) and raised his son George to be a Protestant, and a Protestant he became to the extent of joining the Orange Order, a sectarian political society dedicated to sustaining the memory of King William III and Protestant domination of Ireland. However, George Allgood also married a Catholic, Margaret Harold. Like his father, he then tried to raise his children as Protestants. This was difficult to do, living where he did, utterly surrounded in Dublin's northside by Catholics.

George Allgood insisted on proper deportment in his brood: the children had to rise when he entered the room, and remain silent unless spoken to. He himself never visited the rooms of other tenants, and wished his children not to do so, in vain. While he could not afford to send them to a fee-paying Protestant school, he had them registered as Protestant at the Marlborough Street National School (almost all the other students were Catholic).

In defiance of her husband, but with the assistance of the clergy at Presentation Convent on George's Hill, just four blocks west of the Allgood's dwelling, his wife Margaret took the children each in turn for secret instruction and ultimately confirmation as Roman Catholics.

While his children were taking forbidden instruction in the one true faith, George Allgood was working long weeks as a proofreader in the Queen's Printing Office, Abbey Street. Reading, he believed, was the best path in life for his children. He would bring home proofs of poems – Thomas Hood's 'Song of the Shirt' was one, and William Allingham's 'The Fairies' another. To please him in the evenings after work, his daughter Sara recited them, and he exclaimed at her brilliance. In 1896 George Allgood fell ill. From his deathbed he said again and again to his wife of the children from whom he was about to part, 'Educate them, educate them.'

There were a lot of them to educate. When George Allgood passed away on 2 August 1896, 38-year-old Mrs Allgood had a babe in arms of five months and seven other children, Sara being the oldest. Although she had begun acting lessons with Frank Fay the year before (voice production, deportment, breathing exercises, poetry recitation), Allgood had to go to work upon the death of her father to help support the family. She got a job not far from the family's residence at the time, Ormond Quay, at P.J. Walsh's antique shop in Bachelor's Walk, where she learned about Chippendale furniture, Morris-designed cretonne, and Aubusson carpets, in order to assist the 'Quality' who shopped there.

It is remarkable that of the great Abbey actors, the Shields brothers and the Allgood sisters came from inner-city Dublin Protestant fathers who were artisans in the printing trades. Audiences generally credited these actors with authenticity in their representations of Synge and Gregory's Catholic peasants from the West of Ireland or O'Casey's Catholic Dubliners. Yet they were not so much examples of typical Irish people as they were students of the art of mimicry of Irish characteristics, who lived at close quarters with those they studied.

Sara's sister Molly was the famous beloved, a beautiful tease who inspired even the somewhat morose J.M. Synge with a rage of love, and later wed G.H. Mair (1886–1926), an Oxford scholar and writer for *The Manchester Guardian,* and finally (but not permanently) married the great actor Arthur Sinclair.[27]

Yet Sara Allgood also attracted romantic attention in her early years at the Abbey. Frank Fay gave her editions of Synge's plays and Yeats's poems, then a ten-guinea bicycle (which her brother pawned). Still, she was surprised to receive, when on an Abbey tour of England in March 1904, Frank Fay's written proposal of marriage. She claimed to have been 'quite unconscious' of his intention up until that moment. Around 1908 J.M. Kerrigan, an Abbey actor, also presented her with a wristwatch and a proposal of marriage. She kept the wristwatch but refused the proposal. Kerrigan later asked for the watch back, and then stamped it to bits on the floor of the Abbey green room. Next Arthur Sinclair, in tight trousers and with golden hair parted in the middle like Oscar Wilde's, gave her another wristwatch (one suspects that the actress was often late for appointments). Allgood showed off her latest prize to Lady Gregory.

'Am I to congratulate you?' Gregory inquired.

'What? Does a wristwatch mean a proposal of marriage?'

Her hand having been forced by Lady Gregory, Allgood had to give the watch back to Sinclair (rather than wear it or pawn it).

Sean O'Casey's diagnosis many years later was that Sara Allgood was 'an odd mixture; one minute primed with prudery, the next one leppin' with sex'.[28]

6

One can guess at certain configurations in Sara Allgood's psyche from such anecdotes of her early life: Daddy's girl and child star; a child of mixed marriage who had to play two parts, one Protestant, the other Catholic; tenement girl who was taught stage deportment and the best shop-assistant manners; a professional actress to whom the profession was alone what had lifted her out of poverty and into sporadic, flush paydays; daughter of a mother of eight who may have come to equate reproduction with destitution. Yet the real secret of her later life seems to lie in Australia.

And Allgood meant those subcontinental years to remain largely secret. In the 1940s, when she set down her 'Memories', she recalls some facts. The London members of the cast of *Peg o' My Heart* embarked for Australia in January 1916. In 1917 she married Gerald Henson, an Australian actor who played 'Sir Gerald' in the play.[29] They bought 'Alton', a small cottage on Misman Bay, Sydney. In 1918 Mr and Mrs Henson were in New Zealand touring a production when the influenza epidemic forced the closing of theatres. By the time they reached a hotel in Wellington, New Zealand, people were 'dying like flies', Gerald Henson felt weak and Sara had a cough. A doctor could not be obtained for five days. Gerald Henson died a week later. En route to Sydney, Sara Allgood was quarantined for a week on a leper island. (This is where, it may be, her son John was born and died.) Because of the epidemic, the theatres in Australia remained closed until June, when she was happy to get back on stage in *Out There* by Hartley Manners, author of *Peg o' My Heart*. When she left Sydney on 17 March 1920, she took along her pet parrot and a dog named 'Yen'. They both died en route.

As her niece Mrs Hague noted on the manuscript of the memoir, it is strange that Allgood makes no mention of a baby: 'I am quite certain Sally had two children, Mary first, then John, both of whom she lost. She told me so herself. However, she never spoke of her children and rarely of her husband.' There is an obituary in the *Times* of a daughter, unnamed, born prematurely on 17 January 1918, who 'survived a short time only'.[30] Of the second baby, whom Mrs Hague calls 'John', no record has been traced.

It is also noteworthy that Allgood makes no mention of the fact that her husband, like her father and grandfather, was a Protestant, and that Allgood agreed to marry him in a Methodist Church. In *Daughters of Erin*, Elizabeth Coxhead speculates that Sara Allgood saw the deaths of her children and husband as 'a judgment upon her for having married a Protestant, and religious observance became expiation as well as relief'.[31] However, greater relief than confession and the Mass may have been the regular thunder of applause from pit, boxes and gallery, the whole house in a roar, for it was that she sought from city to city, year by year.

7

In January 1940 Arthur Shields called upon Sara Allgood for help in an emergency. As explained in Chapter III, Shields, with young producer Eddie Choate, had taken the Maxine Elliott Theatre for a production of Paul Vincent Carroll's *Kindred*, and it had been an immediate failure. He, now with Aideen O'Connor on his hands, was facing bankruptcy with no way back to Dublin in wartime. His plan was to recoup the *Kindred* losses by means of a revival of *Juno and the Paycock* featuring its original Abbey stars, Barry Fitzgerald and Sara Allgood. She was promised 10 per cent of the profits if she would take the part on short notice and perform with little rehearsal.[32]

Things were not peaceful backstage. Sara Allgood was always a prima donna. When she was not getting all the attention on stage by her acting, she contrived to get it offstage by making trouble. Yet *Juno* got off to a decent start:good audiences if not great reviews. Since Arthur Shields had been forced into hospital with TB, it was Eddie Choate who had to have a talk with the troublesome leading lady. He explained what this revival meant to her, financially and artistically.[33] She had a chance for a season to be the greatest tragic actress on the New York stage, and take down 10 per cent of the gate receipts each night. Allgood's career, like Barry Fitzgerald's, had been borne aloft on the plays of O'Casey, and *Juno* gave each their classic roles one last time, but the last performances of those roles could be the jumping-off point to a repertoire of kindred parts, both on Broadway and in Hollywood. In the play's final act, Sara Allgood could reign over the stage, tough but warm-hearted, standing up sorrowfully with her pregnant, abandoned daughter for mothers of all helpless babies. With her magnificently musical voice, Allgood could summon all that was down under.

Having been brought to an appreciation of the situation, according to

Choate, Sarah Allgood was 'very, very happy'. Thereafter, she 'reveled' in the continuing publicity. (One can see how delighted she is with herself at the time in Carl Van Vechten's portrait.) *Juno* ran until 13 April 1940 – 105 performances, not bad on Broadway for a revival sixteen years after the play's opening. The triumph in O'Casey's tragedy brought Sara Allgood renewed attention from Hollywood. In October 1940 she got eight and a half weeks' work from Alexander Korda in *That Hamilton Woman*, as the improbably short, plump and lower-class mother of the naturally cultured beauty, Emma, Lady Hamilton (played by most-beautiful-skinny-woman-in-the-world, Vivien Leigh).[34] Upon Allgood's arrival in Hollywood, Alfred Hitchcock sent a car for her and she spent the weekend at his Bel Air estate. Fellow Catholics, she and the Hitchocks attended Mass together on the Sunday morning.

Early in January 1941 Allgood got a small part as the wife of a hopelessly schizophrenic mental patient in *Dr Jekyll and Mr Hyde*. Then came her biggest break yet: John Ford cast her as Beth Morgan, the mother of many sons and one beautiful daughter in *How Green Was My Valley*, produced by Twentieth Century Fox. This story of the despoliation of both coal-miners and the Welsh countryside is taken from a best-selling poetic novel by Richard Llewellyn. Owing to World War II, and attacks on Atlantic shipping, it could not be filmed in Wales and in colour, as planned. It was shot in the Santa Monica hills above Malibu, and therefore in black and white, so that greenness in that semi-arid, dull olive landscape might at least be imagined.[35]

The film script was primarily the work of Philip Dunne. John Ford was brought in by Darryl Zanuck as a replacement for William Wyler, the initial director. Ford and Dunne were old friends, both admirers of Robert Emmet, Michael Collins and other heroes of the Irish rebel tradition. They annually celebrated St Patrick's Day together by getting drunk at the House of Murphy, 410 South Vincente, a hangout of the Hollywood Irish.[36] Dunne asked Ford if he had anything to add to the script of *How Green Was My Valley*. He offered, as if in an afterthought, 'Make the other prize-fighter a sort of second or handler for Dai Bando, and I'll throw the part to that poor bastard Barry Fitzgerald, who can't get a job.'[37] This was untrue. Fitzgerald could get a job; his career was flourishing. Just as Ford had added Arthur Shields to *Drums Along the Mohawk*, he made room for his brother in *How Green Was My Valley*. He liked to create connections with the Abbey Theatre and the Irish Revival.

Although Ford made little further alteration to the screenplay, by other means he gave a new vision to the film as a whole; through casting, for instance, Ford Hibernicized the whole story. Not only was Barry Fitzgerald added, but Arthur Shields was brought in to play the deacon of the village church. Sara Allgood became Beth Morgan, mother of the family of miners, and her daughter was played by Maureen O'Hara. The film of *How Green Was My Valley* almost became an Abbey Theatre production, and the ensemble playing of the cast – 'all star at the right moment' – was perfect for the episodic, multi-threaded nature of the narrative.[38] None of these Irish actors spoke in Welsh accents, their own accents being deemed sufficiently Celtic for movie audiences. Donald Crisp (1880–1974) played the father, Gwilym Morgan, and Crisp, long resident in the United States, had been born in London. In one scene Ford made even him sing an obviously Irish drinking song. When Philip Dunne complained of this alteration to the script, Ford retorted, 'Ah, go on! The Welsh are just another lot of micks and biddies, only Protestants!'

Filming went forward in July and August 1941. On one visit to the set, Philip Dunne found that Sara Allgood was 'kicking up a fuss'.[39] She had notions of herself as Dublin's Sarah Bernhardt and Eleanor Duse rolled into one, yet in Hollywood after the talking pictures arrived, most bit-part actors had been stage stars somewhere else.[40] No matter how great they were on the stages of their home countries, character actors in Hollywood were not supposed to require extra consideration, where every minute was costing thousands of dollars, and accountants were reporting daily progress – page by page of the script – to the studio chief, Darrryl Zanuck.

On the day Philip Dunne made his visit to the set, the local minister, Gruffydd (Walter Pigeon) was explaining a maths problem to young Huw Morgan (Roddy McDowell). How long does it take to fill a hundred-gallon bath at ten gallons a minute if the bath has a hole that empties at five gallons a minute? Sara Allgood as Beth Morgan is meant to scoff at the problem – 'Who would pour water in an old bath full of holes?' – and thus at the idea of education altogether, which her husband favours and she does not. Yet, after a few unusable takes, Allgood complained that the scene was badly written and therefore would not 'play'. John Ford winked at Dunne, and then explained that Sara Allgood had a problem with the scene. Dunne (deliberately re-enacting one of Ford's own fabled tales of the bullying of a troublesome star) ripped the page out of Allgood's script, and said, 'Now it plays.' Ford then told Allgood that since the son-of-a-bitch writer would not help, they would just have to film it as written.

It is unclear what other trouble Allgood caused on set, but she made herself 'distinctly unpopular' with the whole crew, even with the Shields brothers.[41] 'A member of the cast told [Dunne] she was the one truly discordant member of the company; she got on with nobody.' Ford made it plain to Dunne that he did not like Sara Allgood, in language that if recorded 'would blister the page'.[42] More importantly, fault was found with her performance. The role ought to have been perfect for the actress who had made her name in *Juno and the Paycock*. 'If our father was the head of the house,' the narrator Huw Morgan says, 'our mother was its heart'. But as played by Allgood, the heart was not equal to the head, or the woman to the man.

Allgood makes a thunderous impact in one scene. Many miners, including several Morgan boys, want to organize a strike against the owner. Gwilym Morgan, the patriarch, opposes unions. So the younger miners hold a night-time meeting around a bonfire on the hills. They accuse old Morgan of being in league with the mine-owner. Beth Morgan, taking along her youngest son Huw, goes out in the winter night to speak to the men. With her button nose and short, stout figure, snow swirling around, she stands up to the dark-coated men. In a voice of a deep vibrato with womanly higher registers and a bit of a burr, she gives the following speech:

> I have come up here to tell you what I think of you all, because you are talking against my husband. You are a lot of cowards to go against him. He has done nothing against you and he never has and you know it well. How some of you, you smug-faced hypocrites, can sit in the same chapel with him I cannot tell. To say he is with the owners is not only nonsense but downright wickedness. There's one thing more I've got to say and it is this. If harm comes to my Gwilym, I will find out the men and I will kill them with my two hands. And this I will swear by God Almighty.

It is an immense speech for a movie, and it is delivered with theatrical immensity. Hearing it and seeing her in that setting, one woman holding a child's hand against so many men, one can understand why Allgood was nominated for an Academy Award for Best Actress in a Supporting Role.

So why did some, including members of the production team, find fault with Allgood's performance? Andrew Sarris, the American film critic, thinks that the storyline was to blame for a weak Beth Morgan: 'The emotional authority of the mother is fatally undermined when her youngest son Huw (the film's point-of-view narrator) chose to leave home to live with and support his widowed sister-in-law (Anna Lee) for whom he feels a childhood longing of extraordinary delicacy.'[43] Sarris is usually brilliant, but not here. Audiences know that Huw goes to his sister-in-law out of his own tender feelings, not because his mother does not give him the love he needs.

Philip Dunne, the scriptwriter, naturally thinks the script was not at fault.

Before filming, he expected Sara Allgood to 'steal the picture'. Some of the best lines in the script were hers, yet, Dunne says, she threw them away:

> When Morgan offers Huw money for every bruise and scrape he incurs fighting in school, including a broken nose, she interjects, 'fiercely' according to my stage direction, 'Break your old nose then! Break your mother's heart every time you go from the house!' This is aimed not at the boy but at his father. It is a direct confrontation, a questioning of his authority ... It is an expression of the age-old differences between man and woman over the raising of a child. On the screen it comes off as none of these, merely a petulance.[44]

Dunne is not fair. Allgood's rendering comes off as a heartfelt and deep criticism of her husband's values, and of love for her frail youngest child, who had never really recovered from pneumonia after a drenching that snowy night when she confronted the miners' union. Yet the delivery of that line is, according to Dunne, not Allgood's only failure.

> Perhaps the most powerful line in the entire movie was hers in the poignant scene after son Ivor has been killed and grandson born to the new widow, Bronwyn. Morgan says piously, 'Give one, take the other,' and she responds, 'fiercely' according to the stage direction, 'Go to that girl up there and say that to her.' 'Hisht, now Beth,' says Morgan, shocked, 'do not kindle the wrath.' She replies, 'To hell with wrath!' She raises her eyes directly to heaven and adds, 'And I said it to be heard.' This should have all the power and passion of the dying Beethoven shaking his fist at a louring sky. It is a direct and unequivocal defiance and daring of her God, in this deeply religious family, a deliberate and naked blasphemy. I had to negotiate a special waiver from the industry's internal censorship for the line, including the word 'hell', which was then forbidden by the 'Code'. What is more, I had intended it to pave the way for her line at the end of the picture when she senses that her husband is dead and tells [her daughter] Angharad of 'the glory' [s]he has seen. I was trying to show that at last she was at peace with her God, and her blasphemy forgiven. But there had been no blasphemy; the line was thrown away casually as [Allgood] exited the scene.[45]

Basically, the problem with Allgood's performance, as Dunne sees it, is that she was meant to match Donald Crisp as the father, with a woman's values given equal weight to the man's, but when she is called upon to challenge him, she does not do it. She may criticize and complain, but in the end stays in her place, the obedient wife, in the kitchen, at the hearth, or in the sickroom.

Many explanations may be offered for such a lapse in courage by Sara Allgood, if that is what it was. It could be said, for instance, that during that period of history Irish women were generally more deferential to men than

American women were. That generalization, however, would not cover the screen personality of Maureen O'Hara, often depicted throwing a roundhouse punch at a man. Or it could be said, on the assumption that individual psychology is the real source of acting, that Sara Allgood carried from childhood a certain deference toward her strict father. That suggestion, however, is contradicted by Allgood's success in the portrayal of Juno Boyle. In the last act, Juno passes the dreadful judgment on stage that it would be better for a child to have no father at all, so long as that child had both a mother and a grandmother.

It could be said that in an Irish play, as in Irish Catholic culture of the era, oaths that took 'the Lord's name in vain' were hardly regarded as a serious challenge to God or even blasphemies much worth confessing. That is one of the sources of satirical, sectarian comedy in *The Playboy of the Western World* and throughout O'Casey's Dublin plays. Nor is blowing one's top – kindling the wrath, as Gwilym puts it – a serious matter in Irish Catholic culture, though it *is* in the restrained households of Welsh Methodists. Sara Allgood, in short, may have been just playing Beth Morgan as an Irishwoman, because that is what John Ford wanted her to do, even though it clearly was not what Philip Dunne had indicated through his stage directions in the screenplay.

It is not evident from *How Green Was My Valley* that John Ford saw no difference at all between Welsh Protestants and Irish Catholics, as if they were all indistinguishable 'micks and biddies'. Protestantism is in fact vividly set forth as a distinctive way of life and philosophy, an admirable philosophy too. 'Prayer is just another name for good, clean, direct thinking,' the preacher Mr Gruffydd (and love interest for Maureen O'Hara) teaches Huw, who has during his winter of convalescence lost the power to walk. 'When you pray, *think*. Think well what you are saying. Make your thoughts into things that are solid. In that way, your prayer will have strength, and that strength will become a part of you, body, mind, and spirit.' Thus taught, Huw learns to stand on his own two legs and walk again, walk like a man.

Irish Catholic attributes are depicted as well, affectionately, but not always admiringly. In a scene with lines added by Ford during filming, Barry Fitzgerald as Cyfartha is among a group at the head of the mine while far down the shaft at the coal-face, trapped by a cave-in, are Gwilym Morgan and others. Mr Gruffydd asks who will join a party to rescue Gwilym Morgan:

> Dai Bando (Rhys Williams): I, for one. He is the blood of my heart. Come, Cyfartha.
>
> Cyfartha (Barry Fitzgerald):Tis a coward I am. But I will hold your coat.

How Green Was My Valley, *1941, left to right: Morton Lowry as Mr Jonas, Rhys Williams as Dai Bando and Barry Fitzgerald as Cyfartha. (Lilly Library)*

The line (an ad-lib invention by Ford and Fitzgerald) has become a classic moment of Hollywood's Golden Age. It's a good line, and could have been delivered effectively by Bob Hope; perhaps the only things that make it Irish are the syntactical inversion ('Tis a coward I am' for 'I am a coward') and the fact that Barry Fitzgerald says it, and he carries from his stage-past qualities of Captain Boyle from *Juno and the Paycock*, work-shy and full of fighting words; and of Fluther Good, who is so fabulously trained for barroom boxing.

One of the accidental consequences of Ford's Hibernicizing of various parts in the play is that this reproduced the Allgood family household of the 1890s: a mixed marriage between a strict, bookish, working-class Protestant father and a Catholic mother of many children. Margaret Allgood did not share George Allgood's view that children should be brought up strictly and everything sacrificed for their education. She obviously did not want them brought up as Protestants and, worse yet, Catholic-hating Protestants; however, she did not demand that Mr Allgood agree to them being raised as Catholics. No, she just brought them secretly to the Presentation Convent on George's Hill, Dublin.

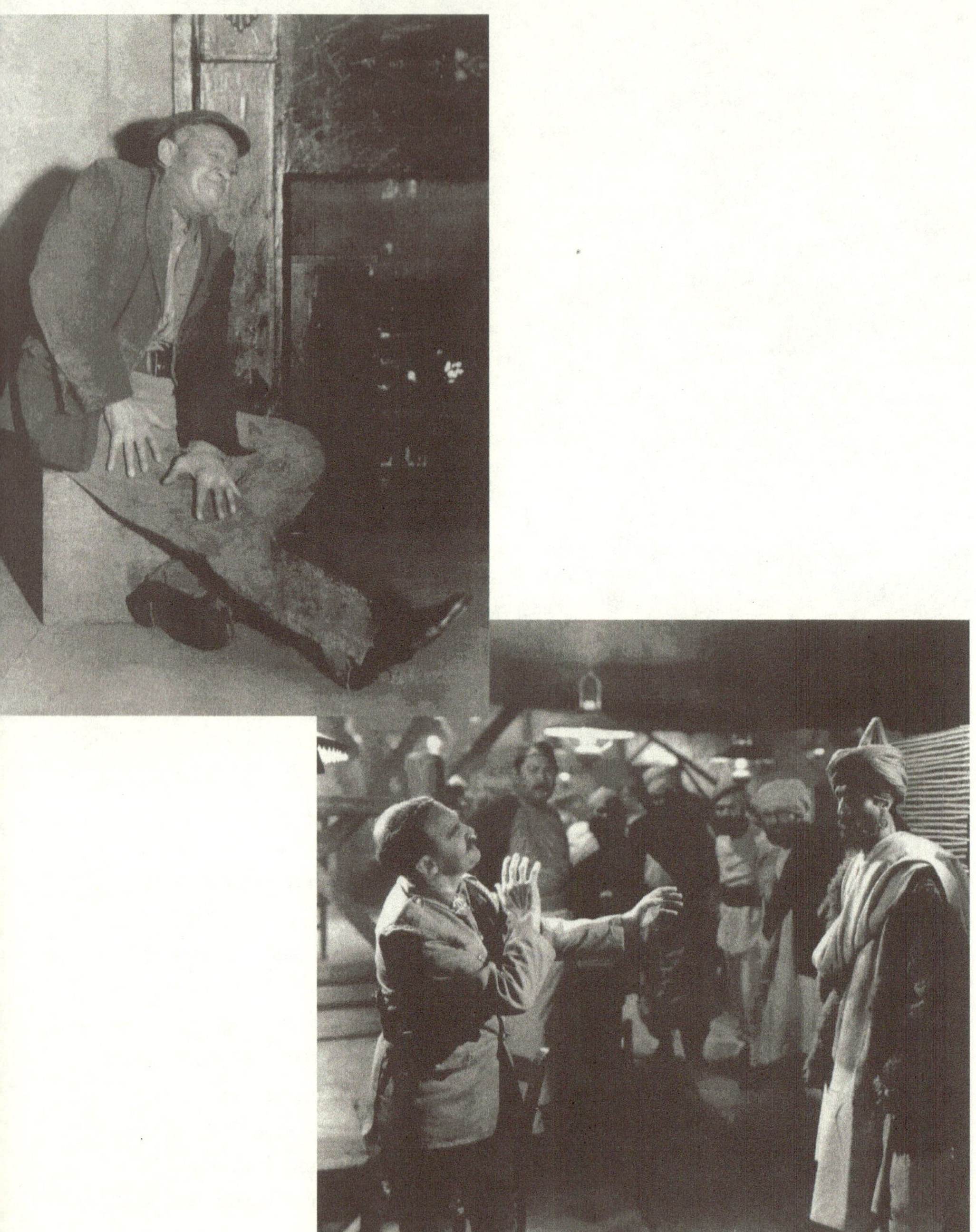

Top: *Barry Fitzgerald, as Captain Boyle in* Juno and the Paycock, *1936;* bottom: *in an encore performance as Fluther the barroom fighter from* Four Men and a Prayer, *1938. (Shields family papers)*

In a perhaps similar way, Sara Allgood as Beth Morgan does not agree with her husband on every matter, and she does not pretend to agree with him; but she does not fight him openly. While Gwilym Morgan wants his youngest son Huw to be able to box his corner, to make the grade at school, and to pursue one of the learned professions, instead of becoming a miner, Beth Morgan establishes a deep compact with him on another basis. Part of that compact is based on their love of the valley, in their love of the mining culture of their hometown where they live in a row of workers' houses, but most of all in their love of family and especially of its head, Gwilym Morgan, who may sometimes be wrong, but is certainly good at heart.

How this compact between mother and youngest son is forged has something to do with the plot. They go out together on that snowy night when Beth speaks up for her husband. On her return, she falls into an icy pond and Huw saves her. They survive, but spend the whole winter in their bedrooms, he downstairs, she upstairs, communicating by knocks of a stick on his floor which is her ceiling. Ultimately, that non-verbal compact between Beth and Huw Morgan is visually realized, as in a film it must be. The picture below tells the story, as Huw communes with his mother after the death of his father, Gwilym. Huw looks upon his mother, and sees her seeing into another world, her lost past, a retrospective attitude that will become his own as an adult.

Sara Allgood and Roddy McDowell in How Green Was My Valley, *1941. (Lilly Library)*

8

Sara Allgood was pleased with her 'wonderful eight weeks' on set with John Ford. It was not, in respect of Sara Allgood, wonderful for him, and she had no idea at the time it would be her last engagement with John Ford. Still, at the close of shooting, she got a seven-year contract from Darryl Zanuck with Twentieth Century Fox.[46] She gloried in her stardom. To celebrate, Una O'Connor took her out to dinner. Allgood could hardly contain her excitement; she was about to become very rich. By 28 October 1941, when *How Green Was My Valley* came out, Una O'Connor had been in Hollywood for ten years and had appeared in forty-three films; she knew the ropes.

'Sally,' she said, 'don't be too optimistic. Look again at your contract. I think you'll find that each year there is an "option clause".'[47] The studio had options but she did not: it was Twentieth Century Fox work or nothing. And as soon as one signed a contract, one went on a 'lay off' for twelve weeks, which meant no salary at all, unless one was cast in another Twentieth Century Fox film.

After five weeks Allgood did get called for a new Twentieth Century Fox project. Now as a contract player, she evidently felt herself to be even grander than she had before felt herself to be. However, she was in for a rude shock. In the 'Memories' that she tearfully and self-consolingly began to write during the unemployed hours at her disposal afterwards, she recalls the painful incident: 'What puzzles me is that no matter what the reputation and background an actor brings with him to Hollywood, one is put through the mill just as if one were a nonentity ... The director kept nagging me about the intonation of a certain line. I kept practising and practising, doing all I could to please him, but at the end of the second day I was dismissed ... I nearly had a nervous breakdown ... for I thought I was disgraced forever.'[48]

That was not, of course, the end of Sara Allgood's film career, though it may have been the end of her 'airs and graces' on Hollywood film sets. She was not nominated again for an Academy Award, but settled into regular work, at first for Twentieth Century Fox and later for other studios, twenty-six more films after *How Green Was My Valley*:

Roxie Hart (1942), Mrs Morton
This Above All (1942), Waitress in a Tea Room
It Happened in Flatbush (1942), Mrs 'Mac' McAvoy
The War Against Mrs Hadley (1942), Mrs Michael Fitzpatrick
Life Begins at Eight Thirty (1942), Robert's Aunt
City Without Men (1943), Maria Barton

Top: *Una O'Connor (photo by Otto Dyar, Fox Studios, date unknown);* bottom: *Una O'Connor as Ellen Bridges in* Cavalcade, *1933. (Fox Films Library, Academy of Motion Picture Arts and Sciences, Hollywood, California)*

Forever and a Day (1943), Cook
The Lodger (1944), Ellen
Jane Eyre (1944), Bessie
Between Two Worlds (1944), Mrs Midget
The Keys of the Kingdom (1944), Sister Martha
The Strange Affair of Uncle Harry (1945), Nona
Kitty (1945), Old Meg
The Spiral Staircase (1946), Nurse Baker
Cluny Brown (1946), Mrs Mailie
The Fabulous Dorseys (1947), Mrs Dorsey
Ivy (1947), Martha Huntley
Mother Wore Tights (1947), Grandmother McKinley
My Wild Irish Rose (1947), Mrs Brennan
Man from Texas (1948), Woman at wedding
One Touch of Venus (1948), Mrs Fogarty
The Girl from Manhattan (1948), Mrs Beeler
The Accused (1949), Mrs Conner
Challenge to Lassie (1949), Mrs MacFarland
Sierra (1949), Mrs Jonas
Cheaper by the Dozen (1950), Mrs Monahan

As a character actress, Allgood continued to suffer from what as an ex-star she felt to be lack of consideration by directors. At one point she was called in to replace Constance Collier in a bit part. Collier (1878–1955) was a tall, statuesque actress who had been a star on the London stage from 1901 to 1916. Oddly, like Sara Allgood, Constance Collier had lost her husband Julian L'Estrange, also an actor, in the 1918 influenza epidemic. With the arrival of the sound era, she became a leading voice coach in Hollywood (pupils included Eva LaGallienne and Marilyn Monroe), while continuing to take bit parts in films.

When Allgood arrived on the set to rehearse in place of Constance Collier, the director kept commanding her to relax her face, to 'unfreeze' her expression, as if she need not act at all. The direction confused Allgood. After three days she was dismissed, and went home crushed. The next day she found on returning to her apartment a gift of flowers and a letter of admiration from Constance Collier, a wise and articulate woman. That was a balm to the injured pride of the Irish actress. Allgood came to think of Los Angeles as the 'city of lost angels', a metropolis where the great actresses from the stages of the world wandered, well-paid but not decently respected.[49] Still, actresses of her own age and even greater past celebrity, former stars like Lilian Gish, Judith

Anderson and Ethel Barrymore, could not get roles on such a regular basis as Sara Allgood.[50] Admittedly, Allgood was given only a little to do in any one film, often a minute or less on screen, yet she did it well. Her ponderosity and gravity of voice made a vivid impression without stealing the scene.

The Strange Affair of Uncle Harry shows her later career to advantage. The story centres on the Quincys, once the most important family in a small town, who have lost their money in the Depression. Harry Quincy, a middle-aged bachelor, has two sisters, one of them a widow, the other a pretty hypochondriac who reads the poems of Edgar Allan Poe in a room crowded with houseplants. Harry designs flower patterns for napkins in the town's cloth factory. As the film begins, Harry has just painted his 6000th rosebud. Sara Allgood plays Nona, a servant who has practically become part of the family. Once a week she goes to the cowboy pictures with her suitor, a milkman, whom she will never marry. She and the two sisters fight over who is to be allowed to bake Harry's pies, serve Harry his dinners, give Harry womanly advice. The conflict in the story is introduced by Mrs Brown, a modern and pretty company executive from New York, who takes a shine to Harry, as he does to her, causing the hypochondriac sister to make endless mischief, and worse than mischief: the other sister winds up dead from a cup of poisoned cocoa.

Allgood does not have many lines, but she is responsible for creating the sense that the Quincys have lived a long time together, too long in fact, trapped in a series of set routines that are driving them all crazy. During one argument between the sisters, Nona intercedes, in Allgood's penetrating tones, 'I don't like what's going on here.' We understand that her words apply not just to the sisters' quarrel but to the whole sick way of life of small-town American pseudo-cultured Anglo-aristocrats. The moral appears to be that, whatever about the old times, people like the Quincys have no value in the new capitalist democracy.

The Strange Affair of Uncle Harry is not the only film of the 1940s in which Sara Allgood played a kitchen maid, the sort of role that her former Dublin admirers found to be a sad embarrassment for their Cathleen ni Houlihan. In *Jane Eyre, The Lodger* and other films she played a maid, but to her credit she did not play them all the same way; each is significantly individual.

Certainly, in a Hollywood film, where the romantic plot dominates and youth and beauty are the coin of the realm, a woman who is past the age of sixty, wide-faced and wide all around, cannot come within an ass's roar of getting a part as the female lead. This casting-by-appearance was less common in theatre, *a fortiori* in a repertory theatre with a small ensemble of players like the Abbey. There Sara Allgood, even though already short and round, could play the heroine Pegeen Mike in spite of the fact that physically she did not look the part of a Mayo publican's pretty daughter.[51]

She also easily suited roles as a tinker's daughter or a woman of the Sidhe; an old woman or a young girl; Emer, wife of Cuchulain; or Dervogilla, the Queen of Breffny. That was a key aspect of the art of acting that theatre audiences in Ireland enjoyed and still enjoy, the play-acting aspect, in which bodily endowments are shown to matter very little compared with power of imagination, and Allgood had imagination. Rather than just being pretty, she could capture through acute observation and with a certain interpretive exaggeration how a pretty woman behaves. Without being a queen, she could satisfyingly ape grandiosity. Yet in Hollywood where there was nearly an infinite supply of actors of all ages, shapes and sizes, it was common practice to cast not against type but true to it. Where a beautiful woman was required, one of the many glamour girls was called up from Central Casting, and plenty of them had acting ability and screen personality on top of their beauty.

In England and the United States, the main markets for Hollywood films of the 1940s, middle-class people did have live-in servants, and often those servants were Irish (though more often still they were African-American).[52] Films were often set in the present day, and pretended to provide a look at middle-class lives; these scenarios often enough had parts for a domestic. Furthermore, throughout the canon of novels and plays, there were roles for maids as gossips, know-it-alls and facilitators of the plot. Sara Allgood was good at getting all such parts and doing them well. Her own solitary status in life – decades away from any dating game – may have given her a certain sympathetic understanding of how to play one who is a close witness of, but not a participant in, matrimony. By playing maids, she made enough money to take a Hollywood flat off Santa Monica Boulevard and employ a maid herself.

In her second-to-last screen performance, *Cheaper by the Dozen* (1950), Allgood again plays a maid. The movie is a classic representation of post-war America, an X-ray of its sociology. In part, it is a biopic of Frank Gilbreth, a time-and-motion analyst, and thus the archetype of Taylorization, the scientifically efficient version of capitalism pioneered by United States corporations. It is also vividly representative of the place of fatherhood in the postwar period, when women, 'liberated' by their experience of doing men's jobs while the war continued, were plunged back into a family role. Frank Gilbreth (Edward Buchanan) has twelve children (thus the title), all but one of whom are girls, and he struggles in a mildly choleric way to impose a business-like efficiency on his large brood of females, to the tolerant, affectionate reaction of his wife (Myrna Loy) and daughters, who enter gamely into his schemes (even the wholesale removal of tonsils in a single day) but genially ignore his patriarchal commands about resisting fashion and pop-culture.

Sara Allgood does not have a big role. She has one line towards the start, and that line is not significant. Just as the family heads off packed into a car toward their new home in New Jersey, Allgood says, 'Have a nice trip. We'll see you Friday morning' – nothing at all for an actress to work with. She has a second moment on screen bringing in the dishes to the family dinner in the new home just as Frank Gilbreth has learned that his proposal to give a scientific paper in Europe may not be accepted, but there is again no chance for her to do anything telling. Her final appearance on camera is after Frank Gilbreth has died of a heart attack, just before he was to give the scholarly paper that might have vindicated his theories. The children are crying on the front steps of the family home. Sara Allgood is comforting the little boy. He looks up to say, 'Our daddy's dead.' The death of the father was an event frequent in families of the world in the 1940s, when sixty-two million died in war alone. But after daddy dies, Mrs Gilbreth gives his lecture for him and goes on to become a leading industrial engineer in her own right; in 1948, she was America's Woman of Year. While Sara Allgood has little to say or do in *Cheaper by the Dozen*, her mere presence as female family stalwart is significant. It evokes Juno Boyle, and her astonishing line that a child who has no father may still have what is better, two mothers.

When during the 1940s Sara Allgood wrote letters to friends in Dublin, or when she recorded her memories, she was inclined to look upon the days in the past as her glory days, and to say, 'O I wish I was on the Abbey stage again.'[53] She had, in fact, been saying just that since 1914, when she was working with the Liverpool Repertory Company; she said it when she was in Australia; she said it when she was a star of London's West End. She had become 'hardened', she said, by doing bit parts in Hollywood studio pictures. Yet it paid well and placed her on a common footing with the greatest actors in the world. There is every sign that Sara Allgood liked it in the United States. She had her hotel apartment at 1015 Larrabee Street in Hollywood, just east of Beverly Hills, between Santa Monica and San Vincente boulevards, overlooking the valley, and only a short distance from the homes of Barry Fitzgerald and Arthur Shields, whom, along with Una O'Connor, she saw regularly. A sister of the Shields brothers moved into the same district, along with her family. This area was a little Dublin within Hollywood. Sara Allgood became the godmother of

Christine, daughter of Aideen and Arthur Shields, born on 16 October 1946. Five years after she settled in Los Angeles, and after the war had ended, when she could easily have returned to Dublin, Sara Allgood took US citizenship.

V

IRISH HOLLYWOOD IN THE 1940S

Previous page: *Barry Fitzgerald as a seaman (1944), a role he played in* Juno and the Paycock, The Long Voyage Home, The Sea Wolf, The Amazing Mrs Holliday *and* Corvette 225. *(Shields family papers)*

When English novelist Evelyn Waugh and his companion arrived in Hollywood in 1947, he recorded his impressions of the city in a diary:

> Arrived at Pasadena at 9 am and were met by a car from MGM. We drove for a long time down autobahns and boulevards full of vacant lots and filling stations and nondescript buildings and palm trees with a warm, hazy light. It was more like Egypt – the suburbs of Cairo or Alexandria – than anything in Europe. We arrived at the Bel Air Hotel – very Egyptian with a hint of Addis Ababa in the smell of the blue gums.[1]

This passage touches upon several of the paradoxes of 'LA'. It was a rapidly growing metropolis (the population of Los Angeles County increased from 3 million to 4.7 million between 1940 and 1950) but also had spacious vacancies and dilapidated structures between its newly rude erections and monuments of opulence. It offered the citizen a surfeit of broad speedways to go by private car from place to place, but few self-sufficient places in which one could simply dwell or walk about (it is a city often without sidewalks). Waugh's comparison with Cairo is triggered by more than the arid climate, the palms and the collocation of the squalid and the grand. Los Angeles is exotic to a European in a way other US cities are not.

But it is a Cairo without the Egyptians. The nineteenth-century population of Indians, settlers of Spanish descent, gold-miners and ranchers had been rapidly increased by surges of African-Americans from the former slave states, Chinese workers (not yet Korean ones), Okie homesteaders from the Dustbowl disaster, the extraterritorial population of Mexico, and, in Hollywood, Beverly Hills and Santa Monica, immigrants of genius from Germany, France, Britain, Scandinavia and Ireland. In March 1941 the *New York Times* estimated that up to 25,000 refugees from the war in Europe had already arrived in LA.[2] In the 1940s its residents included four of the greatest writers of the century: Bertholt Brecht, Thomas Mann, William Faulkner and F. Scott Fitzgerald. However, as Fitzgerald observed, in the screenwriting combines of the big studios, the better men were soon 'weeded out from the needs of speed, with the emphasis as in a mining camp on the lower virtues'.[3] One looks in vain for any great movies developed mainly from the scripts by any one of these geniuses.

In order to milk the talent, studios employed contracts that were at once liberal and tight-fisted. Even as the money poured in and the product poured out, the artists did not feel secure. If they were actors, they could not as in a theatre measure while they worked the subtle signs of audience appreciation. If they were writers, their work was not professionally assessed as it would be in the case of a book review. The star, the studio, the director, or the story might be spotlighted by movie critics, but almost never the work of the writers who invented the story and the words. The successful in Hollywood, James Mason lamented, are 'scared and mistrustful of an achievement for which they cannot confidently take much of the credit'.[4] Even to the nostrils of a Hollywood prince like Budd Schulberg, 'The smell of fear mingled with the scent of orange blossoms.'[5] You may have been a Nobel Prize-winning novelist, star of the London stage, or, like Schulberg, the son of a producer, but once in Hollywood, as writer J.B. Priestley put it, you were 'wrecked on an island that does nothing but make films … you must get into films, stay in films, or perish'.[6]

During World War II, Los Angeles was the manufacturing hub of American world-domination: the aviation and shipbuilding industries and the film industry. The (Henry) Fordist organizational supremacy of the first also characterized the second. Movie-making was a factory business and the artists – no matter how superior their genius – were assembly-line workers, not bosses.

2

If LA looked like Cairo to Evelyn Waugh, it can hardly have appeared less exotic to the Abbey actors. They arrived from Dublin, a wet, grey, low-rise, undynamic city in 1940. The Shields brothers did not record their impressions of Hollywood and its architecture, but one must try to picture them in that setting. Laid down over the original Spanish mission and ranchero styles of Los Angeles and their endless recent architectural echoes at the bungalow level were buildings of a bizarre whimsicality. The principal restaurant – the Brown Derby – actually was in the shape of a brown derby. Up in the foothills were the outdoor Greek theatre and the Hollywood Bowl, a vast, upturned, cement earphone for outdoor concerts. The picture palace used for major studio releases was Graumann's Chinese Theatre, an inexplicable cultural reference, because there were no picture palaces in China in 1940. The silly, stupendous eclecticism of the city was astonishing.

Arthur Shields and Barry Fitzgerald found their way to a cosy little neighbourhood just north of Sunset Boulevard, about two and half miles east of Sara Allgood's apartment. Fitzgerald lived at 1734 North Gardner Street in an Arts and Crafts style seven-room bungalow, perched on a rise above the wooded quiet street. Two blocks down the hill and one block over at 1535 North Sierra Bonita Avenue was the house where Arthur Shields and Aideen O'Connor eventually settled.[7] The Sierra Bonita house was similar in style to Fitzgerald's: clapboard-sided; among its windows, several had leaded glass; there was a veranda on two sides. An Anglican church between the two houses gave a centre to the little community. Three miles to the west of this neighbourhood was Beverly Hills and the sight-seeing splendours of the mansions of the stars. South down the hill into the valley were the Hollywood studios; the production lots of Studio City were over the mountain to the north. It was an easy commute to work in either direction.

The climate of southern California proved a shock to the Irish. The heat made Barry Fitzgerald feel lazy, and he liked that. It had the same effect on Arthur Shields, but he hated it. So did Aideen O'Connor; to her the September heat was actually 'sickening'.[8] While at Christmas-time the Shields family could afford a turkey, English plum pudding and all the fixings, the sunshine still blazing away outdoors made the holiday seem unnatural.

The health of Arthur Shields had been broken by his collapse from tuberculosis at the time of the Broadway failure of *Kindred* and the sudden mounting of *Juno and the Paycock*. He continued to require weekly treatments for his lungs. Easily tired, he chose for pastimes stamp-collecting and reading. In books, his interests were Irish authors and scholarship on the Irish Literary Revival. Mostly what he had on his mind were Aideen O'Connor and his son Adam.

Aideen had been able to take a part in the January 1940 Broadway production of *Juno and the Paycock*. After *Juno* closed, she was cast in another New York play in April 1940. However, once rehearsals had gotten underway, Equity (the actors' union) pressured Aideen to leave the show unpaid.[9] The citizenship bar to the pursuit of her career proved an irremovable obstacle. While the rights of residency and of work were arranged for Arthur Shields by Twentieth Century Fox, Aideen could not share in those rights because the two were not married. Furthermore, they could not be married, divorce being illegal in Ireland.

Misfortune seemed to dog Aideen in Los Angeles. She had to have an appendectomy in October 1940. In June 1940 she had begun the tedious process of preparing the documentation to enter the USA under the quota system for Irish immigrants. Finally, on 8 January 1942, she left the USA for Vancouver, and then crossed back into the country with the right of residency for five years under the quota system.[10] She then got a bit part in *Gentleman Jim* (uncredited, Warner Brothers, 25 May 1942), but her non-naturalized status remained an impediment to obtaining employment.[11] In her idle hours, Aideen followed the war carefully through newspapers, both American and Irish ones. The Irish policy of neutrality distressed her, especially de Valera's refusal to allow the Allies to use Irish ports. She volunteered for Red Cross work in Los Angeles, but it did not seem that there was anything she could do even in that line. At some point she began to drink.

Because of the war, Arthur Shields could do nothing for Adam except to send money to Bazie Shields. On 24 October 1943 Bazie died. Arthur Shields and Aideen O'Connor were married seventeen days later, on 10 November 1943. Owing to attacks on Allied shipping, there was still no way to bring Adam to Hollywood. He was looked after in Dublin by his legal guardian under Bazie's will, her brother Guy Mehigan. With no little Mehigans as companions for Adam, Guy found the motherless, unfathered 13-year-old boy difficult to manage. Adam mitched from Belvedere College and then destroyed the teachers' letters home concerning his truancy. After he was caught and suspended, the head prefect offered Adam an opportunity to return to Belvedere provided he accept punishment. Adam declined the offer.

So Guy Mehigan took him to Arthur Shields's sister's home, and left him there.[12] Marie 'Bid' Shields Mortished, who had children the boy's age, looked after Adam from June 1945 until the summer of 1946. At that time, Barry Fitzgerald, returning like a hero to Ireland after his Oscar-winning performance in *Going My Way*, collected the boy and brought him back to Hollywood. By then, Aideen was pregnant, and Mr and Mrs Shields were settled into

1535 North Sierra Bonita Avenue. Adam joined the family at last and entered Hollywood High School. The following month, on 16 October 1946, Aideen gave birth prematurely to a little girl, Christine Frances Shields.

In November 1946 'Bid' Shields Mortished and her daughter Una came to Hollywood. In March 1949 Una married a Chicago-born actor and former prize-fighter, Nate Slott.[13] He had created a radio programme based on a 'salty, rascally, warm-hearted Judge Fitz', a part Barry Fitzgerald took over in 1945.[14] Slott went on to a career as an assistant director on films such as *The Big Knife* (1955; written by Clifford Odets, directed by Robert Aldrich). The Slotts lived five blocks east of the Shields brothers, also just off Sunset Boulevard, at 1530 Formosa Avenue. They had two daughters, Susan (now Stoddard) and Judy (now Lunny).

Barry Fitzgerald never cooked; he dined with his brother and Aideen three or four times a week, sometimes with the Slotts, and the rest of the time at restaurants. His pleasure was to cruise the Californian motorways on his big motorcyle, eventually buying a weekend house up the coast in the hills of Santa Barbara. He played golf badly but with satisfaction.[15] Early in his residence in Los Angeles he took in a roommate, Angus Taillon (1888–1953). Taillon was Fitzgerald's stand-in on film sets from 1938. He was a full-blooded Iroquois, born in Ontario, Canada.[16] He had been married in Reno, Nevada, to a woman named Daisy; they had one child. In 1920 Daisy sued Angus Taillon for divorce on the grounds of desertion and failure to provide for the child.[17]

In Hollywood Taillon occasionally got non-speaking parts in films – Renoir's *This Land is Mine* (1943), *The Brighton Strangler* (1945), *OSS* (1946), *Top o' the Morning* (1949) and others. In 1950 Barry Fitzgerald and Angus Taillon collaborated on the story for a melodrama with a Mexican setting.[18] Not much else is known about Taillon or his friendship with Barry Fitzgerald. On 8 May 1953, Barry Fitzgerald returned to 1734 North Gardner Street from a holiday at his Santa Barbara house. In the back garden he found his long-time companion slumped dead in a chair, a bag of groceries scattered at his feet. Taillon, sixty-five years old, had been dead for two or three days, of natural causes, according to police.[19]

3

After *The Long Voyage Home* (1940) and *San Francisco Docks* (1941), Barry Fitzgerald was cast a third time as a seaman – 'Cooky' in the Warner Brothers production of *The Sea Wolf*, from a Jack London story, starring Edward G.

Robinson, and directed by Michael Curtiz (who the following year would make *Casablanca*). Like Fitzgerald's character in *The Long Voyage Home*, 'Cooky' is a nasty, tattling, cackling piece of work, nothing at all like Fluther Good in *The Plough and the Stars* and with faults not laughable like those of Captain Boyle in *Juno and the Paycock*. The keynote of Fitzgerald's portrayal is an annoying glee at the misfortunes of others.

While more exciting and dramatic than *The Long Voyage Home*, *The Sea Wolf* is an equally literary film. The main character is 'Wolf' Larsen, a pirate and seal-hunter, whose sailing ship, *The Ghost*, works between Japan and San Francisco. Larsen's library in his ship's cabin is stocked with books by Nietzsche, Darwin, Schopenhauer, Herbert Spencer and Milton. He quotes with approval Satan's lines in *Paradise Lost*: 'Better to reign in Hell than serve in Heaven!' Only the Nietzschean will to power matters to Wolf; he bullies everyone, except for his brother, Death Larsen. The brother never appears on screen, but, sailing in the same Pacific waters, Death Larsen hunts Wolf from an iron freighter mounted with cannon. The allusions to great literature and the allegorical plot are, as any summary makes obvious, crude and unconvincing, but the acting is so good it carries viewers along.

As the movie begins, Larsen is looking for a crew in the bars of San Francisco, but the old salts know the reputation of *The Ghost*: 'No man survives a ship like that,' one warns. So, using drugs, drink and a billy club, Larsen shanghais a crew for his next voyage. As the new recruits are rowed out half-conscious from the dock to the ship, Cooky (Barry Fitzgerald) cackles drunkenly, 'One thing you'll pray for above all – to tear out of your heart the cold merciless fingers of Wolf Larsen,' and then he laughs and laughs, until the first mate shuts him up with a punch.

A man (John Garfield, handsome) and a woman (Ida Lupino, beautiful), though not a couple, yet, are the only two on the deck of a ferryboat moving through the foggy bay. He is reading a book; she is looking around nervously. When two detectives arrive in obvious search of someone, the woman runs to the man and begs him to pretend to be her companion if anyone asks questions. Initially, he covers for her, but when told by the detectives it is a crime to harbour a fugitive, he gives her up. Before she can be taken prisoner, the ferry crashes into an iron steamer and sinks. The man who had been reading – Van Weyden is his name – saves the fugitive woman (Ruth Webster is hers) from drowning. Then out of the fog appears *The Ghost* and the couple are pulled from the sea.

The next morning the first mate of *The Ghost* is dying of wounds from a fight. Van Weyden and Ruth Webster are forced to come along on the seal-hunting expedition, and work their passage; all hands are needed. The girl's job will be to keep the captain company; Van Weyden is sent to the kitchen as potboy. Cooky so annoys the gentle Van Weyden that they ultimately get in a knife fight. Cooky finds the manuscript Van Weyden has been working on and reads from it with dripping sarcasm. The book is a righteous descriptive denunciation of the captain and crew of *The Ghost.* Cooky declares with slimy pomposity: 'It's my duty to turn the [pages] over to the authorities' – Wolf Larsen.

Larsen, however, proves happy to find that he has a novelist on board. He has always wanted to be the subject of a book. 'You write very well' is his judicious assessment. Then, speculatively, he adds, 'I wonder what you'll be like when the voyage is over,' and unpredicatably punches Van Weyden in the stomach, just to make him a better author, because, to Larsen's mind, Van Weyden is soft, like a woman, spoiled by his rich parents; he has no sense of reality. He cannot yet understand what it is to be the child of peasants of the sea, plunged into the struggle for survival. Now Larsen has triumphed. He has a ship where, he boasts, 'my will and my will alone rules'.

Van Weyden later finds an answer to the Captain's defence of the will to power. In his novel, he explains to Wolf Larsen, the supposedly self-sufficient captain will be represented as a complex man who wants to protect his inner dignity, but he can only do that by retreating to a world where he is surrounded by inferiors. Afraid to expose his ego in a world where he might meet his equal, Larsen feeds his sense of superiority by degradation of his dependants.

Larsen is indeed a genius of degradation. He so humiliates the ship's doctor that the man climbs the mast and throws himself to his death. He beats senseless the one shanghaied sailor who had the nerve to show some self-respect. His betrayal of Cooky is premeditatedly brutal. After Cooky has revealed the sailors' plan to mutiny, Wolf Larsen calls everyone on deck, explains that he knows all about their plot, and then, to win their favour, gives the sailors free liquor. Next, astonishingly, he orders them then to keelhaul Cooky for being an informer. The crew laugh and laugh while Cooky is dragged behind the ship; then a shark appears. By the time they are able to drag him back on deck, Cooky has one leg less. But Cooky is not finished yet. He comes to notice that the captain suffers from spells of dizziness, and during those spells, falls blind. Wolf Larsen has such an attack just when his brother, Death Larsen, has located *The Ghost* and fired upon it with cannon. As Larsen stumbles on deck, Cooky cries out with glee: 'He's blind, I tell you, blind!' and trips him up, laughing and laughing.

By the end of the picture, the novelist and the woman alone are saved from the sinking ship, but *The Sea Wolf* remains the story of a wonderfully evil man. Edward G. Robinson (a committed liberal) plays Wolf Larsen as a 'Nazi in everything but name', and Barry Fitzgerald's Cooky is a deliberately undignified projection of the captain's immoralism. [20] He is like a wholly corrupted colonial lackey who extends the evil of the nasty imperialist.

4

The Sea Wolf proved that Barry Fitzgerald could be something in addition to lovable. With his next good part he was again put into the role of an old sea dog, 'Timothy Blake' in *The Amazing Mrs Holliday.* Timothy has been the first mate for thirty-one years of a San Francisco millionaire, Commodore Holliday. Fitzgerald received his highest billing thus far in Hollywood – third in the cast list – but effectively *The Amazing Mrs Holliday* is a vehicle for Deanna Durbin (b. 1921), one of the biggest-grossing movie-stars of the period. A child star in the body of a young woman, Deanna Durbin had a wide-eyed, innocent personality of a kind no longer in vogue, yet it once had the greatest charm. Not absolutely beautiful in appearance, short-legged and with the cheeks of a chipmunk, she had a lovely singing voice and radiated a sunny nature. Deanna Durbin plays Ruth, the daughter of missionaries who has been adopting war orphans in China. On her way back with her brood to the USA, Ruth was promised protection by Commodore Holliday, but the ship sinks, and the captain has evidently gone down with it.

As the movie begins, Ruth is trying to pass her eight orphans through immigration. She is having no luck, so 'Timothy' (Barry Fitzgerald) steps up to handle the matter. Fitzgerald projects great dignity and a bit of sternness throughout as the Captain's Chief Mate. The two are told by the immigration officials that they must find someone to post a $500-bond for each of the children. Timothy takes Ruth off to meet Commodore Holliday's family.

They prove to be stuffy, rich, Anglo people. No, they could not put $4000 in escrow to save eight children – because of the war, taxes have gone up. Their refusal sets up Barry Fitzgerald's great scene. Sad yet indignant, he contrives a piece of cleverness which drives the whole plot: 'Thirty-one years I served [the Commodore], thirty-one years, but I never thought to see the day they'd turn out his widow and children.' Widow and children! With that combination of moral righteousness, human condescension and outright lying, the story is sprung. Ruth does not catch on immediately, but soon, delicately, in a friendly and fatherly way, Timothy explains that she now must play the part of the

Commodore's widow; that is the only way to save the children. The Hollidays have no way to disprove the claim of a shipboard wedding, and Ruth goes in a moment from a benevolent pauper to a millionaire widow.

This is Hollywood and a comedy, so in the heel of the hunt, Durbin marries the Commodore's son and the Commodore astonishingly reappears at a ball. Deanna Durbin sings a song, all is made right, and it ends with a kiss. Barry Fitzgerald's function is to be Providence's ghostwriter, who works in His Own Way. Barry Fitzgerald had great range as an actor – one had to, as a member of the Abbey repertory. But how did writer-director Leo McCarey get the idea he was able for a co-starring role with Bing Crosby in *Going My Way*? Perhaps he saw *The Amazing Mrs Holliday.*

5

In *Going My Way* Barry Fitzgerald was billed second, behind Bing Crosby in the lead. In 1943 Bing Crosby was the top draw among movie actors. For *Going My Way* Paramount paid Crosby $150,000 and Barry Fitzgerald $8750 (still a good fee for four weeks' work: $102,000 in current money). Fitzgerald's steady approach toward top billing was the result of a growing reputation as a 'scene-stealer'. Actually, this term is misapplied to his acting. Correctly used, 'scene-stealer' is a term of criticism for an actor of talent and egotism who appropriates more than his fair share of attention and thus distracts the audience from the central action. What Barry Fitzgerald did was to shine in small parts, doing what he was supposed to do extremely well. The audience awakened to delight when he appeared on screen because of the acute and often humorous depiction of individual manners. Robert Browning fittingly describes the value of art – he is talking of painting, but the lesson applies as well to the art of acting:

> ... [W]e're made so that we love
> First when we see them painted, things we have passed
> Perhaps a hundred times nor cared to see;
> And so they are better, painted – better to us,
> Which is the same thing. Art was given for that;
> God uses us to help each other so,
> Lending our minds out.[21]

Fitzgerald did not steal scenes; he 'lent his mind out' by means of the depiction of human character. Characters are illuminated from within by his enactments, and we recognize as if for the first time features of human behaviour we had seen a hundred times before, and not bothered to notice. But whether or not he could carry a whole story from beginning to end, and provoke movie-goers to identify with him in the vicissitudes of his experience, was a thing unknown.

The movie was Leo McCarey's project. He wrote it; he promoted it to Paramount; he helped finance it by foregoing his director's fee in favour of a percentage of profits; he cast it; he directed it; and he completed it under its $1,050,000 budget.[22] McCarey (1898–1969), the son of a California boxing promoter, was an Irish Catholic, and very sentimental about things Irish and Catholic.[23] He had been directing movies since he was twenty-three years old. He had directed the Marx Brothers in *Duck Soup* (1933) and Cary Grant in *The Awful Truth* (1937) – McCarey suspected that Grant had copied McCarey's off-screen, debonair mannerisms in crafting his own star persona.

The idea for the picture was a contrast between two types of Irish priest, both affectionately observed – the crusty old conservative priest born in Ireland, Father Fitzgibbon, played by Barry Fitzgerald, and the modern, liberal, college-educated Irish-American clergyman, Father O'Malley, played by Bing Crosby – effectively, the contrast between Irish-born immigrants and Irish-Americans. The young priest has been sent by the Bishop to rescue an impoverished New York parish church run by the old priest.

Bing Crosby's Father O'Malley is a miracle-working populist. He does not preach; instead, he plays the piano, baseball and golf. By means of his fluent charm, he organizes the local gang of juvenile delinquents into a boys' choir, and writes a hit song for them to sing, sales of which replenish the church funds. The plot is so far-fetched, it is a wonder that the two actors are able to hold the movie together and give it emotional power.

Part of the interest of the movie is that, granted that it is McCarey's defence of Catholicism to America, it is also his well-intentioned critique of the Catholic clergy. McCarey said his favourite description of the movie was 'gently disrespectful'.[24] If American Catholicism was characterized at the time by the authoritarianism of the clergy and virtuous submission of the parishioners, an emphasis on guilt, belief in modern miracles, and rite rather than reason, then Bing Crosby's Father O'Malley is hardly typical of the Church.[25] Instead, he is an argument by example that Roman Catholic clergy should catch up with American Catholic laymen and embrace modernity. In his straw boater and priest's collar, or in his baseball uniform, Father O'Malley is McCarey's portrait of what priests ought to be in the future, not what they are already. His

Barry Fitzgerald (left) as Father Fitzgibbon and Bing Crosby as Father O'Malley in Going My Way, *1943. (Corbis)*

easygoing pastor is a good entertainer (the best crooner in the world in 1943), a clever businessman, a friend to old and young alike, sympathetic to lovers (and helpful in regularizing their situation), fond of contemporary popular culture, as American as apple pie, and attractive to women – not homosexual, not at all.

One can measure the aggressive novelty of McCarey's priest by the censors' reaction to the script. Joe Breen of the Production Code Administration asked the director to contact Father Devlin, the technical advisor appointed by the Archbishop of Los Angeles to consult on all movies bearing upon Catholicism.[26] Breen himself thought Father O'Malley undignified in speech and conduct. Once consulted, Father Devlin took the same view. He disapproved of Father O'Malley introducing himself as 'Chuck, to my friends.' Father Fitzgibbon should not, the Church's 'technical advisor' explained, give the impression that he asks his housekeeper for advice. The whole subject of relations between priests and their housekeepers required very sensitive treatment. The Bishop should not serve sherry in his office; he would never keep a bottle there. Father Fitzgibbon should not appear to be peddling raffle tickets to increase church funds, because Catholics are 'sometimes accused of resorting to gambling as a device to bolster Church finances'.[27] The Church's 'technical advisor' found offensive, in other words, the very elements of humanization of the clergy that were McCarey's theme. McCarey, however, was well equipped with the Irish charm called *plámás* – Sure, Father, whatever you say, I'm a Catholic myself, don't you know, and would never do anything to bring the clergy into disrepute, just the opposite, you can rest assured – and so went suavely on about his business just as already planned.

Barry Fitzgerald's problem was to play the foil to all-virtuous Father O'Malley without losing the audience's sympathy. A principal way in which he solved that problem was to portray Father Fitzgibbon as not so much a priest as just an old man. Film critic James Agee thought Fitzgerald's was 'the finest, funniest, and most touching portrayal of old age that has yet reached the screen'.[28] He is not an authoritarian, just a crotchety old man, kind at heart, and with a right to his irritability.

When Father O'Malley makes his first appearance at St Dominic's, he is dressed in the sports gear of the St Louis Browns baseball team. Father Fitzgibbon cannot restrain his astonishment at the shape of the man he's been sent as an assistant: 'Even the Archbishop wouldn't do a thing like this to me!' (There is obviously a history with the Archbishop.) Trying to ingratiate himself, Father 'Chuck' attempts to light the old priest's pipe, and fails, knocking things over. 'Young man,' Fitzgibbon regretfully declares, 'you're off to a very bad start.' He does not yet know that Father O'Malley is not a trainee, but already the manager in charge of the parish. Again and again he is provoked to ask of the younger man, 'How did you ever become a priest?' He is nothing like what he ought to be, in the old man's view, while to the audience Bing Crosby is a dreamboat clergyman.

Barry Fitzgerald could do more than brighten a scene; he could also carry the story. This is illustrated in his performance after Father Fitzgibbon has made a trip to the Archbishop's office in an effort to have Father O'Malley transferred. Barry Fitzgerald returns home obviously crestfallen. He asks Father O'Malley to step into the study by the fire. Barry Fitzgerald settles into the armchair; O'Malley stands, pensive, worried.

'I went to the Bishop … to have you transferred.'

'Sorry you dislike me.'

'I don't dislike anyone; I just disagree with you. The Bishop said you were capable, progressive. He even told me you two had a nice talk before you reported to me. He didn't tell me what was said.'

And here Fitzgerald managed a wonderful change of register, into something wise, hurt and heartfelt: 'He didn't tell me what was said. He didn't have to. The Bishop is a kind man, and would not want to hurt anyone.' Father

Fitzgibbon remains in the easy chair, his hands together, their fingers interlaced. 'The Bishop wouldn't hurt anyone. I put him at his ease. "Bishop," I said, "what is on your mind is exactly what's on mine. I want you to put Father O'Malley in charge of St Dominic's." '

Wincing, Father O'Malley says, 'Why can't we go on as we are?'

'No,' replied Father Fitzgibbon. He would rather live in reality, not in an old man's dreamworld. 'Is there anything you'd like me to do?'

'No, Father,' O'Malley indicated, and by replying signalled his implicit acceptance that he was himself now outright master of the parish.

Father Fitzgibbon then ends the conversation: 'Then I think I'll go lie down.'

By emphasizing so gently and wisely, with the raising of one shaggy eyebrow a half-inch higher than the other, the Bishop's tact, the Bishop's kindness, and the Bishop's desire not to hurt anyone, Barry Fitzgerald revealed Father Fitzgibbon's own tact, kindness and gentleness. While Father O'Malley originally came on as the one whose superior training and modern ways would handle the old priest, who would never be the wiser, Father Fitzgibbon is shown to be not foolish at all. He sees what the situation is, and he accepts it, though he is terribly hurt by the change and now feels useless, and old as well, in need, at present, of a nap.

O'Malley makes the mistake of running away on a wet night and must come back to the worried household, wet, bedraggled and shamefaced. The two priests make peace over a whiskey in Father Fitzgibbon's bedroom. They toast their mothers, and by request, Bing Crosby sings a lullaby that Father Fitzgibbon's mother used to sing, 'Toora Loora Loora', while the old man sinks off apparently to sleep. It is a sentimental song capping an extremely sentimental scene. But at the last moment, when the clever, condescending Father O'Malley is turning out the light, Father Fitzgibbon opens his eyes to say 'Goodnight'. It is yet another sign he is not so silly an old man as one might think, and the Bing Crosby character is not quite as slick and smooth as he believes himself to be.

In fact, over the course of the whole movie, in which a huge star was matched with an actor who had only played small parts in films, it is Barry Fitzgerald who becomes the central emotional pole of the drama. Bing Crosby just plays off him, in a charming and smooth but on reflection quite shallow way. *Life* magazine called Fitzgerald's performance 'one of the half-dozen finer things in fifty years of motion pictures'. John Ford wrote that the scenes between Crosby and Fitzgerald 'were the most beautiful I have seen on the screen'.[29] Movie critics recognized Barry Fitzgerald's achievement by taking the unique step of nominating him for Oscars in two categories: Best Actor in a Leading Role and Best Supporting Actor. He won the Supporting Actor award, while Crosby took the Oscar for Best Actor in a Leading Role, itself a testament to the work of the supporting actor – no upstaging or scene-stealing here.

Sara Allgood had been nominated for an Academy Award for her supporting role in *How Green Was My Valley*, but for an Abbey Theatre regular to win an Oscar in the golden age of Hollywood was a great thing.

In fact, it was a great day for Catholics the world over. The vice-president of Notre Dame University wrote Leo McCarey, 'I can hardly express to you the appreciation I feel as a Catholic priest.'[30] Even the Pope had his favourite scene in the movie – the toasting of the mothers and singing of 'Toora Loora Loora'.[31] When Barry Fitzgerald's plane landed at Shannon in June 1946 there was a crowd of priests waiting to greet him. He was on that day the most popular Protestant in Ireland, so popular it was forgotten that he was a Protestant.

Going My Way was a strange kind of war movie. It is reminiscent of a famous episode of John Cleese's *Fawlty Towers*, in which, since there are German guests in the English seaside hotel, the line 'Don't mention the war!' is used again and again, and thus the war is again and again mentioned, to the consternation of the foreign guests. But in *Going My Way*, there is, in contrast, no word of the war at all. There did not have to be. It was understood by viewers of 1944 that so many men had been drafted, few who were not either very young or very old were left behind to carry on with life – just priests, farmers, doctors and Irishmen, for Ireland stood aside in World War II. To judge by the story of *Going My Way*, home was safe for the time being in the hands of priests and Irishmen.

6

In March 1944, while the praise was first flooding in for his performance in *Going My Way*, Barry Fitzgerald was on set working in a superior film that never got its proper praise. *None but the Lonely Heart* was developed by Clifford Odets from a story by Richard Llewellyn (the author of *How Green Was My Valley*). Cary Grant had heard about the story, and liked it.[32] Once he had seen Clifford Odets's script the star was sold. It represented the life he had lived as a young man, as opposed to the life of 'Cary Grant', an imaginary identity he sustained in Hollywood. 'I was usually cast as a well-dressed, sophisticated chap ... This time I was an embittered cockney. In many ways, the part seemed to fit my nature better than the light-hearted fellows I was used to playing.'[33] In Pauline Kael's brilliant phrase, Cary Grant plays the part of Ernie Mott with 'an almost stricken look, a memory of suffering'.[34]

Odets was accustomed to working on stage, and had never directed a movie, but Cary Grant insisted on his taking over *None but the Lonely Heart.* The script is, to a literary taste, brilliant – dialogue, like that of Beckett or Pinter, with the pulse and fingerprint of its author. Barry Fitzgerald plays Henry Twite, a little old man who happens upon the hero, Ernie Mott, at the Tomb of the Unknown Warrior in London:

> Twite [looking at the statue]: Might be my son.
> Mott: Might be my old man.
> Twite: Might.
> Narrator: Ernie Mott didn't know he might become the unknown warrior of another era. This is the story of Ernie Mott who searched for a free, beautiful, a *noble* life in the second quarter of the 20th century.

When one reads a script like that, the high aspiration of mid-twentieth-century movies takes one's breath away. Their cultural ambition has been largely abandoned.

Jane Wyatt and Ethel Barrymore are splendid in supporting roles as the sexually warm, all-forgiving girlfriend and the cross, cancer-afflicted mother. Cary Grant shows things – the old circus actor he had been, the rogue he was – that he rarely shows elsewhere to the same extent. Barry Fitzgerald's part is small. Good, but small. He plays a short guardian angel to tall Cary Grant's heart-of-gold, ne'er-do-well charmer. The part does not give him much to do except project wisdom, friendliness and significance without a lot of accompanying dialogue. He accomplishes this miracle with grace. Grant was nominated, properly, for Best Actor, but was beaten for the Oscar by Bing Crosby for his silky performance in *Going My Way. None but the Lonely Heart* lost money, and that was the end of Cary Grant's roles as an over-sexed, rebellious, politicized Cockney.

7

In 1946 and 1947 Barry Fitzgerald made three films with Irish-Australian writer-director John Farrow: *Two Years Before the Mast* (1946), *California* (1946) and *Easy Come, Easy Go* (1947). Fitzgerald also worked with René Clair – a great director on some occasions – in an Agatha Christie detective story,

And Then There Were None (1945), a film that is no better than it had to be.

The Stork Club (1945), in which Fitzgerald plays a millionaire who, having been saved from drowning by a beautiful young girl (who works at the Stork Club), decides to make all things possible for his rescuer by a secret endowment – no more need be said, except perhaps that Fitzgerald was paid $5000 a week for his work on the film, from 16 April to 9 June 1945, a total of $35,000 (the value in 2011 would be approximately $420,000).

There were, inevitably, spin-offs from *Going My Way*, such as *Duffy's Tavern* (1945), in which Fitzgerald plays Bing Crosby's father. *Welcome, Stranger* (1947) recycles the story of *Going My Way*, with Crosby and Fitzgerald playing doctors, as opposed to priests; otherwise, it is good, but not as good as *Going My Way*. *Top o' the Morning* (1949) – fictionally set in Ireland, but not filmed there – is painfully condescending to the Irish. Fitzgerald plays a policeman, Eileen Crowe a woman with second sight, and Bing Crosby an American who sorts out the lovable idiots in the old country.

Barry Fitzgerald as policeman, after a fall from a bicycle into the mud, in Top o' the Morning, *1949. (Shields family papers)*

The best film in which Barry Fitzgerald took part after *None but the Lonely Heart* was *The Naked City* (1948). Directed by Jules Dassin (one of those soon to be blackballed by the House Un-American Activities Committee), and filmed in a semi-documentary style by William H. Daniels, this police-procedural story was utterly original. It fathered hundreds of successful television and movie imitations. Many will remember the final tag-line of the narrator: *There are eight million stories in the naked city. This has been one of them.* It is a premise that keeps on giving. Every crime takes one intimately into the lives of complicated individual humans, who suffer from passions and poverty and simple misfortune, and whose embarrassed lies must be sorted out by compassionate, high-principled detectives.

Barry Fitzgerald (left) in The Naked City, *1948. (Shields family papers)*

It was filmed in New York City, not on a sound-stage. The opening shot is of the city from an airplane. This is followed by shots of an empty bank, a theatre, people sleeping, getting up in the morning, a day like any other. The city itself is a character. There were scenes shot in the City Morgue, Roosevelt Hospital, the Roxy Theatre and at the Williamsburg Bridge. Scenes were photographed on the street from a van through a tinted window, so only the paid actors knew that a movie was being filmed. The narrator has a working-class New York accent.

The story proper begins with a *corpus delecti.* Jane Dexter, a model, has been found by a house-cleaner murdered in her apartment (all we see is the house-cleaner's mouth open in a scream). Homicide detectives Dan Muldoon (Barry Fitzgerald) and Jimmy Halloran (Don Taylor) are assigned to the case. When Detective Muldoon arrives on the scene, he asks simply, 'What's the story?' He is sorrowful, polite, businesslike. He sadly reprimands people for moving the body, and junior police too for jumping to conclusions: 'Jimmy, it's an obligation to wait for the medical examiner.' He gives orders to the assistant detectives to pursue certain lines of investigation, but things are not just business as usual for him: 'This seems like a heavy case, a heavy case.' It becomes his refrain. When he is later charting the course of the investigation on a police department blackboard, he mutters again, 'A heavy case.'

Suspicion falls on characters who have a connection to a string of jewel thefts from apartments. A burglar is found dead who was a known associate of a man named Willie. He was reputed to be a former wrestler, who played the harmonica in his spare time. Once he is located, a frantic chase begins, and Willie climbs to the top of the Williamsburg Bridge, firing a handgun at the police below. They then bring him down with a volley of return fire.

Naked City stands up very well in a comparison with the many shows to which it gave birth, down to all the *CSI* serials in 2007 and after, the innumerable stories in the naked cities of Las Vegas, Miami and New York. What Barry Fitzgerald brought to the genre, at its origin, is the idea of playing the chief detective as a priest. He is, according to the plot, a widower – but he acts as if he is clerically celibate, sadly identified with the lot of humanity, and firmly determined to gain a confession.

8

In the 1940s and 1950s Arthur Shields was in a lot of movies – even more than Barry Fitzgerald or Sara Allgood – but he often had to settle for small parts. At the Abbey Theatre in the 1920s and 1930s, Shields was normally cast as the handsome lead, Christy Mahon, in *The Playboy of the Western World.* In Hollywood, he was not young enough, handsome enough, American enough, or magnetic enough to take lead roles.

If Barry Fitzgerald's career grew from his two big stage roles as Fluther

Good and Captain Boyle into a variety of loquacious, heavy-drinking, cowardly pugilists and old mariners, Arthur Shields was primarily typed by casting directors on the basis of his success as a clergyman in Paul Vincent Carroll's *Shadow and Substance*. John Ford solidified this public perception of Shields by casting him as a preacher in *Drums Along the Mohawk*, a deacon in *How Green Was My Valley*, and the ship's philosopher in *The Long Voyage Home*.

To be an Irish priest was not a minor role, sociologically speaking. In the Irish Free State, the Catholic Church had the operation of all social services under its control: education, hospitals, delinquency, adoption of children, charity cases of every description. The Irish Free State social system was both like and unlike democratic socialism: it was public and non-profit, but it was completely under the control of the Church. This vast scope of affairs under the power of the Church required the production of lots of clergymen and nuns; they had to run public services for the whole nation. The required numbers of clergy were achieved, and not only the number required. An overflowing tide of Irish nuns and priests poured out toward Africa, Central America, the United States and Canada.

The 'devotional revolution' in Ireland began well before the establishment of the Irish Free State. By 1901, upon his return to Dublin after twenty years away, George Moore was surprised by an astonishingly long 'black queue stretching right across Dublin, from Drumcondra along the Merrion Road' of 'seminarists all along the pavement, groups of threes and fours, and full-blown priests'.[35] The great number of priests and nuns, and the vast powers handed to them by the Free State government, led to a widespread clericalization of the intelligentsia. Those who refused, or were excluded from, the summons to service in the Church nonetheless took upon themselves the manners and roles of priests. Yeats, Joyce, Beckett and even crusading atheists like George Moore, or actors like Barry Fitzgerald and Arthur Shields, became adept at sacerdotal fashions of life and a hieratic manner of authority. When Yeats read his poems, he sounded like a clergyman chanting the evening liturgy. The leader of the country, Éamon de Valera, dressed, spoke, acted and thought like a bishop. Priests in Ireland were obvious models for emulation of every sort, competitive, admiring or parodic.

While in the United States of the period there was a separation of Church and state, the hierarchy of the American Catholic Church was dominated by Irish priests. In 1900 62 per cent of the bishops were Irish, most of them born in Ireland.[36] So when a casting director required an actor to play a priest, an Irishman naturally came to mind, and Shields was not only Irish but had starred on Broadway as a priest. Eleven times in the 1940s Shields was assigned it parts as a clergyman:

1942 *This Above All*, Chaplain
1942 *Gentleman Jim*, Father Burke
1942 *The Black Swan*, The Bishop
1943 *The Man From Down Under*, Father Polycorp
1944 *Keys of the Kingdom*, Father Fitzgerald
1945 *Roughly Speaking*, The Minister
1945 *The Picture of Dorian Gray*, Street Preacher
1946 *Gallant Journey*, Father Kenton
1946 *The Verdict*, Reverend Holbrook
1948 *Tap Roots*, Reverend Kirkland
1949 *Red Light*, Father Redmond

Arthur Shields could make a living as Hollywood's all-purpose man of the cloth, but he could not show his range as an actor. He did get other semi-clerical parts, as a doctor, chemist, inspector and such, but they were usually small roles and handled by directors who did not, like John Ford, make time for individualized cameo performances by members of the supporting cast.

In August 1941, right after completing *How Green Was My Valley*, Shields did get an interesting part in *Confirm or Deny*. The story is set in England during the Blitz. A handsome, hyper, 'can-do' American newspaperman (Don Ameche) sets up a wire service during the Blitz, and aims to telegraph bulletins about the imminence of a Nazi invasion of Britain. Over the course of a romance begun during a blackout and a retreat to a Tube bombshelter for the night, he and an English teletype operator (Joan Bennett) come into conflict over his efforts to elude the British censorship in providing stories for the American newsprints.

Arthur Shields has what his wife Aideen called 'a grand showy part' as an 'oldish, blind telegraphist', who lost his sight during World War I.[37] He has developed a unique capacity to identify the models of German aircraft by the sound of their engines. A strangely erect, mystical figure, he embodies the wisdom, calm and fortitude of the British nation in the midst of war.

In this part Shields found a new use for the famous 'Abbey stare', that look into the far distance in which a character saw the future or the meaning of things or the spirits of the next world. The character and the stare ultimately derived from the plots of W.B. Yeats's plays. Shields acts blindness as if it were Yeatsian second sight. The aura of this romantic style of acting proves surprisingly effective when thrust into a fast-paced, suspenseful action movie.

9

The production company created by Arthur Shields and Eddie Choate to serve as a New York centre for Irish drama came to nothing, as a result of the failures of Paul Vincent Carroll's *Kindred* (opened 26 December 1939, closed after eleven performances) and Louis D'Alton's *Tanyard Street* (opened 4 February 1941, closed after twenty-one performances).

In January 1947, however, Shields got another chance to direct, when Eugene O'Neill chose him to supervise the first production of *Moon for the Misbegotten.* Although the play is set in New England, O'Neill believed that 'the mystic quality' of the three main characters and the 'mercurial changes of mood' were distinctly Irish features, and required a director of Irish birth to bring them out. Columbus, Ohio, was chosen as the city in which to open. The plan was for success there to lead to productions in other Midwestern cities (Pittsburgh, Detroit, St Louis) and ultimately to a New York debut.

O'Neill and the producer cast the play prior to Shields's arrival in Ohio; he did not fancy the choices they had made. J.M. Kerrigan had one of the key roles, but Kerrigan did not like the play, believing it to be offensive to the Irish. Mary Welch, in the female lead, liked the play, but she was a beginner on the stage.[38] Shields could not get the cast to hold their places until there was some signifying purpose for them to move: 'The eternal moving about! They simply wouldn't stand still!'[39] Furthermore, O'Neill confused Shields by saying he wanted the first two acts played for broad comedy, with tragedy emerging at the close.[40] Shields did his best to follow the author's wishes, but he was working in the dark. Directing for an author he did not really know, with actors who neither knew one another nor possessed a common stage practice, and in an American Midwest of which he had no understanding, made for a highly unfamiliar experience for Shields.

Midwestern American audiences did not care whether the first acts of *Moon for the Misbegotten* were done as comedy, tragedy, or high farce; they thought that 'the whole theme is obscene' and 'a slander on American motherhood'. In Detroit in March 1947 a policeman demanded that the actors say 'louse' wherever the script read 'bastard' and 'tart' wherever the script had 'whore'. As for Eugene O'Neill and his Nobel Prize, the policeman said he did not care what kind of prize the man had won: 'He can't put on a dirty show in my town.'[41] It was worse than what Dublin did to O'Casey, because for less cause. The production never made it to Broadway.

10

John Ford had frequently been an angel of mercy for Arthur Shields. Ford had brought him to Hollywood in 1936 for *The Plough and the Stars*. In 1939, at a difficult time in the actor's life, Ford fetched him back from the Abbey for a role in *Drums Along the Mohawk*. As soon as Shields got out of hospital in April 1940 following the *Kindred* disaster, there was a part waiting for him in *The Long Voyage Home*. After *How Green Was My Valley* (1941) was completed, however, Ford went into military service. Shields found employment in Hollywood with other directors, but it was often journeyman work. Then in October 1948 Ford called again upon Arthur Shields, this time for the part of a Wild West doctor in *She Wore a Yellow Ribbon*. Shields was to be paid $1250 a week for four weeks' work (approximately $17,000 a week in current money).

The story opens at a cavalry outpost, Fort Stark, in 1876, after General Custer's defeat. Many different tribes have united in one last effort to drive the white man from the red man's hunting grounds. Made up to look twenty years older than he was, John Wayne plays Nathan Brittles, the second-in-command of the regiment, just days from retirement after forty years in the service. His aide, played by Victor McLaglen, is also just about to retire. Against his better judgment, Brittles is ordered to lead a brigade of cavalrymen to investigate the Indian activity, and, at the same time, to escort the niece and wife of the fort commander to Sudro's Wells, where they can catch a stagecoach back east and out of the danger zone. Dr O'Loughlin, the character played by Arthur Shields, accompanies the regiment on its journey.

In the script by Laurence Stallings and Frank Nugent, 'Dr O'Loughlin' is a very Irish part. When he first appears in the script, the travellers are just setting out from Fort Stark.

> Dr O'Loughlin: Sure, everything worked out beautifully. Mrs Jameson had her baby. The survey sergeant's boils are draining nicely. Mrs Carneal will not bless Fort Stark for another week with offspring. And here I am for as gay a time as I could be wishing, with the prospect of two lovely ladies' company to Sudro's Ford and of escorting Mrs Allshard back with half of me heart that isn't broke with waving Miss Olivia off fer iver, at Sudro's Ford railroad station!

This speech was lost in editing, but that and more like it was the kind of dialogue that gave an actor a chance. The back story, even when dropped, coloured the moments of Shields's performance that were left in the final cut.

There is a lot to enjoy in *She Wore a Yellow Ribbon* – one of John Wayne's best performances, Victor McLaglen as his comical, whiskey-loving sergeant,

George O'Brien in a return to Ford films as the Major, horse-riding by Ben Johnson (including a breathtaking leap over a gorge too wide for the Indians in pursuit to attempt), and the colour photography of an age when colour was as precious to cameramen as gold leaf was to medieval painters. The blue of the cavalry uniforms and pinks and oranges of Monument Valley sand and rock are striking, as are the cloud castles of the western sky, and the yellow ribbon of the title and theme song:

> Around her hair she wore a yellow ribbon
> She wore it for her lover who was far, far away
> And when they asked her why she wore it
> She wore it for her true love in the US Cavalry
> Cavalree, Cavalreee!

Arthur Shields's key scene comes when one of the scouts returns to the wagon train having been wounded by a band of Indians. Dr O'Loughlin rides to the head of the wagon train to beg Nathan Brittles for time to operate on the wound:

> Dr O'Loughlin: The bullet's right near his heart. It has to come out. It's a risky operation at best. Can't you halt?
> Captain Brittles: You know I can't.
> Dr O'Loughlin: Just for twenty minutes, Nathan. It's a man's life.
> Captain Brittles: Not even for five minutes. I couldn't do it if it was my own son. McLean's a soldier; he'll have to take a soldier's risk.
> Dr O'Loughlin: He knows that. I know that. It's I who am begging.
> Captain Brittles: I'll give you all I can.
> Dr O'Loughlin: Thanks, Nathan.

The soldiers dismount and walk their horses forward. The sky darkened by thunderclouds is now and again lit up by flashes of lightning. The troopers are dead quiet as the operation continues; only the clop, clop, clop of horses' hooves and rolling thunderclaps can be heard.

Inside the covered wagon Dr O'Loughlin is assisted by the Major's wife, Mrs Allshard (Mildred Natwick), who administers doses of whiskey to the patient, and alternately takes some herself, until both patient and nurse break out into a drunken chorus of 'She Wore a Yellow Ribbon'. Dr O'Loughlin, his glasses tipped up on his forehead, works away intensely with forceps. Finally, Captain Brittles can stand the tension no longer and rides up to the back of the wagon. Peering inside, he demands, 'Well, how is he?'

'I think I can safely say,' Dr O'Loughlin replies with a grin, 'he'll live to see sergeant.' Captain Brittles sends the word down the line – 'He's doing fine! Now mount up!' When those in the wagon train at last reach the stagecoach depot at Sudro's Wells, they find that an Indian war party has already been there, and killed all present. It is Dr O'Loughlin (drawing upon Arthur Shields's long service as a Hollywood clergyman) who reads the burial rite for the dead.

She Wore a Yellow Ribbon is by common consent one of the best Westerns ever made. It does not have much of a plot – superficially, just the story of the fort commander's niece flirting with two young lieutenants. But the real love in the picture is the director's love for the military. John Ford affectionately details the relations among officers, between officers and troops, between military men and their women, whether they are married, widowed or in love, and between cavalry officers and Indian chiefs, who are depicted as entitled to honour and respect.

Regardless of the degree of pleasure one takes in things military, the movie gains a deeply enjoyable quality from the tried-and-true performances of every one of the cast. They are all members of the John Ford 'stock company'. They respected one another, and enjoyed the respect of the director, who delighted in giving them all chances to display their merits. There is an encore quality to its elements, as if the motion picture were just a sequence of old favourites by star performers of an earlier era, but drawn together by the director into a comical, sentimental and exciting story.

Joseph Hone (son of the biographer of George Moore and W.B. Yeats) left a perceptive account of John Ford as a director, based on Hone's experience as his assistant in the making of *The Rising of the Moon*. 'You learnt most from Ford not by talking to him, which was nearly always a hair-raising experience, but by watching how he looked at things.' 'He never looked through the viewfinder, or watched the daily rushes, and he consulted the script once in a blue moon. The only piece of film lore I ever heard pass his lips was: "Everything's all right with a picture as long as the audience isn't conscious of the machine." ' What Ford really liked were the comic touches by character actors invented on the set. 'This sort of blunt, knockabout comedy was very much to Ford's taste, and he filmed it with relish and fluency, like a man interpreting a recurrent happy dream for the fiftieth time.'[42]

That recurrent happy dream could include scenes repeated from earlier movies. In *She Wore a Yellow Ribbon*, for instance, as in other Ford movies, a man at dusk beside the grave of his wife discusses the day's events, an old sergeant tries to hide his love for his men as he gruffly inspects the troops on parade, an officer suppresses a show of compassion for a wounded enlisted man, and a worldly frontier doctor has the know-how to take over in an emergency.

11

In February 1949, Arthur Shields turned fifty-three. He had just completed a part as an Ulster businessman in St Louis in *Fighting Father Dunne*, another celebratory portrait of a Catholic priest (played this time by Pat O'Brien) working miracles with juvenile delinquents. Its corny piety and the soppy sentimentalism of some of its holy father/naughty delinquent scenes capture some of the worst elements in *Going My Way*, while that Oscar winner's best elements escape the grasp of its imitator.

In April a studio called upon Shields to give voice lessons to Shirley Temple, in preparation for her part as an Irish colleen in *Always Sweethearts.*[43] What mostly kept Shields busy in early 1949 was his part-interest in a new television series sponsored by Lucky Strike cigarettes: *Your Show Time.* It dramatized classic short stories from world literature in weekly episodes; Shields was the host and narrator.

Aideen was not well – 'Never quite right since the birth of Christine,' Shields wrote to Eddie Choate.[44] A photograph from this period shows her greatly aged. Adam Shields had joined the Air Force and was stationed near Chicago. He would not get leave until October 1949.

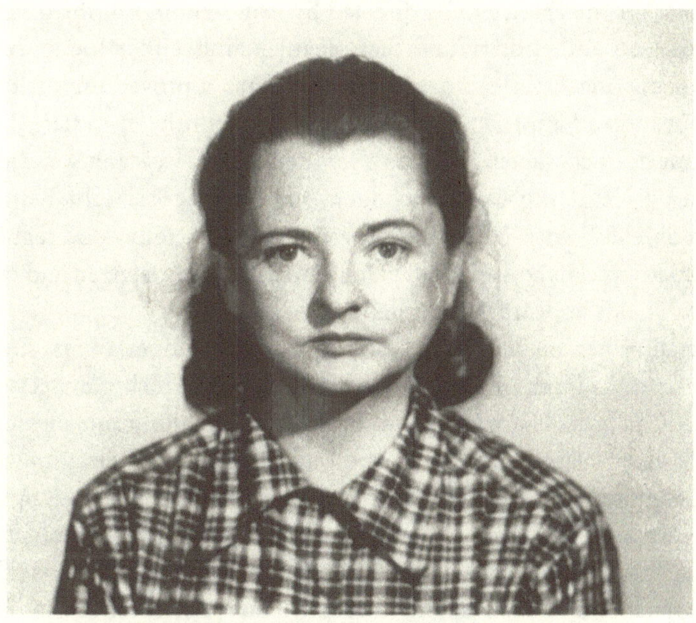

Aideen O'Connor Shields, c.1949–50. (Shields family papers)

Arthur Shields's most exciting artistic opportunity during this period came from Jean Renoir (1879–1974), son of the Impressionist painter and director of two of the greatest films ever made, *La Grand Illusion* (1937) and *La Règle du jeu* (1939). Renoir had bought the rights to *The River* (1946), a novel by Rumer Godden. Godden was an Englishwoman raised in India, where her father ran a steamship line. Her second novel, *Black Narcissus* (1939), made a sensation with its tale of European nuns culturally at sea running a mission in northern India. In 1947 Michael Powell and Emeric Pressburger turned that novel into an immediately famous film. *The River* then became an attractive literary property. Renoir wanted to film the story on location in Calcutta, and in colour, and with native actors in the supporting roles. He sought funding from the new independent government of India, but he sought it in vain.

Meanwhile, Ken McEldowney, a Hollywood florist whose wife was an MGM executive, had become determined to show he could make a better movie than his wife's studio turned out. Although he had never produced a film anywhere at any time, he wanted to make his movie in India, where he had served during the war, and in colour. He located an Indian maharajah willing to fund a movie, and then started to look for a literary property. Before long, he found *The River* and Renoir.

Many Hollywood regulars wanted a part in the movie, including Ronald Reagan, just for the chance to be directed by Jean Renoir. But the director had set his heart on authenticity, and that meant mainly either Indian or British actors. For the one American part (Captain John), it proved impossible to get an appropriate and affordable star to spend five months in India. Ultimately, for the American character, who has a wooden leg, they cast an American with a wooden leg. His acting was also wooden, but the price was right. Renoir knew and liked Shields's work. The Irish actor was the only Hollywood regular to be cast in *The River*. (His contract called for his salary to be deferred and taken out of profits. Shields appears never to have been paid.)[45]

The story centres on Harriet, a girl of poetic temperament, about thirteen years old, and one of the many daughters of a British manager of a jute factory in Calcutta. The movie is a flashback from the point of view of an adult narrator, Harriet. She tells of one year in the life of her family and that of their neighbour, the widower Mr John (Arthur Shields), his young Eurasian daughter Melanie and their American cousin Captain John, who is trying to come to terms with his war wounds and the loss of a leg. Three of the girls, Harriet, Melanie and their slightly older friend Valerie, all fall in love with Captain John. As Harriet's father says, they are babies but they behave like tragedy queens in love, and Captain John does duty as their Lord Byron. When Harriet sees Captain John kissing Valerie, the narrator recalls with feverish melodrama: 'The kiss on her lips was terrifying, fascinating. It was my first kiss, but received by another.'

While most of the story concerns the innocent pains of first love, set against the panorama of life on the River Ganges and the sequence of Hindu seasonal festivals, there is an intermittent story of the one boy in Harriet's family, Bogey. With his Indian playmate, Bogey loves to collect turtles and lizards. Ultimately, he becomes fascinated with cobras, one of which lives in a gigantic holy tree, where women bring it ritual offerings of milk. Bogey follows suit, attracting the serpent with bowls of milk. He then tries, like the men he has seen in the market, to play the flute to the snake. The climax of the three girls' pursuit of romance is suddenly undercut by the heavily foreshadowed death by snakebite of Bogey.

The primary characters in the story are Europeans living in grand houses behind walls; the only Indians in their lives are their servants. However, the narrator's view of life, and the attitudes of nearly all the characters, become shaped by the enveloping Hinduism of the culture, and the film as a whole, while featuring colonists, is paradoxically a celebration of Hinduism and of India.

Arthur Shields looks great on screen – tanned, existentially enthusiastic, full of love for his daughter, philosophical without being preachy, and open to ideas and experience. His is one of few satisfactory acting performances, for while *The River* is a great movie, it is acted in an amateur way. Renoir's device of the voice-over narration and large amounts of travelogue footage save the situation, so that the performances look like stylized illustrations of a narrative rather than lifelike enactments of it.

Mr John, the character played by Shields, has a profound attraction to Hinduism. He married an Indian woman, and at her death was left to raise their Eurasian child, Melanie. He dotes on Melanie, yet frets over the fact that she is caught between cultures: 'Sometimes I think I've put you in a frightful position. Perhaps you should never have been born' [this sentence delivered with tenderness].' 'But I am born,' Melanie abruptly replies, 'some day perhaps I shall find out where I belong.' She is so young to be sadly, beautifully wise. When Captain John pouts about his dreadful position – too many pretty teenagers in love with him, and one leg too few – he cries out to Melanie:

> Captain John: What are we going to do?
> Melanie: Consent.
> Captain John: To what?

> Melanie: To everything. You don't like having one leg. But you cannot go to a country of one-legged men. I don't like …
> Captain John: What?
> Melanie: Well, something …

Mr John has learned, evidently from his wife, his half-caste daughter and India itself something of a Hindu attitude to life. When Bogey, the little boy, is found dead, he muses, 'Perhaps we should celebrate that a child died a child, that one escaped.' In the West, such a response would be cold, depressed pessimism; in its Calcutta setting, it is the Hindu wisdom of acceptance.

12

Arthur Shields arrived in Calcutta on 18 January 1950, his last scenes were shot on 20 April, and he boarded a Pan Am airplane for his return on the next day. When he arrived in Hollywood, after a short stopover in Dublin, he found Aideen in poor condition. She was suffering from liver failure. She had had the disease for three years; the situation was now hopeless. He managed to admit to his old friend Eddie Choate that he was all broken up about it; he could not settle. Words failed him. On 1 July 1950 Aideen fell into a coma. Yet there was nothing to do but consent. The parts actors play can sometimes help them get through life's passages, and something of Mr John's Hindu calm came in aid to Arthur Shields. 'It is all hopeless, and the sooner God takes the poor thing, the easier it will be for her.'[46] On 4 July 1950 Aideen Una Mary Shields died of cirrhosis of the liver. After a funeral mass at St Mary Magdalen Church, she was buried in Holy Cross Cemetery, Culver City, California.

VI

THE QUIET MAN AND *THE PLAYBOY OF THE WESTERN WORLD*

Previous page: *Barry Fitzgerald as Shaughraun; Maureen O'Hara as Mary Kate Danaher, in* The Quiet Man, *1952. (Lilly Library)*

On Saturday morning, 23 March 1935, Aideen O'Connor was in rare good form. She wrote her father from Hotel Sir Francis Drake in San Francisco, the next stop on the Abbey tour after five days in Hollywood.

> We played *Juno* last night and the critics have just gone crazy in this morning's papers ... By the way, they seem to consider me good-looking in this city, all the critics have mentioned me as being 'pretty', or 'lovely'. One even said, 'Aideen O'Connor looks as though she might have come out of a painting,' etc. It will be funny to go home and settle down as the least good looking of the family.[1]

Since it was her father she was addressing, the Shipping Master of Dublin Port, Aideen played down the adoration of actors as just craziness. To her sisters Eileen and Maeve, however, she showed a different side of herself. She could not hide her delight, or fail to tell all about her giddy whirl through the house of fame, with a purse full of cash, changing as the days went by from her afternoon frock to her dinner frock and finally getting into her evening frock. One shopping spree on Wilshire Boulevard was worth a whole paragraph:

> One day in Hollywood, Frolie, Maureen O'Sullivan, and I went shopping in Bullock's, Wilshire, the rendezvous of all the stars. I bought some lovely beach things, a pair of white shorts with a blue strip down the sides. The 'top' consists of a blue handkerchief with white anchors on it, which goes around the neck

and ties at the back … cool, that! I also got a beret in white rubber, and white rubber shoes. Then I got a glorious wool bathing suit in royal blue and beige for myself, a lighter blue one for you and a reddish mixture for Maeve. That left me financially embarrassed for the rest of the week! But you've yours … You simply say, 'swim suits' – it's the thing in Hollywood! I also bought the loveliest stockings in Hollywood! We had lunch with Maureen [O'Sullivan] and of course were photographed …

She was chuffed by all her encounters with the Hollywood Irish and other screen personalities:

Una O'Connor has a movie camera and she took at least ten rolls of me doing different things. She's a pet, and I got awfully fond of her. Wait till you see the lovely jade bracelet and dress clip she gave me …

Dudley and Mrs Digges are a pair of dotes too. Everyone likes Una, Dudley, and Mary [Digges].

Joe Kerrigan is a scream. You just can't stop laughing at him …

Maureen [O'Sullivan] was rather shy at first, but she and Frolie and I have become great friends. She is not a bit spoiled and doesn't like Hollywood much. Her fiancée, John Farrow, is a darling. He reminds me of John Coughlan … talks just like him, and behaves in the same crazy way. He and Maureen are crazy about each other. I think they will be able to get a dispensation all right [Farrow was divorced]. Maureen has a glorious engagement ring.

Victor McLaglen is quiet and refined. He loved our plays and was there every night. He asked Frolie and me out to play tennis with his children, but we weren't able to go.

Pat O'Brien and his wife are as jolly as possible. They have a nine month old baby and are daft about it.

Ralph Bellamy is so good-looking that when I was introduced to him, I just gaped in a half-witted way. He has bright golden hair that waves adorably, huge blue eyes, a marvellous smile, perfect teeth, and a fascinating voice. He's the best looking thing in men I've ever seen.

He and Dudley [Digges] and Joe [Kerrigan] and Maureen [O'Sullivan] all played in the crowd scenes in *Playboy* with us. Such fun! The stars got more of a kick out of it than out of anything since they had come to Hollywood.

Elissa Landi is very charming and quiet. She is not nearly so pretty off screen as on.

Edward G. Robinson and I had a long discussion on James Stephens's poetry, and whether *The Crock of Gold* could be dramatised. Anything less like a gangster I never saw. His wife talked to me about her baby boy, likewise did Mrs Pat O'Brien about her baby daughter, Mavourneen.

Impulsively girlish, uninhibited, intelligent and scatty, the letter goes on for several more pages, offering younger sister Maeve advice about pre-menstrual cramps (Aideen was given drugs for them in Los Angeles but they made her sleepy), chatting about a Chicago photographer who while snapping her portrait fell in love with her, and providing more details about her romance with Bob, a divorced man – he was planning to come to the Dublin Horse Show in August (this was before the start of Aideen's affair with Arthur Shields).

From Molly Allgood's Pegeen Mike to Sara Allgood's Juno, and from Ria Mooney's Rosie to Maureen O'Hara's Mary Kate Danaher, arguments continued about the nature of the Irish woman. What was she really like? To the minds of patriots, she had to be represented as modest, chaste, noble and obedient, a lovely embodiment of family, home and nation. Irish women of the period, although not culturally silent, did not prominently step forward in such debates to say that they were nothing of the kind. Indeed, before the publication of *The Field Day Anthology of Irish Writing: Irish Women's Writing and Traditions* (2003), it was hard to locate instances from 1900 to 1960 in which the free-spirited, uncensored and unpremeditated words of Irish women could be read, although James Joyce invented some plausible and provocative reveries for Molly Bloom.

But Aideen O'Connor's letter to her family of 23 March 1935 has another value too. It conveys the excitement not just of Aideen for Hollywood, but of Hollywood for the Abbey Theatre players. Stars of Irish birth like Dudley Digges, Joe Kerrigan (Abbey veterans themselves) and Maureen O'Sullivan, those of Irish descent like John Farrow, Pat O'Brien and Ralph Bellamy, and those of no Irish descent at all, but with an interest in Irish literature, like Joan Crawford, Heather Angel, Victor McLaglen and Edward G. Robinson, were all swept up in enthusiasm for the revivals of the classics of the Irish stage, especially *The Playboy of the Western World*, performed on 9 March 1935.[2] The happy hilarity of the film actors going on stage in the crowd scenes of that play is easy to picture. What a lark for them to be able to join in with seasoned performers like Arthur Shields as Christy Mahon, Barry Fitzgerald as Michael James and Eileen Crowe as Pegeen Mike, professionals who had all done this play many times already, and were free and at ease in Synge's fantastical language and knew how to get the most of the plot's breathtaking turnabouts. It was like a group of international concert artists joining in a rollicking 'session' with famous traditional musicians in a country pub – a great night's fun!

2

That same week in Hollywood was also the week when John Ford gave his banquet for the Abbey players on the set of *The Informer*, and conceived his plan for a series of Irish films starring the Abbey actors: first *The Plough and the Stars*, then *Juno and the Paycock* and *The Quiet Man*.[3]

This last piece was a short story by Maurice Walsh that first appeared in the 11 February 1933 issue of *The Saturday Evening Post* and was expanded for publication in a volume of interrelated tales, *Green Rushes*, published in 1935. On 25 February 1936, while *The Plough and the Stars* was still in development, Ford bought the film rights to the story.[4] But because *The Plough* turned out to be a financial failure for RKO, there was no chance of that company taking up an option on *The Quiet Man*. In 1937 Ford told the young Irish journalist Michael Morris (Lord Killanin of Spiddal) that he still meant to make a film of 'The Quiet Man' from *Green Rushes*.[5] By 1939 Ford evidently had a producer in mind, because in March of that year, after a spree in New York with Ford, Liam O'Flaherty remarked on the plan to make *The Quiet Man* in Ireland.[6] O'Flaherty hinted that a movie about the IRA would not at the time be popular in England, 'owing to the recent activities of "the boys" ' – a reference to the current IRA bombing campaign on English soil, a renewed protest against the 1920 partition of the country into the twenty-six-county Free State and the six-county Northern Ireland.

But was *The Quiet Man* necessarily going to be a film about the IRA? In Walsh's story the 'quiet man' is Paddy Bawn Enright, a smallish fellow (obviously not the shape of John Wayne, who plays the character in the movie). He had returned around 1920 to Kerry from America where for fifteen years he had been working in steel mills and, under the name Tiger Enright, boxing professionally in the welterweight class. He just wanted to settle down quietly in the Enright family's hillside cottage, but it had been grabbed by a land-hungry farmer, Red Will O'Danaher, a huge figure of a man, and famously short-tempered ('O'Danaher' became 'Danaher' in the film). Rather than fight for his rights, Paddy Bawn Enright quietly accepted the situation, and paid to regain the cottage from O'Danaher. In consequence, he was held in contempt by his neighbours.

Prior to the beginning of the tale, and in episodes dramatized by the earlier stories from *Green Rushes*, Enright had been drawn secretly into service with a flying column of the IRA in its war against the Black and Tans. One of its members was a former student for the priesthood, a 'lean, grave man' named

Mickeen Oge Flynn (obviously nothing like Barry Fitzgerald, who plays that part in the movie). Another Volunteer, Hugh Forbes, proved himself a military commander of genius.

The story proper begins once the war is over and the land is at peace. Paddy falls in love with a red-haired woman he sees at church, Ellen Rose O'Danaher, sister of Red Will. However, Red Will does not allow suitors near his sister; she is useful as a house servant. Once a wealthy neighbour woman becomes a widow, the land-hungry O'Danaher proposes, but she will not make a match so long as Ellen Rose remains in the O'Danaher house. Red Will decides to dispose of his sister by marriage to Paddy Bawn Enright, and he puts up a £100-dowry, provided there's a good harvest and he has spare cash at the time of the wedding.

Paddy knows that Ellen Rose does not love him, but he hopes when they are married she will come to do so. After the wedding he buys her a horse and trap, hires a serving-maid to help with the housework, and chats to her long hours by their fireside about his life in America. Gradually, she does get to like him, and even love him, but it needles her that Red Will has never paid the hundred pounds, her 'fortune'. So though he himself sets no store on the money and simply wants peace and quiet, Paddy Bawn Enright asks Red Will for the dowry, and, refused, asks again. The wealthy widow had by then married another, and Red Will was not happy with his bargain. Forced to ask a third time, 'Go to hell out o' that!' and a hard shove in the public market is all the answer Paddy Bawn Enright gets. To the dismay of onlookers eager for a showdown, once again he does not fight back. He and his wife quarrel, with him saying that maybe with all her care about money, she's just a Danaher after all, and she saying, placing her hand under her breast, 'I am a Danaher. It is a great pity that the father of this, my son, is an Enright coward.'[7] That was the first Paddy Bawn Enright knew he was going to be a father, and this news arrived with the information that his wife had lost all love and respect for him.

Husband and wife go home together to a sad house. During a sleepless night Paddy realizes that he was going to have 'to do a thing so final and decisive that never again could it be questioned'. The next morning he asks Ellen Rose if she will come with him to see Red Will, and they walk together to the field where O'Danaher is threshing corn with his men. Once the brother flatly refuses to hand over the promised dowry, Paddy springs his surprise:

> 'Right. That breaks all bargains.'
>
> 'What's that?'
>
> 'If you keep your hundred pounds, you keep your sister.'[8]

But the public return of his sister without her virginity, and pregnant, puts Red Will in a spot. Watched by forty men, he decides to pretend that he was only joking with the little Yank, and now will hand over the dirty money, and give him a beating to boot. In two minutes O'Danaher is back with the banknotes, and he thrusts them into Paddy's hand with a curse and a threat. Paddy turns, and walks toward the threshing machine. Ellen Rose, anticipating him, throws open the firebox door, and he pitches the crumpled bills into the blazes.

With a cry of 'My money, my good money!' Red Will comes running to batter Paddy Enright. At last there is the long-awaited fight in the field, followed blow by blow by forty onlookers, with Mickeen Oge Flynn taking bets on the outcome. His own money is on Paddy Bawn Enright, because he knows about his past in the ring as Tiger Enright. In the clinch Enright proves unhittable, while O'Danaher is defenceless against the array of quick punches from the smaller man. For five minutes he gives it to O'Danaher. Eight times, Red Will is knocked down, and eight times he comes back for more, until a combination of a left below the breastbone and a right uppercut to the jaw lifts O'Danaher up off his feet, and he falls flat, out cold. Ellen Rose, satisfied at last, declares of her husband, 'Mother o' God! The trouble I had to make a man of him!' Mickeen Oge corrects her: 'God Almighty did that for him before you were born!'[9]

3

It seems that at one time John Ford fancied making much of the involvement of the man from America in an IRA flying column. Ford himself had been to Ireland in early December 1921, at the very end of the Anglo-Irish war, and he had seen the cottage of his kinfolk in Spiddal left in ashes by the Black and Tans. He liked to fantasize that he had had been involved in the struggle. It was probably in 1929 that he got to know Ernie O'Malley, a head organizer of IRA flying columns; in that year O'Malley was in Hollywood raising money for the Fianna Fáil party. Ford later hired O'Malley as advisor on the set of *The Quiet Man*, and at one time considered having him make an appearance on screen.[10] Liam O'Flaherty had done service with the IRA too, and that won him great favour with Ford.

But fundamentally, 'The Quiet Man' as a short story does not feature either the War of Independence or the Civil War. It begins after war has ended, and concerns Irishmen fighting not with Englishmen but with each other over land

and a woman. The essential elements of its plot are the return of a man from America seeking a peaceful life, a love story with a proud red-haired woman, a point of honour connected with the dowry system, and a fist fight at the end. Leave out any one of those elements, and you do not have *The Quiet Man*; put in action about the flying columns, and you strain the unity of the tale.

But John Ford would have a lot of time to consider what the real story of *The Quiet Man* ought to be. Six months after Liam O'Flaherty asked him if he was coming to Ireland to film it on location, World War II broke out.

4

If there is anything at all to the *auteur* theory of film – that great movies are the self-expression of great directors – then *The Quiet Man* ought to register the effect of World War II upon John Ford. The war was the most significant experience in his life. Already in the Naval Reserve, he enlisted for active duty on 11 September 1941, well before the December attack on Pearl Harbor. Serving in Washington DC as a commander in the Office of Strategic Services (forerunner of the CIA), Ford recruited many from his usual crew of photographers, soundmen, editors and special-effects experts to work under him in the Field Photographic Unit. Their brief was to develop the potential of film for training, propaganda, documentation of combat, and reconnaissance.[11]

Ford's military service record is unusual. He shot with a camera and not with a rifle, but there cannot have been many servicemen who were wounded in action at the Battle of Midway (4 June 1942),[12] accompanied the tank invasion of North Africa (16 November 1942),[13] set up operations in Argentina and Brazil (April–May 1943), covered the fields of operation in Southeast Asia, travelled secretly behind Japanese lines into China ([?] November 1943 to 14 January 1944),[14] and went ashore in the D-Day invasion (29 July–4 August 1944 at Grandcamp Les Bains).[15] He was first wounded in the Battle of Midway while shooting film of the dive-bomb attack of Japanese zeros from the 'top of the power house, a hot place to be during an air raid', as his commanding officer noted.[16] Again and again Ford put his life at risk when he could have remained behind the lines. For having done so, he wanted the medals and ribbons, and when he got them he wore them unblushingly.

Ford had friends, and the sons of friends, who were killed among the three hundred men under his command. Twelve are memorialized at the Field Photo Farm he set up for veterans after the war. He saw men and women of all backgrounds thrown together in a common war effort, to sink or swim by their unity.

As a top man in the intelligence service, Ford was briefed not just about the enemy, but about America too. Upon Ford's request, Elmo Roper (of 'Roper Polls') provided a summary of studies on possible chinks in 'America's moral armour'. A main problem, Roper reported, was the 'northern negro': 'he feels discriminated against', as indeed he was.[17] Another problem was anti-Semitism. 'Too many people' thought Hitler had to be 'licked' but that he was not all wrong about the Jews. In the Midwest, people had little sympathy for Britain, and thought the British ought to carry more of the burden of war than they already did, though their country had been bombed to bits. Finally, a majority did not believe that the Soviet Union could be trusted as an ally, especially once war had ended. Ford himself had had many of these attitudes that Roper counted as chinks in America's moral armour, but he probably had not before thought of them in that light. A strong nation, it was implied, was a multi-ethnic nation with tolerance and equality at home, and respect for other nations who were not openly at war with the United States.

These profound experiences mattered to Ford's sense of himself as both an American and an Irishman. A *Quiet Man* after the war was not likely to be the same as a *Quiet Man* made before it.

5

In October 1944, upon leaving active military service, Ford visited the set of *The Spanish Main*, a swashbuckler directed by Frank Borzage and starring Maureen O'Hara. Ford called Borzage over to witness a conversation: 'Maureen, I am going to make a movie in Ireland called *The Quiet Man*, and I would like you to play the female lead.' Ever since they had worked together on *How Green Was My Valley* (1941), Ford had kept O'Hara in mind for this project.[18]

But Ford would make a lot of other movies before he made *The Quiet Man* with Maureen O'Hara in the female lead:

1945 *They Were Expendable*
1946 *My Darling Clementine*
1947 *The Fugitive*
1948 *Fort Apache*
1948 *Three Godfathers*

1949 *She Wore a Yellow Ribbon*
1950 *When Willie Comes Marching Home*
1950 *Wagon Master*
1950 *Rio Grande*
1951 *This is Korea!*
1952 *The Quiet Man*

Some of the continuing delay in making *The Quiet Man* had to do with the difficulty encountered by Merian Cooper, Ford's partner in Argosy Pictures, in finding money for a production in Ireland. It would have been easier, no doubt, had *The Fugitive*, made in Mexico, not been such a failure. That gave a bad name to Ford's pet notions and to filming on location with native actors.

Ford was not wasting his talent in directing the other movies. *My Darling Clementine*, made with Twentieth Century Fox under Darryl Zanuck, and the cavalry trilogy – *Fort Apache*, *She Wore a Yellow Ribbon* and *Rio Grande* – made with Argosy Pictures, are some of the best Westerns of all time.

Fundamentally, the films of the Cavalry trilogy are war movies, but in a form acceptable to a movie-going public tired of propaganda films about World War II servicemen.[19] Because of this displacement, they are more philosophically broad in their representation of life and also take a longer view historically than movies about the wars against the Germans and the Japanese. While patriotic, they are not first and foremost American propaganda. They take it upon themselves to examine critically the formation of the nation. Fundamental to all of them is that the Indian wars are a backdraft of the Civil War. Some of the soldiers in the cavalry fought for the South, others were Yankees, and now they must unite to advance the interests of a single nation. Yet the 'enemy' are the original inhabitants of the land. It is a fraught situation and now and then is recognized to be so.

If one sees the movies allegorically, a cavalry outpost in the west does duty for service abroad in World War II, and the Indians in a complicated way stand in for the foreign enemy, while also being sometimes acknowledged as natives in their own land – people of another language, and with their own customs, wishing to defend their buffalo-hunting way of life against invaders. The comparable desires of Japanese people to defend their rice-growing, samurai-honouring way of life, or the Germans their steel-smelting, music-making way of life, are not explicitly evoked, but a degree of cultural doubt and a momentary question over ethnocentrism are indicated by the representation of native Americans in *She Wore a Yellow Ribbon* and *Fort Apache*. Fundamental to the 'cavalry trilogy' is the case of General Custer, personification of bloody-minded aggression and idealistic nationalism.

The questions that underlie the plots (one could hardly say the questions are 'raised') are anything but simple or easy, nor are the implied answers. What is civilization and what savagery? How can one weigh up the stakes, when common security ('freedom') is bought at the cost of individual liberty? How do people cope with their part in the tribal and global murder of others, and go on to propagate their individual futures? How do women manage to get along with men who have done such things in war, and have thrilled in the doing of them? The allusions to Custer in *She Wore a Yellow Ribbon* and *Fort Apache* do not directly evoke Hitler, but nonetheless they force one to consider a basic problem of leadership, whether elected or military: what if the leader is wholly in the wrong, so that doing one's duty makes one an evildoer?

Overall Ford gave a picture of the military that was not a nightmare of moral contradictions. His picture is instead sentimental, full of affection for the military as a way of life and an ethical way of life. The deep, sorrowful, mutually reliant friendships between officers, the almost wifely loyalty of aides to their commanding officers among the career veterans, the fatherly care of the officers for the boys who enlisted, and the pride among the rank-and-file in being led – all this is depicted as the best life has for the giving. It may be that the military offers 'a life of suffering and hardship, an uncompromising devotion to your oath and your duty' (as Lt. Col. Yorke tells his son in *Rio Grande*), but it is still the best life. Duty stands unquestioned at the top of the scale of human virtues.

Curiously, Ford mixes family life and military life in each of the films, although the anomaly of women and children on an imperilled outpost has to be explained away again and again. In *Fort Apache*, widower Lt. Col. Owen Thursday (Henry Fonda) brings his daughter (Shirley Temple) with him when assigned to command of the outpost, and she falls in love with Sgt. O'Rourke's son – unworthy on two counts in Thursday's view: Irish and the child of a mere enlisted man. A plot about free choice in marriage then runs side-by-side with the story of a Custer-like general who leads his men into a massacre. *She Wore a Yellow Ribbon* also has a romantic plot involving the younger generation within the frame tale of an Indian rebellion and senior officers at Fort Stark, who this time do not make Custer's mistake.

6

Rio Grande is a particularly interesting case, because it was envisioned as a sort of diptych with *The Quiet Man* and a down-payment on it. John Wayne at the time was under a seven-year contract at Republic Pictures, mostly a producer of B-movies. He tempted its owner, Herb Yates (frightened by the new competition from television), with the opportunity of making an A-list movie directed by Duke's pal John Ford. All 'old man' Yates had to do was give Ford money for *The Quiet Man*. The producer, a Scots Presbyterian and basic businessman, suspected that Ford's pet project was, like *The Informer* or, worse, *The Fugitive*, another 'phoney art-house movie'.[20] So he insisted Ford first make a successful cowboy movie with the 'same director, same producer, same cast and crew, same everybody.'[21] Thus, Yates could cut overheads, and pay for *The Quiet Man*.

While Ford and Merian Cooper directed and produced both movies, the cast and crew for *Rio Grande* and *The Quiet Man* are not in fact identical. James K. McGuinness (a right-wing Irish-American and old friend of Ford's) wrote the Western; Frank Nugent did the script for the Irish film. Bert Glennon photographed *Rio Grande* in black and white; Winton Hoch was the Oscar-winning cinematographer for the Technicolour *Quiet Man*.

But the principals for both movies were John Wayne and Maureen O'Hara, and they were supported in each by Victor McLaglen. The two stars play characters older than their real age in the first film, and younger in the second. In the first, they have been married for over sixteen years, have a son, and are long since separated; in the second, they are a courting couple who marry and then work out their differences. In the first, the embers of the couple's old passion, though clearly still alive, are buried under ash, and never burst visibly again into flame; in the second, their desires are licking flames from their first sight of one another. So 'same cast, same crew, same everybody' superficially seems to have produced nothing except proof that two talented actors can represent a wide variety of individualities.

A basic motif of *Rio Grande* is children. In the opening scene of the movie, a detail of cavalry is returning to base after a police expedition among hostile Apaches. Children within the fort race for the gates to see their fathers arrive, as if they are simply coming home after a day's work or an out-of-town business trip. It is not in their minds that their dads might come back wounded, or dead. The situation is different for the row of wives who wordlessly watch the men file into the fort. The delight of those catching first sight of their fathers and husbands on horseback, tired and dusty (all but those four troopers lost in action) tells a tale. Some Apache prisoners have been taken, and they are put with others in a detention centre. The end of the movie will repeat the scene of the soldiers' return to the fort, but this time Maureen O'Hara will have joined the waiting wives, as she searches the file of tired troops for the faces of her son and her husband.

There is a great deal of 'back story' in the plot of *Rio Grande*. The past emerges bit by bit in the present, as the central characters try to heal old wounds from the time of the Civil War. Kirby Yorke (John Wayne) is a lieutenant colonel in the 7th Cavalry, serving under Lieutenant General Philip Sheridan (1831–88), and based near the Mexican border. The area has been harassed by raids of Apaches, who escape to sanctuaries across the Rio Grande. Colonel Yorke has requisitioned 180 additional troopers to handle the problem. Instead, he gets eighteen, and one of them is his teenage son, Jeff, who, lying about his age, has enlisted after being expelled from West Point for failing mathematics. York has not seen his son since 1864, fifteen years earlier. In that year General Sheridan introduced tactics of 'total war' in the Shenandoah valley campaign, burning out the crops and destroying the farms of the confederacy. A Yankee platoon under Kirby Yorke's command carried out an order to burn down the plantation home of his wife Kathleen's family, and she has not lived with him since.

Jeff is called to a short meeting in his father's tent, and gruffly told that he will be treated with the same rough discipline as the other recruits. However, Kirby Yorke has a hard time hiding his fatherly concern, as the boy risks his neck learning horse-back stunts, and has to stand up for himself in fistfights with older troopers. Just as Jeff has proudly gotten his first black eye, Mrs Kathleen Yorke (Maureen O'Hara) arrives at the fort to buy out his commission and bring him home to school and safety. Kirby Yorke sees that his wife is still beautiful, and longs for her love, but he refuses to sign the release. Jeff does the same (he has to keep his word and prove himself), so Kathleen stays on in the fort to try to get her way. At dinner parties in Kirby's tent, and listening to serenades of Irish songs by the regimental singers ('I'll Take You Home Again, Kathleen'), the couple try to come to terms. At one point, Yorke admits he is tempted to agree that if she would sleep with him, he would let their son go, but decides he could not even then release Jeff; the boy has to grow up.

One night the Apaches raid the fort, shoot up the place, and free the captives from the stockade. Colonel Yorke decides it is time to send his wife along with the other troopers' families out of harm's way, and assigns Jeff to guard the caravan, supposedly safe duty.

General Sheridan finally gives Yorke secret permission to engage in the sort of total war that had brought victory in the Shenandoah valley. He is to lead the 7th Cavalry across the Rio Grande in pursuit of the Apaches, and wipe them out. If the mission fails, Sheridan will deny he gave the order and Yorke will be court-martialled, but Sheridan promises that the officers who try him will be picked from those who participated in the raid on the Shenandoah valley, men with experience of justifiable atrocity.

The caravan carrying Mrs Yorke and the other wives and children is raided by Apaches. She survives, but many of the children are taken captive across the Rio Grande, and one of the soldiers' wives is raped and murdered. Trooper Tyree (Ben Johnson) followed the Apaches into Mexican territory, and learned that the children are being held in a village church. According to his reconnaissance, the Apaches have been drinking all day in a tribal festival, and are not prepared to defend themselves. Tyree volunteers to lead a commando party to break into the church and protect the children while Yorke attacks the village with the main force. Tyree selects Jeff to go with him, and Kirby Yorke, though his face shows worry, has to swallow that decision.

The manoeuvre is a success, the children are rescued, and the Apaches slaughtered, but Yorke takes an arrow in the chest. Returning to consciousness, he asks his son to pull it out. 'Get it done, Johnny Reb,' Tyree says to the hesitant youngster, and, in a weird piece of symbolism, Jeff dis-impales his father. In that moment, he becomes a man, his father becomes old, and the Civil War becomes history. When the cavalry return to the fort with the children, Kirby Yorke drawn along in a litter, Kathleen runs up, and, her heart evidently open to renewed love, takes his hand and paces along by his side. Father, mother and son are united once again.

Although both Colonel Yorke and General Sheridan are depicted as grave, dignified and honourable gentleman, they justify past war crimes and plan and execute new ones. These atrocities, it is acknowledged, have divided Yorke from Mrs Yorke, the North from the South in the Civil War, settlers from Indians, and Americans from Mexicans, but they are necessary to bring an end to conflict and save American lives. This is the same argument that was used to justify dropping the atom bomb on Japan, twice, just five years earlier.

It is sometimes said that the movie allegorically addresses an issue in the Korean War. Should not the United Nations' forces pursue the Chinese armies – fighting in support of the North Koreans – across the Yalu River and into Red China, even at the risk of a wider war? In fact, the North Korean army did not invade the South until 25 June 1950, while *Rio Grande* was in its tenth day of filming in Utah. Chinese communist forces did not enter the fighting until 14 October, by which time the movie was completed. So the Korean War may have been on the minds of the movie-goers who first watched *Rio Grande* in late November 1950, but it cannot have been on Ford's mind when making the movie, much less on that of James Warner Bellah, who published the story on which the movie is closely based in the *Saturday Evening Post* in 1947. The Cold War was hardly underway at that point; the communist takeover of Czechoslovakia occurred in February 1948. The movie is not therefore in any specific way a 'Cold War Western', but it is racist in its depiction of raping, murdering, child-abducting and tequila-drinking Apache and righteously nationalistic in its justification of total war.[22] Indeed, the dehumanization of the Apache is a necessary preliminary to the justification of a strategy to extirpate them.[23]

Strangely enough, *Rio Grande* is more accurately conceived not as a Cold War movie but as a post-World War II, coming-home movie like *The Best Years of Our Lives* (1946), only from a patriarchal and pro-war point of view.[24] In the earlier movie war-wounded veterans return home to find their kids grown up and wives estranged by the passage of years; the soldiers have trouble reintegrating into civil society. In *Rio Grande* the wife and child of Colonel Yorke come to the military fort that is his home. There they have to be cured of their illusions and reintegrate with him and his soldiering way of life. Reality is his world – war on the heels of war, until the end of time to police the earth. His view, not theirs, is realism. Father knows best. They just have to learn to accept that fact. Although kind enough, Lt. Col. Kirby Yorke is too powerful and too damn sure he is right. An arrow in the breast makes him lovable again.

In addition to the humanizing wound, another element in the film draws the couple toward reconciliation, the element of music. After their first candlelit dinner together in the Colonel's tent, Kirby and Kathleen Yorke are serenaded by the regimental singers. She is still stiff with fury at Kirby and his 'arsonist' aide, Quincannon (Victor McLaglen), whose hand it was that, under orders, set fire to her family home. The eight-man chorus sings 'I'll Take You Home Again, Kathleen' with aching slowness:

I'll take you home again, Kathleen,
Across the ocean wild and wide,
To where your heart has ever been,
Since first you were my blushing bride.

The roses all have left your cheek,
I've watched them fade away and die;
Your voice is sad when e'er you speak,
And tears bedim your loving eyes.

Oh! I will take you back, Kathleen,
To where your heart will feel no pain,
And when the fields are fresh and green,
I'll take you to your home again.

Kathleen Yorke melts and leans in toward her husband. Kirby stupidly apologizes that the song was not sung at his request, perceptibly disappointing Kathleen, and confirming the belief that 'real' males are clueless.[25] A few bars later, she turns again toward him, he moves to return her look, she turns aside in embarrassment before their eyes can meet, and at last they both face the music once again, the possibility of an early reconciliation lost.

The importance of the song is not just that Mrs Yorke's name is Kathleen, or that she might wish that Kirby would take her back to where her heart would feel no pain, or even that she would be relieved if he could at least acknowledge that she does feel pain. It is also that the song is always taken to be about Irish-American longing for the old country.[26] Along with the song after their second dinner, 'The Bold Fenian Men' –

Some died on the glenside, some died near a stranger,
And wise men have told us that their cause was a failure.
They fought for old Ireland, and they never feared danger.
Glory O, Glory O, to the bold Fenian men

– it evokes the fact that Kirby and Kathleen are both Irish, as is Quincannon. General Sheridan is a Fenian good old boy too. All of them are Irish-Americans working in the new land to make America great, but not forgetting the roots that bind. The recognition of common ethnicity is a step toward overcoming personal differences.

In the final scene of the movie, music again does all the talking. With Colonel Kirby Yorke back on his feet, and himself, Kathleen and General Sheridan on the review stand for awards to the troops (Jeff Yorke gets one), the regimental singers give a rendition of 'Dixie', by order of General Sheridan. Kathleen twirls her parasol in pleasure, both at the tune and at the long-awaited acknowledgment of herself. That she was well worth it – a fact about which movie-goers can have had no doubt – was all left to Maureen O'Hara to embody. She had few lines and little to do to show it. In a movie that requires a woman to execute one long 'climb down', and to give up everything to a man and a man's values, she never loses her pride, and it is hard to see exactly how she carries it off.

7

The making of *A Quiet Man* at long last in June and July 1951 was a family reunion and family vacation for Irish and Irish-American actors. John Wayne arrived at Shannon Airport with his wife Pilar and kids. Melinda, Michael, Patrick and Toni Wayne all show up in the scenes at the pony races on the strand. John Ford brought his son Patrick, who directed some second-unit photography, while his daughter Barbara stayed in Hollywood to edit the rushes. Her future husband Ken Curtis joined the cast in an uncredited part. Ford's brother Eddie O'Fearna was a second assistant director; his brother Francis had a cameo role as old Dan Tobin with a long prop-room beard. Tobin's daughter is played by Ford's former girlfriend Mimi Doyle.[27] Maureen O'Hara's brothers Charles B. Fitzsimons and James Lilburn had parts as, respectively, IRA man Hugh Forbes and young Father Paul. Victor McLaglen's son Andrew was 'second assistant director'; the 'first assistant director' was Wingate Smith, Ford's brother-in-law. Barry Fitzgerald – who got star billing and top pay along with Wayne and O'Hara – was joined in the cast by his brother Arthur Shields. So in the cast and crew of *The Quiet Man*, there were seven Fords, five Waynes, three Fitzsimons, two McLaglens and two Shields, as well as long-time members of the 'John Ford Stock Company' like Ward Bond and Mildred Natwick, who were the next thing to family.

Fitted out from head to toe in brand-new tweeds from O'Máille's shop in Galway, they were all settled in to the finest hotel in Ireland, Ashford Castle (the hotel was a main reason for the choice of location). One can imagine the pleasure of its manager, Noel Huggard, in February when he received a letter reserving eleven twin-bedded rooms from 1 June 1951 to 1 September 1951, a major booking only to be enlarged by the time summer came.[28]

Ashford is a thirteenth-century Norman castle, to which a nineteenth-century French chateau was added by the Oranmore and Browne family, and Victorian gothic extensions by the Guinnesses later in the century. It is sited at the mouth of a river connecting Lough Mask to Lough Corrib, with some of the best trout and salmon fishing in Europe. Ward Bond tried his luck as an angler both on set as Father Lonergan, and off-set during his free time. In the local pubs of Cong village nearby, 18-year-old whiskey sold for a shilling a glass – fourteen cents in American money – and John Wayne sometimes took advantage of this.[29] The landscaped 'English garden' around the castle (where one first sees Maureen O'Hara as Mary Kate herding a flock of sheep) had been converted to a golf course. This amenity was appreciated by Barry Fitzgerald, who relaxed with a round of golf. Arthur Shields wrote Christine, his five-year-old daughter, a message on a postcard depicting Ashford from the air: 'Isn't this a lovely-looking house? This is where we stay. It is on a river that flows between two lakes. Lots of big fish in the water and plenty of flowers and trees.'[30] Plenty of trees is an anomaly in the west of Ireland. Shields wished Christine were there to enjoy Ashford's loveliness and the gaiety of cast and crew.

Ashford Castle, Co. Mayo. The castle itself never appears in The Quiet Man, *although the crew was lodged there and many scenes were filmed on the grounds.*

Frank Nugent, the screenwriter, came along as well. Adjustments to the script continued up to and then into the period of filming. The complete history of the script of *The Quiet Man* is difficult to trace. A prose treatment was done by Richard Llewellyn (author of *How Green Was My Valley*). Bits of it that survive show that early scenes would depict 'The Troubles', with an IRA Flying Column battling the Black and Tans. An undated version by Nugent that evidently was written after 22 December 1950 and before 22 May 1951 also includes a brief early scene entitled 'The Terror'. The hero (then named 'Sean Burke'), having already married Danaher's sister, but who has not consummated the marriage, goes out at night with an IRA column to defend villagers against Black and Tan terrorism.[31] Armistice then occurs, a blacksmith puts away his rifle and takes out his fishing rod, and the rest of the story proceeds in peacetime.

A note in the script suggests that this treatment of 'The Terror' is abbreviated from an earlier version, as a result of 'our lengthy discussion with Sean Nunan of External Affairs'. The writers were informed by this official that it was the wish of the Republic of Ireland that the film should have as little as possible to do with the Anglo-Irish war. Whether this was out of diplomatic sensitivity to Britain, the hope of warmer winds of tourism blowing from America, or some other reason, it is impossible to say.

In any event, not only were no pre-1921 war scenes shot, the film's action was shifted to a vague time period well after peace had been established. As if this were not sufficient, the IRA characters are hilariously sanitised as apple-cheeked dandies in knee-breeches and tam-o-shanters. When one night Mickeleen O'Flynn (Barry Fitzgerald) says that he thinks he'll go to a pub and meet up with his comrades to 'talk a little treason', it is implied – partly because Barry Fitzgerald, aka 'Captain Boyle', says it – that it will be all talk and harmless talk.[32] *The Quiet Man* is not a war movie.

8

But it may be helpful to compare *The Quiet Man* to post-war, coming-home movies. In that way, if few others, it is like *Rio Grande.* One of the fundamental changes made in the plot of Walsh's short story has to do with the motive of 'the quiet man' for refusing to fight Red Will Thornton for the dowry, when it means so much to his wife. Walsh simply stipulated with circular logic that the quiet man after his time in America wanted quiet and did not care about money. But if that were the case, why did he join the IRA soon after his return to Ireland? That he uses a machine gun in a surprise attack against British soldiers but has compunctions about fighting for his wife's dowry does not make sense.

Ford and Nugent invented a new back-story in which Sean Thornton is in flight from a thing he did in America. He killed a man in a prize fight. That fills him with self-disgust, and especially disgust for any fighting done for money. That is why he will not fight Red Will for the £100.

True, he does not have such an aversion to money that he has given his own to charity. Mickeleen O'Flynn says to the IRA boys that Thornton is a millionaire, 'like all the Yanks' (a knowing joke by Ford). As a matter of fact, Thornton is indeed rich, at least relative to the villagers of Innisfree. He has a brand-new set of tweeds; he buys back the family cottage, 'White O' Morn', from Widow Tillane for £1000. Having bought it, he comes into the village pub and offers to buy everyone a drink. He hires a crew to thatch his cottage. He gets himself a fine hunter, a big, dark steed. After his marriage, he buys his wife a pony and trap. The Yank throws his money around. Indeed, part of what is so infuriating to his wife is his attitude to her pittance – what's a hundred pounds? He implies he has so much more as to make that amount nothing. Why bother with the brother? The Yank has so much money he cannot understand its social meaning.

Ford kept World War II out of *The Quiet Man* nearly as completely as he did the Irish War of Independence, yet there is one direct allusion to military service: Sean Thornton was known in the ring, the Reverend Playfair recollects, as Trooper Thornton. War service was, along with working in a Pittsburgh steel smelter, among those unmentionable 'other things' that Thornton says hardened him in the USA. Along with this slight 'Trooper Thornton' reference to the military, the fact that Sean Thornton is 'coming home' to Ireland traumatized by having killed a man, a decent man who had a wife and kids, makes *The Quiet Man* comparable to the sub-genre of post-war, coming-home movies.[33]

The Quiet Man is a diptych with *Rio Grande* by virtue of being, among 'coming-home movies', its opposite: it explores the anti-war position. Against the ethic of the most engaged, militarily aggressive and ethically vociferous nation, Ford is matching the ethic of a small nation with a policy of neutrality. Ireland would not fight even against Hitler, nor did Irish men enlist in World War II to the degree that they volunteered for World War I. The first film explores a politics of engagement; the second, of disengagement. In *The Quiet Man*, disengagement proves impossible for Sean Thornton, although the slow-paced, dreamy life of a country that forgot the war and was forgotten by Europe seems idyllic.

9

The Quiet Man is often taken to be an idealization of Ireland, even ridiculously so. That it is idealized is certainly true cinematographically. Although 1951 had a good summer, the best the people of Cong had seen in years, it was not good enough for the cinematographer, Winton Hoch. He photographed only when sunshine of Californian brightness broke out, so that the movie is made up of the best minutes of a fair season.

The Quiet Man also packs into its fictive little townland of Innisfree the sightseeing splendours of three counties. The production company was based, as mentioned, at Ashford Castle, but the film crew ranged around to all the beauty spots within a day's drive: Yeats's castle, the Tully strand, the Maumturk mountains, Ballyglunin station, the streets of Tuam – they were all magically made part of the immediate vicinity of Innisfree (Cong village). *The Quiet Man* became the 'beautiful travelogue' that Ford intended: turn one way, and you are in Mayo, another and there is Galway; a short stroll, and you are standing on the sea cliffs of Clare.

The movie leaves out Ashford Castle itself, but it frequently features the Castle's mock-Gothic stone bridge and the artificial landscape of its 'English garden'. The slopes and valleys and plantings of the parkland had been constructed between 1860 and 1890 by thousands of post-Famine workers, employed by Lord Ardilaun of the Guinesss family.[34] Even the picturesque church is actually a decorative Protestant estate chapel that normally had at its door no such papist feature as a stoup of holy water (from which Sean Thornton cups a handful for Mary Kate to bless herself). The interior of the church in the movie, however, comes from the Catholic church of Cong, because Ford wanted to include on film its stained-glass masterpiece by Harry Clarke. The Ireland of *The Quiet Man* is an assembly, and a magnificent one.[35]

10

But Ford did not just idealize Ireland, he critiqued it. The critique, like the idealization, comes about through his practice of loading every rift with ore. Ford and Nugent drew into the tale by Maurice Walsh references to many Irish literary classics. 'Innisfree', the name of the townland, obviously alludes to Yeats's most popular poem, 'The Lake Isle of Innisfree'. *Innis* means 'island' in Irish, and the movie's village is on the mainland, so the name does not make sense. It is apposite as a literary allusion. Like the speaker of Yeats's poem, Sean Thornton was heartsick on the roadway and the pavements grey; he dreamed that he would arise and go to a small cabin. Indeed, Thornton not only dreamed of doing it, he bought the cabin.

'To begin at the beginning,' as Father Lonergan says, the movie first introduces, though she has no particular plot reason for being there, May Craig at the 'Castletown' railway station. May Craig was the Abbey's most veteran actor, someone present at the beginning of the Irish Dramatic Revival, and on stage in the first production of *The Playboy of the Western World* in 1907. That is why she is there at the Castletown station.

Stepping off the newly arrived train, Sean Thornton (John Wayne) sparks off a complex little comedy just by asking the guard (Joseph O'Dea), 'Can you tell me the way to Innisfree?' Thornton gets an hilarious amount of useless help. O'Dea says, 'Do you see that road over there?' Yes. 'Well, don't take that one. It will do you no good at all.' As the train guard quickly falls into a fight with the railway porter about Irish history, May Craig butts in with her offer of assistance. Her sister's 'third young one' lives in Innisfree and will be only too glad to show Thornton the way. That's great. '*O, no, if she was here*,' which she is not.

The train driver is played by Eric Gorman (1882–1971), with the Abbey since 1909. He next steps to centre stage in the conversation, but then cannot get it out of his head that the Yank is not in the West of Ireland for the fishing. In his own tales of trout and salmon he has himself caught, 'as long as my arm' (he points with his right hand to the full length of his left arm, elbow to ring finger), he forgets all about Innisfree. The train porter joins in the melee, everyone talking at once, while the fireman watches closely. Finally, without a word, Mickeleen Oge Flynn (Barry Fitzgerald), arrives and walks off with Thornton's cases to his horse and buggy.

This comedy of country confusion is a skilful pastiche of a play by Lady Gregory, with her signature combination of condescension to, and appreciation of, Irish country people. *Spreading the News* (1904) works in ways similar to the opening episode of *The Quiet Man.* Eric Gorman, May Craig and Joseph O'Dea were old hands at playing Lady Gregory's one-acts; their performances in such plays were beloved by Abbey audiences and audiences across America during the Abbey's tours.

'Justified complaints about "American cultural imperialism",' Fintan O'Toole observes, 'can sometimes miss the point that American mass culture may well contain buried elements of other cultures.'[36] This Lady Gregory moment in *The Quiet Man*, of course, is hardly buried. It is a conscious tribute by John Ford, blazoned at the movie's beginning, to her type of comedy and the players who brought it to life again and again over the previous forty years. *The Quiet Man* is full of 'cover versions' of Top Forty Hits of the Irish Revival.

The casting of Barry Fitzgerald as Mickeleen Oge Flynn manages to bring one of O'Casey's characters into play, and enables the film to offer another 'cover version' of an old favourite, or a medley of such. The part of Mickeleen was expanded and diversified into a combination of jarvey, family friend, matchmaker, chaperone, bookie, veteran of the old IRA, secular priest and boxing referee. He even has different costumes for different roles. When going about his business as a *shaughraun*, he puts on a top hat and greatcoat like a character out of Boucicault.

Fitzgerald evokes Captain Boyle from *Juno and the Paycock* by means of his vocabulary. In one of the best lines in the movie (ad-libbed by Fitzgerald),[37] Mickeleen, having carried the crib into the Thorntons' bedroom following their wedding night, sees that the bed has been toppled and a corner of the mattress has dropped to the floor. Ford allows Fitzgerald plenty of time to silently take in the scene, and set the stage for his first judgment, which he addresses toward the viewer as if from the apron of a stage: 'Impetuous!' On further consideration of what he thinks must have been epic love-making, Mickeleen adds, 'Homeric!' The chief identifying feature of Captain Boyle in *Juno and the Paycock* is the utterance of the unexpectedly bookish polysyllable, an incongruous exactitude that is irresistibly comic.[38]

After Sean Thornton outbids Squire Danaher in the Widow Tillane's parlour for 'White O' Morn', Thornton proposes to Mary Kate Danaher, but the Squire, having lost to Sean Thornton a property he thought some day would be added to his own, will not hear of such a match. And Mary Kate could not, and would not, marry without her brother's consent. The Yank finds her deference to her brother and rejection of himself outrageous. We see how angry and frustrated he is by the way he rides his hunter. As if he were an eighteenth-century Irish buck, he jumps gates, gallops through farmers' fields, spurs on the horse, then, dragging hard on the reins, pulls it to a painful stop beside Mary Kate, before digging the spurs again into its wet flanks.

Faced with the spectacle of such public passion, the priest, the vicar, the vicar's wife and Mickeleen agree that something must be done. They concoct a plot to change Danaher's mind. The first part of the plot is to perpetrate a lie. They make out that Thornton is now aiming to marry the Widow Tillane, on whom (or on whose acres) Squire Danaher had always set his sights. At the Innisfree races, the custom is for the unmarried women of the parish to tie their bonnets on high stakes, and the riders in the order of their finish can snatch what bonnet they wish, and thus both prove their mettle and claim their prizes. Sean comes first at the finish, and leaves Mary Kate's bonnet untouched; he takes the Widow's instead. Mary Kate is distressed and Squire Danaher alarmed. Mickeleen and Father Lonergan then spring the second part of their plot. They tell Danaher that were Mary Kate out of his house, the Widow would be happy to come into it as Mrs Danaher.

11

One of the biggest changes to Maurice Walsh's plot was the introduction of pony-racing on the strand. Nothing of the kind occurs in the short story; in the movie, it is important both as spectacle and as a key part of the plot within the plot. It is also an obvious allusion to J.M. Synge's *The Playboy of the Western World*, where such a race occurs offstage in Act III. A movie can do something like this so well, especially a movie by John Ford (past master of filming men on horseback), and a play cannot do it at all. So *The Quiet Man* splendidly supplies a missing scene from a great Irish play, but there may be more of *The Playboy* in *The Quiet Man* than a pony race on the strand.

There is a rhyme between the premises of Synge's play and Ford's film. In Synge's plot, Christy Mahon arrives at a Mayo village having (he thinks) killed a man, his own father. Christy falls in love with the publican's daughter, while a widow also takes a fancy to him. He begins to prove his mettle – that he's not all talk, and a snivelling coward – by winning the races, but he cannot avoid a fight with the old man at the end of the play, watched by the whole village. Then, surprisingly victorious, he walks off alone, and Pegeen Mike is left to despair: 'I've lost the only playboy of the Western World.'

Now compare the story of Sean Thornton. He arrives at a Mayo village having killed a man, a father. He falls in love with the local spinster, while it is falsely rumoured he is courting the village widow. He begins to prove his mettle by winning the races, but still ultimately has to fight old Squire Danaher. Here, however, there is an important change from *The Playboy* pattern: the movie does not end with sexual frustration, but with fulfilment.

Some of these similarities between play and movie are also found between *The Playboy* and Walsh's story, which is riddled with recycled elements from the Literary Revival. Ford evidently perceived the similarities, and both underlined and extended them by the addition of the race scene. This enforcement of the parallel compels a comparison of Pegeen Mike with Mary Kate Danaher.

12

One of the causes of offence taken by Irish nationalist audiences in 1907 to Synge's play was its representation of women. Famously, rioting broke out at the verbal evocation by the playboy of himself being served up with 'a drift of chosen females standing in their shifts' (that is, in their slips). The alexandrine preciousness of the rhyme between *drift* and *shifts* did not mitigate the crime of conceiving of Irish women as willingly coming in a herd, like heifers, to service, or to be serviced by, the playboy. And how could Synge make mention of the undergarments of Catholic Irishwomen?

Synge's fantasies about countrywomen did not stop there. Not a single passionate kiss (according to the stage directions) is exchanged between the actors, but Christy promises Pegeen that in days to come: 'You'll feel my two hands stretched around you, and I squeezing kisses on your puckered lips, till I'd feel a kind of pity for the Lord God is all ages sitting lonesome in his golden chair.' Pegeen skips over the ticklish question of whether God might or might not regret His sexual solitude, and simply says, 'That'll be right fun, Christy Mahon.'[39] Pleased with her receptiveness, he next pictures the two 'making mighty kisses with our wetted mouths … with yourself stretched back unto your necklace, in the flowers of the earth.' Pegeen, 'moved by his tone', murmurs: 'I'd be nice so, is it?' The readiness for love of Pegeen was Synge's wish and part of the point of his play. The audience got that point, and did not like it, especially coming from a Protestant author about characters who were Catholics. Catholic Irish countrywomen were not like that. Not at all. Not a one of them. Never had been.

The riotous reaction to *The Playboy* pretty much put an end to stage representations of Irish women as sexual beings. Synge's play is unarguably a masterpiece, and it quietly took its place in the Abbey repertoire, after some bowdlerizations and the introduction of a demure tradition in the way Pegeen Mike was acted.

13

When Ford finally got around to making *The Quiet Man*, he decided it was going to be a sexy movie, not a movie about IRA heroics. This was not because Hollywood required it to be so, nor because Ford needed to find a way to turn a profit on the movie, nor because it was Ford's custom to dwell on the sexual side of things (it was not), nor even because the IRA activities were small beer after Ford's experiences in the OSS. *The Quiet Man* is far and away the sexiest movie that Ford ever made. Indeed, he claimed it is 'the sexiest picture ever … all about a man trying to get a woman into bed'.[40] He had a reason for making it such.

Sean Thornton's first physical encounter with Mary Kate occurs just after he buys 'White O' Morn'. He is left home by Mickleen Oge Flynn for his first night in his new property, a quite Gothic, Sheridan Le Fanu, ghostly ruin. Yet as he approaches the abandoned cottage, he sees turf smoke coming from its chimney. Thornton opens the cottage door, and the gale outside rushes in, disturbing a little heap of dust beside an abandoned broom. He tiptoes in and fastens the door. He does not (as we do) see Mary Kate Danaher crouching in the shadows, but he does sense the presence of someone else in the building. He gives an Indian war-cry and pitches a stone through a window-pane. Mary Kate (who has been preparing the place for his arrival) gasps, turns, sees her own image in a dusty mirror, screams, and runs for the door, where she is intercepted by the Yank. He pulls the beautiful woman into his arms for a kiss. She, having taken the kiss, stands back, considers her position, then wallops him with a round-house punch.

> Mary Kate Danaher: It's a bold one you are! Who gave you leave to be kissin' me?
> Thornton: So you can talk!
> Mary Kate Danaher: Yes I can, I will and I do! And it's more than talk you'll be gettin' if you step a step closer to me!
> Thornton: Don't worry – you've got a wallop!
> Mary Kate Danaher: You'll get over it, I'm thinkin'.
> Thornton: Well, some things a man doesn't get over so easy.
> Mary Kate Danaher: Like what, supposin'?
> Thornton: Like the sight of a girl coming through the fields with the sun on her hair ... kneeling in church with a face like a saint...
> Mary Kate Danaher: Saint indeed!
> Thornton: ... and now coming to a man's house to clean it for him.
> Mary Kate Danaher: But ... that was just my way of bein' a good Christian act.
> Thornton: I know it was, Mary Kate Danaher. And it was nice of you.
> Mary Kate Danaher: Not at all.

'Saint, indeed!' She both rebukes him for the impiety and phoniness of his courtship metaphor, and indignantly denies being a saint. This Irishwoman is no puritan. After she is done talking, Mary Kate turns to leave, then darts her head back inside the door for one last quick kiss on the lips of the Yank before taking her leave.

When the official courting commences, Mary Kate is as eager as Sean Thornton is to escape the eye of their chaperone, Mickeleen. Together they steal a tandem bicycle – the riding of which even more than paddling a canoe together traditionally symbolizes successful marital relations. Having gotten clear of onlookers, they pause, and Sean wishes to point out aspects of the scenery. Not Mary Kate.

John Wayne, Barry Fitzgerald as chaperone, and Maureen O'Hara, at the beginning of the courting in The Quiet Man, *1952. (Lilly Library, courtesy Republic Pictures)*

She runs off across a field. At a river's edge, she kneels to peel off her silk stockings. Sean catches a glance of her thighs, she catches him looking, and returns to her undressing, then bare-footed prances across the stream. He gives his usual John Wayne double-take, throws one shoulder back, then rears forward to stomp, still wearing his shoes, splashingly after her. Up ahead, she does a Daphne-like pastoral striptease – with her stockings in one hand, she takes off her bonnet with the other, casting flirtatious looks back at him. He shows he is as game as she is by hurling his hat into the next field over. Then she leads him by the hand up the hill.

They arrive at a hilltop churchyard with a ruined chapel.

> Thornton: If anybody had told me six months ago that today I'd be in a graveyard in Innisfree with a girl like you that I'm just about to kiss, I'd have told 'em …
> Mary Kate Danaher: Oh, but the kisses are a long way off yet!
> Thornton: Huh?
> Mary Kate Danaher: Well, we just started a-courtin', and next month, we start the walkin' out, and the month after that there'll be the threshin' parties, and the month after that …

Thornton: Nope.
Mary Kate Danaher: Well, maybe we won't have to wait that month …
Thornton: Yup.
Mary Kate Danaher: … or for the threshin' parties …
Thornton: Nope.
Mary Kate Danaher: … or for the walkin' out together …
Thornton: No.
Mary Kate Danaher: … and so much the worse for you, Sean Thornton, for I feel the same way about it myself!

She opens her arms to be embraced, and he gathers her in to himself. Thunder rolls. Frightened by the lightning-bolts, Mary Kate hugs closely to Sean Thornton's broad chest. He puts his suit coat round her shoulders as the winds rise. Then big raindrops splat one by one on his white nylon shirt, and each makes a little nude pool of transparency, over which Mary Kate spreads and tenses her fingers. Finally, they do kiss. The experience leaves Mary Kate limp. During its shooting, Ford did take after take trying to get the pair to be more passionate.[41] Though only involving a kiss and a rain shower, the action is metaphorically pre-coital, coital, and then post-coital. It is as sexual as a Hollywood movie in 1951 could be.

For the rest of the movie, Ford makes the audience interested in one chief question: when will Sean Thornton and Mary Kate Danaher get on with the consummation of their love? They get married in due course, but at the wedding reception Squire Danaher finally realizes that he has been tricked by a community plot against himself; he punches Sean and scatters the coins across the floor. Mary Kate makes it known to Sean that she will not sleep with him until she gets her dowry, and locks herself in the bedroom.

In a new scene that was suggested by John Wayne (unless he got to do it, he feared he would appear to have 'no balls'),[42] Sean Thornton kicks the bedroom door down, lifts his bride up, and says, 'There'll be no locks or bolts between us, Mary Kate Danaher, except those in your own mercenary little heart,' then tosses her, panting with anger and sexual frustration, onto her own marriage bed, breaking it. So when Mickeleen Oge Flynn says their love-making has been impetuous and Homeric, we know it has as yet been nothing of the kind. They both want it, but because of the missing dowry, they cannot have it.

Each goes to talk to a man of the cloth – Thornton to Church of Ireland Reverend Playfair (Arthur Shields) and Mary Kate to Father Lonergan (Ward Bond). Reverend Playfair knows all about Thornton's history in the ring, and has a scrapbook to illustrate it, but he also knows a lot about local customs of marriage, and, though Protestant, respects them. He gently takes it for granted that now Sean will have to fight for the dowry. By showing a picture of himself on the Trinity College boxing team, he subtly shifts the context from boxing as a fight to the finish to boxing as an athletic competition. That is all the persuasion required. The tact and economy in the script is admirable, as is Shields's performance. His message is: You must fight for that dowry, and it will be good sport on the day.

Mary Kate happens to catch Father Lonergan just as he is stalking a trophy salmon. She whispers to him in Irish of her plight (as if dirty things become clean when spoken *as Gaelige*): no dowry, no consummation, husband in sleeping bag. 'Sleeping bag' in Irish is unfamiliar to Lonergan (a joke on the language revival?), but when he does get the meaning, he is outraged: 'Ireland may be a poor country, God help us, but here a married man sleeps in a bed and not a bag.' His implied message is: Go home and bring your husband to your bed. Which she duly does.

Revd Playfair (Arthur Shields), Mary Kate Danaher Thornton (Maureen O'Hara) and Mickeleen Oge Flynn (Barry Fitzgerald) attend to Sean Thornton (John Wayne) after he has been knocked cold at his own wedding reception, in The Quiet Man, 1952. *(Lilly Library, courtesy Republic Pictures)*

We do not witness the long-delayed nuptials, but the next morning Sean Thornton appears to be mighty pleased with how the night was passed. He is cock of the walk and calls for his wife, but she is not to be found in the kitchen. Mickleen Oge Flynn, waiting at the cottage door, is ready to explain that she is so ashamed of loving a man of whom she could not be proud, she has run away to Dublin. It all has to do with the dowry, and a woman's rights.

Thus, the final fist fight is precipitated, more or less as in the story by Maurice Walsh, apart from Ford's innovation of having Sean Thornton drag his wife brutally from the train station across half the parish to Squire Thornton's fields, where he throws her violently back into the hands of the Squire. It is hard to see what this picturesque and vaudevillian violence is meant to be except either a comic critique of the widespread wife-battering in the Irish Free State, or an endorsement of it. Maybe a public and post-colonial festival re-enactment of the Roman rape of local Sabines?[43] There is a self-conscious element of possible playacting by both Sean and Mary Kate, an over-the-top impersonation of an archaic, primitive custom – is he serious? is she frightened? – that enables the scene to be enjoyed, without requiring one's approval of a social code of female subjugation.[44]

Publicity still from The Quiet Man *of Mary Kate Danaher (Maureen O'Hara) being violently dragged along by Sean Thornton (John Wayne); the use of the image for publicity suggests an expectation that this 'taming of the shrew' would become a favourite part of the movie. (Lilly Library, courtesy Republic Pictures)*

The fight with Red Will Danaher sportily (if not sportingly) won, peace settles back on Innisfree, according to the narrator, Father Lonergan. The whole story has unfolded as if it were his home movie ('See, that's me there …'), and now he is folded back into it in a playful device. In a theatrical 'curtain call' – as Luke Gibbons calls it – the characters each get a final close-up (all pretending to be Protestants, for the benefit of Reverend Playfair and the visiting Bishop).[45] The last to take a bow are Sean Thornton and his wife in their cottage garden. Then Mary Kate whispers in Sean's ear. He is amazed by what he has heard. She sprints off toward the cottage, and, once again rearing back one shoulder, then plunging forward, John Wayne follows after her.

A cult-movie secret is what Ford told O'Hara to whisper in John Wayne's ear before she dashes off – something she at first said she would not dare to say, and then did say. If her words did not have to do with some very pleasurable thing that Wayne has always wanted and will get if he just comes inside, it would be a big surprise. Ford has made the audience wait and wait. Just as the curtain falls, they know impetuous, Homeric consummations are very soon to resume and will long continue.

14

What is even more noteworthy than Ford's thoroughgoing characterization of the Irish woman as a fully adult, pleasure-loving person is how few objections were raised by Richard Hayes, the Irish censor. He cut to ribbons most Hollywood movies submitted for Irish circulation. In the case of *The Quiet Man* Hayes scissored out Mickeleen's two best lines – 'Homeric!' 'Impetuous' – about the presumed feats of love that broke Sean Thornton's big bed, and the appraisal by Feeney (Jack McGowran) of the bed itself: 'Ah, a man'd have to be a sprinter to catch his wife in a bed like that.'[46] While these excisions are ridiculous, they are mild exactions by the standards of the time in Ireland, which were the strictest in the world.

Ford was, of course, unlike Synge, a Catholic. Also, the sex that occurs in *The Quiet Man* occurs within marriage, off screen, and for the most part after the end of the story. Nudity is never an issue. But still it is surprising that no whisper was raised about the 'unhealthiness' of the way Mary Kate is depicted. She is often filmed from low down and in half-profile, so as to make Maureen O'Hara, already well-endowed, appear heroically voluptuous. It would have been silly to make a stink about what is overall such a light and affectionate portrait of Ireland, simply because Mary Kate Danaher's breasts appear to be cinematically large, but the fear of being silly did not always stand in the way of the Irish censorship.

The failure to register the film's two major innovations, its sexualization of Irish womanhood and its thematic concentration on the importance of regular and mutually joyful sexual intercourse to a happy marriage, meant that Ford's chief criticism of Ireland went unnoticed. Like Synge, he saw the Irish rural population as starved of joy by Catholic sexual repression and nationalist chauvinism. He wanted to replace those false images with more natural truths and healthy teachings. A man would not have to be a sprinter to catch his wife in a big bed, because she would most likely not be running away from his embraces, but warmly returning them. This view of women was Ford's gift from America to his homeland, but Ireland was not quite ready to accept the offering, or even to acknowledge it.

The Irish response to *The Quiet Man* was often embarrassment. It was commonly said to be all stereotypes. Squire Danaher as if on cue even produces an Irish bull: 'He'll regret it til his dying day, if he lives that long.' The characters, situations and gags of *The Quiet Man*, however, are not so much stereotypes of a socially regressive kind, as 'old chestnuts' – oft-told tales and pieces of theatrical lumber. Ford's Irish movie is like a Christmas pudding made from an ancient recipe, stuffed with nuts and fruits and coins and candies of every description, then soaked in liquor.

The cast was conscious of the twice-told character of the tale, and they gave to their playing the quality of an encore. They gloried in the recherché quaintness of the game. The acting is quite in the spirit of that Friday night in March 1935 when the Hollywood actors joined the Abbey regulars in a performance of *The Playboy of the Western World*. In *The Quiet Man*, however, the stars are not lost in the crowd; they come forward into central roles. Admittedly, those film stars playing Irish people ham it up in sometimes corny fashion, but Abbey actors had always done that too. Fifteen years after the Abbey actors had come to Hollywood for *The Plough and the Stars*, the dramatic furniture and playing style of the Irish Revival had been taken up into the working vocabulary of international performance. It is remarkable how well Victor McLaglen does as Squire Danaher, and how brilliantly the old football player and cowboy actor Ward Bond carries off the role of Father Lonergan. Irish priests aren't like that? More's the pity.

In a surprising coincidence, just as Ford was making *The Quiet Man* into 'the greatest hits of the Irish Revival', and Hollywood stars were demonstrating that the Abbey playing styles had been affectionately taken up into the vocabulary of global entertainment, the Abbey Theatre itself burned. As its home burned, the style took wing. The *Irish Independent* caught up with the *The Quiet Man* cast on the runway of Shannon Airport, just before their return to Hollywood, and asked them their reactions to the fire. John Wayne said he had known the Abbey actors since they began touring America in the 1930s, and they had become some of his best friends, often visiting his home, so he felt terrible for them; it was as if their own home place had been burnt. Yes, it was a terrible shock, Shields admitted, but the place was always a tinderbox. Anyway, 'fire won't stop the Abbey'.[47]

Barry Fitzgerald agreed. The old, beloved costumes were gone, and perhaps some valuable unpublished scripts, but the actors were still there to act and the playwrights were not going to vanish. It was more than time for the government to build a new and bigger theatre in Dublin. John Ford had the last word. The Irish people could expect the film he was making in Galway to appear in Irish picture houses the following March or April. The greatness of the Abbey Theatre, it was implied, had been captured and, in some degree, immortalized in *The Quiet Man.*

Abbey Theatre interior, intact but blackened after the 18 July 1951 fire. (Photograph made 1 January 1953, Gjon Mili/Time Life Pictures/Getty Images)

AFTERWORD

Arthur Shields was married three times – to Bazie McGee, to Una O'Connor, and, on 17 September 1955, to Laurie Bailey – and he had two children, Adam and Christine, both resident in the United States. Nonetheless, he chose to be buried in Ireland in a single plot alongside his brother Will Shields, known the world over as Barry Fitzgerald.

Although eight years older than Arthur Shields, Will had always been the little boy in the family. As Arthur came of age, his relationship to Will was sometimes a protective one. Neither brother, however, was dominant; they supported one another when support was needed.[1] They went into the Abbey within a few years of one another (1913 for Arthur, 1917 for Will); they left it within a few years of one another (1936 for Will, 1939 for Arthur). They both worked on Broadway in the late 1930s, and sometimes in the same productions. In March 1940, when Arthur Shields was released from hospital after his collapse with tuberculosis, Will drove him from New York to Hollywood, stopping each day in a different town to obtain from the local doctor the required out-patient treatment. Thereafter, they were both settled in California. In their Hollywood hills community Will was a regular at Arthur Shields's dinner table. On weekends Arthur Shields and his family became frequent guests at Will's vacation home in the Santa Barbara hills. Along with the families of their sister and their niece, the Mortisheds and the Slotts, the Shields brothers kept an extended family vitally centred while living in Los

Angeles, where the velocity of centrifugal social forces is often shattering.

The greatest days of their creative achievements came to an end in the summer of 1952 with *The Quiet Man.* The Internet Movie Database lists another thirty-three appearances in television or film for Arthur Shields, and seven more roles for Barry Fitzgerald, but none of these is a highlight of two careers with many earlier brilliant successes.

After *The Quiet Man* was completed, Will Shields learned that he had Parkinson's disease. It is observable in that film that he often holds one hand in another when he has nothing else to grip (the reins of a horse, a pint glass, etc.); a primary symptom of Parkinson's is a trembling of the hands. For the autumn of 1952 Fitzgerald was contracted to star in an Italian movie, *Ha da veni ... Don Calegero!* A foreign country, an unknown director and the early effects of Parkinson's disease made him 'over-tired and out of sorts', so Arthur Shields stayed in Rome for three and a half months to help him out.[2] Afterwards the brothers agreed that Will should not again take on such demanding professional duties.

Will Shields was put on several speculative medications (no single treatment for Parkinson's was known to be successful) and sleeping pills were prescribed on top of the other medications to ensure rest. He occasionally got confused and overdosed himself. Once, on a sudden impulse, Arthur Shields ran round to Will's house on Gardner Street. He arrived just in time to save his brother from death by overdose.

In 1959 Will Shields went to Ireland. Feeling moody and distracted, he went to his friend J.J. Molloy's doctor in July. He was judged to be in a toxic state from the amounts and combinations of medications he was taking.[3] In mid-October he collapsed from a blood clot in the brain. Surgery was carried out at St Vincent's Hospital, Dublin. Back in Los Angeles Arthur Shields was just then opening with Mary Anderson in a production of *The Plough and the Stars* at the Civic Theater. He was unable to come to Ireland until 1 November. After arriving at the hospital room Arthur Shields gave Will a Camel, and Will just let the cigarette burn, never moving at all, even as the lighted end burned down to his fingers – Arthur had to jump up and take it away from him. To see his brother in such a state was heartbreaking. The always gentle little man, so nimble and light on his feet, even had unaccountable, staggering fits of violence. Arthur Shields had a meeting with Dr Donovan, and was not consoled about Will's prognosis.

Only five months later Will himself wrote a letter with this completely unexpected news: 'I've made a good recovery and am looking forward to summer here.' In August 1960, after a season of fishing and yachting, he declared his intention to head back to his home in Gardner Street, Hollywood, live with his sister 'Bid' Shields Mortished, then convalescent, and employ a young couple to look after them both. But in October, before he could put this plan into action, he had to go into St Patrick's Hospital in Dublin. He died on 4 January 1961.

Going through Will's effects in the hospital, Arthur Shields came across a letter of consolation from a Father Lynch, which arrived after the actor had already entered a coma. Shields took the time to write Father Lynch, and reflect on his brother's life:

> Barry was a shy little man ... he was uncomfortable in crowds and really dreaded meeting new people, but he was not a recluse, and did enjoy certain company, especially when 'old chat' was good. He always loved our Christmas parties, when the children were all around, and he could sit back, smoke his pipe, have an odd drink, and open his presents. He never married, not that he disliked the company of women, but I think he was held back from proposing to anyone through shyness.[4]

In all their years together in Dublin, New York and Hollywood, Shields could recall only one quarrel between them. That was in February 1926 after the first production of *The Plough and the Stars.* Sean O'Casey was weighing the possibility of leaving Ireland for London. Will advised him to go; Arthur Shields felt strongly that O'Casey should stay, since both the Abbey and the country needed him, and he needed them too. The two brothers did not speak for twelve days. Then their mother 'told us we ought to be ashamed of ourselves to allow something completely irrelevant to come between us'. Never since, Shields told Father Lynch, had they fallen out with each other.

The funeral service for Barry Fitzgerald was held in St Patrick's Cathedral, Dublin, where Jonathan Swift had once been Dean. An elegy was delivered from the high pulpit by the Archbishop, the Most Revd Dr G.O. Simms – very personal in tone, and giving thanks to God for 'a lovable life, lived with an unusual serenity and simplicity, yet a life of wide influence'. The Cathedral was crowded with old friends from the theatre and many others whom Shields did not know – 'more Catholics in the church than Protestants'. Shields felt it deeply. At the interment in Dean's Grange, he saw Helena Molony at the cemetery gate. He made the others wait while she, old and partly crippled, made her way to the graveside. The great feminist Republican had been an actress in the Abbey, and was the one who in 1916 asked Arthur Shields to hide the printing press on which the Proclamation had been printed.

When Arthur Shields was in Dublin the previous November to look after his brother, he had been invited to call upon President Éamon de Valera at Áras an Uachataráin (formerly the Viceregal Lodge). Shields reported to his wife Laurie that he was 'not at all impressed' by de Valera. 'God bless us, but he has a lot to answer for.'[5] Both men had fought in the Easter 1916 rebellion. Shields had been a leader of the Abbey Theatre and a key figure in the representation of Ireland on Broadway and in Hollywood, while de Valera had been the single most important leader of the Irish state in the century. Yet they did not at all see eye to eye on the new Ireland that followed the national movement for freedom. Shields regarded with horror the Civil War de Valera had started over the Oath to the king and the partition of the Six Counties in the 1922 Treaty.

He resented the constitutional declaration that Gaelic was the 'national' and 'first official' language of the country (afterwards, compulsory for actors employed by the Abbey Theatre). The ban on divorce, and in general the privileged position of Catholic doctrine in the 1937 Constitution, were injurious to him, his son and his second wife Aideen. Neutrality in World War II seemed wrong to Shields – although German on his mother's side, he was all for the Allies. Basically, the new Ireland did not have a place, he felt, for people like himself, a Protestant by background, a secularist, an intellectual and an artist. Still, it could not be said that Arthur Shields was bitter, or had lost his love of Ireland, its people and its literature.

2

After the success of *The Quiet Man*, John Ford dreamed up schemes for further collaborations with the Shields brothers in putting the Irish Revival on screen. One of his first ideas for Four Provinces Films, the production company he formed with Lord Killanin and Brian Desmond Hurst in 1951, was a treatment of James Stephens's *The Demi-Gods*, starring Barry Fitzgerald and Maureen O'Hara.[6] That film was never made, nor did Barry Fitzgerald again act under Ford's direction.

Three years after Barry Fitzgerald's death, Ford was preparing to direct a movie based on the life of Sean O'Casey, *Young Cassidy*. He called upon Arthur Shields – perhaps for the sake of good luck, and the touch of Abbey Theatre authenticity – to serve as a voice coach and play a part. By this time, however, Shields himself was ailing. His old bout with TB, and a lifetime of smoking Camel cigarettes, had left him with emphysema.

Arthur Shields was financially secure. Barry Fitzgerald had shared out his sizable fortune among the extended Shields-Mortished-Slott family. Earlier, Arthur had bought a 10-per-cent stake in Ziv Productions, a television production company, which paid him returns. He also became the pitch man in commercials for Italian Swiss Colony wine; that brought a regular income. This advertising work came about in a period (1957–60) when the California wine industry was just getting on its feet, and Americans were not yet customarily drinkers of wine. The fact that Shields was Irish, and presumably associated with the consumption of whiskey and porter, did not stand in his way. He fitted the stereotype of a cultivated and European gentleman. And who would not trust the word of a priest about wine, even if he were only a stage priest?

His wife Laurie, amazed at all that this kindly, modest gentleman had done before she met him, was determined that he should get his life-story on paper. It seemed important to do not just for his daughter Christine and the wider Shields clan, but for Ireland and for theatre. She facilitated a number of long interviews with theatre scholars from American universities. In his recorded recollections, Shields was very definite in his beliefs. Writers, he thought, were at the basis of theatre, both in creating a sense of self in the audience – 'It was the plays of the Abbey Theatre that made me increasingly aware that I was an Irishman, even before I was a member of the Company' – and in forming the pediment upon which all the actor's work is raised: 'The real greatness of the Abbey was that it was a writer's theatre, not an actor's theatre, director's theatre, electrician's theatre, or a scene-painter's theatre … The playwrights were really in charge. My advice to those who want to start a theatre is that they should start with the playwrights, and make sure they have plays really worth performing.'[7]

Yet strangely enough, after working with three generations of Irish writers – Yeats and Gregory, Robinson and O'Casey, Denis Johnston and Paul Vincent Carroll – Arthur Shields went off to Hollywood, a place where the writers, however essential, were not in charge. In the rank and file of production companies, they came behind the producers, the directors, the stars and sometimes even the cameramen.

In Hollywood, at the very fountain of representations for the world as a whole, Shields and his former Abbey Theatre colleagues – Barry Fitzgerald, Sara Allgood, Una O'Connor, J.M. Kerrigan and others – managed to embody something of the 'real greatness' of the Abbey: the writers' perceptions of the human story at the dayspring of a nation. They did this by the ways they played their parts in movies based on Irish plays, like *The Plough and the Stars*, and in other movies that transmitted knock-on effects of those plays, like *How Green Was My Valley.* The Shields brothers enjoyed a creative and collaborative sympathy with John Ford that parallelled writer and actor relations at the Abbey.

John Ford's movies with Abbey actors drew upon the Irish heritage and also aspired to leave new proofs of the national genius. Movies like *The Long Voyage Home* and *She Wore a Yellow Ribbon* were not marked as essentially Irish; they were multi-ethnic and universal in their range. These too, however, like *The Playboy of the Western World* and *Juno and the Paycock*, are great cultural achievements. The connection has not hitherto been biographically traced between the plays of the Irish Revival and a certain group of distinguished movies of Hollywood's golden age, but the connection is there. That quiet, modest gentleman Arthur Shields may be foremost among those who forged the link.

NOTES

Introduction

1. Alastair Phillips and Ginette Vincendeau (eds), *Journeys of Desire: European Actors in Hollywood* (BFI Publishing: London 2006), p. 7.

2. W.B. Yeats to Edith Shackleton Heald, 4 September [1938], unpublished letter, 'The Collected Letters of W.B. Yeats, Past Masters: English Letters Collection', Online database, OUP: Oxford.

3. Stanley Weintraub (ed.), *Literary Criticism of Oscar Wilde* (University of Nebraska Press 1968), p. 190.

4. *Ibid.* p. 182.

5. See James Pethica, '"Our Kathleen": Yeats's Collaboration with Lady Gregory in the Writing of *Cathleen ni Houlihan*' in Deirdre Toomey (ed.), *Yeats and Women* (Palgrave: London 1997).

6. W.J. McCormack, *Fool of the Family: A Life of J.M. Synge* (London, Weidenfeld & Nicolson/New York: New York UP 2000), p. 362.

I. John Ford as an Irish Author

1. For details of the Screen Directors Guild meeting, see Joseph McBride, *Searching for John Ford* (Faber and Faber: London 2003), pp. 479–84. And for a different, and standard, reading of this episode and of Ford as a director of Westerns, see Jim Kitses, *Horizons West: Directing the Western from John Ford to Clint Eastwood* (BFI Publishing: London 2004), p. 29.

2. Robert S. Birchard, *Cecil B. DeMille's Hollywood* (UP of Kentucky: Lexington 2004), p. 343.

3. David Thomson, *Showman: The Life of David Selznick* (Alfred Knopf: New York 1992), p. 179.

4. McBride, *Searching for John Ford*, p. 191.

5. Edward Bernds, quoted in *ibid.* p. 483.

6. *Ibid.* pp. 139–42.

7. Maureen O'Hara, *'Tis Herself: A Memoir* (Simon and Schuster: New York 2004), p. 60.

8. *Ibid.* p. 139.

9. It is a pleasure to credit this observation to Darcy O'Brien, actor George O'Brien's son, a novelist and distinguished scholar of Irish literature, and my own teacher at Pomona College, California. The observation is recorded by McBride, *Searching for John Ford*, p. 200.

10. Desmond King, *The Liberty of Strangers: Making the American Nation* (OUP: Oxford 2005), p. 67.

11. *Ibid.* p. 60.

12. Emile Durkheim, *Division of Labour in Society*, trans. W.D. Halls (Macmillan: London 1984), pp. 304–8.

13. Herbert J. Gans, 'Symbolic Ethnicity' in John Hutchinson and Anthony D. Smith (eds), *Ethnicity* (Oxford UP: Oxford 1996), pp. 146–52.

14. O'Hara, *'Tis Herself*, p. 104; McBride, *Searching for John Ford*, pp. 549, 650.

15. Brian Spittles, *John Ford* (Longman: Harlow, Essex 2002), p. 20.

16. John Ford to Bob Ford [September 1937?], Bill Brown's Physical Training Farm, John Ford papers, Lilly Library. Bob Ford was the son of the actor and director Francis Ford.

17. Daddy to Dear Ma [26? June 1943], Office of Strategic Services stationery, John Ford papers, Lilly Library.

18. Mary [Ford] to My dearest Jack, 1 June 1943, Lilly Library; the reference is to John Wayne, whose marriage to Josie Saenz was falling apart because of his affair with 17-year-old Mexican actress Esperanza Bauer (1926–61).

19. One threatened exception to Ford's escape from slanderous publicity was avoided in early 1942. Ollie Carey warned Ford that a writer named Tom Wood was preparing a scurrilous article about him. Ford wrote to John Wayne and Ward Bond, asking them to threaten Wood that if one derogatory word was published about Ford, they would 'kick the shit out of [him] regularly each and every day of the week' (Ford to Wayne, 12 January 1942, Lilly Library). He also asked his agent, Harry Wurtzel, to hire a lawyer to put Wood on notice that his work would be examined carefully for libel (Ford to Wurtzel, 12 January 1942). It is not clear what Ford feared Wood would say. Wurtzel got the story, and sent it to Ford for clearance before its publication in *Liberty* in the last week of February (Wurtzel to Dear Pappy, nd, Lilly Library).

20. Leonard Mosley, *Zanuck: The Rise and Fall of Hollywood's Last Tycoon* (Little, Brown and Co.: Boston 1984), p. 242.

21. Mimi [Doyle] to My Darling [December 1938?], Monday, John Ford papers, Lilly Library.

22. Katherine Hepburn to Dearest Sean [John Ford], [?March 1937], Marriot Apartment Hotel, Indianapolis, John Ford papers, Lilly Library.

23. [Katherine Hepburn] to Dear Sean [John Ford], 10 April 1937, Havana Special, Pennsylvania Railroad stationery, Lilly Library.

24. The original name of 'Eve March' was Adalyn Doyle. She got a start in Hollywood as a stand-in for Katherine Hepburn, and, though only 5' 3" tall, was said to resemble

Hepburn. Darryl Zanuck groomed Doyle for feature roles, beginning with a small, uncredited part in *Advice to the Lovelorn* (1933) (*New York Times*, 8 October 1933).

25. Mimi to My Darling [December 1938?], John Ford papers, Lilly Library; William J. Mann, *Kate: The Woman Who Was Katherine Hepburn* (Faber and Faber: London 2006), p. 253.

26. [Frances Rich] to Dearest Pal, 30 April 1937, Cranebrook Academy of Art, Michigan, Ford Papers, Lilly Library. Rich gossips about Ford's romance with Hepburn and confesses that she herself is aiming to sleep with Erro Saarinen, the architect and sculptor, before the week is out. There is no sign that Ford and Rich were a couple.

27. McBride, *Searching for John Ford*, pp. 649–50.

28. *Ibid.* p. 383, Ford to Spig Wead, 11 February 1944, John Ford papers, Lilly Library.

29. [John Ford] to My Darlin' (My loved one, my heart, *Maisin!*), 19 November 1950, 5 December 1950 and 19 January 1951; O'Hara, *'Tis Herself*, pp. 144, 147, 149.

30. O'Hara, *'Tis Herself*, p. 190. Tyrone Power is suspected to be the man.

31. *Ibid.* p. 197.

32. *Ibid.* p. 131.

33. 'A Footnote in the Decathalon', *New York Times* (30 June 1996).

34. McBride, *Searching for John Ford*, p. 651.

35. There is a continuing debate about whether Stepin Fetchit was degrading to African-Americans or satirically exploitative of white prejudices, on the lines of Baron Sasha Cohen. On 14 February 1945, Stepin Fetchit wrote to 'Commander John Ford' to say: 'It would be a life-saver and opening of corporal grace again if you could arrange anything for me.' A year later, Ford suggested to Darryl Zanuck that they cast Stepin Fetchit in *My Darling Clementine* as 'bellboy, porter, night clerk, waiter, bootblack, bartender and chambermaid at the hotel'. Zanuck replied the following day, 5 February 1946, that Walter White, head of the NAACP, had singled out Stepin Fetchit as one who always portrayed the blacks as 'lazy, stupid, halfwit[s]' and they were furious about it.

Everyone who knew him well could agree that Stepin Fetchit was an intelligent, furiously industrious actor with a well-schooled skill in physical comedy, but those who saw his work were not sure who the joke was on. Woody Strode himself recalled defending Fetchit to other black actors in 1965: 'He was one of our greatest comedians and the first black actor to get star billing. I took a stand for him. I said, "If it hadn't been for Stepin Fetchit, I wouldn't be here. Somebody had to start it." They're going to do his story some day and all this history will come out. John Ford loved the guy; so did Will Rogers. In fact, John Ford directed a couple of pictures in which Will and Step shared top billing. As a child [in Los Angeles], the only black movie star I had ever heard of was Stepin Fetchit. He made two million dollars during the 1930s. He owned sixteen cars. I saw him when I was a kid; he was driving a pink convertible Rolls Royce.'

36. Peter Bogdanovich, *John Ford* (University of California Press 1978), p. 97.

37. *Ibid.* p. 104. Ford also told Bogdanovich that it was the American audience that liked 'to see Indians get killed. They don't consider them as human beings – with a

great culture of their own – quite different from ours' (pp. 94–5). This is well said, but it ignores Ford's own role through scores of mass-culture cowboy films made before 1964, which fed the audience's readiness to treat native Americans as not really human.

38. Emile Durkheim quoted in John Rex, 'Multiculturalism in Europe' in Hutchison and Smith, *Ethnicity*, p. 245.

39. Christopher Robbins, *The Empress of Ireland: Chronicle of an Unusual Friendship* (Scribner: London 2004), pp. xi–xii.

40. *Ibid.* p. 335.

41. Hutchison and Smith, *Ethnicity*, pp. 6–7.

42. W.B. Yeats to Edmund Dulac, 6 July [1935], Past Masters, Oxford UP.

43. Brian Desmond Hurst to Dear Jack, 16 July 1951, Renown Film Productions, John Ford papers, Lilly Library.

44. Barbara Naomi Cohen-Stratyner, *The Biographical Dictionary of Dance* (Shirmer Books: New York 1982), pp. 452–4.

45. Spencer Tracy's homosexual life, to the degree that it existed, is documented in William J. Mann's biography *Kate.*

46. Clifton Webb specialized in playing sinister sissies. He was blackballed by the Hays Committee for being homosexual, and was not able to work for many years, until Otto Preminger won permission to use Webb in *Laura.* Webb was nominated for an Oscar in the film, which reactivated his Hollywood career. See Vito Russo, *The Celluloid Closet: Homosexuality in the Movies* (Harper and Row: New York 1987), pp. 45, 59, 94.

47. Robbins, *Empress of Ireland*, pp. 337–8.

48. Abbey Theatre Minute Books, 14 June 1935, NLI, Acc 3961, vol. 4.

49. Daddy to Dear Ma [John Ford to Mary Ford], [August 1942?], John Ford papers, Lilly Library.

50. John Ford to Darling Mary, 23 June 1944; Ford to My darlings, 27 June 1944; Ford papers, Lilly Library.

51. Brian [Desmond Hurst] to Dear Jack [Ford], [24 September 1947], John Ford papers, Lilly Library.

52. Michael Killanin to My dear Jack [December 1947?], House of Lords, John Ford papers, Lilly Library.

53. John Ford to Maureen O'Hara, 10 January 1951, O'Hara, *'Tis Herself*, p. 149.

54. Jack to Brian [Desmond Hurst], telegram, 6 April 1951; Hurst to Ford, 9 April 1951; John Ford papers, Lilly Library.

55. Michael Killanin to My dear Jack, 20 October 1951, Spiddal House, John Ford papers, Lilly Library. Ford told Maureen O'Hara that he had her and John Wayne in mind for *The Demigods*, which seems bizarre (O'Hara, *'Tis Herself*, p. 180); the proposed cast list was later amended to O'Hara and Barry Fitzgerald, with an 'extremely handsome … preferably blonde' boy yet to be sourced (Ford to Killanin, 9 September 1952). After the producers encountered difficulty with the purchase of rights, the film of Stephens's novel was never made.

56. Ford to Michael Killanin, 25 October 1951, John Ford papers, Lilly Library.

57. John Ford to Michael Killanin, 3 December 1951, John Ford papers, Lilly Library.

58. John Ford to Michael Killanin [*c.*20 August 1952], John Ford papers, Lilly Library.

59. Adrian Frazier, '"Quaint Pastoral Numbskulls": Siobhan McKenna's *Playboy* film' in Adrian Frazier (ed.), *Playboys of the Western World: Production Histories* (Carysfort Press: Dublin 2004), pp. 59–74.

60. McBride, *Searching for John Ford*, p. 671.

61. Ford says the plot was changed to comply with film censorship: 'Even today, you can say s--- and f--- on the screen, but you can't have a priest living with a woman,' in Bogdanovich, *John Ford*, p. 86.

62. Max Weber, 'The Origin of Ethnic Groups' in Hutchinson and Smith, *Ethnicity*, p. 35.

63. *Ibid.* p. 45.

64. Ruth Vasey, *The World According to Hollywood, 1918–1939* (University of Exeter Press 1997), p. 108; Gregory D. Black, *The Catholic Crusade Against the Movies, 1940–1975* (CUP: Cambridge 1997), pp. 10–12.

65. Robert Sklar, *Movie-Made America: A Cultural History of American Movies* (Chappel & Co.: London 1978), p. 245.

66. Gaylyn Stuldar and Mathew Bernstein (eds), *John Ford Made Westerns: Filming the Legend in the Sound Era* (Indiana UP: Bloomington and Indianapolis 2001), p. 228. They were quoting from Lewis Jacobs, *The Rise of American Film: A Critical History* (Harcourt Brace and Co.: New York 1939).

67. Dudley Nichols to Lindsay Anderson in Andrew Sarris, *'You Ain't Heard Nothin' Yet': The American Talking Film: History and Memory 1927–1949* (OUP: Oxford 1998), p. 169.

68. Bogdanovich, *John Ford*, p. 52. According to Ford, he did not require Nichols to put in ' "scene so-and-so, camera moves in, zooms in, pans". None of that stuff, because it's none of the [screenwriter's] business.' It soon became an axiom of Nichols's business as scenarist 'to write as a camera', i.e. his scenarios did indicate the close-ups, medium shots, or long shots. Furthermore, he made it clear that the emphasis of the film would be on how the hero reacted to situations. These aspects – writing as camera, essential reaction-shots – characterize the script Nichols produced for *The Informer*. For an analysis of Nichols's occasional pieces on screenwriting, see Patrick F. Sheeran, *The Informer* (Cork UP: Cork 2002), p. 68.

69. Andrew Sarris, *'You Ain't Heard Nothing Yet': The American Talking Film, History and Memory 1927–1949* (OUP: NY, Oxford 1998), p. 169.

70. For a discussion of this ideal and its achievement in *The Informer*, see Sheeran, *The Informer*, p. 66.

71. Bogdanovich, *John Ford*, p. 59.

72. 'A Producer's Lot is Not ...: Cliff Reid, Who Has *The Informer* to his Credit, Confesses that Making Nine Films At Once Has Its Woes', *New York Times* (28 July 1935).

73. Thomson, *Showman*, p. 139.

74. Douglas W. Churchill, 'John Ford: The Man Behind *The Informer*', *New York Times* (5 January 1935). In the John Ford papers, Lilly Library, there are unaccustomedly truthful statements by Ford, in answer to questions in writing from William Hawks (30 May 1946), including this one: 'I tried to peddle [*The Informer*] from studio to studio. I tried unsuccessfully for four years … Eventually, through the offices of J.R. McDonough, Executive Producer, and Cliff Reid, RKO bought it.'

75. Bogdanovich, *John Ford*, p. 61; McBride, *Searching for John Ford*, p. 220.

76. Elia Kazan once asked Ford where he got his ideas about how to stage scenes. 'He said from the set. Not from the script, not from the actors, not from the theme. From the set. The settings he chose were already poetry.' Stuldar and Bernstein, *John Ford Made Westerns*, p. 293.

77. *Sunrise* photo from *Village Voice* article (8 September 2004), and credited to Photofest/Film Forum.

78. O'Flaherty, like O'Casey a communist, actually laid the plot in the Civil War of 1922, immediately after the Anglo-Irish Treaty brought about the departure of the British. The hero betrays the anti-Treaty forces to the new Irish government, not to the British. The film, however, places the story in the IRA's war against the British.

79. Ford, 1936 interview with Howard Sharpe, in Gerald Peary and Jenny Lefcourt (eds), *John Ford Interviews* (UP of Mississippi: Jackson 2001), pp. 16–17.

80. In the fairly rapid boil of the Californian melting pot, one could not certify an American's Irishness by hair or skin colour, body type, accent, place of birth or religion, so any white-skinned person with a Scottish or Irish surname (and McLaglen could be either) would be entitled by Ford to the benefit of the doubt.

81. Philip Liebfred, 'Victor McLaglen', *Films in Review*, 41, 4, 214–20.

82. Sheridan Morley, *Tales from the Hollywood Raj: The British Film Colony on Screen and Off* (Weidenfeld & Nicolson: London 1983), p. 140.

83. Churchill, 'The Man Behind *The Informer*'.

84. Dudley Nichols said the fog was intended in his screenplay to be 'symbolic of the groping primitive mind; it's really a mental fog in which he moves and dies'. McBride, *Searching for John Ford*, p. 219.

85. Sheeran, *The Informer*, p. 40.

86. *Ibid.* p. 69.

87. Saverio Giovacchini, *Hollywood Modernism: Film and Politics of the New Deal* (Temple UP: Philadelphia 2001), p. 49. See also Sheeran, *The Informer*, p. 61, and Sarris, *You Ain't Heard Nothin' Yet*, p. 181.

88. 'Stormy Advices from Hollywood', *New York Times* (29 December 1935).

89. Emanuel Eisenberg, interview with John Ford in *New Theatre* (April 1936); also in Peary and Lefcourt, *John Ford Interviews*, pp. 11–12.

90. Bogdanovich, *John Ford*, pp. 63–4.

91. With some reporters, Ford backtracked and denied that 'McLaglen was tricked

into doing some of the scenes ... That's absurd. Vic is a superb actor.' Churchill, 'The Man Behind *The Informer*'.

92. Peary and Lefcourt, *John Ford Interviews*, pp. 13–14.

93. *Ibid.* p. 14.

94. 'We never worked for Max Reinhardt/Or the Moscow Theatre of Art' are the opening lines. John Ford papers, Lilly Library.

95. Howard Sharpe interview with Ford for *Photoplay* (1936), in Peary and Lefcourt, *John Ford Interviews*, 16.

96. *Ibid.* p. 17.

97. O'Hara, *'Tis Herself*, p. 69.

98. Peary and Lefcourt, *John Ford Interviews*, p. 12.

99. '*The Informer*, RKO, Screenplay by Dudley Nichols from the Novel by Liam O'Flaherty, 18 December 1934', Arts Library Special Collections, UCLA. My friend the late Pat Sheeran of the National University of Ireland, Galway, gives an interesting analysis of the respective contributions of Ford and Nichols to *The Informer* in his book on film treatments of O'Flaherty's novel (Sheeran, *The Informer*, pp. 63–72). According to Dan Ford's book on his grandfather (*Pappy: The Life of John Ford*, Da Capo Press: New York, 1979), in a series of meetings at the director's Odin Street home, Ford shouted at Nichols, insulted him, insisted on Ford's superior knowledge of Ireland, and virtually dictated the script, so he is the real author of *The Informer*. However, Nichols himself said several times that he wrote the script at 'white heat' and there was never a second draft. Neither account is convincing. Nichols wrote a long draft, dated 18 December 1934, and then, before shooting began in February 1935, produced a tighter final version (both drafts are in the Special Collections, Arts Library, UCLA). It is reasonable to conclude that the changes between the first and second drafts were the consequence of discussions between Ford and Nichols on the *Araner* voyage.

100. Lindsay Anderson, 'John Ford: his work is a portrayal of the righteous man', *Films in Review* (2, 2, February 1951), 7.

101. Sklar, *Movie-Made America*, p. 191.

102. Garry Wills entitles a chapter on Ford 'Sadist' in his *John Wayne's America* (Simon and Schuster: New York 1997), pp. 67–76.

103. McBride, *Searching for John Ford*, p. 217.

104. Robert Parrish, *Growing up in Hollywood* (Harcourt, Brace, Jovanovich: New York and London 1976), pp. 132–3.

105. John Ford to Mary Ford [22 May 1942], the Carlton, Washington DC, John Ford papers, Lilly Library. Ford was speaking of a naval officer under his command.

106. Dudley [Nichols] to Dear Sean [John Ford], 26 March [1939], John Ford papers, Lilly Library.

107. *New York Times* (30 April 1935).

108. Scott Eyman, *Print the Legend: The Life and Times of John Ford* (Simon and Schuster: New York 1999), p. 179.

109. McBride, *Searching for John Ford*, p. 328.

110. Charles Ramirez Berg, 'The Margin as Center: The Multicultural Dynamics of John Ford's Westerns' in Stuldar and Bernstein, *John Ford Made Westerns*, p. 75.

II. Barry Fitzgerald and *The Plough and the Stars* on Stage and Screen

1. Photograph of Barry Fitzgerald and Eileen Crowe in *Juno and the Paycock, Chicago Sunday Tribune*, 26 February 1933; reviewed in *Chicago American*, 1 March 1933.

2. '*Juno* at Ambassador', *Daily News* (6 December 1937).

3. The first tour began on 3 October 1931; Robert Hogan and Michael J. O'Neill (eds), *Joseph Holloway's Irish Theatre*, vol. 1, 1926–1931 (Proscenium Press: Dixon, California, 1968), p. 79.

4. Barry Fitzgerald to Sean O'Casey, 8 October 1931, On board Cunard RMS *Aquitania*, David Krause (ed.), *The Letters of Sean O'Casey*, vol. 1 (Macmillan: New York 1975), pp. 436–7.

5. Peter Judge (aka F.J. McCormick) was one such lonely family man. On 26 April 1935 he wrote to Joseph Holloway from Kansas City, Missouri: 'Naturally, after seven months away from the children, I'm anxious to see them, and will get back to the life I like best – Dublin – Dublin – Dublin!' Hogan and O'Neill, *Joseph Holloway's Irish Theatre*, vol. 2, 1932–1937 (Proscenium Press: Dixon, California, 1969), p. 43.

6. Krause, *Letters of Sean O'Casey*, vol. 1, pp. 574–5.

7. Richard Hayes, a government nominee to the board, apparently did not join until 1934; Robert Welch, *The Abbey Theatre 1899–1999* (OUP: Oxford 2000), p. 119.

8. Krause, *Letters of Sean O'Casey*, vol. 1, pp. 341–2.

9. 'The Theatres', *The Times* (10 February 1930), 10.

10. Krause, *Letters of Sean O'Casey*, vol. 1, p. 397; Daniel Murphy (ed.), *Lady Gregory's Journals*, vol. 2 (Colin Smythe: Gerrards Cross, Bucks. 1975), p. 257.

11. In Hitchcock's film (an inept piece of work), Barry Fitzgerald does not play, as he ought to have done, Captain Boyle opposite Allgood's Juno Boyle (that role is taken by Edward Chapman), but a newly invented narrator called 'the Orator'.

12. Krause, *Letters of Sean O'Casey*, vol. 1, p. 397; interview with Barry Fitzgerald, *The Chicago Daily News*, 15 March 1933, Abbey Theatre scrapbook, NLI.

13. Murphy, *Lady Gregory's Journals*, vol. 2, p. 534.

14. *Ibid.* p. 556.

15. Both Shields brothers were in *The Whiteheaded Boy* during the 1932/33 tour.

16. Lennox Robinson to Sean O'Casey, Thursday [nd], NLI MS 27,024.

17. In June 1932 Fred Johnson, a longtime veteran of the Abbey and a teacher as well in the Abbey school of acting, asked for a sizable raise from his two pounds a week; Lennox Robinson, manager at the time, admitted the merit of his request, but could only offer him two pounds ten shillings; Lennox Robinson to Fred Johnson, 27

June 1932, Fred Johnson papers, NLI MS 27,613. For thin audiences, see Murphy, *Lady Gregory's Journals*, vol. 2, p. 579.

18. Gabriel Fallon, 'The celluloid menace', *Capuchin Annual* (December 1937), 248–50.

19. Annie Horniman purchased the Mechanics Institute on Abbey Street in 1903, and it opened to the public as the Abbey Theatre on 27 December 1904.

20. 'Two Actors Relive the Great Days at the Abbey Theatre', *The Times* (28 January 1963), 5.

21. Gabriel Fallon, 'The ageing Abbey – II', *Irish Monthly*, 66 (1938), 344.

22. Ann Saddlemyer, *Theatre Business: The Correspondence of the First Abbey Theatre Directors: William Butler Yeats, Lady Gregory, and J.M. Synge* (Colin Smythe: Gerrards Cross, Bucks. 1982), pp. 269–71; Adrian Frazier, *Behind the Scenes* (University of California Press 1990), pp. 176–9, and *passim.*

23. Joseph Holloway, 23 February 1930, 'Diaries of a Dublin Playgoer', National Library of Ireland.

24. *Storm in a Teacup* was James Bridie's Scottish version of the German extravagant comedy *Sturm im Wasserglass*, concerning how a dispute over a dog licence turns into a crisis in local government; 'Royalty Theatre', *The Times* (6 February 1936), 12.

25. Hogan and O'Neill, *Joseph Holloway's Irish Theatre*, vol. 2, p. 60.

26. Allgood also took leave from the Abbey for a stint with the Liverpool Repertory Theatre in 1914; Sara Allgood to Joseph Holloway, 27 January 1914, Joseph Holloway papers, NLI MSS 22,404.

27. *The Times* (18 November 1926), np.

28. Murphy, *Lady Gregory's Journals*, vol. 2, p. 323; for £200-debt, see p. 33.

29. *Ibid.* p. 257.

30. G.B. Shaw to Yeats [November 1915] in John Cronin (ed.), *Selected Plays of St John Ervine* (Colin Smythe: Gerrards Cross, Bucks. 1988), p. 8.

31. *Ibid.* p. 8.

32. Hogan and O'Neill, *Joseph Holloway's Irish Theatre*, p. 187.

33. 'Obituaries: Mr Arthur Sinclair', *The Times* (17 December 1951), 8.

34. From business stationery of Arthur Sinclair, Arthur Sinclair to Mr Robertson, 12 February 1918, Manning Robertson papers, NLI.

35. When *Old Man Murphy* played in Dublin, 27 February 1932, Holloway had bitter remarks for both Allgood sisters: of Sara – 'once an artist, now a clown', and of Molly – 'her acting has deteriorated into that of a harsh-tongued shrew' (Hogan and O'Neill, *Joseph Holloway's Irish Theatre*, vol. 2, p. 6).

36. *The Times* (26 July 1921), 8.

37. From a discussion of Sinclair's acting by Brinsley MacNamara, Dudley Digges, Maire Quinn and Joseph Holloway, recorded in Hogan and O'Neill, *Joseph Holloway's Irish Theatre*, vol. 2, p. 74.

38. Abbey Theatre scrapbooks, NLI.

39. *The Chicago Daily News* (15 March 1933), Abbey Theatre scrapbooks, NLI.

40. In the interview, Fitzgerald says his brother was thirteen years old in 1912, but this must be a mistake, because Arthur Shields was born on 15 February 1896, in Dublin.

41. *The Chicago Daily News* (15 March 1933), Abbey Theatre scrapbooks, NLI.

42. Christopher Fitz-Simon, *The Boys: A Biography of Micheál Mac Liammóir and Hilton Edwards* (Nick Hern Books: London 1994), p. 42.

43. Murphy, *Lady Gregory's Journals*, vol. 2, p. 263.

44. Gabriel Fallon, *Sean O'Casey: The Man I Knew* (Routledge and Kegan Paul: London 1965), p. 54.

45. Seán Ó Cathasaigh to Lennox Robinson, 23 April 1922, Krause, *Letters of Sean O'Casey*, vol. 1, p. 102.

46. Fallon, *Sean O'Casey*, p. 82; Philip B. Ryan, *The Lost Theatres of Dublin* (Badger Press: Westbury, Wiltshire, 1998), p. 23.

47. As a young man J.J. O'Leary had worked with Fitzgerald in the Irish Land Commission. When Fitzgerald left for the stage, O'Leary left for Fleet Street. He came back to Dublin and bought Cahill's, a major printing works in Dublin, producing everything from bus timetables to bibles. One of its products was *The Irish Digest*, which was edited by Sean O'Faolain. O'Leary then materially assisted O'Faolain in getting *The Bell* up and running. The atmosphere of the new Irish patron of letters, O'Faolain remarked defensively in a letter to Frank O'Connor, was not like that of Yeats and Edward Martyn – 'no grand manner hanging around' – but it was the world of the new Ireland, with the beggars raised up by Daniel O'Connell coming into power. See Maurice Harmon's *Sean O'Faolain* (Constable: London, 1994), pp. 127, 130, 150.

48. 'Two Actors Relive the Great Days', *op. cit.*

49. *The Chicago Daily News* (15 March 1933), Abbey Theatre scrapbooks, NLI.

50. Allan Wade (ed.), *The Letters of W.B. Yeats* (Macmillan: New York 1955), pp. 740–1.

51. Yeats thought O'Casey's depiction of the middle-class character of Nora Clitheroe in *The Plough and the Stars* was shallow because 'O'Casey is there writing about people he does not know, people he has only read about,' as if O'Casey were on much more familiar terms with the wastrels, unmarried mothers, prostitutes, drunks and old-age pensioners who make up the rest of the cast. Yeats's misapprehension of the sphere of O'Casey's social knowledge was to have serious consequences in the handling of his next play, *The Silver Tassie.* Yeats believed the representation of Irishmen who went to World War I was outside O'Casey's experience, and thus outside his ability to dramatize – in both cases, not true. See Yeats to George O'Brien, 10 September 1925, quoted in Robert Hogan and Richard Burnham, *The Years of O'Casey, 1921–1926, A Documentary History* (Colin Smythe: Gerrards Cross, Bucks. 1992), p. 283.

52. Sean O'Casey, *Three Plays* (St Martin's Press: New York 1957), p. 90.

53. Nicholas Grene, *The Politics of Irish Drama* (CUP: Cambridge 1999), p. 122.

54. Grene, *Politics of Irish Drama*, p. 113.

55. O'Casey, *Three Plays*, p. 61.

56. 'Two Actors Relive the Great Days', *op. cit.*

57. Hogan and Burnham, *The Years of O'Casey*, p. 294.

58. Fallon, *Sean O'Casey*, pp. 87–9.

59. Hogan and Burnham, *The Years of O'Casey*, p. 288.

60. Four streetwalkers were shooed off from the Abbey entrance by a policeman as the distinguished patrons left the first night of *The Plough and the Stars*; Joseph Holloway's diary, quoted in Hogan and Burnham, *The Years of O'Casey*, p. 287.

61. M.J. Dolan to Lady Gregory, 1 September 1925, quoted in Hogan and Burnham, *The Years of O'Casey*, p. 282.

62. O'Casey to Lennox Robinson, 10 January 1926, Hogan and Burnham, *The Years of O'Casey*, pp. 283–4.

63. By mid-1936 Fallon had become a sectarian nationalist, follower of Daniel Corkery, and president of the Catholic theatre guild. See, for instance, 'Sitting at the play: those dramatists of Inish', *Irish Monthly*, 64 (August 1936), 614.

64. O'Casey, *Three Plays*, p. 215.

65. *Ibid.* p. 179.

66. W.B. Yeats to Lady Gregory, 15 January 1926, Hogan and Burnham, *The Years of O'Casey*, p. 286.

67. George O'Brien to Lennox Robinson and W.B. Yeats, 13 September 1925, Hogan and Burnham, *The Years of O'Casey*, pp. 283–4.

68. W.B. Yeats to George O'Brien, 10 September 1925, Hogan and Burnham, *The Years of O'Casey*, p. 283.

69. From the *Irish Times* review of *The Plough and the Stars*, reprinted in Hogan and Burnham, *The Years of O'Casey*, p. 289.

70. O'Casey, *Three Plays*, p. 162.

71. *Ibid.* p. 195.

72. F.S.L. Lyons, *Ireland Since the Famine* (Fontana Collins: London 1973), p. 366.

73. Fallon, *Sean O'Casey*, p. 86.

74. *Ibid.* p. 90.

75. *Irish Independent* (13 February 1926), Hogan and Burnham, *The Years of O'Casey*, p. 306.

76. Fallon, *Sean O'Casey*, p. 91; Hogan and Burnham, *The Years of O'Casey*, pp. 295–302.

77. Murphy, *Lady Gregory's Journals*, vol. 2, p. 63.

78. As quoted from *The Manchester Guardian* in R.F. Foster, *W.B. Yeats: A Life*, II. *The Arch-Poet* (OUP: Oxford 2003), pp. 305–6.

79. Murphy, *Lady Gregory's Journals*, vol. 2, p. 67.

80. 'Two Actors Relive the Great Days', *op. cit.*

81. Murphy, *Lady Gregory's Journals*, vol. 2, p. 64; Fallon, *Sean O'Casey*, p. 94.

82. Hogan and Burnham, *The Years of O'Casey*, p. 309.

83. Krause, *Letters of Sean O'Casey*, vol. 1, pp. 178, 179.

84. *Ibid.* pp. 177–80.

85. Review of New York performance, 29 October 1932, Abbey Theatre scrapbooks, NLI.

86. *Pittsburgh Press* (15 December 1932), Abbey Theatre scrapbooks, NLI.

87. O'Casey, *Three Plays*, p. 31.

88. Lennox Robinson and Arthur Duff, 27 August 1935, Hogan and O'Neill, *Joseph Holloway's Irish Theatre*, vol. 2, p. 46.

89. Hogan and Burnham, *The Years of O'Casey*, p. 188.

90. *Chicago Herald-Examiner* (8 March 1933), Abbey Theatre scrapbooks, NLI.

91. Recollection of Shelah Delaney, Hogan and Burnham, *The Years of O'Casey*, p. 293.

92. Ford finished the script with Dudley Nichols in January 1935. *The Informer* was released 1 May 1935; McBride, *Searching for John Ford*, pp. 220, 221, 224.

93. *Ibid.* p. 200.

94. Ford, *Pappy*, p. 72.

95. Barry Fitzgerald to Sean O'Casey, 11 September 1932, Krause, *Letters of Sean O'Casey*, vol. 1, p. 447.

96. RKO papers, Arts Library Special Collections, UCLA.

97. Abbey board meeting of 28 February 1936; Abbey Theatre Minute Books, Acc 3961, vol. 4.

98. Hogan and O'Neill, *Joseph Holloway's Irish Theatre*, vol. 2, p. 60. On 16 March 1936 Fitzgerald played his last role at the Abbey, a small part in Teresa Deevy's *Katie Roche*.

99. Barry Fitzgerald to Sean O'Casey, 8 October 1931, Krause, *Letters of Sean O'Casey*, vol. 1, pp. 436–7.

100. Barry Fitzgerald to Sean O'Casey, nd, Sean O'Casey, *Rose and Crown* (Macmillan: London, 1952), p. 151.

101. Barry Fitzgerald to Sean O'Casey, 11 September 1932, Krause, *Letters of Sean O'Casey*, vol. 1, p. 447.

102. O'Casey did not improve matters by lambasting sanctimonious Roman Catholics in one-and-a-half closely printed columns of *The Irish Press*. Krause, *Letters of Sean O'Casey*, vol. 1, pp. 578–9.

103. Gabriel Fallon, 'Sitting at the play: yellow moons and purple cathedrals', *Irish Monthly* (11 May 1936), 453–7. For Lady Gregory's opinion that Fitzgerald was 'wasted' in a serious role, see Murphy, *Lady Gregory's Journals*, vol. 2, p. 571.

104. Gabriel Fallon, 'The genius of Barry Fitzgerald', *The Leader*, 74, 2 (February 1937), 40–1.

105. F.J. McCormick, quoted in Gabriel Fallon, 'Sitting at the play: darkness before dawn', *Irish Monthly*, 64 (September 1936), 673.

106. Conversation with Eileen Crowe, 6 September 1936, in Hogan and O'Neill, *Joseph Holloway's Irish Theatre*, vol. 2, p. 60.

107. Robert Frost, 'Provide, Provide', *The Poetry of Robert Frost: The Collected Poems, Complete and Unabridged*, ed. Edward Connery Lathem (Henry Holt and Company: New York 1979), p. 307.

108. Conversation with Eileen Crowe, 6 September 1936, in Hogan and O'Neill, *Joseph Holloway's Irish Theatre*, vol. 2, p. 63.

109. 'New films in London', *The Times* (8 February 1937), 10.

110. McBride, *Searching for John Ford*, p. 243.

111. RKO papers, Arts Library Special Collections, UCLA.

112. O'Casey, *Three Plays*, p. 178.

113. Preview reports from RKO employees, RKO papers, Arts Library Special Collections, UCLA.

114. Ford to O'Casey, 9 March 1936, Lilly Library.

115. Wade, *Letters of W.B. Yeats*, p. 741.

116. Abbey Theatre Minute Books, 2 October 1936, 6 October 1936, NLI Acc 3961.

117. Hedda Hopper typescript of interview with Barry Fitzgerald, 22 January 1945, Academy of Motion Picture Arts and Sciences.

118. The contract for *Ebb Tide* is archived at the Margaret Herrick Library, Academy of Motion Picture Arts and Sciences, Beverly Hills, California.

119. For an account of the making of *Bringing up Baby*, see Richard B. Jewell, 'How Howard Hawks Brought Baby Up: An Apologia for the Studio System' in Leo Braudy and Marshall Cohen (eds), *Film Theory and Criticism: Introductory Readings* (OUP: Oxford 2004), pp. 581ff.

120. 'Cliché Expert', *New York Times* (4 March 1938). Howard Hawks himself concluded that the problem with *Bringing up Baby* – it lost more than $350,000 – was that 'There were *no* normal people in it. Everyone you met was a screwball.' See Todd McCarthy, *Howard Hawks: The Grey Fox of Hollywood* (Grove Press: New York 1997), p. 256.

121. McCarthy, *Howard Hawks*, p. 252.

122. '*Juno* at Ambassador', *Daily News* (6 December 1937), previously quoted at the beginning of this chapter.

III. *The Long Voyage Home*: Arthur Shields, John Ford, Eugene O'Neill and Irish Exile

1. L.B. Shields, 'Saturday's Child Has Far to Go …', book proposal by Shields's third wife, Shields Archive, NUI Galway. This is the source of much of the information here about Shields's early life. The romanticism of the Irish nationalists of the period is beautifully expressed by Joseph Campbell in his prison diary: 'I praised the quiet, deep, simple Russian-like Western lads … Even though they have no education, they seem to be so right – to have faith – to believe implicitly in the idea of Cathleen ni Houlihan. They have such a sure contact with the realities – earth, sky, tradition.' See Eileán Ní Chuilleanáin (ed.), *'As I was Among the Captives': Joseph Campbell's Prison Diary, 1922–1923* (Cork UP: Cork 2001), p. 59.

2. Frank Fay had been brought back to the Abbey in order to give voice lessons, but he

was still angry with the company for the way he and his brother had been forced out by Annie Horniman. Shields was something of a pet in the school, and Fay tried to persuade him to leave it and join Fay in a travelling company: 'The O'Brien and Ireland Company'; when Shields refused, the two fell out. 'Frank was a great speaker of verse; unfortunately, he was a very tiny little man, with a big nose, and it sometimes seemed ridiculous, very ridiculous.' From an early 1960s' interview with Herbert J. Gans, Shields family papers.

3. Arthur Shields played Mr Butterfield in *The Lord Mayor* by Edward McNulty on 13 March 1914; see Lennox Robinson, *Ireland's Abbey Theatre* (Kennikat Press: Port Washington, New York 1951, 1968), p. 110.

4. From an early 1960s' interview with Herbert J. Gans, Shields family papers.

5. It was the misfortune of the author of this play, T.H. Nally, that his opening night was the beginning of the Easter Rebellion. It was the end of his career as a playwright.

6. Statement by Lt. Col. Charles Saurin, Collins Barracks, 27 February 1926, Shields family papers. Unless otherwise noted, this statement is the source for the details of Shields's involvement in the Easter Rising.

7. Donal Nevin, *James Connolly: A Full Life* (Gill and Macmillan: Dublin 2005), p. 643.

8. *Ibid.* p. 644.

9. *Ibid.* p. 652.

10. Saurin, Statement.

11. Desmond FitzGerald, *The Memoirs of Desmond FitzGerald* (Routledge and Kegan Paul: London 1968), p. 142.

12. Michael Foy and Brian Barton, *The Easter Rising* (Sutton: Phoenix Mill, 1999, 2004), 225.

13. Max Caulfield, *The Easter Rebellion* (Gill and Macmillan: Dublin, 1963, 1995), 259.

14. Saurin, Statement.

15. Seán O'Mahony, *Frongoch: University of Revolution* (FDR Teoranta: Dublin 1987), p. 44.

16. Arthur Shields to family, 30 [May 1916]; Charlie Saurin to Dear William, 5 June 1916; Arthur Shields to family, 12 [July 1916]. For the 'pray in Gaelic' remark, see Homer D. Swander's article: 'Sometime after [Shields] resigned [from the Abbey], he remarked that he "couldn't have done otherwise very well. If you could say your prayers in Gaelic, you could have got on awfully well at the Abbey. I don't have many prayers, and I don't have any Gaelic." ' Homer D. Swander, 'Shields at the Abbey', unpublished article, Shields family papers, T13/A/399.

17. St John Ervine [signed], Abbey Theatre Regulations, Shields family papers.

18. Shaw to W.B. Yeats, quoted in Cronin, *Selected Plays of St John Ervine*, p. 8.

19. Shields, 'Saturday's Child'.

20. A.J. Leventhal, MS of article published in *Envoy: A Review of Literature and Art* (July 1950), Shields family papers.

21. Swander, 'Shields at the Abbey'.

22. For the 11 March 1919 production of Brinsley MacNamara's *The Rebellion in*

Ballycullen, Yeats asked Arthur Shields to take over as stage manager (or 'director'), and to play the lead. This was the first time Shields was charged with supervising a production, a job he often took later. He directed many of the productions of George Yeats's Dublin Drama League, the Yiddish Theatre, and the Abbey itself. Not until 1927, however, was he formally made assistant producer. For some reason, Lady Gregory did not like him. Shields understood that to be the case, and did not know why it was so, but said in an early 1960s interview that it did not matter; she was a great woman. Her own plays, her courage in defending the Abbey's independence, her admiration for his brother Barry Fitzgerald, and her advice and support for Sean O'Casey, all won his respect and affection. Interview with Herbert J. Gans, Shields family papers.

23. Daniel J. Murphy (ed.), *Lady Gregory's Journals,* vol. 1, books 1–29, 10 October 1916–24 February 1925 (Colin Smythe: Gerrards Cross, Bucks. 1978), p. 57.

24. See James Pethica, ' "Our Kathleen": Yeats's collaboration with Lady Gregory in the writing of Cathleen ni Houlihan', *Yeats Annual,* 6, ed. Warwick Gould (London: Macmillan,1988), 3–31.

25. Herbert J. Gans interview, Shields family papers.

26. She was one of the women in *Old Mag,* a one-act Christmas play by Kenneth Sarr; Robinson, *Ireland's Abbey Theatre,* p. 137.

27. Harry Clarke's father, Joshua, was a Protestant Englishman from Leeds. However, after he settled in Dublin as a stained-glass maker, and married Brigid McGonigal, he became Catholic. Harry Clarke maintained good relations with clients in both Churches. See Nicola Gordon Bowe, *Harry Clarke: Exhibition Catalogue* (Douglas Hyde Gallery: Trinity College Dublin, 12 November to 8 December 1979), pp. 1–11.

28. Bernard Adams, *Denis Johnston: A Life* (The Lilliput Press: Dublin 2002); Denis Johnston journal, 2 February 1926, TCD MSS 10066/165.

29. Merrion Square is a square in Dublin, with the National Gallery and National Museum on one side, terraces of handsome four-storey Georgian houses around the other three sides, and a landscaped garden behind a railing in the centre. On 19 November 1928 Arthur Shields took out a lease on a flat in No. 72 Merrion Square. At this time Yeats lived at No. 82; Æ (George Russell) at No. 89.

30. Denis Johnston journal, 13 October 1926, TCD MSS 10066/165.

31. *Ibid.* 5 August 1926.

32. *Ibid.* 10 November 1926.

33. Adrian Frazier, 'McGuinness and the boys', *Dublin Review* (Summer 2002), 72–86.

34. The play is reproduced in Curtis Canfield, *Plays of a Changing Ireland* (Macmillan: New York 1936).

35. Christopher Fitz-Simon, *The Boys: A Biography of Micheal Mac Liammóir and Hilton Edwards* (Nick Hern Books: London 1994), p. 78.

36. Denis Johnston journal, 5 August 1926, TCD MSS 10066/165.

37. Lennox Robinson, Tom Robinson and Nora Dorman, *Three Homes* (Michael Joseph: London 1938), pp. 217–18.

38. The story had already been published in the USA in 1920; Robinson may not have reflected that in Ireland it would surely cause trouble. See Foster, *W.B. Yeats: A Life*, II, p. 268.

39. Indeed, the story appears to be a spin-off of Moore's heretical Irish tales in *A Story-Teller's Holiday* (1919).

40. 'Unclean Literature: Conference at Ballinrobe', *The Western People* (31 October 1925), 5. See also Adrian Frazier, 'Harry Clarke and modern Ireland', *Textual Practice*, 16, 2 (2002), 314–15.

41. Christopher Murray (ed.), *Selected Plays of Lennox Robinson* (Colin Smythe: Gerrards Cross, Bucks.; Catholic UP: Washington DC 1982), p. 167.

42. Swander, 'Shields at the Abbey'.

43. 'About Town', Kansas City newspaper [April 1935?], Abbey Theatre scrapbook, NLI.

44. Arthur Shields to Lini Saurin, 24 November [1931], Ottawa, Ontario; Arthur Shields to Lini Saurin, 27 October [1931], Altoona, Pennsylvania, Shields family papers.

45. Denis Johnston journal, 31 December 1931, TCD MSS 10066/165.

46. Will Shields to Lini Saurin, 30 December [1931], The New Pfister, Milwaukee, Shields family papers.

47. Denis Johnston journal, 31 December 1931, TCD MSS 10066/165.

48. Information in this paragraph is taken from letters of Arthur Shields to Lini Saurin, who was looking after his son Adam in Ireland (Shields family papers).

49. 'Dubbed "Best Character Comedian", Barry Fitzgerald Sighs for Serious Roles', *New York World Telegram* ([16?] December 1934), Abbey Theatre scrapbooks, NLI.

50. Arthur Shields to Lini Saurin, 30 January 1932, Shields family papers.

51. *Ibid.* 6 March 1932, Shields family papers.

52. *Ibid.* 26 March 1932, Shields family papers.

53. Harry C. Rudden, 'The Abbey Players', nd, Abbey Theatre scrapbooks, NLI.

54. Profile of Arthur Shields in *Philadelphia Public Ledger* ([20?] November 1932), Abbey Theatre scrapbooks, NLI.

55. Edward L. Shaughnessy, *Eugene O'Neill in Ireland: The Critical Heritage* (Greenwood Press: New York, London 1988), pp. 64–5.

56. Clipping [December 1936?], scrapbook, Shields family papers.

57. 'Youth for the Abbey Theatre', clipping, 14 September 1933, Shields family papers.

58. Murray, *Selected Plays of Lennox Robinson*, p. 215.

59. Wade, *Letters of W.B. Yeats*, pp. 740–2.

60. *Evening Mail*, 13 August 1935.

61. Christopher Murray, *Sean O'Casey: Writer at Work* (Gill and Macmillan: Dublin 2004), p. 242.

62. Fallon, 'Those dramatists of Inish', *Irish Monthly* op. cit. 614–22.

63. 'Shadow and Substance', *Irish Independent* (26 January 1937).

64. Paul Vincent Carroll, *Shadow and Substance* (Macmillan: London 1938), p. 34.

65. The point at which the affair became public in Dublin is marked by a letter of W.B. Yeats to his wife George Yeats, published just as *Hollywood Irish* was going to the printer. On 16 March 1937, Yeats wrote: 'Here is what happened at the Abbey which reduced Miss O Connor to such tears. Boss [Arthur Shields] has an impossible wife he has started an affair with Miss O Connor. Some virtuous member of the company sent an anonimous letter to Miss O Connor's father who turned her out; & to Boss Shield's wife who came to the theatre & slapped Miss O Connor. I have sworn not to tell how I know' (*W.B. Yeats & George Yeats: The Letters*, ed. Ann Saddlemyer [Oxford University Press, 2011], p. 459; WBY's spellings maintained throughout).

66. Aideen O'Connor to Eileen, 28 November 1937, Hotel Edison, Shields family papers.

67. Aideen O'Connor to Eileen, 31 January 1938, Shields family papers.

68. Aideen O'Connor to Eileen, 4 March 1938, Shields family papers.

69. Aideen O'Connor to Eileen [5 April 1938], Shields family papers.

70. Phyllis Ryan, *The Company I Kept* (Town House: Dublin 1996), p. 74.

71. James P. McGlone, *Ria Mooney: The Life and Times of the Artistic Director of the Abbey Theatre, 1948–1963* (McFarland & Co.: Jefferson, NC, and London 2002), p. 69.

72. Arthur Shields to Eddie Choate, 28 April 1939, Abbey Theatre stationery, Shields family papers.

73. Aideen O'Connor to Eddie Choate, Abbey Theatre stationery, Shields family papers.

74. Private communication, Christine Shields; the books are now in the Shields family papers.

75. James Matthews, *Voices: A Life of Frank O'Connor* (Atheneum: New York 1983), p. 144.

76. Foster, *Yeats: A Life*, II, p. 631.

77. Matthews, *Frank O'Connor*, p. 145.

78. Shields, 'Saturday's Child'.

79. 'Success of British Plays, New York Stage', *The Times* (31 January 1939), 10.

80. Eddie Choate to Arthur Shields, 4 March 1939, Shields family papers.

81. 'Abbey Players the Most Rehearsed in the World', *New York Post* (6 November 1937), Shields family papers.

82. Eddie Choate to Arthur Shields, 9 March 1939, Shields family papers.

83. Arthur Shields to Eddie Choate, 12 April 1939, Shields family papers.

84. *Ibid.*

85. Hugh Hunt to Eddie Choate, 27 April 1939, Shields family papers.

86. Arthur Shields to Eddie Choate, 12 May 1939, Shields family papers.

87. *Ibid.*

88. Faulkner's version is written in beautiful sentences (he could not help himself), but the story is grotesque, inappropriate (adultery, torture, miscarriage) and dispiritingly ironic; see Twentieth Century Fox papers, Special Collections, Arts Library, UCLA.

89. 5 April 1939, 'Conference with Mr. Zanuck on Temporary Script of 11 March 1939', Special Collections, Arts Library, UCLA.

90. '3 May 1939, Conference with Mr Zanuck on the Final Script of April 24, 1939', Special Collections, Arts Library, UCLA.

91. Robert Parrish, 'Témoignage sur John Ford', *Préscence du Cinéma* 21 (March 1965), 18–20; quoted in Tag Gallagher, *John Ford: The Man and His Films* (University of California Press 1986), p. 175.

92. McBride, *Searching for John Ford*, p. 307.

93. Gallagher, *John Ford*, p. 175.

94. Jeremy Butler, 'The star system and Hollywood' in John Hill and Pamela Church Gibson (eds), *Oxford Guide to Film Studies* (OUP: Oxford 1998), pp. 342–53.

95. McBride, *John Ford*, p. 270.

96. Robin Wood, '*Drums Along the Mohawk*' in Ian Cameron and Douglas Pye (eds), *The Movie Book of the Western* (Studio Vista: London 1996), p. 178.

97. Arthur Shields to Eddie Choate, 23 August 1939, Shields family papers.

98. Eddie Choate to Richard Maney, 6 December 1939, Shields family papers.

99. Memorandum, Eddie Choate to Arthur Shields, 20 January 1940, Shields family papers.

100. Arthur Shields to Eddie Choate, 24 April 1940, Shields family papers.

101. Redilwoth Rust, 'The unity of O'Neill's S.S. *Glencairn*', *American Literature*, 37, 3 (November 1965), 284.

102. Interestingly, after the American panic about immigration in the 1920s (issuing in the Johnson-Reed Act of 1924 that established quotas on national origins), in the late 1930s the USA was beginning to represent 'group-based pluralism' as a national strength. According to a 1938 publication, *The Problems of a Changing Population*, 'Americans have come to realize that while we do not have a wealth of cathedrals, fine carvings, old family customs, or a national folk music and literature, we do possess an abundance of cultural diversity.' Desmond King, *The Liberty of Strangers: Making the American Nation* (OUP: Oxford 2005), p. 92.

103. Stephen A. Black, *Eugene O'Neill: Beyond Mourning and Tragedy* (Yale UP: New Haven: 1999), p. 116.

104. Eugene O'Neill, *Complete Plays 1913–1920* (Library of America: New York 1988), p. 189.

105. Dudley Nichols to John Ford [no date], John Ford papers, Lilly Library.

106. Louis Shaeffer, *O'Neill: Son and Artist* (Little, Brown and Co.: Boston, Toronto 1973), pp. 504–5; Ford, *Pappy*, p. 154.

107. Eugene O'Neill put in his work diary for 12 February 1940: 'Ford and Nichols up from Hollywood – much talk regarding *Glencairn* – like them both a lot.' O'Neill loved the film (see Meta Sterne to Eugene O'Neill [June 1940], telegram; and Carlotta O'Neill to John Ford, 29 June 1940, John Ford papers, Lilly Library).

108. McBride, *Searching for John Ford*, p. 319.

109. While it was Ford's stated practice that 'Everything's all right with a movie as long as the audience isn't conscious of the machine,' he gave Gregg Toland a free hand

to impose his artistry on every scene of *The Long Voyage Home.* See Robert L. Carringer, *The Making of Citizen Kane* (University of California Press 1985), pp. 75–86, and for the Ford quotation, Joseph Hone, 'Autobiography', p. 15. This was later published by The Lilliput Press in 2009 as *Wicked Little Joe.*

110. O'Neill, *Plays*, p. 511.

111. Fintan O'Toole, *The Ex-Isle of Erin* (New Island Books: Dublin 1997), p. 137.

IV. Sara Allgood, *Juno and the Paycock* and *How Green Was My Valley*

1. Sara Allgood to Joseph Holloway, 27 January 1914, Holloway MSS, NLI.

2. Sara Allgood, 'Memories', Belfast Public Record Office, p. 96. In February 1914, Allgood was also in James Sexton's *The Riot Act*, produced by Liverpool Repertory Company; see *The Times* (4 February 1914), 6.

3. Joseph Holloway, diary for 15 April 1939, Hogan and O'Neill, *Joseph Holloway's Irish Theatre*, vol. 3, 1938–1944 (Proscenium Press: Dixon, California, 1970), pp. 25–6.

4. The London production of *Juno* was at the Royalty Theatre; see *The Times* (18 November 1925), 12.

5. The three Hitchcock films in which Allgood appeared were *Blackmail* (1929), *Juno and the Paycock* (1930) and *Sabotage* (1936). For Douglas Byng, see Allgood, 'Memories', p. 98.

6. Retitled *Storm over Patsy*, the play opened on 8 March 1937 at the Guild Theatre and ran for forty-eight performances.

7. A capable actor, hoofer and crooner, Dowling had been given his start as a Broadway producer in 1919 with the Ziegfield Follies. In 1926 he discovered a 200-pound 19-year-old singer, Kate Smith (1907–86), whose rendition of 'God Bless America' became a second national anthem. Now he was breaking into the production of serious literary theatre, a move that would lead him to introduce Tennessee Williams to Broadway with *The Glass Menagerie* in 1945.

8. Ryan, *The Company I Kept*, p. 62.

9. *Katie Roche* by Teresa Deevy opened at the Ambassador Theatre on 2 October 1937, and was a failure both with the audience and the critics; it was taken off after five nights. However, Lennox Robinson's *The Far Off Hills*, which replaced it on stage, ran for six weeks. Aideen O'Connor to Maeve O'Connor, 18 November 1937, Shields family papers, NUI Galway.

10. May Higgins, 'Biographical notes', F.R. and May Higgins papers, NLI.

11. F.R. Higgins to May Higgins, 24 October 1937, F.R. and May Higgins papers, NLI.

12. F.R. Higgins to Eric Gorman, 10 November 1937, Hotel Edison, New York, F.R. and May Higgins papers, NLI. Eddie Dowling's birth name was Joseph Nelson Goucher.

13. In a communication acceding to this arrangement, the Abbey Board – Frank O'Connor, Ernest Blythe, Walter Starkie, and Richard Hayes – expressed its amazement that Higgins had not simply approved the original offer of an Abbey production

of the play on Broadway. Abbey Minute Books, 17 November 1937, Acc 3961, NLI.

14. New Yorker Carl Van Vechten was many things: novelist, dance critic, impresario ('the Harlem Renaissance' was of his manufacture) and friend of an astonishing range of people, including Gertrude Stein, Langston Hughes, George Moore and Zora Neale Hurston. He was also a gifted amateur photographer.

15. Van Vechten spoke with Allgood after a 21 March 1938 performance. Carl Van Vechten to Dorothy Peterson [22 March 1938], Bruce Kellner (ed.), *Letters of Carl Van Vechten*, (Yale UP: New Haven 1987), p. 159.

16. J.M. Synge, *Plays: Book I*, ed. Ann Saddlemyer, in vol. III, *J.M. Synge: The Collected Works* (Colin Smythe: Gerrards Cross: Bucks. and Catholic University of America Press: Washington DC 1982), p. 27.

17. William Hazlitt, *Essays* (Blackie and Son: London, Glasgow, and Bombay: 1906), p. 41. My thanks to Mary O'Malley.

18. C.S. Andrews, *Dublin Made Me: An Autobiography* (Mercier Press: Dublin and Cork 1979), pp. 99, 124. See also the witness statement of Mairín Cregan to the Bureau of Military History, reported in Annie Ryan, *Witnesses: Inside the Easter Rising* (Liberties Press: Dublin 2005). She recalls going with her friends, future leaders of the Free State, to the Abbey Theatre every Saturday night during her university years prior to the 1916 Rising (p. 46). Many more examples could be adduced of future political leaders who had been patriotically inspired by the plays and players of the Abbey Theatre.

19. In *The Old Woman Remembers*, Allgood as Shan Van Vocht recited the sad proud history of Ireland, lighting one candle for every hundred years of suffering, seven candles in all (Abbey Theatre, 31 December 1924).

20. 'Abbey Theatre Ceremony', unidentified newspaper clipping (29 September 1932), Abbey Minute Books, NLI.

21. W.B. Yeats to Frank Fay, 13 August 1906, quoted in Saddlemyer, *Theatre Business*, p. 139.

22. 'Abbey Theatre Ceremony', unidentified newspaper clipping (29 September 1932), Abbey Minute Books, NLI.

23. W.B. Yeats, *Explorations* (Macmillan: New York 1962), p. 364.

24. Speaking literally, this was not the case with *Riders to the Sea*, since Synge drafted the play in the summer of 1902 before he became familiar with Sara Allgood.

25. Hazlitt, *Essays*, p. 41.

26. The story here of Allgood's early life is taken from her unpublished 'Memories' (Belfast PRO, op. cit).

27. See the obituary of G.H. Mair, *The Times* (4 January 1926), 14. After the outbreak of war in 1914, Mair worked 'in a confidential capacity' for the Ministry of Information and was he was the assistant director in the League of Nations Secretariat. Mair and Allgood had a son and a daughter.

28. Sean O'Casey to Frank McCarthy, 6 December 1950: Krause, *Letters of Sean O'Casey*, vol. 2, p. 758.

29. According to other sources, Sara Allgood married Henson in Melbourne at a registry office in September 1916, and in a religious ceremony at Central Methodist Mission in Sydney in January 1917. See Elizabeth Coxhead, *Daughters of Erin: Five Women of the Irish Renascence* (Colin Smythe: Gerrards Cross, Bucks. 1979), p. 202.

30. 'Births', *The Times* (14 March 1918), 1.

31. Coxhead, *Daughters of Erin*, p. 206.

32. Choate-Shields Productions contracts, 15 January 1940, Shields family papers, NUI Galway.

33. Eddie Choate to Robert Edmond Jones, 8 February 1940, Shields family papers, NUI Galway.

34. Charles Drazin, *Korda: Britain's Only Movie Mogul* (Sidgwick and Jackson: London 2002), p. 233.

35. Philip Dunne, *'How Green Was My Valley': The Screenplay for the Darryl F. Zanuck Film Production, Directed by John Ford* (Santa Teresa Press: Santa Barbara, California 1990), p. 20.

36. *Ibid.* p. 25.

37. *Ibid.* p. 26.

38. *Chicago Herald-Examiner* (8 March 1933), Abbey Theatre scrapbooks, NLI.

39. Dunne, *'How Green Was My Valley'*, p. 27.

40. On 16 May 1941, Sara Allgood wrote to Joseph Holloway to thank him for writing of her in the newspaper as being in the company of Duse and Bernhardt; Robert Hogan and Michael J. O'Neill, *Joseph Holloway's Abbey Theatre: A Selection from his Unpublished Journal*, vol. 3 (Southern Illinois UP: Carbondale and Edwardsville, Illinois; Feffer and Simons: London and Amsterdam 1967), p. 60.

41. Aideen O'Connor to Eddie Choate, 23 August 1941, Shields family papers, NUI Galway.

42. Dunne, *'How Green Was My Valley'*, p. 32.

43. Sarris, *You Ain't Heard Nothin' Yet*, p. 197.

44. Dunne, *'How Green Was My Valley'*, p. 31.

45. *Ibid.* p. 32.

46. 'Fox has signed Sara Algood to a term contract', *New York Times* (29 August 1941).

47. Allgood, 'Memories', p. 106. For details on Hollywood contracts, see Tino Balio, *Grand Design: Hollywood as a Modern Business Enterprise, 1930–39* (Scribner's Sons: New York 1993), p. 145.

48. Allgood, 'Memories', p. 108. It is unclear what director dismissed Allgood; perhaps Reuben Mamoulian or William Wellman. According to *The New York Times* of 30 October 1941, Allgood was to play opposite Henry Fonda in *Rings on her* Fingers (directed by Reuben Mamoulian), but does not appear in the final cast. She was also initially to be in the cast with Fonda in *The Oxbow Incident* (directed by William Wellman) and then replaced by Florence Bates (*New York Times*, 17 June 1942). My guess is that it was Mamoulian, because, under Wellman's direction, Allgood performed

adequately as the matron of a women's prison in *Roxie Hart*, before filming began on *The Oxbow Incident*.

49. Allgood, 'Memories'. Allgood does not identify the director or film in question.

50. Charles Affron, *Lillian Gish: Her Legend, Her Life* (University of California Press 2002), p. 303.

51. Sara Allgood played Pegeen Mike only when her sister Molly was not in the cast; when she was, Sara played the Widow Quin, as in the opening production in 1907.

52. In the 1860, in a population survey of Jersey City, NJ, 76 per cent of the Irish female workforce was employed in domestic service. Generally, an Irish maid washed on Monday, swept on Tuesday, courted on Thursday, cleaned on Friday, and baked on Saturday; every day of the week, she cooked, served food, answered the door, and took messages. She never made enough money, obviously, to retire at ease. See J.P. Dolan, *The American Catholic Experience* (University of Notre Dame Press: Notre Dame 1992), *passim.*

53. A wish reported in a letter from Gabriel Fallon to Maire [nic Shiublaigh], 20 November 1947, NLI MS 27631.

V. Irish Hollywood in the 1940s

1. Michael Davie (ed.), *The Diaries of Evelyn Waugh* (Phoenix: London 1976, 1995), p. 672.

2. Saverio Giovacchini, *Hollywood Modernism: Film and Politics of the New Deal* (Temple UP: Philadelphia 2001), p. 114.

3. Matthew J. Bruccoli (ed.), *The Love of the Last Tycoon: A Western* (Simon and Schuster: New York 1941, 1993), p. 150.

4. Morley, *Tales from the Hollywood Raj*, p. 212.

5. Budd Schulberg, *Moving Pictures: Memories of a Hollywood Prince* (Ivan R. Dee: Chicago 1981), p. 326.

6. Morley, *Tales from the Hollywood Raj*, p. 142.

7. The first years of Aideen O'Connor and Arthur Shields in Hollywood were spent at 1843 North Cherokee; the North Sierra Bonita house was purchased in 1946.

8. Aideen O'Connor to Eddie Choate, 1 September 1942, Shields family papers.

9. Arthur Shields to Eddie Choate, 24 April 1940, Shields family papers; and 6 April 1940 contract for Aideen O'Connor for a play at the time entitled *Thumbs* produced by a man called Cooper. This may be Irving Cooper's production of *Grey Farm*, a melodrama by Terence Rattigan (3 May–1 June 1940, at the Hudson Theater).

10. Aideen O'Connor to Eddie Choate, 20 January 1942, Shields family papers.

11. Aideen O'Connor to Eddie Choate, 25 May 1942, Shields family papers.

12. Guy Mehigan to Arthur Shields, 13 June 1945, Shields family papers.

13. *Joplin Globe* (8 May 1945), 12.

14. 'Coming Your Way', *Radio Life* (4 November 1945).

15. Aideen O'Connor to Eddie Choate, 12 January 1943, Shields family papers.

16. US military records for World War I give 11 October 1890 (and not 1888) as Angus Taillon's birthdate; his birthplace is recorded there as Alexandria, Ontario.

17. *Reno Evening Gazette* (17 November 1920); *Variety* (13 May 1953).

18. 'Fitzgerald Authors Own Starring Subject', *Los Angeles Times* (21 November 1950). It appears the film was never made.

19. 'Barry Fitzgerald Finds Stand-in Dead', *Los Angeles Times* (9 May 1953).

20. Edward G. Robinson, with Leonard Spiegelgass, *All My Yesterdays: An Autobiography* (W.H. Allen: London 1974), p. 218.

21. Robert Browning, *Fra Lippo Lippi*, lines 300–5.

22. Paramount Inter Office Communication, 2 July 1943, Academy of Motion Picture Arts and Sciences.

23. Wes D. Gehring, *Leo McCarey: From Marx to McCarthy* (The Scarecrow Press, Inc.: Lantham 2005), *passim.* See also Lawrence McCaffrey, '*Going My Way* and Irish-American Catholicism' in Ruth Barton (ed.), *Screening Irish-America: Representing Irish-America in Film and Television* (Irish Academic Press: Dublin 2009), pp. 186–7.

24. Gehring, *Leo McCarey*, p. 183.

25. Dolan, *The American Catholic Experience, passim.*

26. Joe Breen to Luigi Luraschi, Paramount Pictures (12 August 1943), Academy of Motion Picture Arts and Sciences. For a further account of censorship and *Going My Way*, and much more about Breen himself, see Thomas Doherty, *Hollywood's Censor: Joseph I. Breen & The Production Code Administration* (Columbia UP: New York 2007), pp. 191–4.

27. Luigi Luraschi to Frank Butler and Leo McCarey (19 August 1943), Academy of Motion Picture Arts and Sciences.

28. James Agee, *Agee on Film*, vol. 1 (Grosset and Dunlap: New York 1969), p. 347.

29. John Ford to Bing Crosby [February 1944?], Lilly Library.

30. John Cavanaugh to Leo McCarey, 9 March 1944, Academy of Motion Picture Arts and Sciences.

31. Gehring, *Leo McCarey*, p. 175.

32. Warren G. Harris, *Cary Grant, A Touch of Elegance* (Doubleday: New York 1987), pp. 125–7.

33. Graham McCann, *Cary Grant: A Class Apart* (Columbia UP: New York 1996), p. 161.

34. *Ibid.*

35. George Moore, *Salve* (William Heinemann: London, 1912), p. 331.

36. Dolan, *The American Catholic Experience*, p. 143.

37. Aideen O'Connor to Eddie Choate, 23 August 1941, 1843 North Cherokee, Shields family papers.

38. Sheaffer, *O'Neill*, pp. 592–3.

39. Arthur Shields, quoted by Homer Swander, 'Shields at the Abbey: A Friend of Cathleen', article, Shields family papers.

40. Black, *Eugene O'Neill*, p. 492.

41. Sheaffer, *O'Neill*, p. 595.

42. Hone, 'Autobiography', pp. 14–16.

43. 'Shirley Temple Gets Coaching', *Los Angeles Times* (9 April 1949).

44. Arthur Shields to Eddie Choate, 14 March 1949, Shields family papers.

45. Vernon Jacobson [lawyer for Arthur Shields] to Edmund Granger, Oriental International Films, 17 September 1951.

46. Arthur Shields to Eddie Choate, 2 July 1950, Shields family papers.

VI. *The Quiet Man* and *The Playboy of the Western World*

1. Una [Aideen] O'Connor to My dear Daddy, 23 March 1935, Shields family papers, NUI Galway.

2. For the attendance of Heather Angel and Joan Crawford at the Abbey plays, see Joan Harvey, 'Hollywood Beauty Gossip', *Los Angeles Times* (20 March 1935); for the Abbey schedule, *Los Angeles Times* (1 March 1935).

3. An article in the *Los Angeles Times* alludes to talk of a Hollywood film starring the Abbey players, but says the idea is 'sheer nonsense' (16 March 1935).

4. Gerry McNee, *In the Footsteps of the Quiet Man* (Mainstream Publishing: Edinburgh and London 1990, 2004), p. 23.

5. Killanin, interview in McNee, *In the Footsteps of the Quiet Man*, p. 50.

6. Liam O'Flaherty to My dear Jack [15 March 1939], Lilly Library.

7. Maurice Walsh, *The Quiet Man and other stories* (Appletree Press: Belfast 2002), p. 140.

8. *Ibid.* p. 145.

9. *Ibid.* p. 149.

10. My thanks to Cormac O'Malley. See also Richard English, *Ernie O'Malley: IRA Intellectual* (OUP: Oxford 1998), pp. 30–7.

11. McBride, *Searching for John Ford*, p. 337.

12. Frederick S. Foote, Lt. Comdr, USNR, medical history of John Ford, 4 June 1942, Lilly Library.

13. James S. Simmerman, Major, 13th Armed Regiment, report on service of Commander Ford, 8 July 1943, Lilly Library.

14. OSS record of recent travel, John Ford, 24 January 1944, Lilly Library.

15. OSS record of recent travel, John Ford, 1 September 1944, Lilly Library.

16. Unsigned to Col. William J. Donovan, 15 June 1942, Lilly Library.

17. Elmo Roper to Dear John, 9 July 1942, Lilly Library.

18. O'Hara, *'Tis Herself*, pp. 100–1.

19. As André Bazin noted, 'The world conflict not only provided Hollywood with spectacular scenes, it also provided, and indeed, forced upon it, some subjects to reflect

upon, at least for a few years.' André Bazin, *What is Cinema?*, vol. 2 (University of California Press 1971), p. 151.

20. Randy Roberts and James S. Olson, *John Wayne: American* (The Free Press: New York 1995), p. 360.

21. O'Hara, *'Tis Herself*, p. 136.

22. Richard Slotkin, *Gunfighter Nation: The Myth of the Frontier in Twentieth-Century America* (Atheneum: New York 1992). According to his own son, James W. Bellah, author of the story on which the film was based, was a 'fascist, a racist, and a world-class bigot' (Roberts and Olson, *John Wayne: American*, p. 324). These qualities suffice to explain the story's righteous defence of aggression. The fact that the remark comes from Bellah Jr may suggest something about the theme of bringing a son to heel.

23. No doubt when released on 15 November 1950, just as Chinese Communist forces were overrunning divisions from the USA and South Korea, and especially after President Truman threatened on 30 November 1950 to use atomic weapons against the Chinese army, *Rio Grande* was seen in light of debates about the conduct of the Korean War. It could have been predicted from the movie that Ford would support General Douglas MacArthur's aggressive strategy, and he did. See McBride, *Searching for John Ford*, p. 504.

24. For a wide-ranging discussion of post-war Hollywood movies in this light, see Peter Biskind, *Seeing is Believing: How Hollywood Taught us to Stop Worrying and Love the Fifties* (Henry Holt: New York 1983), pp. 251ff.

25. After the song, Kathleen says goodnight to Kirby, and apologizes for taking his bed, and he in turn apologizes for having more forcefully dispossessed her fifteen years earlier. 'You've grown more thoughtful.' But has he? His broody sucking on a cigar is the movie's main way of suggesting that he thinks.

26. In fact, the 1875 song was by a German-American, Thomas P. Westendorft, and makes no direct reference to Ireland.

27. The interior scene involving Mimi Doyle was filmed in the Republic studio; there is no evidence that she made the trip to Ireland.

28. Lee Lukather to Noel Huggard, Ashford Castle, 28 February 1951, Lilly Library.

29. Frank Nugent, 'Pubs, Pictures, and "Nice Soft Days" in Eire', *New York Times* (8 August 1951).

30. Arthur Shields to Christine Shields, 9 June 1951, Shields family papers.

31. In the script, it is assumed that Denis O'Dea would play Mickeleen O'Flynn, driver of the sidecar. O'Dea agreed to be in the film on 22 December 1950; by 22 May 1951, the cast had been set and O'Dea was not in it. The version must have been written in the interval, and probably closer to December than May. Frank Nugent, undated draft, 'The Quiet Man', Lilly Library.

32. In an influential monograph on *The Quiet Man* (Cork UP: Cork 2002), Luke Gibbons makes a case that the 'quiet' of *The Quiet Man* is a false quiet, just a surface; underneath it, sectarian conflict seethes, and the IRA is a constant and respected presence biding its time before it renews the Republican mission. The flashback in which Sean

Thornton kills a man in the ring is said to be a 'displacement' of the 'violence simmering ... under the Irish landscape' (p. 50), rather than simply a replacement of it. In all outward show, Ford removed the Troubles – present in some early drafts of the scenario – from the finished film. Gibbons also argues that Sean Thornton was a trauma victim, injured psychically not just by the accident in the boxing ring, but by American capitalism.

33. Edward A. Hagen also comments on Sean Thornton as a returning veteran in 'From "Peace and Freedom" to "Peace and Quiet": *The Quiet Man* as a Product of the 1950s' in James Silas Rogers and Matthew J. O'Brien, *After the Flood: Irish America 1945–1960* (Irish Academic Press: Dublin 2009), pp. 102–3.

34. George Moore describes the construction of the castle extension and gardens in 'A Castle of To-Day', *Parnell and His Island* (1887). The history of English gardens in Ireland is learnedly discussed in relation to *The Quiet Man* in Eamonn Slater, 'The Hidden Landscape Aesthetic of *The Quiet Man*', Seán Crosson and Rod Stoneman (eds), *The Quiet Man ... And Beyond* (Liffey Press: Dublin 2009), pp. 139–58. Ford expresses his early intention to make *The Quiet Man* a 'travelogue' in a letter of 9 August 1946 to Lord Killanin (McNee, *In the Footsteps*, p. 32).

35. Luke Gibbons argues that the viewer is intended by Ford to detect the film's artifice, and so Ford arranged that the joins between the assembled parts be made in a deliberately clumsy fashion (Gibbons, *The Quiet Man*, p. 19). What is obvious about 'Innisfree' is that it is jam-packed with beauty spots from far and wide on the Western seaboard (see the screenplay instructions from Ford to Nugent in Des MacHale, *Picture the Quiet Man* [Appletree Press: Belfast 2004], p. 134.).

36. O'Toole, *The Ex-Isle of Erin*, p. 21.

37. McNee, *In the Footsteps*, p. 132.

38. Fitzgerald himself made this point about Captain Boyle: 'He was a Dublin original, a strutting Paycock, fond of his drink and vociferous with malapropisms.' 'Star System Opposed by Celebrated Irish Comedian', *Los Angeles Times* (3 March 1935). Fitzgerald gets the same sort of O'Casey quality into his pronunciation of the syllables of Sean Thornton's supposed American home city: 'Pittsburgh, Massachusetts' and his disgusted one-word comment on America: 'Pro-hi-bi-tion!'

39. Synge, *Playboy of the Western World*, p. 67.

40. MacHale, *Picture the Quiet Man*, p. 131.

41. McNee, *In the Footsteps*, p. 133.

42. Roberts and Olson, *John Wayne*, p. 365.

43. At the end of *The Quiet Man*, Mary Kate significantly throws the stick away – the same stick that the old woman gave Sean 'to beat the lovely lady with', and that, after her rebuke from the parish priest, Mary Kate herself handed to Sean for that purpose.

44. For an interesting meditation on these complexities from the point of view of a contemporary Irish feminist, see Dióg O'Connell's 'Feminist Icon or Prisoner of Patriarchy: An Exploration of Mary Kate's Character in *The Quiet Man*', *The Quiet Man ... and Beyond* (pp. 203–13).

45. It is tempting to suggest that this scene of the Innisfree villagers pretending to be Protestants is John Ford's inside joke on the Abbey custom of Protestants pretending to be Catholics, with a kind of triumphalist smirk at the fact that there were scant few Protestants left in Ireland after thirty years of Catholic and Gaelic self-rule, but the tone of the scene is in fact simple and cheerful. There is, however, a Hollywood inside joke on the name of the Innisfree pub, Cohan's. 'We pronounce it,' Mickeleen says, 'Co-Hans,' a slightly anti-Semitic, because unnecessary, correction. Would Mickeleen be likely to know much of Cohens or Cohns? Or that a prominent Hollywood producer was Harry Cohn? Shortly after completing *The Quiet Man*, John Wayne formed a production company with Robert Fellows, saying, 'It had to be better than working with men like Yates and Cohn'. Ronald L. Davis, *Duke: The Life and Image of John Wayne* (Norman: University of Oklahoma Press 1998), p. 164.

46. See Kevin and Emer Rockett, *Irish Film Censorship: A Cultural Journey from Silent Cinema to Internet Pornography* (Four Courts Press: Dublin 2004), p. 13.

47. 'Former Players High Hopes for the Future', *Irish Independent* (20 July 1951), 7.

Afterword

1. Laurie Bailey Shields, Notes for a proposed biography, Shields family papers.
2. Arthur Shields to Eddie Choate, 27 August 1951, Shields family papers.
3. J.J. Molloy to Arthur Shields, 7 July 1959, Shields family papers.
4. Arthur Shields to Father Lynch, 24 January 1960, Shields family papers.
5. Arthur Shields to Laurie Shields, 7 November 1959, Shields family papers.
6. John Ford to Michael Killanin, 9 September 1952, Lilly Library.
7. Homer Swander, 'Shields at the Abbey', p. 2.

BIBLIOGRAPHY

MANUSCRIPT COLLECTIONS

Abbey Theatre Minute Books. NLI Acc 3961. National Library of Ireland.
Sara Allgood, 'Memories.' Belfast Public Record Office.
F.R. and May Higgins Papers. National Library of Ireland.
Joseph Holloway papers. 'Diary of a Dublin Playgoer'. National Library of Ireland.
Joseph Hone, 'Autobiography.' Private collection.
Hedda Hopper archive. Margaret Herrick Library, Academy of Motion Picture Arts and Sciences, Beverly Hills, California.
Denis Johnston Papers. TCD MSS 10066. Trinity College Dublin.
John Ford Archive. Lilly Library. University of Indiana.
Maire nic Shiublaigh Papers. NLI MSS 27631. National Library of Ireland.
Paramount Papers. Margaret Herrick Library, Academy of Motion Picture Arts and Sciences, Beverly Hills, California.
RKO Papers. Special Collections, Arts Library, UCLA.
Shields Family Papers. Special Collections, National University of Ireland, Galway.
Twentieth Century Fox Papers. Special Collections, Arts Library, UCLA.

WORKS CITED

Adams, Bernard, *Denis Johnston: A Life* (The Lilliput Press: Dublin 2002).

Affron, Charles, *Lillian Gish: Her Legend, Her Life* (University of California Press: Berkeley, Los Angeles, London 2002).

Agee, James, *Agee on Film*, vol. 1 (Grosset and Dunlap: New York 1969).

Anderson, Lindsay, 'John Ford: his work is a portrayal of the righteous man', *Films in Review*, February 1951.

Andrews, C.S., *Dublin Made Me: An Autobiography* (Mercier Press: Dublin and Cork 1979).

Balio, Tino, *Grand Design: Hollywood as a Modern Business Enterprise, 1930–39* (Scribner's Sons: New York 1993).

Barton, Ruth, *Acting Irish in Hollywood: From Fitzgerald to Farrell* (Irish Academic Press: Dublin 2006).

Barton, Ruth (ed.), *Screening Irish-America: Representing Irish-America in Film and Television* (Irish Academic Press: Dublin 2009).

Bazin, André, *What is Cinema?*, vol. 2 (University of California Press: Berkeley and Los Angeles 1971).

Birchard, Robert S., *Cecil B. DeMille's Hollywood* (UP of Kentucky: Lexington 2004).

Biskind, Peter, *Seeing is Believing: How Hollywood Taught us to Stop Worrying and Love the Fifties* (Henry Holt: New York 1983).

Black, Gregory D., *The Catholic Crusade Against the Movies, 1940–1975* (CUP: Cambridge 1997).

Black, Stephen A. *Eugene O'Neill: Beyond Mourning and Tragedy* (Yale UP: New Haven and London, 1999).

Bogdanovich, Peter, *John Ford* (University of California Press: Berkeley and Los Angeles 1978).

Bowe, Nicola Gordon, *Harry Clarke: Exhibition Catalogue* (Douglas Hyde Gallery: Trinity College Dublin, 12 November to 8 December 1979).

Braudy, Leo and Marshall Cohen (eds), *Film Theory and Criticism: Introductory Readings* (OUP: Oxford and New York 2004).

Butler, Jeremy, 'The star system and Hollywood', *Oxford Guide to Film Studies* (OUP: Oxford and New York 1998).

Cameron, Ian and Douglas Pye (eds), *The Movie Book of the Western* (Studio Vista: London 1996).

Campbell, Joseph, *'As I was among the captives': Joseph Campbell's Prison Dairy, 1922–1923*, ed. Eileán Ní Chuilleanáin (Cork UP: Cork 2001).

Canfield, Curtis, *Plays of a Changing Ireland* (Macmillan: New York 1936).

Carroll, Paul Vincent, *Shadow and Substance* (Macmillan: London 1938).

Caulfield, Max, *The Easter Rebellion* (Gill and Macmillan: Dublin 1963, 1995).

Cohen-Stratyner, Barbara Naomi, *The Biographical Dictionary of Dance* (Shirmer Books: New York 1982).

Coxhead, Elizabeth, *Daughters of Erin: Five Women of the Irish Renascence* (Colin Smythe: Gerrards Cross, Bucks. 1979).

Crosson, Seán and Rod Stoneman (eds), *The Quiet Man … and Beyond: Reflections on a Classic Film, John Ford, and Ireland* (Liffey Press: Dublin 2009).

Doherty, Thomas, *Hollywood's Censor: Joseph I. Breen & The Production Code Administration* (Columbia UP: New York 2007).

Dolan, J.P., *The American Catholic Experience* (University of Notre Dame Press: Notre Dame 1992).

Drazin, Charles, *Korda: Britain's Only Movie Mogul* (Sidgwick and Jackson: London 2002).

Dunne, Philip, *How Green Was My Valley: The Screenplay for the Darryl F. Zanuck Film Production, Directed by John Ford* (Santa Teresa Press: Santa Barbara, California 1990).

Durkheim, Emile, *Division of Labour in Society*, trans. W.D. Halls (Macmillan: London 1984).

English, Richard, *Ernie O'Malley: IRA Intellectual* (OUP: Oxford 1998).

Ervine, St John, *Selected Plays of St. John Ervine*, ed. John Cronin (Colin Smythe: Gerrards Cross, Bucks. 1988).

Eyman, Scott, *Print the Legend: The Life and Times of John Ford* (Simon and Schuster: New York 1999).

Fallon, Gabriel, 'Sitting at the play: those dramatists of Inish', *Irish Monthly*, 64 (1936): 614.

Fallon, Gabriel, 'The ageing Abbey – II', *Irish Monthly*, 66 (1938), 344.

Fallon, Gabriel, 'The celluloid menace', *Capuchin Annual* (1937), 248–50.

Fallon, Gabriel, 'The genius of Barry Fitzgerald', *The Leader*, 74, 2 (1937), 40–1.

Fallon, Gabriel, *Sean O'Casey: The Man I Knew* (Routledge and Kegan Paul: London 1965).

FitzGerald, Desmond, *The Memoirs of Desmond FitzGerald* (Routledge and Kegan Paul: London 1968).

Fitzgerald, F. Scott, *The Love of the Last Tycoon: A Western*, ed. Matthew J. Bruccoli (Simon and Schuster: New York 1941, 1993).

Fitz-Simon, Christopher, *The Boys: A Biography of Micheal Mac Liammóir and Hilton Edwards* (Nick Hern Books: London 1994).

Ford, Dan, *Pappy: The Life of John Ford* (Da Capo Press: New York 1979).

Foster, R.F., *W.B. Yeats: A Life, II: The Arch-Poet* (OUP: Oxford 2003).

Foy, Michael and Brian Barton, *The Easter Rising* (Sutton: Phoenix Mill 1999, 2004).

Frazier, Adrian (ed.), *Playboys of the Western World: Production Histories* (Carysfort Press: Dublin 2004).

Frazier, Adrian, 'McGuinness and the boys', *Dublin Review* (Summer 2002), 72–86.

Frazier, Adrian, *Behind the Scenes: Yeats, Horniman, and the Struggle for the Abbey Theatre* (University of California Press: Berkeley and Los Angeles 1990).

Frazier, Adrian, *George Moore: 1852–1933* (Yale UP: London and New Haven 2000).

Gallagher, Tag, *John Ford: The Man and His Films* (University of California Press: Berkelely and Los Angeles 1986).

Gehring, Wes D., *Leo McCarey: From Marx to McCarthy* (The Scarecrow Press Inc.: Lanham 2005).

Gibbons, Luke, *The Quiet Man* (Cork UP: Cork 2002).

Giovacchini, Saverio, *Hollywood Modernism: Film and Politics of the New Deal* (Temple UP: Philadelphia 2001).

Gregory, Augusta Isabella, *Lady Gregory's Journals*, vol. 2, ed. Daniel Murphy (Colin Smythe: Gerrards Cross, Bucks. 1987).

Grene, Nicholas. *The Politics of Irish Drama (*CUP: Cambridge 1999).

Harmon, Maurice. *Sean O'Faolain* (Constable: London 1994).

Harris, Warren G., *Cary Grant, A Touch of Elegance* (Doubleday: New York 1987).

Hazlitt, William, *Essays* (Blackie and Son: London, Glasgow, and Bombay 1906).

Hogan, Robert and Michael J. O'Neill (eds), *Joseph Holloway's Abbey Theatre: A*

Selection from his Unpublished Journal (Southern Illinois UP: Carbondale and Edwardsville, Illinois; Feffer and Simons: London and Amsterdam 1967).

Hogan, Robert and Michael J. O'Neill (eds), *Joseph Holloway's Irish Theatre*, vols 1–3 (Proscenium Press: Dixon, California, 1968, 1969, 1970).

Hogan, Robert and Richard Burnham, *The Years of O'Casey, 1921–1926, A Documentary History* (Colin Smythe: Gerrards Cross, Bucks. 1992).

Hutchinson, John and Anthony D. Smith (eds), *Ethnicity* (OUP: Oxford 1996).

Jacobs, Lewis, *The Rise of American Film: A Critical History* (Harcourt Brace and Co.: New York 1939).

Kellner, Bruce (ed.), *Letters of Carl Van Vechten* (Yale UP: New Haven 1987).

King, Desmond, *The Liberty of Strangers: Making the American Nation* (OUP: Oxford 2005).

Kitses, Jim, *Horizons West: Directing the Western from John Ford to Clint Eastwood* (BFI Publishing: London 2004).

Krause, David, *The Letters of Sean O'Casey, 1910–1941*, vol. 1 (Macmillan: New York 1975).

Krause, David, *The Letters of Sean O'Casey, 1942–1954*, vol. 2 (Macmillan: New York 1980).

Lathem, Edward Connery (ed.), *The Poetry of Robert Frost: The Collected Poems, Complete and Unabridged* (Henry Holt and Company: New York 1979).

Lyons, F.S.L., *Ireland Since the Famine* (Fontana Collins: London 1973).

MacHale, Des, *Picture the Quiet Man* (Appletree Press: Belfast 2004).

Mann, William J., *Kate: The Woman Who Was Katherine Hepburn* (Faber and Faber: London 2006).

Matthews, James, *Voices: A Life of Frank O'Connor* (Atheneum: New York 1983).

McCormack, W.J., *Fool of the Family: A Life of J.M. Synge* (Weidenfeld & Nicolson: London 2000).

McBride, Joseph, *Searching for John Ford* (Faber and Faber: London 2003).

McCann, Graham, *Cary Grant: A Class Apart* (Columbia UP: New York 1996).

McCarthy, Todd, *Howard Hawks: The Grey Fox of Hollywood* (Grove Press: New York 1997).

McGilligan, Patrick, *Alfred Hitchcock: A Life in Darkness and Light* (Wiley: London 2003).

McGlone, James P., *Ria Mooney: The Life and Times of the Artistic Director of the Abbey Theatre, 1948–1963* (McFarland & Co.: Jefferson, NC, and London 2002).

McNee, Gerry, *In the Footsteps of the Quiet Man* (Mainstream Publishing: Edinburgh and London 1990, 2004).

Moore, George, *Salve* (William Heinemann: London 1912).

Morley, Sheridan, *Tales from the Hollywood Raj: The British Film Colony on Screen and Off* (Weidenfeld & Nicolson: London 1983).

Mosley, Leonard, *Zanuck: The Rise and Fall of Hollywood's Last Tycoon* (Little, Brown and Co.: Boston 1984).

Murray, Christopher (ed.), *Selected Plays of Lennox Robinson* (Colin Smythe: Gerrards

Cross, Bucks.; Catholic UP: Washington DC 1982).

Murray, Christopher, *Sean O'Casey: Writer at Work* (Gill and Macmillan: Dublin, 2004).

Nevin, Donal, *James Connolly: A Full Life* (Gill and Macmillan: Dublin 2005).

O'Casey, Sean, *Three Plays* (St Martin's Press: New York 1957).

O'Casey, Sean, *Rose and Crown* (Macmillan: London 1952).

O'Hara, Maureen, *'Tis Herself: A Memoir* (Simon and Schuster: New York 2004).

O'Mahony, Seán, *Frongoch: University of Revolution* (FDR Teoranta: Dublin 1987).

O'Neill, Eugene, *Complete Plays 1913–1920* (Library of America: New York 1988).

O'Toole, Fintan, *The Ex-Isle of Erin.* New Island Books: Dublin, 1997.

Parrish, Robert, *Growing up in Hollywood* (Harcourt, Brace, Jovanovich: New York and London 1976).

Peary, Gerald, and Jenny Lefcourt (eds), *John Ford Interviews* (UP of Mississippi: Jackson 2001).

Phillips, Alastair, and Ginette Vincendeau (eds), *Journeys of Desire: Europeans Actors in Hollywood* (BFI Publishing: London 2006).

Robbins, Christopher, *The Empress of Ireland: Chronicle of an Unusual Friendship* (Scribner: London 2004).

Roberts, Randy and James S. Olson, *John Wayne: American* (The Free Press: New York 1995).

Robinson, Edward G. with Leonard Spiegelgass, *All My Yesterdays: An Autobiography* (W.H. Allen: London 1974).

Robinson, Lennox, Tom Robinson and Nora Dorman, *Three Homes* (Michael Joseph: London 1938).

Robinson, Lennox, *Selected Plays of Lennox Robinson*, ed. Christopher Murray (Colin Smythe: Gerrards Cross, Bucks.; Catholic UP: Washington, DC 1982).

Robinson, Lennox, *Ireland's Abbey Theatre* (Kennikat Press: Port Washington, New York 1951).

Rockett, Kevin and Emer, *Irish Film Censorship: A Cultural Journey from Silent Cinema to Internet Pornography* (Four Courts Press: Dublin 2004).

Rogers, James Silas and Matthew J. O'Brien, *After the Flood: Irish America 1945–1960* (Irish Academic Press: Dublin 2009).

Russo, Vito, *The Celluloid Closet: Homosexuality in the Movies* (Harper and Row: New York 1987).

Rust, Redilworth, 'The unity of O'Neill's S.S. *Glencairn*', *American Literature*, 37, 3 (1965), 284.

Ryan, Annie, *Witnesses: Inside the Easter Rising* (Liberties Press: Dublin 2005).

Ryan, Philip B., *The Lost Theatres of Dublin* (Badger Press: Westbury, Wiltshire 1998).

Ryan, Phyllis, *The Company I Kept* (Town House: Dublin 1996).

Saddlemyer, Ann, *Theatre Business: The Correspondence of the First Abbey Theatre Directors: William Butler Yeats, Lady Gregory, and J.M. Synge* (Colin Smythe: Gerrards Cross, Bucks. 1982).

Sarris, Andrew, *'You Ain't Heard Nothin' Yet': The American Talking Film: History and Memory 1927–1949* (OUP: Oxford 1998).

Schulberg, Budd, *Moving Pictures: Memories of a Hollywood Prince* (Ivan R. Dee: Chicago 1981).

Shaeffer, Louis, *O'Neill: Son and Artist* (Little, Brown and Co.: Boston, Toronto 1973).

Shaughnessy, Edward L., *Eugene O'Neill in Ireland: The Critical Heritage* (Greenwood Press: New York, London 1988).

Sheeran, Patrick F., *The Informer* (Cork UP: Cork 2002).

Sissons, Elaine, *Pearse's Patriots: St Enda's and the Cult of Boyhood* (Cork UP: Cork 2005).

Sklar, Robert, *Movie-Made America: A Cultural History of American Movies* (Chappel & Co.: London 1978).

Slotkin, Richard, *Gunfighter Nation: The Myth of the Frontier in Twentieth-Century America* (Atheneum: New York 1992).

Spiegelgass, Leonard, *All My Yesterdays: An Autobiography* (W.H. Allen: London 1974).

Spittles, Brian, *John Ford* (Longman: Harlow, Essex 2002).

Stuldar, Gaylyn and Mathew Bernstein (eds), *John Ford Made Westerns: Filming the Legend in the Sound Era* (Indiana UP: Bloomington and Indianapolis 2001).

Synge, J.M., *Plays: Book I*, ed. Ann Saddlemyer, vol. 3, *J.M. Synge: The Collected Works* (Colin Smythe: Gerrards Cross: Bucks., and Catholic University of America Press: Washington, DC 1982).

Thomson, David, *Showman: The Life of David Selznick* (Alfred Knopf: New York 1992).

Toomey, Deirdre (ed.), *Yeats and Women* (Palgrave: London 1997).

Tynan, Kenneth, *Theatre Writings*, ed. Dominic Shellard (Nick Hern: London 2007).

Van Vechten, Carl, *Letters of Carl Van Vechten*, ed. Bruce Kellner (Yale UP: New Haven and London 1987).

Vasey, Ruth, *The World According to Hollywood, 1918–1939* (University of Exeter Press: Exeter 1997).

Walsh, Maurice, *The Quiet Man and other stories* (Appletree Press: Belfast 2002).

Waugh, Evelyn, *The Diaries of Evelyn Waugh*, ed. Michael Davie (Phoenix: London 1976, 1995).

Weintraub, Stanley (ed.), *Literary Criticism of Oscar Wilde* (University of Nebraska Press: Lincoln 1968).

Welch, Robert, *The Abbey Theatre 1899–1999* (OUP: Oxford 2000).

Wilde, Oscar. *Literary Criticism of Oscar Wilde*, ed. Stanley Weintraub (University of Nebraska Press: Lincoln 1968).

Wills, Garry. *John Wayne's America* (Simon and Schuster: New York 1997).

Yeats, W.B., *Explorations* (Macmillan: New York 1962).

Yeats, W.B., 'The Collected Letters of W.B. Yeats. Past Masters: English Letters Collection', online database, OUP: Oxford.

Yeats, W.B., *The Letters of W.B. Yeats*, ed. Allan Wade (Macmillan: New York 1955).

INDEX

Abbey Festival, 127, 128–9
Abbey Theatre, 57–8, 59, 241; *see also Juno and the Paycock*; *Playboy of the Western World*; *Plough and the Stars*
Allgood portrait, 154
burnt, 238
Carroll play rejected, 129
Silver Tassie rejected, 78, 92
Abbey Theatre company, 6, 57–9, *58*, 139, 185
'Abbey stare', 196
Abbey 'style', 78–80, 95, 153
acting school, 60–1, 67–8, 102, 118, 129
Allgood in, 149, 150
Catholicism in, 129
conflicts, 68–70
departures from, 62–5, 95
Fitzgerald in, 95, 160, 239
and Ford, 46, 47, 48, 54, 80–4, 210
founded, 149
government influence, 4–5, 73–4
and Hollywood, 7, 8–10, 27–8, 178–81, 243–4
How Green Was My Valley, 161
O'Connor letter, 1935, 207–9
The Quiet Man, 237–8
Protestantism in, 110–14, 129
rehearsals, 66, 131
relationships, 126, 157
salaries, 62
sets, 131
Shields in, 101, 102, 107–10, 129, 194, 239, 242
Silver Tassie, 120–1
US tours, 2, 3–4, 53, 57–60, 62, 80–2, 140
1931, 114–18
1934, 119–20
1937, 123–6, 130
1938, 151–2
Academy Awards, 8, 15, *40*, 44–6, 47, 142, 191, 217
Allgood, 162
Fitzgerald, 180, 190
The Informer, 44–5, 45–6
Academy of Motion Picture Arts and Sciences, 8
acting, discussion of, 152–6
Africa, 16, 195, 213
African-Americans, 172, 178, 214
Agee, James, 53, 188
Alabama, 115, *116*, 117
alcoholism, 18, 24
Aldrich, Robert, 181
Alexandra College, 110
All-Ireland Labour Conference, 101
Allenby, General, 40
Allgood, George and Margaret, 156–7, 165
Allgood, Molly (Maire O'Neill), 62, 64, 65, 149, 150, 153, 157, 209
Allgood, Sara, 5–6, 10, 58, 65, 110, 135, *147*, 194

career, 28, 58, 149–53, 156–74
in Hollywood, 4, 159, 160–74, 179, 243
character parts, 171–2
difficulties, 159, 161, 170–1
How Green Was My Valley, 160–7, *167*
Oscar nomination, 190
Juno and the Paycock, 63, 137–8, 209
leaves Abbey, 62
'Memories', 168
portrait of, 154
Shadow and Substance, 150–2
Allgood family, 156
Allingham, William, 156
Always Sweethearts, 201
Amazing Mrs Holliday, The, 176, 184–5
Ameche, Don, 196
American Civil War, 25, 215, 218, 219
American Declaration of Independence, 93
American Revolution, 93, 94
And Then There Were None, 192
Anderson, Judith, 170–1
Anderson, Lindsay, 49–50
Anderson, Mary, 240
Andrews, C.S., 154
Angel, Heather, 209
Anglo-Irish Treaty, 1921, 70
anti-Semitism, 214
Apollo Theatre, London, 58
Aran Islands, 15, 80
Araner (ketch), 16, 18, 20, 21, 33, 49, 50, 80, 85
Ardilaun, Lord, 226
Argentina, 213
Argosy Pictures, 13, 33–4, 140, 215
Arizona, 15
Arrowsmith, 27
Ashford Castle, County Mayo, 28–9, 222–3, 226
Asia, 16, 213
Auden, W.H., 9
August, Joe, 39, 47, 48, 52
Australia, 62, 64, 149–50, 158, 173
auteur theory, 46–7
Awful Truth, The, 186

Baghdad, 40
Bailey, Laurie, 239
Balanchine, George, 58
Ballinrobe, County Mayo, 113
Baltimore, 57
Barry, Kevin, 29, 76
Barrymore, Ethel, 171, 191
Baudelaire, C.P., 108
BBC, 61
Beckett, Samuel, 191, 195
Belfast, 26, 63
Bellah, James Warner, 220
Bellamy, Ralph, 208, 209
Belvedere College, 180
Bennett, Joan, 196
Bernhardt, Sarah, 161
Big House, The (Robinson), 59, 113
Big Knife, The, 181
Big Tree, Chief, 135
Black and Tans, 54, 210, 212, 222
Black Narcissus, 202
Blackmail, 62
Blight (O'Connor and Gogarty), 66
Blythe, Ernest, 75–6, 121, 129
Blythe, Mrs, 121
Bogdanovich, Peter, 25, 45, 142
Boise, Idaho, 115
'Bold Fenian Men, The', 221
Bond, Ward, 18, 33, 135, 140, 222
The Quiet Man, 233–4, 237
Borzage, Frank, 214
Boston, 115
Boucicault, Dion, 228
Brazil, 213
Brecht, Bertholt, 178
Breen, Joe, 35, 187

Brighton Strangler, The, 181
Bringing up Baby, 95–8
Briskin, Sam, 85, 93
Britain, 16, 36, 54, 64, 76, 137, 172, 214; *see also* London
Abbey tours, 103, 110
Allgood, 149, 150
McLaglen, 39–40
Broadway *see* New York
Browning, Robert, 185
Buchanan, Edward, 172
Bush, George W., 36
Byng, Douglas, 150

Caesar and Cleopatra (Shaw), 28
California, 15, 136, 243
California, 191
California Studio, 38, 39, 80–1
Campbell, Mrs Patrick, 149, 154
Canada, 40, 59–60, 114, 115, 181, 195
Capra, Frank, 13, 50
Carey, Dobe, 19, 22, 23
Carnegie Libraries, 113
Carroll, Paul Vincent, 5, 62, 123, 135, 243
Kindred, 130–2, 137–8, 159, 197
Shadow and Substance, 123, 150–2, 195
The White Steed, 129–31
Casablanca, 182
Cathleen ni Houlihan (Yeats/Gregory), 9, 102, 109, *109*, 112–13, 154
Catholic League of Decency, 35
Catholic Truth Society, 113
Catholicism, 8, 23, 26, 77, 236
in Abbey, 4, 70–3, 123, 129
and blasphemy, 163, 164
'devotional revolution', 195
Ford, 19–20, 33–4
in Hollywood, 164, 186–8, 190
in Irish Free State, 82, 112–14, 120–1, 195, 242
Sinn Féin, 106–7
in USA, 10, 16, 195–6
Cavalcade, *169*
censorship, 4–5, 35, 113, 236
Censorship Act, 1929, 113
Central America, 195
Cheaper by the Dozen, 172–3
Chekhov, Anton, 59
Cheyenne Autumn, 25
Chicago, 60, 79, 117, 209
Chicago Daily News, 65, 68
Chicago Times, 60, 62, 65
China, 178, 213, 219
Choate, Eddie, 130–1, 136, 137, 159–60, 197, 201, 204
Christie, Agatha, 192
Church of Ireland, 121
Cincinnati, Ohio, 114
Citizen Kane (Welles), 142
Civic Theatre, Los Angeles, 240
Civil War, 5, 75–6, 80, 212, 242
in *Juno and the Paycock*, 57, 68, 70
Claidheamh Soluis, An, 106
Clair, René, 191–2
Clare, County, 226
Clarke, Harry, 110, 120, 226
Clarke, Mrs Tom, 76
Clarke, Tom, 105
Cleese, John, 190
Cleopatra (DeMille), 15
Clifford, Tommy, *126*
Clifton, Harry, 27
Cochrane, Charles, 58–9
Colbert, Claudette, 134, 135
Cold War, 220
Collier, Constance, 170
Collins, Michael, 160
Colorado, 115
Columbia, 38
Committee on Interstate Commerce, 35–6
communism, 13, 80
Confirm or Deny, 196

Cong, County Mayo, 222, 225, 226
Connecticut, 117–18
Connolly, James, 6, 93, 101, 104, 105
Connolly, Seán, 63, 103, 104, 106
Constitution of Ireland, 1937, 242
Cooper, Merian, 13–14, 215, 217
Cork, 122
Cork Opera House, 113
Corkery, Daniel, 121, 128–9
Corvette 225, 176
Coughlan, John, 208
Coward, Noel, 32
Coxhead, Elizabeth, 159
Craig, May, 73, 226–7
Crawford, Joan, 209
Crisp, Donald, 161, 163
Crock of Gold, The (Stephens), 208
Crosby, Bing, 185–90, 191, 192
Cross Roads, The (Robinson), 113
Crowe, Eileen
  Ford film of *The Plough and the Stars*, *83*, 84, 90
  in Hollywood, *81*, 82, 84, 192, 209
  and O'Casey plays, 57, 71, *71*, *72*, 73
Crucible, The (Miller), 150
CSI, 194
Cukor, George, 27
Curling [Wall], Kitty, 81, 110, 115, *115*, 118, *127*
Curragh camp, 75
Curtis, Ken, 222
Curtiz, Michael, 182
Custer, General, 215, 216
Czechoslovakia, 220

D-Day, 213
D'Alton, Louis, 197
Daniels, William H., 193
Darragh, Florence, 154
Dassin, Jules, 192
Days Without End (O'Neill), 118
de Valera, Éamon, 74, 75, *122*, 180, 195, 242
Deirdre of the Sorrows (Synge), 154
Deirdre (Yeats), 154
Delaney, Maureen, 76, 79, *79*, *128*
DeMille, Cecil B., 13, 14
Detroit, 197
Devlin, Father, 187–8
Dietrich, Marlene, 40
Digges, Dudley, 60, 62, 208, 209
Digges, Mary, 208
Dishonored, 40
Dolan, M.J., 72, 73, *115*, 118
domestic service, 171, 172
Donahue, Ed, 85
Donovan, Dr, 240
Dostoevsky, F.M., 39
Douglas, Kirk, 24
Dowling, Eddie, 150–1
Doyle, Mimi, 22, 222
Dr Bull, 15
Dr Jekyll and Mr Hyde, 160
Drago, Kathleen, 62, 64
Drama at Inish (Robinson), 119–20, 122–3
Drumcliffe, County Sligo, *122*
Drums Along the Mohawk, 15, 36, 49–50, 132–6
  Shields in, 6, 132, 133, 135–6, 160, 195, 198
Dublin, 3, 4, 6, 10, 61, 82, 95, 159, 178–9, 204; *see also Informer, The*
  Abbey box-office, 57–8, 59
  Catholicism, 82, 195
  Easter Rising, 103–7
  Fitzgerald death, 241
  housing, 66
  MGM talent scouts, 81
  mimicry, 67–8
  and O'Casey, 73–7, 164, 197
  Protestantism, 95, 156, 157
  social classes, 68–9
Dublin Castle, 66, 68

Dublin Drama League, 110, 112
Dublin Horse Show, 111, 209
Duck Soup, 186
Duffy's Tavern, 192
Dundalk, County Louth, 123, 131
Dunne, Philip, 160–4
Durbin, Deanna, 184–5
Durkheim, Emile, 16, 25
Duse, Eleanor, 161
DuWorld Pictures, 27

Easter Rising, 1916, 6, 7, 9, 68, 75, 78, 92
  and Abbey Theatre, 62–4
  in *The Plough and the Stars*, 74–5, 76
  Proclamation, 93, 103, 241
  Shields in, 7, 63, 101, 103–7
Easy Come, Easy Go, 191
Ebb Tide, 95
Edinburgh, 150
Edison Hotel, New York, 151
Edmonds, Walter, 132
Education, Department of, 70
Edwards, Hilton, 111
Egypt, 177
Eliot, T.S., 112
Eller, Jack and Coughlan, Reed, 35
Emmet, Robert, 160
Equity, 138, 180
Ervine, St John Greer, 63–4, 66, 107
ethnicity, 9–10, 14, 24–5, 54
  fictional identities, 34–6
  of Ford, 15–17
  images of the Other, 25
  Irish, 16, 19–20, 26–7
Ever the Twain (Robinson), 112
External Affairs, Department of, 223

Fagan, J.B., 64, 150
Fairbanks, Douglas, 108
Fallon, Gabriel, 66, 73, 78, 121–3
Farmer, Frances, 95
Farrow, John, 191, 208, 209
Faulkner, William, 132, 178
Fawlty Towers, 190
Fay, Frank, 60–1, 95, 102, 153, 157
Fay, W.G., 60–1, 153
Feeney, John, 15, 80, 92
Fetchit, Stepin, 24–5, *25*
Fianna Fáil, 212
Field Day Anthology of Irish Writing, 209
Field Photo Farm, 213
Fighting Father Dunne, 201
Films in Review, 49–50
Fitzgerald, Barry, 7, 10, *55*, *67*, *71*, *79*, *81*, *141*, *166*, *175*, *192*, *193*
  in Abbey Theatre, 5–6, 66–8, 80, 107–8, 114–18, 153
    Juno and the Paycock, 57, 78–9, 137–8, 159–60, 195, 228
    The Plough and the Stars, 73, 76
    The Silver Tassie, 120–1
  and brother, 239–44
  death, 241
  health, 240–1
  in Hollywood, 82, 125; 173, 178–81, 181–94
    Bringing up Baby, 95–8
    How Green Was My Valley, 160, 165, *165*
    The Long Voyage Home, 138, 143–6
    The Plough and the Stars, 83, 83–98, 88–90, *91*, 94–5
    The Quiet Man, *205*, 211, 222–4, 227–8, *232*, *234*
    stereotypes, 94–5, 98
  in London, 4, 58–9
  love of USA, 57–8, 81, 82
  nationalism, 65–6
  and O'Casey, 58, 59, 66–8, 110, 135, 195
  salary, 192
  'scene-stealer', 185

The White Steed, NY, 129–31
will, 243
FitzGerald, Desmond and Mrs, 121
Fitzgerald, F. Scott, 58, 178
Fitzsimons, Charles B., 222
Florida, 115
Fonda, Henry, 15, 18, 33–4, 36, 134–6, 216
Ford, Barbara, 222
Ford, Francis, 43
Ford, Henry, 178
Ford, John, *21*, *51*, 125, 196, 242; *see also Informer, The*; *Plough and the Stars, The* (O'Casey); *Quiet Man, The*
and Abbey Theatre, 2, 3–4, 6–7, 54, 80–2, 168, 189–90, 244
Shields, 132, 195, 198–200
and Allgood, 168
Catholicism, 23, 26, 33–4
as director, 7–8, 10, 14–15, 46–53, 200, 215
depiction of women, 32–3
dialogue, 88
'stock company', 47–8, 140–2, 200, 222
Westerns, 25, 198–200, 215–21
films
Drums Along the Mohawk, 132–6
How Green Was My Valley, 160–7
The Long Voyage Home, 138–46
The Plough and the Stars, 153
Rio Grande, 216–21
The Rising of the Moon, *31*
She Wore a Yellow Ribbon, 198–200
and Hollywood blacklist, 13–14
Irish links, 15–17, 18–20, 26–7, 28–9, 32, 36–7, 53
as Irish author, 13–54
in Spiddal, *16*
and Nichols, 37–8
personality, 19
bullying, 50–3
dishonesty, 19
drinking, 18
fighting, *18*, 18–19
flirtations, 20–3
handkerchief chewing, 22
relationships, 22, 23–4, 26–7, 32
smoking, 22
World War II service, 8, *11*, 13–14, 20, 23, 212–14
Ford, Mary, 20, 30
Ford, Patrick, *16*, 33, 222
Ford, Wallace, 137
Fort Apache, 14, 215, 216
Foster, Preston, 43–4, 81, 85–7, *87*, 93
Four Courts, 121
Four Men and a Prayer, 22, *166*
Four Provinces Films, 29, 30, 242
Fox Studios, 15, 37, 38
France, 46, 122, 137, 213
Franco, General F., 95
Franklin, Benjamin, 93
Frongoch camp, 106
Frost, Robert, 84
Fugitive, The, 33–4, 215, 217

Gaelic League, 106
Gallipoli, Battle of, 26
Galway, 5, 26, 57, 222
Galway, County, 28–9, 226
Gans, Herbert, 9
Garbo, Greta, 22
Garfield, John, 182
Gasworkers' Union, 101
Gate Theatre, 66, 111–12
Gentleman Jim, 180
Geoghegan, J., 121
Germany, 16, 36, 39, 85, 101, 137, 215, 242
Gibbons, Luke, 236
Gielgud, John, 131
Gilbreth, Frank, 172–3
Gish, Lilian, 170–1

Glasgow, 61, 95, 123
Glennon, Bert, 52, 217
Godard, Jean-Luc, 46
Godden, Rumer, 202
Gogarty, Oliver St John, 66, 97
Going My Way, 180, 185–90, 191, 192, 201
Golders Green Hippodrome, London, *63*
Goldwyn, Sam, 15
Goor, M et Mme, 120
Gorman, Eric, 227
Graham, Sheilah, 58
Grahame, Margot, 42, *51*, 52
Grand Illusion, La, 202
Grant, Cary, 95–7, 186, 190–1
Grapes of Wrath, The, 15, 36, 132, 142
Green Rushes (Walsh), 210
Greene, Graham, 33–4
Gregory, Augusta Lady, 58, 59, 65, 243
  and Allgood, 62, 157
  and Fitzgerald, 66
  and O'Casey, 85
  plays, 9, 30, 63, 102, 112–13, 154, 227
  Protestantism, 4, 129
  on stage, 109, *109*
Grene, Nicholas, 68–9
Gresham Hotel, 128
Guerlet, M et Mme, 120
Guinness family, 222, 226
Guiry, Philip, 106

Ha da veni ... Don Calegero!, 240
Hague, Mrs, 158
Hairy Ape, The (O'Neill), 111
Hancock, John, 93
Hangman's House, A, 26
Hardwicke, Sir Cedric, 151, 152
Harrison, Rex, 151
Hawks, Howard, 46, 95, 96
Haydon, Julie, 152
Hayes, Richard, 236
Hays, Will, 35
Hazlitt, William, 152–3, 155–6
Henderson, Captain Leo, 103
Henry, Patrick, 94
Henson, Gerald, 158–9
Hepburn, Katherine, 20–1, *21*, 22, 23, 52, 96–7
Herald and Examiner, Chicago, 79
Higgins, F.R., 121, 126, 127, *127*, 129, 132, 151
Hinduism, 203–4
Hitchcock, Alfred, 46, 58, 59, 62, 150
Hitler, Adolf, 137, 214, 216, 225
Hoch, Winton, 47, 217, 225
Hokusai, K., 8
Holloway, Joseph, 64, 75, 84, 108, 121
Hollywood, 16, 27, 39, 40
  Abbey actors in, 2–10, 54, 58, 60, 62, 81–2, 153, 178–81
    O'Connor letter, 1935, 207–9
  Allgood in, 159, 160–74
  blacklist, 13
  collaborative art, 44, 46–7
  description of, 177–9
  and ethnicity, 35–6
  homosexuality, 27
  Irishness in, 186
  marriage, 20
  Production Code, 35, 87, 163, 187
  role of actors, 178
  Shields in, 107, 136, 138, 239–40, 242–4
  studio system, 37, 38
  writers, 178
Hollywood Bowl, 179
Hollywood High School, 181
Home Rule Bill, 1914, 102
homesickness, 145–6
Homolka, Oscar, 95
homosexuality, 22, 23–4, 26–7, 32, 111–12
Hone, Joseph, 200
Hood, Thomas, 156
Hope, Bob, 165

Hopper, Hedda, 20
Horniman, Annie, 7, 61
House of Murphy, Hollywood, 160
House Un-American Activities Committee (HUAAC), 13, 192–4
How Green Was My Valley, 160–7, 168, 190, 214, 244
  Irishness in, 160–1
  Shields in, 160–1, 195, 196, 198
Howth gun-running, 102–3
Huggard, Noel, 222
Hughes, Howard, 22
Hungry Hill, *28*
Hunt, Hugh, 82, 123, 126, 130, 131
Hunter, Ian, 142
Hurst, Brian Desmond, 26–32, *28*, 242

Ibsen, Henrik, 74
Idaho, 115
immigration, 10, 16, 26–7, 36, 54, 186
  homesickness, 145–6
  in *The Long Voyage Home*, 138–9
India, 202–4
Informer, The (O'Flaherty), 3, 27, 47, 48, *51*, 53, 80–1, 88, 217
  draft screenplay, 49
  filming, 38–44
  planned, 37–8
  set, *2*
  success of, 44–6
Internet Movie Database, 240
Invisible Man, The, 60, 62
Irish Citizen Army, 63, 85, 104
Irish Free State, 36, 60, 74, 75, 83, 92, 103, 154, 235
  Catholicism in, 4, 82, 108–9, 112–14, 120–1, 195, 242
  Protestantism in, 6, 68, 95, 110–14, 121–3, 129, 242
  in *The Quiet Man*, 213, 215, 222–30
Irish Independent, 123, 238
Irish language, 6, 16, 80, 106–7, 108, 242
Irish Literary Revival, 54, 110, 179, 226, 237
  and Fitzgerald, 65–6
  and Ford, 29, 32, 36, 50, 227–9, 242, 244
Irish Monthly, The, 121
Irish National Theatre Society, 4, 60, 64
Irish Renaissance, 16
Irish Republican Army (IRA), 16, 70, 92, 109, 212, 222, 230
  English bombing campaign, 210
  in *The Informer*, 43–4
  in *The Quiet Man*, 54, 222
Irish Revival, 4–5, 6–10
Irish Times, The, 76, 121
Irish Volunteers, 102–7
Ito, Michio, 27

Jacobs, Lewis, 36–7, 53
Jane Eyre, 171
Japan, 8, 213, 215, 219
Jefferson, Thomas, 93
Jellett, Mainie, 121
John, Augustus, 58
Johnson, Ben, 199, 219
Johnson, Nunnally, 18
Johnston, Denis, 28, 110–12, 112, 243
  US tour, 1931, 114–18
Jones, Beulah Hall, 135
Joyce, James, 8, 26, 111, 195, 209
Judge, Peter *see* McCormick, F.J.
Judge Priest, 15, 24, 25
Juno and the Paycock (O'Casey), 3, *55*, 95, 244
  Abbey production, 78, 80
  Allgood in, 4, 5, 149, 150, 159–60, 162, 164
  characterization, 68, 69–70
  in Chicago, 57
  Fitzgerald in, *55*, 66–8, 68, 165, *166*, 176, 182, 228

Ford film plan, 53, 210
Hitchcock film, 59, 62
O'Connor in, 119
Shields in, 110
in USA, 5, 137–8, 159–60, 179, 180, 207

Kael, Pauline, 191
Kahane, B.B., 38
Kanin, Garson, 27
Kelly, P.J., 60
Kennedy, Hugh, 75–6
Kennedy, John F., 38
Kennedy, Joseph, 38
Kerrigan, J.M., 6, 65, 102, *126*, *139*, 153
and Allgood, 157
Ford's *Plough*, *83*, 84
in Hollywood, 3, 125, 208, 209, 243
The Informer, 43, 47, 53, 81
The Long Voyage Home, 139–46
Moon for the Misbegotten, 197
and Shields, 103
Kerry, County, 30, 210
Key, Francis Scott, 94
Kildare Street Club, 6, 129
Killanin, Michael Lord, 28, 29, 30, *30*, 210, 242
Kincora Dramatic Club, 102
Kindred (Carroll), 130–2, 137–8, 159, 179, 197
King Kong, 13
King of Kings, The, 15
Knutsford camp, 106
Kochno, Boris, 58
Korda, Alexander, 28, 36
Korea, 178
Korean War, 219–20

LA Times, 52
Lafayette Theatre, New York, 138
LaGalienne, Eva, 170
Landi, Elissa, 208
Lang, Fritz, 36
Las Vegas, 194
Last Hurrah, The, 22
Lee, Anna, 54
Leigh, Vivien, 151, 160
Lennox Hill Hospital, NY, 138
L'Estrange,Julian, 170
Leventhal, A.J., 108
Levine, Sonya, 132
Liberty Valance, 24
Life, 189
Lilburn, James, 222
Lincoln, Abraham, 14–15, 24
'Little Theatre' movement, 118
Liverpool Repertory, 149, 173
Llewellyn, Richard, 160, 190, 222
Lloyd, Harold, 96
Lodger, The, 171
London, 28, 32, 61, 77, 82, 125, 150, 161
Abbey actors in, 58, *63*, 64–5, 110, 153
Allgood in, 62, 149, 158, 173
O'Casey in, 4, 78, 241
The Silver Tassie, 121
London, Jack, 181
London Irish Players, 150
Long Gray Line, The, *18*, 23
Long Voyage Home, The, 138–46, 176, 181–2, 195, 198, 244
Longford, Earl and Countess of, 121
Look at the Heffernans (Macnamara), 112
Lorentz, Pare, 44
Los Angeles, 10, 22, 84, 125, 239–40; *see also* Hollywood
Abbey actors in, 53, 80–1
climate, 179
Hurst in, 26–7
population, 177–8
Lost Patrol, The, 38
"Lovey", Otho Lovering, editor, 53
Lowry, Morton, *165*
Loy, Myrna, 173

Lucky Strike, 201
Lupino, Ida, 182
Lynch, Father, 241

Mac Liammóir, Micheál, 32, 66, 108, 110, 111–12
McBride, Joseph, 22, 24, 26, 46, 135
McCarey, Leo, 185, 186–8, 187, 190
McCarthy, Joseph, 13
McCormack, Count John, 125, 126
McCormack, W.J., 5
McCormick, F.J., 55, 57, 67, *72*, *81*, 82, 153
  in Ford's *Plough and the Stars*, 83–4, 86–7
  in *The Plough and the Stars*, 70–1, 73, 76
McDermott, Sean, 106
MacDonald, J. Farrell, 37
McDonough, J.R., 38, 47
McDowell, Roddy, 161, *167*
McEldowney, Ken, 202
MacEntee, Seán, 154
McGee, Bazie, 110
McGonigal, Maurice, 120
McGowran, Jack, 236
McGrail, Walter, 37
McGuinness, James Kevin, 37, 38, 217
McHugh, Michael J., 30
Macken, Monsignor, Dean of Tuam, 113
McKenna, Siobhan, 29, 30
McKenna, Stephen, 104
McLaglen, Andrew, 222
McLaglen, Victor, 26, *40*, *41*, *51*, 198, 208, 209
  The Informer, 39–44, 44–6, 47, 50
  The Quiet Man, 217, 222, 237
MacNamara, Brinsley, 82, 112, 119, 121
McNeill, Eoin, 103
McNeill, James and Mrs, 121
Madame Butterfly, 27
Mair, G.H., 157
Man Who Shot Liberty Valance, The, 32–3
Manchester Gaiety, 149
Manchester Guardian, The, 157
Manhunt, 36
Mankiewicz, Joseph L., 14
Mann, Thomas, 178
Mann, William J., 21, 22
Manners, Hartley, 158
Manning, Mary, 111–12
March, Eve, 22
Margaret Gillan (MacNamara), 119
Marlborough Street National School, 156
Marx Brothers, 186
Mary of Scotland, 15, 20, *21*, 52
Mary Pickford Company, 95
Masefield, John, 149
Mason, James, 178
Massachusetts, 134, 135
Masses and the Man (Toller), 112
Maxine Elliott Theatre, NY, 137, 159
May, Ada, 58
Mayo, County, 9, 226
Mehigan, Guy, 180
Melville, Herman, 138
Men Without Women, 32
Merchant Tailors' School, 102
Meredith, Bess, 132
Meredith, Burgess, 131
Merivale, Gladys and Philip, 129
Methodism, 159, 164
Mexico, 215
MGM Studios, 38, 44, 81, 82, 177, 202
Miami, 194
Michigan, 114
Midway, Battle of, 14, 213
Milland, Ray, 95
Miller, Arthur, 150
Milton, John, 70
Milwaukee, 114
Mitchell, Susan, 110
Mitchell, Thomas, 139

Moiseiwitsch, Tanya, 131
Molloy, J.J., 240
Molony, Helena, 103, 241
Monroe, Marilyn, 170
Monument Valley, Utah, 39
Moon for the Misbegotten (O'Neill), 197
Moon in the Yellow River, The (Johnston), 114
Mooney, Ria, 28, 72, 76, 77, 111, 126, 209
Moore, George, 7, 113, 195, 200
Morgan, Sydney, 64, 65
Morosco Theatre, New York, 129
Mortished, Marie 'Bid' Shields, 180, 181, 241
Mortished, Una, 181
Mortished family, 239, 243
Motion Picture Producers and Distributors Association (MPPDA), 35
Muckross Park Convent, 118
Mulhern, Frolie, 126
Murnau, F.W., 39
Murphy, Jack, 37
Murphy, Maurice, 37
Murray, T.C., 66, 102
music halls, 66–7
My Darling Clementine, 15, 24, 33, 50, 215

Naked City, The, 192–4
National Theatre of Ireland, 149
National University of Ireland, Galway, 5
nationalism, 4, 32, 39, 54, 60, 112–13, 120–1, 154
Native Americans, 25, 215, 217–20
Natwick, Mildred, 199, 222
Nevada, 181
New England, 115
New York, 6, 10, 20, 52, 77, 134, 138, 210
- Abbey actors in, 4, 57, 60, 65, 80, 115, 123, 124, 140, 151–2
  - *Juno and the Paycock*, 78–9, 80
  - permanent outlet, 130
  - *The Plough and the Stars*, 77, 78, 80
  - *Shadow and Substance*, 151–2
- Allgood in, 5, 150, 151–2
- Drama Critics Awards, 123, 130, 152
- Equity, 180
- Fitzgerald in, 116, 239
- *Kindred*, 136, 179, 197
- *The Naked City*, 192–4
- Shields in, 5, 137–8, 239, 242
- *Spring Meeting*, 129
- *The White Steed*, 129–31

New York Times, 38, 44–5, 96, 178
New York World, 37
nic Shiublaigh, Máire, 108
Nicholls, George, 85
Nichols, Dudley, 33–4, 43, 45, 47, 88, 95
- *Bringing up Baby*, 95, 97
- and Ford, 37–8, 49, 50
- *Long Voyage Home*, 140
- *Plough*, 85
- *Stagecoach*, 52

None but the Lonely Heart, 190–1, 192
Northern Ireland, 74, 131, 210
Norton Anthology of English Literature, The, 6
Notre Dame University, 190
Nugent, Frank, 198, 217, 222, 224, 226
Nunan, Sean, 223

Oakland, California, 5
Oberon, Merle, 28
O'Brien, George, 37, 39, 73–4, 85, 88, 199
O'Brien, Pat, 201, 208, 209
O'Casey, Sean, 58, 146, 153, 197, 243; *see Juno and the Paycock; Plough and the Stars, The*
- and Allgood, 135, 150, 157, 158
- and Fitzgerald, 58, 59, 66–8, 135, 195
- Ford's interest in, 7, 36, 53, 92–3, 242
- leaves Ireland, 4, 78, 241

Protestantism, 110, 123
satire, 164
Shadow of a Gunman, 66, 68–9, 75
The Silver Tassie, 58, 78, 82, 92, 120–1
O'Connor, Aideen *see* O'Connor, Una (Aideen O'Connor)
O'Connor, Eileen, 124, 207, 208, 209
O'Connor, Frank, 7, 30, 128–9
O'Connor, Joseph, 66
O'Connor, Maeve, 207, 208, 209
O'Connor, Robert Emmett, 37
O'Connor, Una, 6, 102, 125, *169*, 173, 208
and Allgood, 168
in Hollywood, 3, 125, 243
The Informer, 43, 47, 53, 81
leaves Abbey, 62
O'Connor, Una ('Aideen O'Connor'), 5, 6, *124*, *125*, *127*, 130, 239, 242
in Hollywood, 207–9
illness and death, 201, 204
Kindred, 137–8
and Shields, 118–20, 123–6, 131, 132, 174, 196
marriage, 179–80
Spring Meeting, 129
O'Dea, Denis, 3, 42, 53, 81, 82, *83*, 84, 125
O'Dea, Joseph, 227
Odets, Clifford, 181, 190–1
O'Donovan, Fred, 62, 64
Of Mice and Men, 137
O'Fearna, Eddie, 52, 222
O'Feeney, Sean Martin Aloysius *see* Ford, John
Office of Strategic Services (OSS), 28, 213, 230
O'Flaherty, Liam, 3, 7, 26, 27, 29, 36, 47, 80, 210, 213
The Informer, 37–8
Tomorrow, 113
O'Hara, Maureen, 161, 164, 209, 242
and Ford, 16, 19, 23, 26, 32, 33, 48
The Quiet Man, 9, *205*, 214, 222, *232*, *234*, *235*, 236–7
Rio Grande, 217–18, 221
O'Higgins, Kevin, 75–6
Ohio, 37, 114
O'Kelly, Fergus, 104
Oklahoma, 15, 25
Old Man Murphy, 64
Old Woman Remembers, The (Gregory), 154
O'Leary, J.J., 67
Olivier, Laurence, 131
Olympic Games, 24
O'Máille's shop, Galway, 222
O'Malley, Ernie, 212
On Baile's Strand (Yeats), 64
O'Neill, Eugene, 7, 39, 118, 151, 197
The Hairy Ape, 111
The Long Voyage Home, 138–46
O'Neill, Maire *see* Allgood, Molly
O'Neill, Sally, 37
Ontario, 114
O'Rahilly, The, 106
Orange Order, 106–7, 156
Oranmore and Brown family, 222
O'Rourke, J.A., 62
Oscars *see* Academy Awards
OSS, 181
O'Sullivan, Maureen, 95, 125, *126*, 207–8, 209
O'Toole, Fintan, 145, 227
Oughterard, County Galway, *31*
Out There (Manners), 158
Owsley, Mr and Mrs, 120
Oxford University Dramatic Society, 82

pacifism, 92
Paramount Studios, 27, 95, 185, 186
Paris, 26
Parsons, Louella, 20
Payne, Ben Iden, 61

Peacock Theatre, 111
Pearl Harbour, 213
Pearse, Mrs, 76
Pearse, Patrick, 74, 76, 85, 89, 93, 104, 105, 106
Pearse, Willie, 106
Peg o' My Heart, 149, 158
Pennsylvania, 114
Philadelphia, 57, 118
Pickford, Mary, 88, 95
Pigeon, Walter, 161
Pilkington, Charlie, 111
Pinter, Harold, 191
Pirandello, Luigi, 119
Pittsburgh, 57, 197
Pius XI, Pope, 60
Playboy of the Western World, The (Synge), 65, 70, *71*, 127, *128*, 137, 140, 226, 244
  depiction of women, 9
  film, 30
  Hollywood extras, 3, 208–9, 237
  Molly Allgood, 154
  pony-racing, 229
  riots, 4, 8, 229–30
  satire, 164
  Shields in, 108, 127, *133*, 194
  in USA, 5, 152, 208, 209
Player Queen, The (Yeats), 154
Plotinus, 104
Plough and the Stars, The (O'Casey), 3–4, 5, 46, 53, 68, 119, 241
  characterization, 69
  Fitzgerald in, 182
  Ford film, 81, 82, 83–98, 153, 210, 243
    alterations, 92–4
    lack of dialogue, 88–91
    outdoor sets, 85
    use of Tricolour, 93–4
  opposition to, 70–7
    riots, 4, 76–7, 120
  Shields in, 110
  in USA, 78, 80, 237, 240
Plunkett, Sir Horace, 59
Plunkett, Joseph, 104
Poe, Edgar Allan, 27, 171
Poland, 137
Portland, Maine, 20–1
Powell, Jack, 58–9
Powell, Michael, 202
Presentation Convent, George's Hill, 156, 165
Pressburger, Emeric, 202
Price, Will, 33
Priestley, J.B., 178
Prisoner of Shark Island, 15
Proclamation of Independence, 93, 103, 241
Production Code, 35, 87, 163, 187
prostitution, 72, 73–4
Protestantism, 8, 19, 26, 156, 157
  and Abbey, 4, 6, 82, 158, 159
  'Ascendancy', 121–2
  in *How Green Was My Valley*, 164
  in Irish Free State, 29, 95, 110–14, 121–3
  and nationalism, 59, 112–13, 128–9
  O'Casey, 69, 73, 90, 92
  Shields family, 82, 101–2, 106–7, 242
Provincetown Players, 118, 138
Purefoy, Tom, 111
Purser, Sarah, 121, 154

Qualen, John, *141*
Queen's Printing Office, 156
Quiet Man, The, 4, 7, 10, 15, 23, 30, 95, 216, 240, 242
  compared with *Playboy*, 229
  critique of Ireland, 226–8, 237
  image of Ireland, 225–6
  Irish response to, 237–8
  Irish womanhood in, 9, 236–7

making of, 222–30
original story, 53, 54, 210–12
planning, 28–9, 210–13
pony-racing, 229
sentimentality, 36
sexual relations, 230–6
and World War II, 224–5
Quigley, Martin, 35
Quinn, Maire, 60

racism, 24–5
Rank, Arthur, 29
Reagan, Ronald, 202
Red Cross, 180
Redgrave, Sir Michael, 32
Règle du jeu, La, 202
Reid, Cliff, 38, 50–1
Reissa, Miss, 82
Renoir, Jean, 181
The River, 202–4
Republic Pictures, 217
Republican Club, 78
Republican Party, 14, 35
Richards, Shelah, 73, 76, 77, 110–11, 113
US tour, 1931, 114–18
Richardson, Ralph, 28
Richmond Barracks, 106
Riders to the Sea (Synge), 27–8, *147*, 152, 155
Rio Grande, 215, 216–21, 224, 225
Rising of the Moon, The, 30, *31*, 200
Riskin, Robert, 50
River, The, 202–4
RKO Studios, 2, 3, 15, 38, 53, 81, 210
The Informer, 37–40, 46
The Plough and the Stars, 85, 90, 93
Robbins, Christopher, 26, 32
Robinson, Edward G., 181–4, 208, 209
Robinson, Lennox, 110, 120, 121, *122*
Abbey Festival, 127
and Allgood, 62, 154
as director, 80
Drama at Inish, 119–20, 122–3
and MGM talent scouts, 81, 82
and O'Casey, 72–3
plays, 59, 66, 112, 113, 243
The Whiteheaded Boy, 117, 150
Protestantism, 112–14, 122–3
US tours, 58, 114–18
Robinson, Mrs, 121
Rogers, Will, 15
Rome, 240
Roper, Elmo, 214
Royalty Theatre, London, 62
Ruggles, Charlie, 97
Ruzicka, Madame, 120
Ryan, Phyllis, 126, 150

St Louis, 60, 197
St Patrick's Cathedral, Dublin, 241
St Patrick's College, Drumcondra, 123, 160
St Patrick's Day, 16
St Patrick's Hospital, Dublin, 241
St Vincent's Hospital, Dublin, 240
Salomé (Wilde), 111, 112, 154
San Francisco, 124, 207
San Francisco Docks, 181
Sarris, Andrew, 162
Saturday Evening Post, The, 210, 220
Saurin, Charlie, 103, 105, 106, 114
Savoy Theatre, London, 64
Schulberg, Budd, 178
Screen Directors Guild, 13–14, 15, 29, 36
Screenwriters Guild, 45
Sea Wolf, The, 176, 181–4
Seanad Eireann, 75
séances, 108
Searchers, The, 25
sectarianism, 4, 70, 73, 107, 121, 128–9, 156
Sellers, Peter, 144
Selznick, David O., 50

Sergeant Ruttledge, 24, 25
Shadow and Substance (Carroll), 5, 123, *124*, 126, 137, 195
  Broadway, 1938, 150–2
Shadow of a Gunman (O'Casey), 66, 68–9, 75
Shadow of the Glen (Synge), 60
Shakespeare, William, 4, 53
Shannon Airport, 190, 238
Shaw, George Bernard, 5, 28, 107, 137, 153
She Wore a Yellow Ribbon, 198–200, 215, 216, 244
Sheehan, Winfield, 15, 37
Sheehy Skeffington, Francis, 78
Sheehy Skeffington, Hanna, 76, 78
Shelbourne Hotel, Dublin, 151
Shields, Adam, 114, 136, 138, 179, 180–1, 201, 239, 242
Shields, Adolphus, 101–2, 103
Shields, Arthur, 10, 59, *81*, *124*, *125*, *127*, *128*, *133*, 150, 153
  in Abbey Theatre, 66, *109*, 114–18, 127–8
    The Playboy of the Western World, 127, *128*
    The Plough and the Stars, 70–1, 73, 76
    The Silver Tassie, 120–1
  archive, 5–6
  and brother, 239–44
  career of, 101–20, 243–4
  and Choate, 130–1
  director, 197
  Easter Rising, 7, 63, 101, 103–7
  first marriage, 110
  health, 138, 179, 239, 243
  in Hollywood, 82, 173, 178–81, 194–6, 201–4
    Drums Along the Mohawk, 132, 133, 135–6, 160
    Ford contract, 132
    How Green Was My Valley, 161
    The Long Voyage Home, 138–46
    The Plough and the Stars, 84, *89*, 91, 93
    The Quiet Man, 222, 223, 233–4, *234*
    The River, 202–4
    salary, 198
    She Wore a Yellow Ribbon, 198–200
  and Johnston, 111–12
  library of, *99*
  New York productions, 129, 159–60
    Juno and the Paycock, 137–8
    Kindred, 130–2, 137–8
    Shadow and Substance, 151–2
  Protestantism, 114, 135
  and Una O'Connor, 118–20, 123–6, 131, 132, 174, 196
    marriage, 179–80
  and Yeats, 75, 127, 129, 146
Shields, Bazie (Mac), 111, 123, *125*, 136, 138, 180, 239
  US tour, 114–18
Shields, Christine, 5, 173–4, 181, 201, 222, 239, 243
Shields, Fanny Sophie Ungerland, 101–2
Shields, Laurie, 101, 242, 243
Shields, Lini, 114
Shields, Will *see* Fitzgerald, Barry
Shields family, 157
Shubert brothers, 130, 150
Silver Tassie, The (O'Casey), 58, 78, 82, 92, 120–1
Sinclair, Arthur, 62, *63*, 64, *64*, 66, 150, 153, 157
Sinn Féin, 106, 109, 154
Slott, Judy, 181
Slott, Nate, 181
Slott, Susan, 181
Slott family, 239, 243

Smith, Mary McBryde *see* Ford, Mary
Smith, Wingate, 222
Smyllie, Mr and Mrs R.M., 121
Solomons, Dr and Mrs Bethel, 120
Song of My Heart, 126
Soviet Union, 73, 214, 220
Spain, 95
Spanish Civil War, 19
Spanish Main, The, 214
Spartacus, 24
Spiddal, County Galway, 15, *16*, 29, 80, 92, 210, 212
Spreading the News (Gregory), 227
Spring Meeting (Farrell and Perry), 6, 129, 131
Squaw Man, The, 15
Stagecoach, 36, 52–3, 132
Stalin, Joseph, 137
Stallings, Laurence, 198
Stanislavski, 155
Stanwyck, Barbara, 81, 85–7, *91*
'Star-Spangled Banner, The', 94
Starkie, Madame, 121
Starkie, Mrs J.M., 121
Starkie, Walter, 58
Steamboat Round the Bend, 15, 24
Steinbeck, John, 137
Steiner, Max, 47
Stephens, James, 29, 208, 242
Stevens, Ruby *see* Stanwyck, Barbara
Stevenson, Robert Louis, 95
Stewart, Jimmy, 50
Stork Club, The, 192
Storm in a Teacup, 150, 151
Strange Affair of Uncle Harry, The, 171
Strode, Woody, 24
Stuart, Francis, 113
studio system, 37, 38
Sullivan, Joan *see* Shields, Bazie
Sun Shines Bright, The, 24
Sunday Independent, 103
Sunrise (Murnau), 39
Swift, Jonathan, 155, 241
symbolic ethnicity, 9–10
Synge, J.M., 36, 62, 66, 102, 104, 153, 157; *see also Playboy of the Western World, The*
  and Allgood, 64, 149, 154
  O'Connor lecture, 128–9
  portrayal of women, 229–30, 237
  Protestantism, 4, 9, 129
  Riders to the Sea, 27–8, 152, 155
  The Shadow of the Glen, 60

Taidbhearch Theatre, Galway, *31*
Taillon, Angus, 181
Taillon, Daisy, 181
Tanyard Street (D'Alton), 197
Tarzan's Secret Treasure, 95
Taylor, Don, 194
Taylorization, 172
television, 201, 243
Tell-Tale Heart, The (Hurst), 27
Temple, Shirley, 14, 15, 201, 216
Tennyson, Alfred Lord, 145
Texas, 115
Thalberg, Irving, 50
That Hamilton Woman, 36
The Old Lady Says, 'No!' (Johnston), 112
Theatre Guild, Broadway, 60
Theatre Royal, Dublin, 66–7
Things That Are Caesar's, The (Carroll), 62, 123
This Land is Mine, 181
This Lion Had Wings, 28
Thornton, Michael, 16, 92
Times, The, 65, 84–5, 158
Toland, Gregg, 47, 142
Toller, Ernest, 112
Tomorrow (magazine), 113
Top o' the Morning, 181, 192
Tracy, Spencer, 27, 37, 88

Traynor, Oscar, 104–5
Trinity College Dublin, 121, 234
Trotti, Lamar, 132–3
Truffaut, F., 46
Tuam, County Galway, 226
Tullubov, art director, 53
Tuskegee University, Alabama, *116*, 117
Twentieth Century Fox, 6, 14, 15, 20, 140, 160, 215
  Allgood contract, 168
  and Shields, 132, 136, 180
Two Years Before the Mast, 191

UCLA, 24
Ulster, 29, 102, 106–7
Ulysses (Joyce), 111
Unemployment, Department of, 59, 107
Unionism, 63, 102
United Artists, 88
United Services Club, Hollywood, 40
United States of America, 36, 64, 93–4, 172, 186–7, 195–6, 214, 224
  Abbey tours, 3–4, 5, 59–60, 114–20
    Abbey 'style', 78–80
    black audiences, 116–17
  cinema audiences, 60
  ethnicity, 13, 16, 54
  Protestantism in, 135–6
  Shields on, 116–18
  theatrical culture, 117–18
Universal Studios, 38
US Congress, 16, 35–6
Utah, 134, 136, 219

Van Vechten, Carl, 152, 153, 160
Vancouver, 115, 116, 180
Vanity Fair, 44
Verlaine, P., 108
Vigilance Committees, 113
Voltaire, 34
von Juhlmann, Herr and Frau, 120

Waco, 115
Waddell, Helen, 121
Waddell, S., 121
Wales
  How Green Was My Valley, 160–7
Wall, Joseph P., *127*
Walsh, Maurice, 7, 226, 229, 235
  The Quiet Man, 53, 54, 210–12
Walsh, P.J., antique shop, 157
Wanger, Walter, 140
War of Independence, 5, 16, 29, 68, 154, 212, 223, 224, 225
Warner Brothers, 180
Wasatch Mountains, Utah, 134
Washington, George, 85
Washington State, 115
Waugh, Evelyn, 177
Wayne, John, 18, 24, 26, 125, 238
  and Ford, 33, 50, 216–17
  The Long Voyage Home, *141*, 141–2, 143
  The Quiet Man, 23, 210, 222, 227, *232*, 233, *234*, *235*
  Rio Grande, 217, 218
  She Wore a Yellow Ribbon, 198–200
  Stagecoach, 36
Wayne, Josephine, 125
Wayne, Pilar, 222
Wayne family, 222
Webb, Clifton, 27
Weber, Max, 9, 34–5
Wee Willie Winkie, 14
Weenink, Mons, 120
Weismuller, Johnny, 95
Welch, Mary, 197
Welcome, Stranger, 192
Welles, Orson, 142
White Steed, The (Carroll), 129–31, 137
Whiteheaded Boy, The (Robinson), 59, 80, 117, 150
Widowers' Houses (Shaw), 107

Wilde, Hagar, 95
Wilde, Oscar, 8, 9, 32, 97, 108
    Salomé, 111, 112, 154
Wilder, Billy, 13
Williams, Rhys, *165*
Willmore, Michael *see* Mac Liammóir, Micheál
Wills, Garry, 50
wine industry, 243
Winnipeg, 115
Wisconsin, 114
womanhood, Irish, 9, 209, 229–30, 235–6
Wood, Robin, 136
Words upon the Windowpane (Yeats), 155
World War I, 26, 37, 40, 60, 62, 142, 178, 196, 225
    and Easter Rising, 85
    in O'Casey, 90, 92
World War II, 28, 33, 46, 159, 160, 196, 215
    declared, 137
    Ford's naval service, 8, *11*, 13–14, 20, 23, 212–14
    and *Going My Way*, 190
    Irish neutrality, 53–4, 180, 242
    and *The Quiet Man*, 224–5
    US neutrality, 35–6
Wright, Richard, 39
Wright, Udolphus, 60, *61*, 62, 64, 65
Wyatt, Jane, 191
Wyler, William, 13, 160
Wyoming, 25

Yates, Herb, 217
Yeats, Anne, 120–1, 131
Yeats, George, 110, 120
Yeats, Mrs Jack, 121
Yeats, W.B., 7, 27, 61, *77*, 109, 126, 137, 151, 200, 226
    and 'Abbey stare', 196
    and Abbey tours, 58
    on actors, 154–5
    and Ervine, 63
    funeral, *122*
    and Literary Revival, 32, 36, 65
    and O'Casey plays, 68, 73–7, 85
        rejects *The Silver Tassie*, 92, 120, 121
    O'Connor on, 128–9
    plays, 9, 64, 109, 112–13, 243
    Protestantism, 4, 110, 123, 129, 195
    and Shields, 6, 102, 127, 129, 146
Young Cassidy, 242
Young Mr Lincoln, 15, 36, 49–50, 132
Your Show Time, 201
Youth's the Season (Manning), 111–12

Zanuck, Darryl, 20, 160
    and Allgood, 161, 168
    and Ford, 15, 36, 49–50, 132–4, 140, 215
Ziv Productions, 243

www.ingramcontent.com/pod-product-compliance
Lightning Source LLC
LaVergne TN
LVHW050955080826
845145LV00006B/1500

* 9 7 8 1 8 4 3 5 1 1 8 1 6 *